OUR DYNAMIC WORLD

CORE BOOK

PATRICK O'DWYER & BARRY BRUNT

My-etest

Packed full of extra questions, **my-etest** lets you revise –
at your own pace – when you want – where you want.
Test yourself on our FREE website **www.my-etest.com**
and check out how well you score!

Teachers!

Print an etest and give it for homework or a class test.

GILL & MACMILLAN

Gill & Macmillan Ltd
Hume Avenue
Park West
Dublin 12
with associated companies throughout the world
www.gillmacmillan.ie

© Patrick O'Dwyer & Barry Brunt
0 7171 3518 7
Design, colour illustrations and print origination in Ireland by Design Image, Dublin
Colour reproduction by Ultragraphics, Dublin

*The paper used in this book is made from the wood pulp of managed forests. For every tree felled,
at least one tree is planted, thereby renewing natural resources.*

CORE UNIT 1: PATTERNS AND PROCESSES IN THE PHYSICAL ENVIRONMENT

	Content description	National settings	International settings
1.1	**The tectonic cycle** [Chapter 1] Statement: **The mobility of the earth's crust produces endogenic forces, which give rise to geological structures within it. Crustal structures are created, modified and destroyed as part of the tectonic cycle.** Students should study: • the internal structure of the earth • the plate tectonics model • plate boundaries as zones of crustal construction and destruction • the geography of volcanoes and earthquakes and how they and their effects may be predicted.	The position of Ireland in relation to plate boundaries now and in past geological periods. Antrim basalt extrusion in relation to the opening of the Atlantic.	Global geography of lithospheric plates. Global geography of volcanic and seismic activity.
1.2	**The rock cycle** [Chapter 2] Statement: **Rocks are continually formed, modified, destroyed and reconstituted as part of the rock cycle. They are formed and modified by endogenic forces: they are destroyed by exogenic forces of erosion on exposure to weather and climate; they are reconstituted by the deposition of sediments.** Students should study: • the geotectonic setting of the formation of igneous (both plutonic and volcanic), metamorphic and sedimentary rocks • the processes of weathering (both physical and chemical). • mass wasting and erosion by rivers, sea, ice and wind. (**N.B.** This can be studied in conjunction with section 1.5 below) • The human interaction with the rock cycle, paying particular attention to **one** of the following: mining, extraction of building materials, oil/gas exploitation, geothermal energy production.	Irish rock types as illustrations of plutonic, volcanic, metamorphic, and sedimentary settings. Appropriate national examples.	The North American continent with its active and trailing plate margins. Appropriate international examples.

	Content description	National settings	International settings
1.3	**Landform development (i)** [Chapter 3] Statement: **The development of landforms is influenced by geological structures which have resulted from the operation of the tectonic cycle** Students should study the effects of the following on landform development: • volcanic and plutonic structures, lava flows, volcanoes, joints etc • sedimentary structures, bedding planes, joints etc • structures of deformation including folding, doming and faulting (by both vertical and horizontal displacement).	Appropriate examples e.g. Landforms of the Antrim plateau and the Leinster batholith. e.g. Dartry-Cuilcagh upland e.g. South Ireland ridge and valley province, Armorican thrust front, Donegal thrust and tear faults etc.	Appropriate examples e.g. Hawaii, Iceland Devon and Cornwall. e.g. Paris, Basin, Brecon Beacons etc. e.g. The Appalachians, The Weald, The Alps.
1.4	**Landform development (ii)** [Chapter 6] Statement: **The development of landforms is influenced by rock characteristics which have resulted from the operation of the rock cycle** Students should study: • landforms associated with particular rock types • the way in which spatial variations in rock type may influence the physical landscape.	Appropriate Irish examples e.g. The Burren, Marble Arch upland, Mask-Corrib lowland, Wicklow Granite landscapes.	Appropriate examples e.g. Slovenia, S.W. China, Kentucky, Jamaica. Appropriate examples e.g. Dartmoor.
1.5	**Landform development (iii)** [Chapter 7] Statement: **The development of landforms is influenced by surface (exogenetic) processes which may vary (both spatially and temporally) in their intensity and frequency of operation.**		

	Content description	National settings	International settings
1.5	**Landform development (iii) (contd.)** Students should study all of the surface processes listed and focus in detail on **one** of the following: • mass movement processes and the factors governing their operation • fluvial processes, patterns, and associated landforms • coastal processes, patterns and associated • glacial processes, patterns and associated landforms	Appropriate Irish examples e.g. Antrim coastal landslides, bog bursts in N.W. Ireland etc. Appropriate Irish examples. Appropriate Irish examples. Appropriate Irish examples.	for example, mudslides in Italy. Middle East, S. America etc.
1.6	**Landform development (iv)** **[Chapter 8]** Statement: **All landforms represent a balance between endogenetic and exogenetic forces; this balance may change through time.** Students should study the way in which landforms result from a combination of crustal uplift (in response to isostatic readjustment) and denudation by surface processes, and that sometimes landscapes illustrate that these opposing forces are temporarily out of balance. Students should study: • isostasy • fluvial adjustment to base level • cyclic landscape development and peneplains.	Rivers of N.W. Ireland. Planation surfaces in Munster.	
1.7	**Human interaction [Chapter 9]** Statement: **Human activities can impact on the operation of surface processes.** Students should study **one** of the following: • mass movement processes and the impact of overgrazing, overcropping and deforestation • river processes and the impact of hydro-electric dams, canalisation and flood control measures • coastal processes and the impact of recreational pressures, coastal defence work, conservation and management measures.	Appropriate Irish examples.	Appropriate examples.

CORE UNIT 2: REGIONAL GEOGRAPHY

	Content description	National settings	International settings
2.1	**The concept of a region** [Chapters 10–17] Statement: A region is an area of the earth's surface which can be identified by selected criteria operating at a variety of scales. Single or multiple indices may be used to study these regions. Students should study: ● climatic regions, in particular the cool temperate oceanic ● geomorphological regions including: – Karst landscapes – Munster ridge and valley – Northern European plain. ● Administrative regions at different scales ● Cultural regions – regions associated with language – regions associated with religion ● socio-economic regions – less-developed regions – core regions – peripheral regions – regions of industrial decline ● nodal/city/urban regions – urban areas and hinterland	Irish climate. e.g. Burren. e.g. South Munster. Local council/corporations, constituency boundaries, county divisions. Examples in Ireland. Examples in Ireland. **Regional examples chosen here can be linked with 2.2, Irish regions.** Irish cities	North West Europe. French departments. Belgium. The Islamic world. Examples in Europe. **Regional examples chosen here can be linked with 2.2, European regions.** European cities
2.2	**The dynamics of regions** [Chapters 18–21] Statement: The study of regions show how economic, human, and physical processes interact in a particular area. Students should study: ● two contrasting Irish regions: the study of each region should include: – physical processes e.g. climate, soils, relief, drainage – economic processes – primary activities e.g. agriculture, forestry, fishing, mining/energy – secondary activities e.g. patterns in manufacturing activities – tertiary activities e.g. tourism and transport		

Content description	National settings	International settings
2.2 **The dynamics of regions (contd.)**		

2.2 **The dynamics of regions (contd.)**

- human processes, e.g. language, religion, urban and rural development and population dynamics

● **two contrasting European regions. Students can choose one region from Scandinavia and/or one from western/central Europe (including the United Kingdom) and/or one from the Mediterranean. The study of the region should include:**
  - physical processes e.g. climate, soils, relief, and drainage
  - economic processes
  - primary activities e.g. agriculture, forestry, fishing, mining/energy
  - secondary activities e.g. patterns in manufacturing activities
  - tertiary activities, e.g. transport and tourism
  - human processes, e.g. language, religion, urban and rural development and population dynamics

European regions.

● **one continental/subcontinental region. The study should include:**
  - physical processes, e.g. climate, soil, relief and drainage
  - economic processes,
  - primary activities e.g. agriculture, forestry, fishing, mining/energy
  - secondary activities e.g. patterns in manufacturing activities
  - tertiary activities, e.g. transport and tourism.
  - human processes, e.g. language, religion, urban and rural development and population dynamics.

A non-European region.

	Content description	National settings	International settings
2.3	**The complexity of regions (i)** [Chapters 22–24] **Statement:** The study of regions illustrates the geographical complexity of the interaction between economic, cultural and physical processes. Students should study: • the interaction of economic, political and cultural activities • the interaction of different cultural groups and political regions • the future of Europe and the European Union, with particular reference to the issues relating to political union, economic union and sovereignty.	The Republic of Ireland and Northern Ireland.	European examples. The EU.
2.4	**The complexity of regions (ii)** [Chapters 25–28] **Statement:** The boundaries and extent of regions may change over time. Students should study: • changes in the boundaries and extent of language regions • urban growth and the expansion of city regions • European Union development and expansion • changes in political boundaries and their impact on cultural groups.	Gaeltacht areas from 1850. Dublin Council structures. Irish economic regions.	Appropriate examples. Post-war development, eastern European expansion.

CORE UNIT 3: GEOGRAPHICAL INVESTIGATION AND SKILLS

Stage	Activities
Chapter 28 (pp 309–315) Introduction: **Posing the problems and devising a strategy**	● the selection of a topic for investigation ● a clear statement of hypothesis or aim ● an outline of the objectives ● identification of the types of information required
Planning: **Preparation of the work to be carried out**	● the selection of methods for the collection and gathering of information ● the design of a questionnaire or recording sheets ● decisions on locations for the investigation
Collection of data	● the use of instruments to make measurements ● records of observations made in the field ● the use of questionnaires and surveys as appropriate ● the use of a variety of secondary sources, e.g. documentary sources ● a discussion of the problems encountered
Preparation of the report	● the organisation of data ● the use of illustrations, graphs, maps, and tables ● the use of ICT, where appropriate, to prepare and present results and conclusions
Conclusion and evaluation	● analysis and interpretation of results ● the drawing of valid conclusions ● the comparison of findings with established theory ● the evaluation of hypotheses ● the examination of the validity of the investigation and suggestions for improvements

CONTENTS

INTRODUCTION

This textbook was written for the new Leaving Certificate Geography course. It forms the core text for both Ordinary and Higher level students. Great care was taken by the authors to ensure that both the text and style of presentation are suited to both levels.

The content adheres to the Department of Education syllabus, guidelines and concepts. Its aim is that students who use this book will be adequately prepared for the Leaving Certificate examination.

Guidelines are given to teachers and students at appropriate places, such as pages 93 and 143, for choosing optional areas of study where some parts only need be studied.

This core text creates settings, such as India and southern Italy, for continued study in the Elective and Option units to develop the concept of region and to reduce the material content as much as possible in keeping with syllabus aspirations.

ACKNOWLEDGMENTS

The writing and completion of this text would have been impossible without the assistance of a number of individuals. Their interest, support and advice deserve our acknowledgement and thanks.

Patrick O'Dwyer would like to thank the Geological Survey of Ireland and the Department of Geology at University College Cork for their advice on aspects of the physical section of this book.

Special thanks are due to Hubert Mahony, Educational Publishing Director, for his constant expert advice and support. Tess Tattersall, Managing Editor, and Helen Thompson, picture researcher, also deserve special mention for their constructive work to make this book a reality. As editor Picot Cassidy provided an effective critique of the text. Her attention to detail was most impressive, and we thank her sincerely.

Sincere thanks to Dara O'Doherty and her team at Design Image for their creative and elegant design of this book.

Finally, a sincere appreciation has to be extended to our families for their constant support throughout the preparation and writing of this text.

Patrick O'Dwyer
Barry Brunt

SECTION 1 (CHAPTER 1)
EARTH'S INTERNAL FORCES AND STRUCTURES

This section is about the workings of the earth's interior and how these processes create, change and destroy the earth's crust. It explains how mountains, deep sea trenches and volcanoes are formed and why earthquakes happen. It covers:

- The internal structure of the earth
- The theory of plate tectonics
- Plate boundaries
- The geography of volcanoes and earthquakes
- How volcanoes, earthquakes and their effects can be predicted.

Tectonics studies the processes that gave the earth's surface its structure and shape. These processes — folding, faulting, melting and convection — are dynamic, because they are always changing and they never stop. The theory of plate tectonics is a revolutionary idea. It is so far-reaching that it can be considered the basis for studying all other geological and geographical processes.

Most of our knowledge of this theory was only discovered during the past fifty years. Before that most scientists believed that the continents and the ocean basins were fixed. Later we learned that continents gradually migrate across the globe and crash into each other, forming mountain ranges and mineral deposits inside, while ocean floors are sucked into the interior of the earth and destroyed. As landmasses split apart, new oceans are created between the separating blocks.

- Chapter 1   The Tectonic Cycle

Lava flow on Mt Etna

Black smokers on a mid-ocean ridge

Buildings sink into the ground during an earthquake in San Francisco.

CHAPTER 1
THE TECTONIC CYCLE

KEY IDEA!

The ability of the earth's crust to move about produces forces that create different rock layers within the earth.

THE PLANET EARTH

The planet earth is some 4.6 billion years old. It formed from a cloud of dust that became solid and then became molten from the impact of meteorites crashing into it. As it cooled, heavier materials sank and lighter materials stayed at the surface, forming the different layers of the earth's crust. **The earth is still cooling, and its molten rock continues to rise from its core to the crust.** This liquid rock brings heat to the surface for release, so the earth does not overheat.

Don't sell your Junior Certificate Geography textbook. It may help you with map and photograph activities.

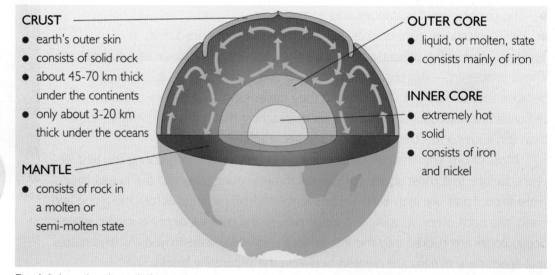

CRUST
* earth's outer skin
* consists of solid rock
* about 45-70 km thick under the continents
* only about 3-20 km thick under the oceans

MANTLE
* consists of rock in a molten or semi-molten state

OUTER CORE
* liquid, or molten, state
* consists mainly of iron

INNER CORE
* extremely hot
* solid
* consists of iron and nickel

Fig. 1.1 A section through the earth

The rising molten rock forms **convection currents** that create earthquakes, volcanoes and mountain ranges that shape our life-bearing lands and seas. The currents driving these vast movements within the earth sweep slowly through the underlying mantle rock. The idea that solid rock can flow is hard to understand because rock seems unchanging in our lifetime. Yet over millions of years, rock can flow like glacier ice and it moves about as fast as our fingernails grow.

Fig. 1.2 Convection currents in a heated pot

2

The Earth's Crust
The Earth's Crust Has Two Layers
Continents have an upper layer of light **rocks** called **sial**. Their lower layer, called **sima**, is heavy and extends under the ocean and consists of basalt. Continents appear to 'float' like icebergs in the heavier basalt rock underneath.

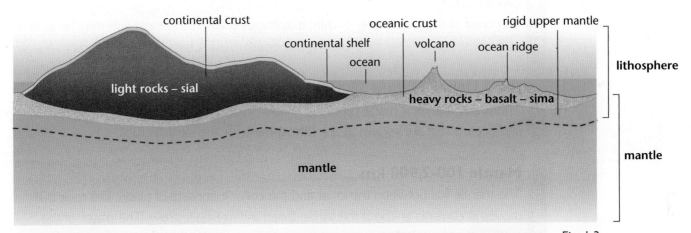

Fig. 1.3

Land is formed of sial, which is light. Ocean floors are formed of sima, which is heavy.

Activity
1. Which part of the crust is made up of light rocks?
2. What are these light rocks called?
3. Which part of the crust is made up of heavy rocks?
4. What are these heavy rocks called?
5. What type of rock are these heavy rocks?

3

Lithosphere

Crust 0-50 km

Continental Crust

The crust of the continents is **thick** compared to that of the ocean floor. It has an average thickness of 45 km and is up to 70 km in thickness under the mountain ranges. The rocks that form the continental crust are **light** in weight.

Ocean Crust

The crust of the ocean floor is **thin**; it averages 8 km in thickness and may be as thin as 3 km in places. The rock forming the ocean crust is basalt, which is **heavy**.

Rigid Upper Mantle 50-100 km

The upper mantle is made up of rigid rocks. These rocks and the continental crust and ocean crust are known as the **lithosphere**, or the earth's crust.

Mantle

Mantle 100-2,900 km

The mantle lies between the crust and the core. It consists of plastic-like rock that moves in currents at about the same speed as fingernails grow. The plates of the earth's crust are carried about on these slow-moving convection currents.

Rocks are cooler, stronger and more rigid in the lithosphere than in the mantle. According to the theory of plate tectonics, the lithosphere is broken into plates. The plates, which are much like segments of cracked shell, move relative to each other, sliding on the underlying mantle.

Core

Core

At the centre of the earth is the heaviest of the three layers, the **core**. The core is composed mainly of **iron** with some **nickel**.

Make sure you know the different parts of the earth's make-up. These parts will be mentioned again and again.

Activity
1. How thick is the continental crust?
2. How thick is the ocean crust?
3. What is the earth's mantle?
4. What is the name for the continental crust, the ocean crust and the upper mantle?
5. The theory of plate tectonics helps us to understand the structure of the lithosphere. Explain.

PLATE TECTONICS

Global Distribution of Plates

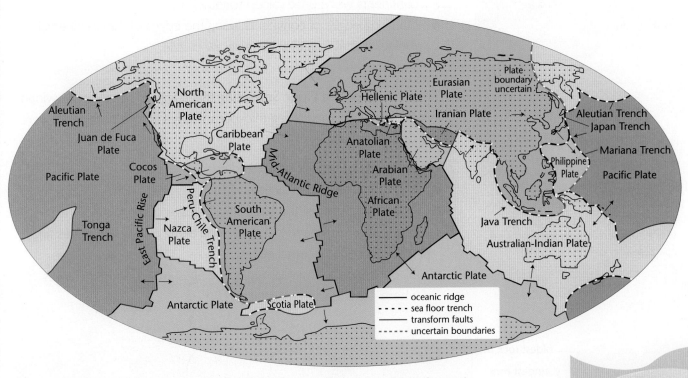

Fig. 1.4 Six large plates of the crust and several smaller ones cover the earth's surface and move steadily in the directions shown by the arrows.

Learn the main plates of the earth's crust.

In geology terms, a **plate** is a large, rigid slab of solid rock. The word '**tectonics**' comes from the Greek word for to build. Putting these two words together, we get the term '**plate tectonics**', which refers to how the earth's surface is built of plates.

These huge plates of rock float on the layer of heavier, '**plastic-like**' **rock** called the **mantle**. The plates move relative to each other, carried along by **convection currents** within the mantle. To us this movement is very slow, but in terms of geological time it is fast. Over time, the plates separate, collide and in some places slide past each other. These movements cause **folding, faulting, volcanic activity and earthquakes**. This entire process repeats itself in an endless cycle over hundreds of millions of years. Plate tectonics combines two theories: continental drift and sea floor spreading.

● **The Theory of Continental Drift** that suggests the continents are carried across the globe on the plates of the earth's crust. **This movement is powered by convection currents that are located within the earth's mantle.**

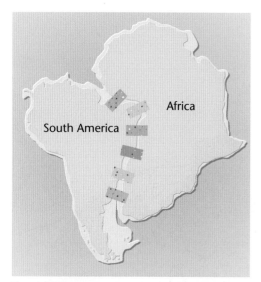

Fig. 1.5 This shows the best fit of South America and Africa along the continental slope at a depth of 500 fathoms (about 900 metres). Areas where continental rocks are examined and match appear in different colours.

Proofs of Continental Drift

- Matching rocks found on continents that are thousands of miles apart.
- Matching fossils that are found in precise locations where the continents were once joined together.
- Matching edges of continents along the edges of the continental shelves that fit together like a jigsaw puzzle.

- **The Theory of Sea Floor Spreading** that suggests ocean floors widen as new rock is formed along mid-ocean ridges where continents were split apart originally.

Some Proofs of Sea Floor Spreading

- The existence of mid-ocean ridges.
- The varying ages of the sea floor: The age of the sea floor is youngest where new rock is formed along mid-ocean ridges and oldest along continental edges.
- Glacial deposits of similar types and ages are found in the areas where continents were attached.

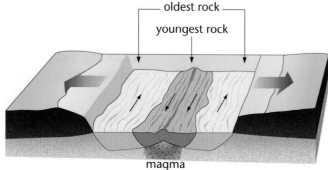

Fig. 1.6

When hot magma cools on the sea floor at mid-ocean ridges, it splits in two. One half forms part of the plate to the west, the other half forms part of the plate to the east.

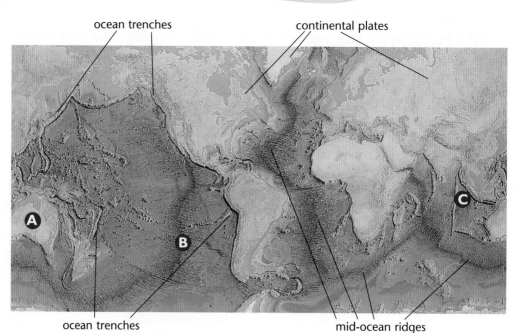

Fig. 1.7 Can you identify the features at A, B and C?

Convection Currents within the Earth

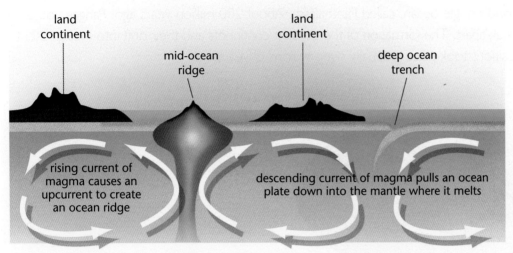

Fig. 1.8 Convection currents make the plates of the earth's crust move about.

What three parts form the lithosphere? Explain your answer.

On average the ocean crust is about 8 km thick, while on average continents are between 35 and 40 km thick.

Water that is heated in a saucepan expands and rises. As it rises, it starts to cool, flows sideways and sinks, eventually to be reheated and to pass again through the same process.

Though much slower than convection in a saucepan, the principle is the same here. Hot rock rises slowly from deep inside the earth. It cools, flows sideways and sinks. The rising hot rock and sideways flow are believed to be the factors that control the positions of oceans and continents.

Activity

1. Explain in your own words what continental drift means.
2. What are convection currents?
3. What relationship, if any, exists between continental drift and convection currents?

Switch on a lava lamp to see how the 'magma' heats and rises in your room – just as it happens in nature.

Fig. 1.9 How convection works

Continental Drift

The theory of continental drift suggests that the continents have moved great distances on the earth's surface and are still moving today. According to the theory, the continents once formed part of a single landmass, called Pangaea, which was surrounded by the world's single ocean, called Panthalassa. About 200 million years ago, Pangaea began to break apart. The formation of the present continents and their drift into their present positions took place gradually over millions of years.

Fig. 1.10

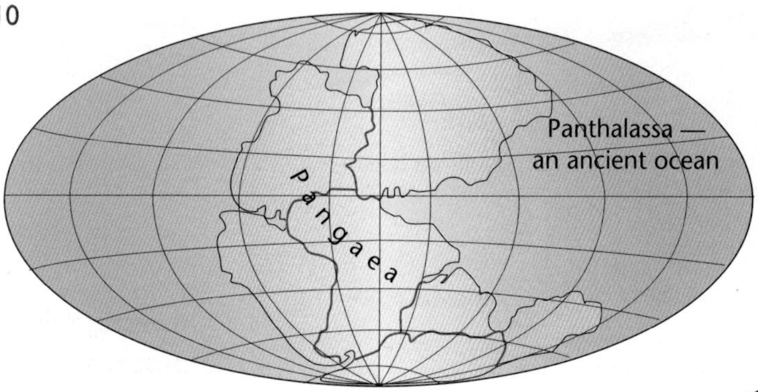

(a) Pangaea: The supercontinent of 200 million years ago

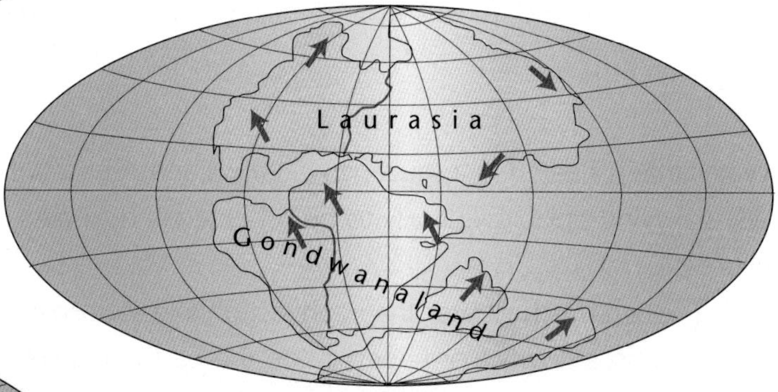

(b) Convection currents in the mantle send the landmasses wandering. Pangaea split into two continents.
● *Name the two continents.*

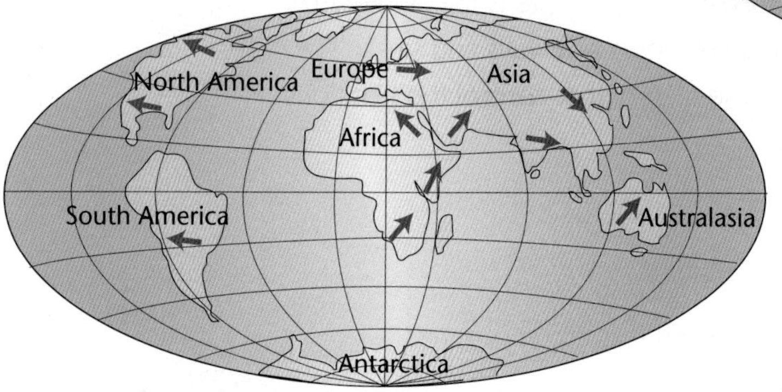

(c) Tomorrow's world: 50 million years from now

Activity
1. Look at Fig. 1.10 and do the following.
2. Find India in each of the diagrams.
3. For each of the diagrams a, b and c, explain the processes involved as India's location changed.

Continents continue to split apart today. Africa is splitting apart along the African Great Rift Valley fault line.

Although Pangaea split up 200 million years ago, the continents were moving much earlier; Pangaea itself was formed by the collision of many small continents. Recent work shows that continents have been in motion for the past two billion years (some geologists say four billion). For half or more of the earth's history, the continents appear to have collided, welded together, then split and drifted apart, only to collide again, over and over in an endless, slow dance.

PLATE BOUNDARIES

KEY IDEA!

Forces within the earth create, change and destroy rock and landforms where plates collide and separate.

Types of plate boundaries

At plate boundaries rock and rock structures are formed, changed or destroyed. There are three types of plate boundaries.

- **Boundaries of Construction**

  Here, new rock is formed to create mid-ocean ridges. Plates formed from this new rock separate and move away from each other, e.g. the Mid-Atlantic Ridge.

- **Boundaries of Destruction**

  Here, rock is **destroyed** or **changed**. There are three types of destructive boundaries.
  - Where two ocean plates meet, called **ocean-ocean**.
  - Where an ocean plate and a continental plate meet, called **ocean-continent**.
  - Where two continental plates meet, called **continent-continent**.

  Where destruction occurs, one plate sinks into the mantle beneath the other plate and melts. A deep **sea trench** is formed on the sea floor. This process is called **subduction**.

- **Passive Boundaries**

  Land is neither created nor destroyed at these boundaries. Plates simply **slide past each other**.

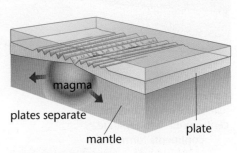

magma

plates separate

mantle

plate

1. constructive

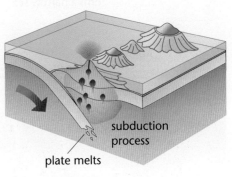

subduction process

plate melts

2. destructive

plates slide past each other

3. passive

Fig. 1.11

Activity
1. Explain what happens at boundaries of destruction.
2. Explain why boundaries of construction are different from boundaries of destruction.
3. Explain why passive boundaries are different from both boundaries of construction and destruction.

Continental Break-up and Sea Floor Spreading
How a New Sea Floor, Mid-Ocean Ridge and Ocean are Formed

Practise and memorise these simplified diagrams before you begin this section.

A a rising current of magma splits a continent and its crust and is stretched. Volcanoes appear at the centre

convection currents carry each side away from the centre until two separate continents form

B ocean water spills in and fills the newly created valley to form a narrow sea

a mid-ocean ridge forms at the centre

new continent

new continent

the rising magma current continues to push each newly created continent apart

C the narrow sea gets wider to form a new ocean

continent

continent

a mid-ocean ridge forms along cracks on the sea floor

a new sea floor is created as the rising magma forms basalt rock at the mid-ocean ridge

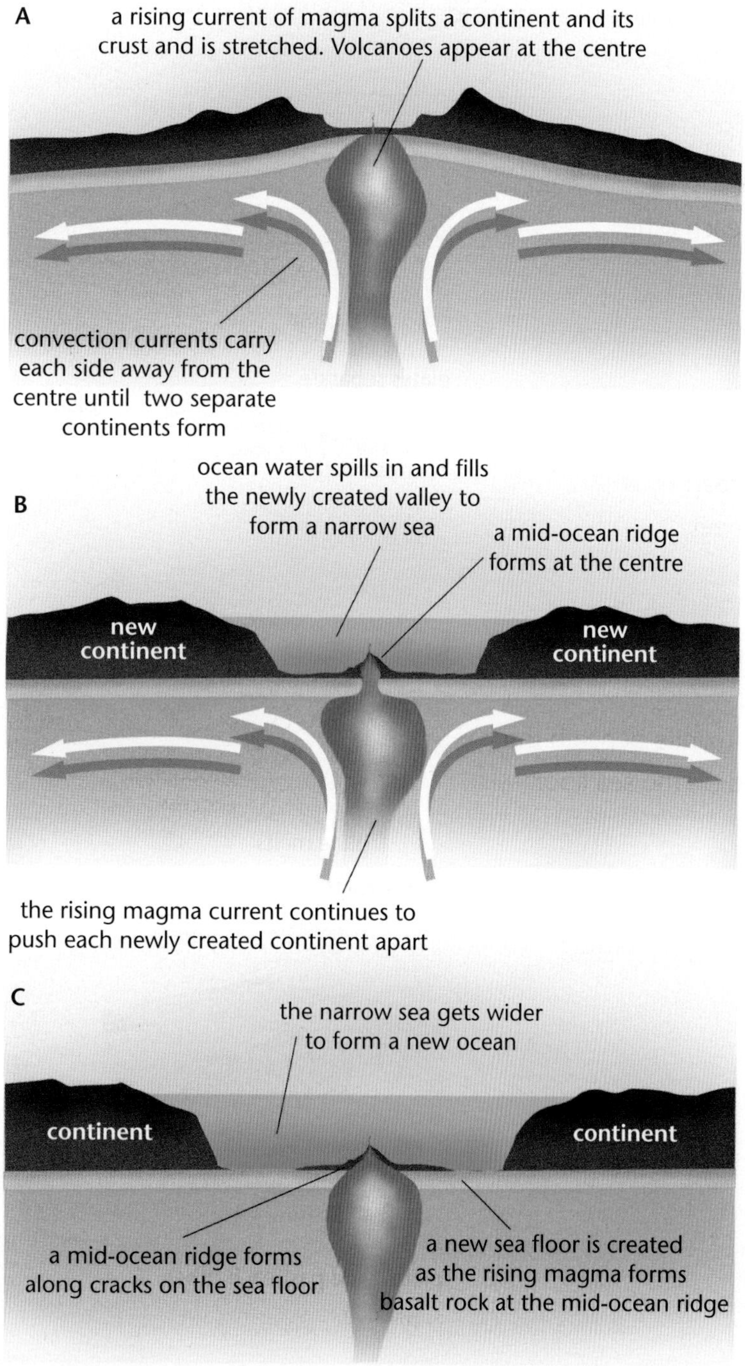

Fig. 1.12 Stages in the formation of a new sea floor, a mid-ocean ridge and ocean

This process is called rifting.

A. A hot current of magma, called a plume, rises from the mantle towards the surface, stretches the crust of the continent and splits the continent into two parts. New volcanoes appear along the cracks that appear on the surface.

An example of this process in action is the East African Rift Valley, in eastern Africa.

B. As the plates separate and the continent splits into two new continents, seawater floods into the new valley that forms. Hot magma rises from the mantle in the middle of the valley and cools quickly, forming basalt rock when it meets the cold seawater.

This basalt forms the new sea floor or ocean crust and a mid-ocean ridge directly over the rising magma.

C. The plates continue to separate, widening the sea to form an ocean. As the continents move apart, their edges are no longer supported and dip into the sea forming shallow continental shelves.

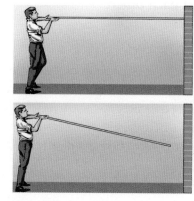

Hold a long pole against a wall so that it is exactly horizontal. Now move back a step back and the pole will dip when the wall no longer supports it. In the same way continental shelves form when continents split apart.

Fig. 1.13

Destructive Plate Boundaries
Some Landforms are Created While Others are Destroyed

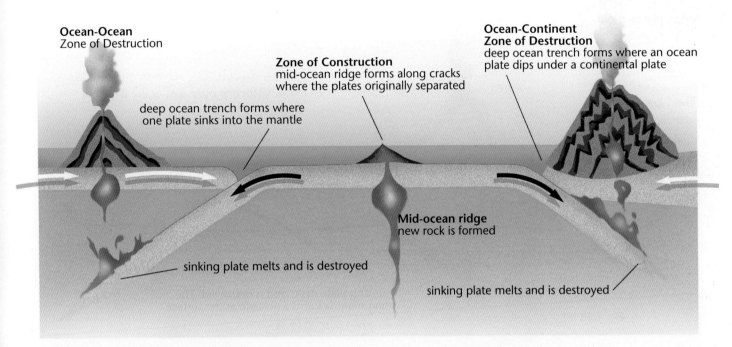

1.14 Constructive and destructive plate boundaries

Two plates move towards each other at destructive or converging boundaries. Generally, when this happens, one plate is pulled down into the mantle and destroyed. This process is called **subduction**.

The character of the boundary depends partly on the types of plates that collide. There are **three types** of destructive or converging boundaries.

● ocean-ocean
● ocean-continent
● continent-continent.

Activity
1. What happens when a continent splits into two separate land areas?
2. What process occurs to allows two plates to approach each other and eventually collide?

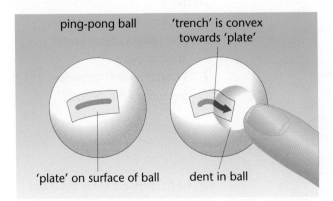

A curved **deep sea trench** occurs at all destructive boundaries. These trenches form the deepest parts of the oceans.

island arc
A curved chain of volcanic islands near deep ocean trenches.

1.15 This sketch explains why deep sea trenches are curved.
● *Can you now explain why they are curved?*

Ocean-Ocean Boundaries

Where two ocean plates collide, one plate is pulled under the other.

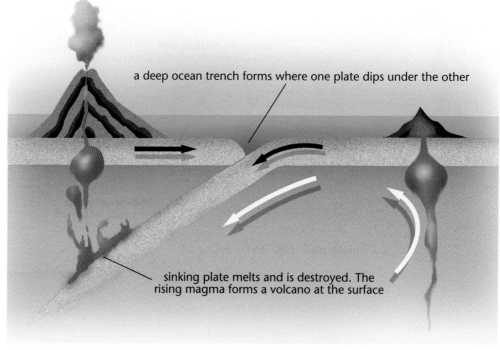

a deep ocean trench forms where one plate dips under the other

sinking plate melts and is destroyed. The rising magma forms a volcano at the surface

Fig. 1.16

Volcanic island arcs form where two ocean plates meet.

The Lipari Islands near Sicily, in Italy, also form an arc shape.

- The descending plate bends downward forming a deep, curved ocean trench. As the plate descends, it melts, because:
  - Heat radiates from the hot magma in the mantle.
  - Heat increases due to compression (being squeezed).
- Because the descending plate is saturated with water, it melts quickly.
- Magma then rises and forms volcanic cones on the ocean floor. Dry land eventually emerges from the ocean depths to form an island arc, a curved string of islands parallel to the ocean trench.

The islands of Japan were formed when many volcanoes joined along an ocean-ocean boundary.

Did you know that 10 per cent of all active volcanoes are located in Japan?

Volcanic island areas include the curved chains of islands in the Pacific Ocean.

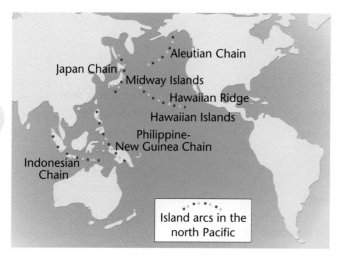

Aleutian Chain
Japan Chain
Midway Islands
Hawaiian Ridge
Hawaiian Islands
Philippine-New Guinea Chain
Indonesian Chain

Island arcs in the north Pacific

Activity
1. Explain what happens when one plate is pulled under another plate.
2. What landform develops because of this process?

Fig. 1.17 There are many island arcs in the Pacific Ocean.
- *Name some island arcs.*

Ocean-Continent Boundaries
Case Study: How the Rockies were formed

Fig. 1.18

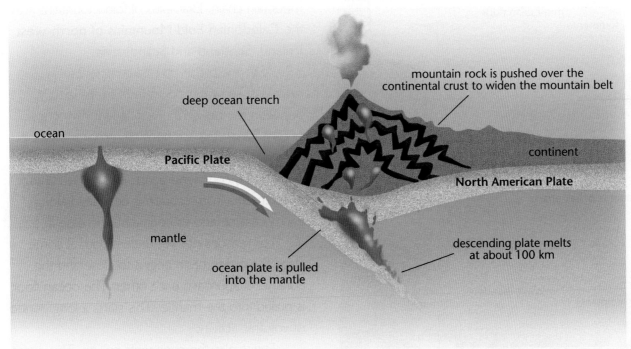

mountain rock is pushed over the
continental crust to widen the mountain belt

deep ocean trench

ocean

continent

Pacific Plate

North American Plate

mantle

descending plate melts
at about 100 km

ocean plate is pulled
into the mantle

When an ocean plate and a continental plate collide, the heavy ocean plate is pulled under the lighter continental plate. The ocean plate sinks into the **mantle** and **melts** at a depth of about **100 km**.

Meanwhile, the continental plate scrapes layers of sediment and islands off the descending ocean floor to form layers of rock along the seaward edge of the continent. Eventually these layers of rock are **compressed** (squeezed) and **folded** (buckled) to form fold mountains. In other places some rock is **metamorphosed** (heated and changed). This has happened in the Rocky Mountains in North America and in counties Donegal, Galway and Wicklow in Ireland.

Squeezing caused by the colliding plates causes **faulting**. Constant pressure over millions of years cracks the rock (faulting) and pushes some of it forward either horizontally or at a low angle for many kilometres, so increasing the width and the thickness of the mountain belt. The faults created by this action are called **thrust faults**. Such faults are found in the mountains of **Donegal,** such as the **Gweebarra Fault,** and the Rockies in North America.

Activity
1. Which two plates have collided to form:
   a. the Rockies?
   b. the Andes?
2. What is a thrust fault?
3. How are some fold mountains formed?

Continent-Continent Boundaries

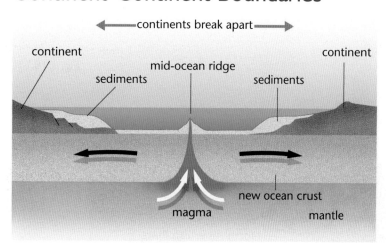

Stage 1 Continents break apart.

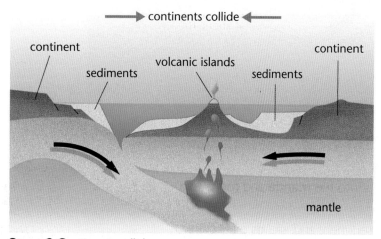

Stage 2 Continents collide.

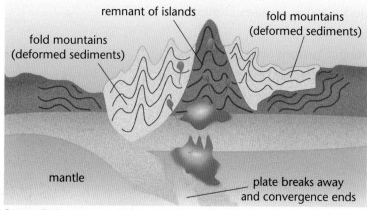

Stage 3 Continents continue to press into each other.

Fig. 1.19

When two continental plates approach each other and collide, they will form a high fold mountain chain. Examples of fold mountains are the **Caledonian Fold Mountains of north-west Ireland, Scotland and Scandinavia.**

After the break-up of a continental landmass, seawater pours in to fill the area between the new continents and forms a new ocean. When this happens new rock is created at a mid-ocean ridge to form an ocean floor, so pushing the continents apart. Also a thick wedge of sediments from erosion is deposited along each coastline and so continents increase in size.

For reasons not yet understood, at some stage the ocean basin begins to close and the continents approach each other. The ocean floor is pulled into the mantle. This starts a long period of volcanic activity.

Eventually, the continents collide. This event buckles, deforms and metamorphoses the crust and trapped sediments washed in by rivers and the island arc to form **fold mountains.**

Faulting, thrusting and folding of the trapped sediments occurs in the fold mountains. The **Himalayas** formed as a consequence of the continent-continent collision of India and Asia.

Activity
1. Name the northern part of Sweden that forms part of the Caledonian Fold Mountains.
2. Explain in your own words what happens when continents approach each other.

In some cases, continents that break apart collide with landmasses other than those from which they separated originally.

Case Study: Formation of the Indian Subcontinent – A Natural Region

Stage 1: India approaches Asia

As the Indian plate moved north, rivers deposited huge amounts of sediment on the ancient sea floor. Also, the ocean floor on top of which India floated was pulled down (subducted) into the mantle and melted.

> The Indian plate is a huge terrane (see page 17).

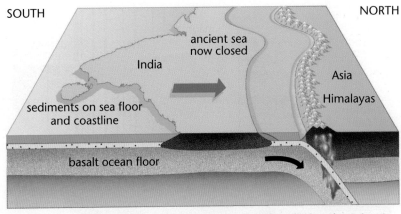

Stage 2: India crashes into Asia

As India came nearer Asia, the sediments on the sea floor were scraped off the descending plate, were squeezed against the Asian coast and were buckled to form mountains. Some were so squeezed that they heated, changed and formed metamorphic rock. The crusts of Asia and India were also buckled as the two plates collided.

Stage 3: The Himalayas formed from folded rock layers

Because these two continents collided less than 20 million years ago, they are still very high and have not been lowered by weathering and erosion.

Very destructive earthquakes continue to occur along fault lines within the Himalayan Mountains.

> India is a natural region because it was formed by nature.

> The Deccan Plateau in India once formed part of a much larger African plateau region.

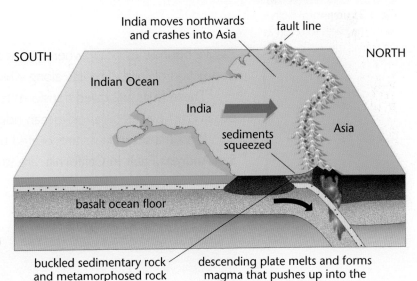

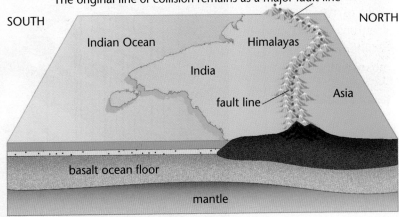

Fig. 1.20

15

EARTH'S INTERNAL FORCES AND STRUCTURES

Passive Boundaries

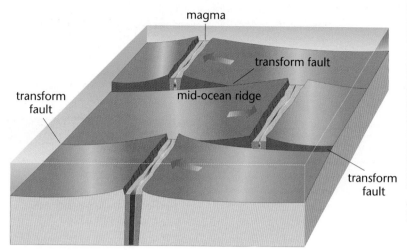

magma

transform fault

mid-ocean ridge

transform fault

transform fault

Fig. 1.21 Transform faults allow the earth to retain its circular shape.

A mid-ocean ridge and numerous transform faults in the Indian Ocean

Passive boundaries occur where plates slide past each other without the creation or destruction of crust. The line along which the plates slide is called a fault line.

These faults are called transform faults and they provide the means by which the ocean crust created at a mid-ocean ridge can be carried to a boundary of destruction.

Most transform faults are located under the oceans, but a few, including the **San Andreas Fault in California**, are situated within continents.

Some rock is buckled along the San Andreas Fault.

mid-ocean ridge
A volcanically active ridge of mountains that runs continuously on the ocean floor between the continents.

A mid-ocean ridge is not straight. Many faults are offset and cross it at right angles so that it may fit on the curved surface of the earth.

Activity

1. Can you explain why there are no volcanoes along the San Andreas Fault?

16

How Fold Mountains and Continents Increase in Width

As ocean plates move, they carry chunks of land such as islands and ocean plateaus to subduction zones where plates sink into the mantle. At subduction zones, the upper layers of these slabs are peeled from the descending plate and pushed in relatively thin sheets against the nearby continent. This process adds to the width of the continent and to the fold mountain.

A fault is a weakness or crack in the earth's crust.

These added chunks of crust are called **terranes**. Terranes vary in size. Some are no bigger than islands. Others, such as the entire **Indian subcontinent**, are huge.

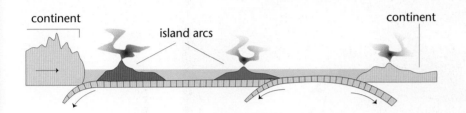

Fig. 1.22 The continent increases in width as more terranes are added at the edge.

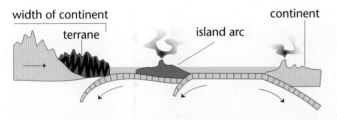

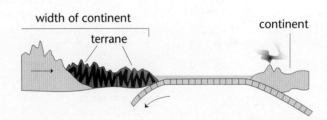

How Ireland Formed

Ireland is made up of many different pieces, each called a terrane. **Each terrane is separated from the next by a major fault line.** Most of these fault lines lie buried deep under layers of rock, such as limestones, sandstones and shales. Ireland's oldest faults are exposed in its oldest mountain regions, such as the Donegal mountains. One of these faults is called the **Gweebarra Fault** in the Derryveagh Mountains in County Donegal.

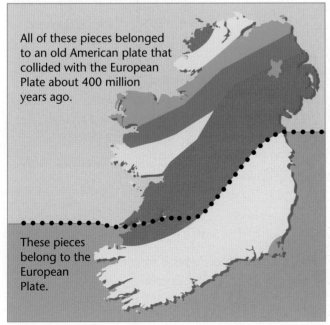

All of these pieces belonged to an old American plate that collided with the European Plate about 400 million years ago.

These pieces belong to the European Plate.

Fig. 1.23 Ireland's buried terranes

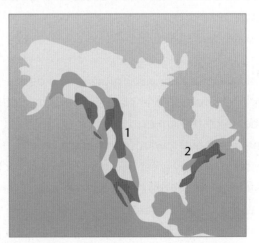

Fig. 1.24 North America's mountains are formed of many terranes that were squashed together to form its Rocky and Appalachian mountain ranges.
● *Identify the mountain ranges marked 1 and 2.*

THE GEOGRAPHY OF VOLCANOES AND EARTHQUAKES

KEY IDEA!

Volcanoes and earthquakes are located where plates separate or collide, but earthquakes also occur where plates slide past each other.

Fig. 1.25 Most volcanoes and earthquakes occur around the **rims of the Pacific and Indian Oceans** and along **mid-ocean ridges** where the edges of many crustal plates meet.

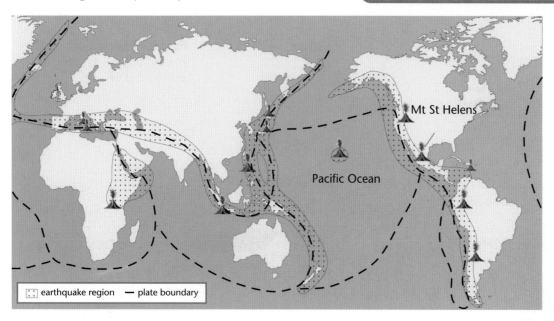

Mt St Helens

Pacific Ocean

⬚ earthquake region   — plate boundary

Volcanoes

A volcano refers to a pipe-like outlet, called a vent, through which molten rock, gases, rock fragments and dust erupt and form a cone-shaped landform made of these materials. Volcanoes are found at the following locations:

● destructive plate boundaries
● constructive plate boundaries
● hot spots.

Most volcanic activity occurs along constructive and destructive plate boundaries. At all boundaries of destruction one plate sinks under another. When the sinking plate reaches a depth of 100 km or more, it starts to melt. The melting creates masses of magma that move towards the surface.

If these masses meet any great thickness of folded rock, the magma pushes its way up into the folds or squeezes into cracks or faults. Here, it cools deep in the crust to form masses of granite rock.

Some magma, however, finds its way to the surface of the buckled rock to form volcanoes. This is why volcanoes occur in fold mountains such as the Rockies in North America and the Andes in South America.

At ocean-ocean boundaries, mid-ocean ridges and

What is silica?
Silica is a white or colourless substance and is a mineral formed of silicon and oxygen.

Magma with a high content of silica is thick and traps gases. It forms the most dangerous volcanoes of all.

Magma with a low content of silica is runny and gases can escape freely.

Class activity
1. What is silica and how does it affect magma?
2. Where do most volcanoes occur?
3. Why do the volcanoes occur at these locations?

hot spots, the magma simply melts its way to the surface where it creates volcanoes and volcanic islands.

Because magma is lighter than surrounding rocks, it works its way towards the earth's surface. When magma reaches the surface it is called **lava**. When lava and other volcanic materials reach the surface they are called **extrusive** materials. The landforms that are created by extrusive materials vary from tiny **volcanic cones** to widespread **lava flows**.

Materials that are pushed into the crust are called **intrusive** materials. They may be later exposed at the surface by erosion of the overlying rocks. Both extrusive and intrusive materials cooled from magma are called **igneous rocks**.

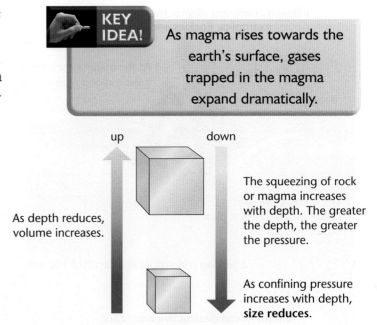

KEY IDEA! As magma rises towards the earth's surface, gases trapped in the magma expand dramatically.

up

down

As depth reduces, volume increases.

The squeezing of rock or magma increases with depth. The greater the depth, the greater the pressure.

As confining pressure increases with depth, **size reduces**.

Fig. 1.27 Pressure within the earth

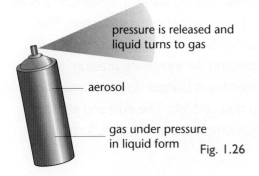

pressure is released and liquid turns to gas

aerosol

gas under pressure in liquid form

Fig. 1.26

A   Molten rock (magma) from the earth's mantle forms a chamber as much as ten kilometres (six miles) below the surface. As the magma rises, gases dissolved in the molten material expand and bubble off, as water does when it is boiled.

B   The resulting froth creates tremendous outward pressure that forces the magma upward. As the molten material comes into contact with groundwater near the surface, the volcano becomes like a pressure cooker.

C   The volcanic mountain bulges. Finally, the froth and compressed gases push through cracks in the volcano. When they reach the surface, the pressures are suddenly released, the bubbles expand dramatically and the volcano erupts in an explosion of ash and molten rock. Vast 'clouds' of hot ash and gases may rush down the mountainside destroying everything in their path.

clouds of steam, gases and hot ash rush down the mountainside

gases expand as they rise

magma chamber

Fig. 1.28 Why a volcano explodes

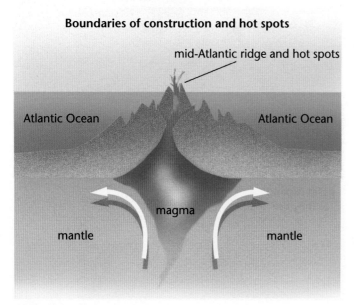

**Ocean-continent destructive boundary –
examples: Rockies and Andes**

4 Volcanoes form
at the surface.

deep ocean trench

3 As the magma rises, its
gases expand massively.

1 The ocean plate sinks
under the continental plate.

2 Sinking plate melts at a depth of 100 km.

**Ocean-ocean destructive boundary –
example: Japan Islands and the Philippines**

4 Volcanoes and volcanic islands
appear at the surface.

deep ocean trench

3 As the magma rises, its
gases expand massively.

1 One ocean plate sinks
under another.

2 Sinking plate melts at a depth of 100 km.

Boundaries of construction and hot spots

mid-Atlantic ridge and hot spots

Atlantic Ocean

Atlantic Ocean

magma

mantle

mantle

Volcanoes at Destructive Plate Boundaries

Volcanoes that are formed at subduction zones are among the most violent and potentially dangerous forces on earth.

Why are these volcanoes the most dangerous? Magma at **destructive plate boundaries**, such as in Japan, has a high content of silica. The gases cannot escape because the magma is too thick.

When gases rise within the magma they expand rapidly as they approach the surface, occupying hundreds of times the original volume than when they were deep down within the mantle. The thick magma **prevents** these rapidly and **massively expanding gases** from escaping. This leads to a build-up of intense pressure within the mountain. The volcano mountain **bulges**. Finally the mountain is unable to withstand the increasing pressure and the entire mountain top is blasted skywards and its rock is pulverised to dust and ash. The dust and ash from explosive eruptions falls near the vent, forming a steep cone.

Volcanoes at Constructive Plate Boundaries

Mid-ocean Ridges and Hot Spots

Magma at **constructive plate boundaries** has **low silica** content. Massively expanding **gases** within the magma can **escape freely**, because the magma is runny. The escaping gases help to blast lava, rock and rock particles, called **pyroclasts**, hundreds of metres into the air forming lava flows and 'lava fountains' on land. The escaping gases also help push the flowing lava forward. The hot temperature of 1,000°C also makes the magma runny.

Because runny lava allows the gases to escape with ease, it prevents a build-up of pressure and so these volcanoes are relatively 'safe'. Lava fountains, such as those at Mauna Loa in Hawaii, are regularly included in tourist itineraries.

Fig. 1.29

Hot Spots

Some volcanic activity occurs **away from plate boundaries**. It is localised and is confined to specific spots on the earth's crust, such as in Hawaii or the Canary Islands. These places are called hot spots. Some hot spots are located at plate boundaries, eg Iceland.

Distribution of Hot Spots

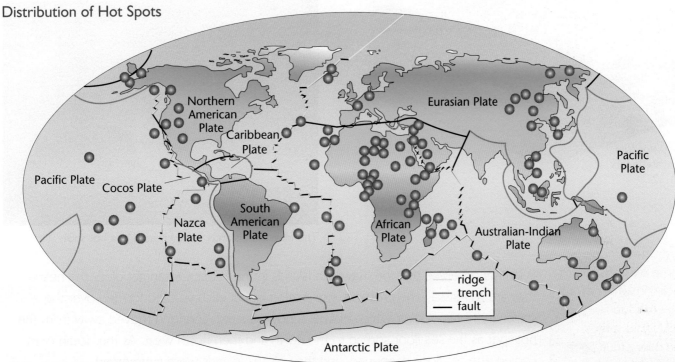

Fig. 1.30 Long-lived hot spots at the earth's surface, each a centre of volcanic activity.
● *Which spot represents Hawaii?*

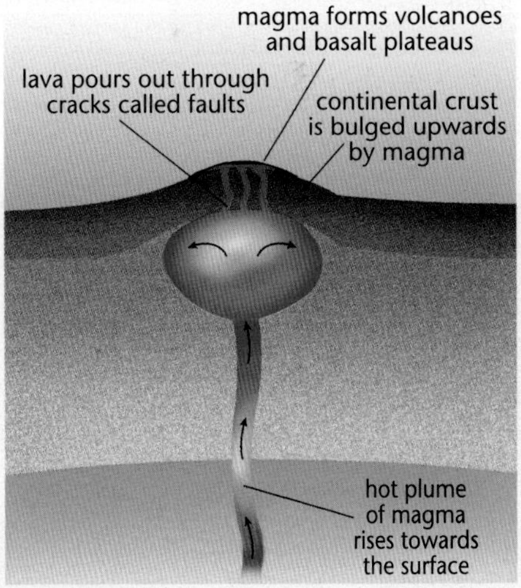

Most evidence indicates that hot spots remain stationary. Only about 20 of the 120 hot spots that are believed to exist are near plate boundaries.

What are Hot Spots?

Hot spots are unusually warm areas found deep within the earth's mantle. Some geologists believe that narrow columns of hot magma called **plumes** rise through the mantle to the surface, much as smoke rises through a chimney. These plumes can split continents or create volcanoes, such as in Hawaii.

A hot spot beneath Iceland is thought to be responsible for the regular volcanic activity on the island, which is sited on the Mid-Atlantic Ridge. Another hot spot is believed to exist beneath the Canary Islands.

Fig. 1.31 Plume at hot spot

Class activity

1. Why are volcanoes that form near deep ocean trenches the most dangerous?
2. Why are some volcanoes not as explosive as others?
3. Search the Internet for information about volcanoes in Iceland.

Case Study: Hawaiian Islands at a Hot Spot in the Pacific Ocean

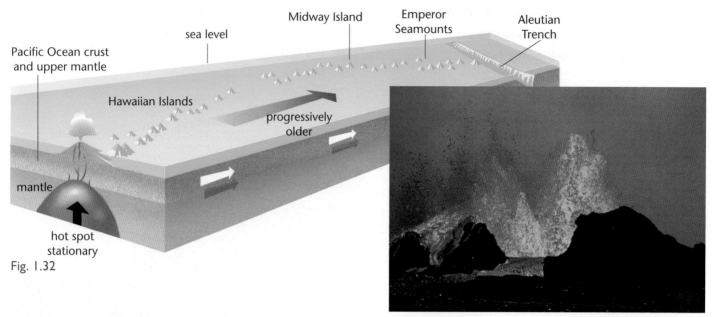

Fig. 1.32

The Hawaiian Islands were created at a hot spot.

Hydrothermal areas
These are areas where cooling magma near to the earth's surface creates hot springs, and boiling mud pools and geysers.

Scientists observed that the Hawaiian Islands in the Pacific Ocean get older the nearer they are to Alaska. The probable explanation is that each volcano formed over the stationary hot spot over which Hawaii is now situated, and then moved away from the hot spot as the sea floor spread to the north and then north west. As the ocean crust cooled, the sea floor deepened, and the volcanic islands were submerged.

Black smokers are found at mid-ocean ridges.

Other Forms of Volcanic Activity: Hydrothermal Areas

● **Geysers** are **jets of hot water** and **steam** that shoot into the air, often rising 30 to 60 metres, at regular intervals. Hot water is ejected first. After the jet of water stops, a column of steam rushes out, usually with a thundering noise. The most famous geyser in the world is Old Faithful in Yellowstone National Park, in the USA.

● **Hot springs** occur when groundwater circulates **at great depths** and becomes **heated.** If the water rises to the surface, it may emerge quietly as a hot spring. Hot springs are common in Iceland and Italy.

● **Black Smokers**
Super-hot water at 700°C gushes from chimney-like openings in the ocean floor at mid-ocean ridges. This water has many minerals dissolved in it.

How Volcanoes And Their Effects Can Be Predicted

Many steps are involved in forecasting volcanic eruptions and their effects. Firstly, geologists (people who study rock and rock structures) draw upon their **background knowledge** of the way volcanoes are formed, how they are composed, the type and date of deposits that form the volcano and the **patterns of events** that have been associated with past volcanic eruptions and the **settings** in which volcanoes erupt.

Patterns of Events

The type, date and patterns of deposits are useful information to geologists.

- The **types of materials** found on the sides of volcanoes help geologists to determine the power and explosive nature of past eruptions. The **dating** of these deposits helps to establish a rhythm – whether the volcano erupts regularly, every hundred years or once every thousand years.
- The **distribution of ejected material** and its relation to the local landscape is studied. This suggests where ejected material is likely to collect and so helps geologists pinpoint the places most likely to be affected by an eruption.

Earthquakes

There is often an increase in the frequency of minor earthquake tremors (mild shaking of the ground) prior to an eruption. Having decided that a volcano may erupt in the foreseeable future, geologists set up a number of **seismographs** (instruments that measure earthquakes) around the sides and the summit of the volcano. These help to track the location, severity and frequency of earthquakes. Geologists also install **tiltmeters** to detect ground swelling or other movements.

Class activity

1. Why are volcanoes on some Hawaiian islands extinct, while on other islands they are active? Explain.
2. What are hydrothermal areas?
3. Identify three types of hydrothermal activity.

Some geologists take great risks with their personal safety so that we can increase our knowledge of volcanoes and magma.

Geologists study rock samples around a volcano.

Column of ash, hot gases and pulverised rock

A geologist installs a seismograph to detect earthquakes.

23

Poisonous gases escape from the sides of some volcanoes.

Lahars cause great damage to towns and villages.

Other patterns

Ground tilting and earthquakes are only two of the signs that are monitored by geologists. Other signs include:

● Changes in the quantity and type of gases escaping from the vent.
● Changes in the heat escaping from the crater.
● Changes in local groundwater.
● The appearance of geysers, hot springs or steam vents in the region.

By integrating this information, geologists hope to improve their forecasting abilities.

Past volcanic eruptions

Knowing the effects of volcanoes that erupt suddenly helps to warn people or to evacuate residents who may be affected if an eruption is likely. These effects include:

● **Lahars**
Lahars are mud flows created by the sudden melting by hot ash and lava of ice on elevated ice-capped volcanic cones. Because lahars occur suddenly, they can cause great loss of life and destruction to property near active or dormant volcanic cones. Torrents of hot, thick mud, ash and rubble can race down the valleys of nearby rivers that radiate from the volcano, devastating everything in their way.

● **Nuée Ardente**
When expanding hot, poisonous gases and glowing ash are ejected from a volcano, they may produce a heavy fiery grey cloud called a nuée ardente. Also referred to as glowing avalanches, these devastating clouds of steam, poisonous gases and ash flows, which are heavier than air, race down steep volcanic cones at speeds up to 200 kilometres per hour.

These ground-hugging clouds are suspended from the ground by hot, expanding gases, much as a hovercraft travels over land or water. Some of their deposits travel more than 100 kilometres from their source.

Nuées ardentes regularly cause loss of life during volcanic eruptions.

The Position of Ireland Now and in the Past

About 450 million years ago Ireland as we know it today did not
exist. Instead bits and pieces of it were separated from each other
as islands in an ancient ocean, with the European Plate on one side
and the American Plate on the other (see Terranes, page 17). This
ocean disappeared about 400 million years ago when the American
and European plates moved together to form a great European-
American plate.

The various pieces were squeezed and welded together to form
Ireland. A line joining Limerick to Dundalk separates the parts to the
north that originally belonged to the American Plate from those
south of this line that belonged to Europe.

As the margins grew closer, seafloor sediments were squeezed
and buckled into folds and pushed up to form high mountains. These mountains were
called the **Caledonian Fold Mountains** and their remnants are found in Galway, Mayo,
Donegal and Wicklow in Ireland. The Appalachians in North America, the Scottish
Highlands and the Scandinavian Highlands were also formed as part of this crushing
movement . They all have a north-east to south-west trend. When they were formed
first, they were as high as the Himalayas are today.

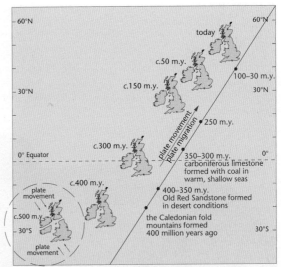

Fig. 1.33

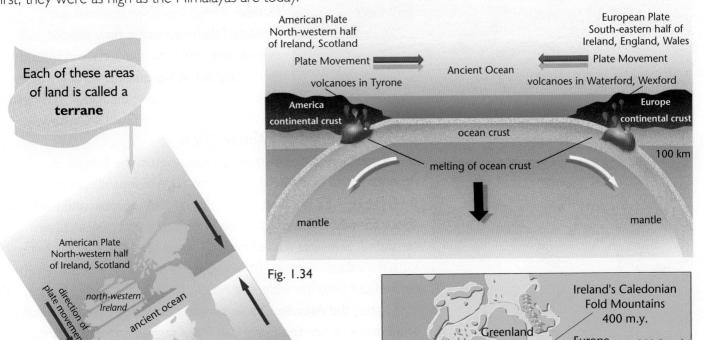

Each of these areas
of land is called a
terrane

Fig. 1.34

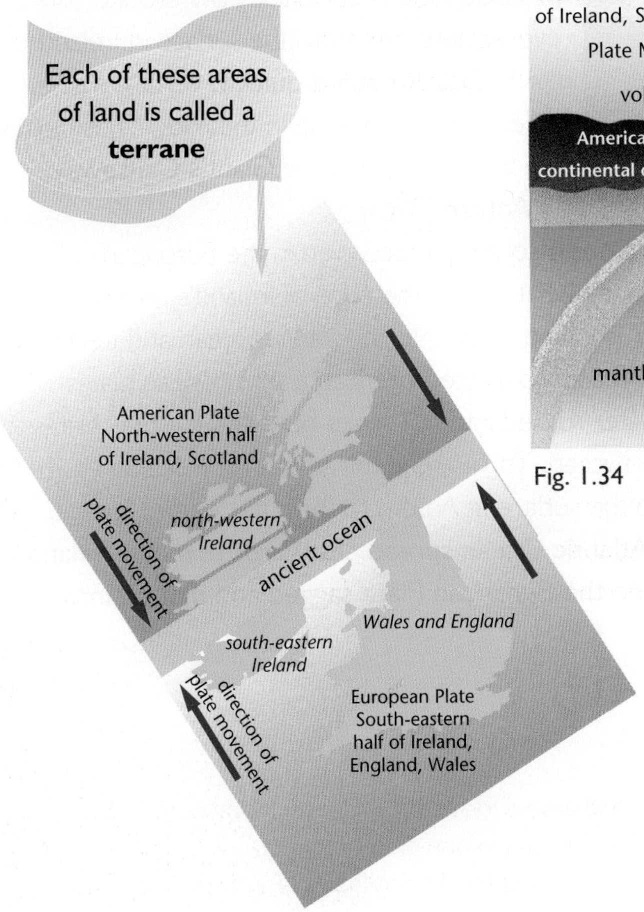

Fig. 1.35 The birth of Britain and Ireland about 400 million years

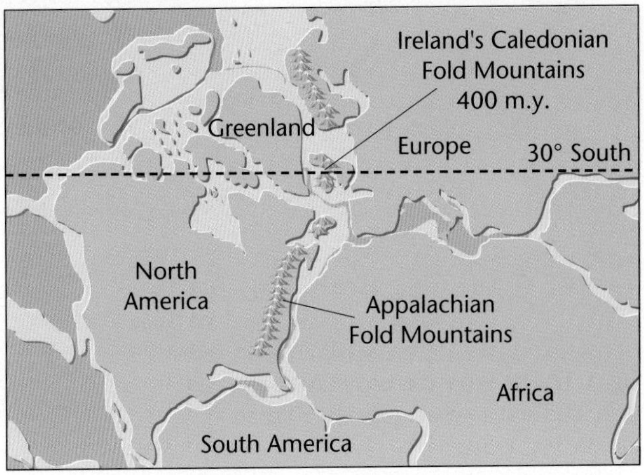

Fig. 1.36 Ireland's position at 30° South when the Caledonian
Mountains were formed about 400 million years ago.

25

The Antrim Plateau is formed from numerous lava flows that cooled quickly on the surface.

As the rock layers were folded, hot magma rose from the mantle and forced its way into the folds and there it **cooled slowly** to form huge masses of granite rock (see page 42). Today, most of the covering rock has been eroded and this granite is exposed at the surface in Connemara, Mayo, Donegal and Wicklow (see pages 49 and 50).

Today's Ireland

About 65 million years ago, the great **European-American plate** began to **split apart**. As it did so, surface rocks were stretched, and some cracks appeared that allowed magma to rush to the surface. These cracks appeared in what is now Antrim, where lava poured out onto the chalk surface and cooled quickly to form basalt rock. **These and later lava flows built up to form the Antrim Plateau.** These lava flows covered and protected the chalk that is now eroded everywhere else from the surface in Ireland. As the **basalt cooled quickly,** vertical cracks, called joints, appeared in the rock. These joints are clearly visible at the **Giant's Causeway in Antrim**.

Then a great north-south split occurred in the European-American plate along what is now the edge of Ireland's continental shelf. Figure 1.37 is a map of the North Atlantic Ocean and Ireland about 55 million years ago as the American and European plates separated. Seawater rushed into the space between the two plates to form the Atlantic Ocean. Throughout this separation, lava flows poured out onto the surface at Antrim to form the Antrim Plateau.

Later, the Atlantic Ocean spread eastwards towards Ireland and Europe when the European Plate sagged and dipped into the sea.

Fig. 1.37 The American and European plates separated and a new ocean, the Atlantic Ocean, was created

Activity

1. Was Ireland always located at its present location? Explain.
2. Was Ireland always in one piece? Explain.
3. When and why did the Antrim Plateau form?

Earthquakes

What is an Earthquake?

An earthquake is a shaking, rolling or sudden shock of the earth's crust. There may be as many as a million earthquakes in a single year. Most of them take place beneath the surface of the sea, and few of these cause any damage. But earthquakes that occur near large cities can cause much damage and loss of life, especially if the cities are on soft ground, e.g. Mexico City.

Earthquakes create a vibration of the earth's surface. These vibrations radiate in all directions from its source, the **focus**, in the form of waves, something like the ripples produced by dropping a stone into a calm pond. Just as the impact of the stone sets water waves in motion, an earthquake generates **waves** that radiate throughout the earth. Even though this energy decreases quickly with increasing distance from the focus, instruments located throughout the world record the event.

> An earthquake is a sudden tremor or vibration of the earth's crust.

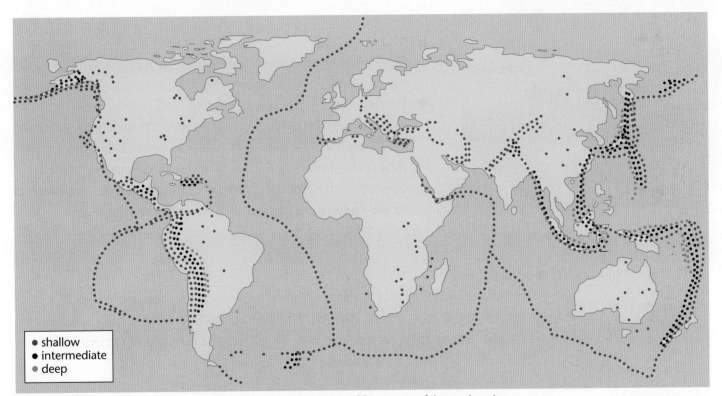

- shallow
- intermediate
- deep

Fig. 1.38 World distribution of earthquakes. The epicentres of over 99 per cent of the earthquakes that occur each year are confined to the boundaries of the earth's crustal plates.

Class Activity

Look at the world distribution map of earthquakes above and the world distribution map of earthquakes and volcanoes in Figure 1.25, page 18. What similarities can you see between these maps?

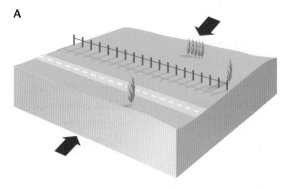

A

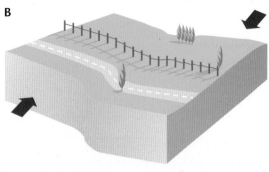

B

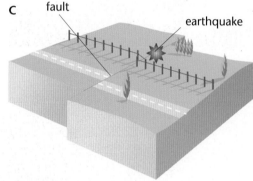

C

What Causes an Earthquake?

Earthquakes occur for a number of reasons.

- Slipping

  As plates move very slowly, they deform the rocks on both sides of a fault line. Under these conditions, rocks are bending and storing 'elastic energy' the way a wooden stick would if bent. Eventually, the plate slips at the **weakest point**, called the **focus**, causing an earthquake.

  > Rocks behave elastically, as a stretched elastic band does when it is released.

- Sinking Plates

  The melting of plates creates earthquakes, as the plates sink into the mantle.

- Ice Age

  Earthquakes may also be associated with the melting of the great ice sheets that covered much of North America, Europe and Asia thousands of years ago. Melting relieved the load that pushed down the crust, and the theory is that the **strain** was **transferred to old faults** as the crust rose slowly to its original level.

Fig. 1.39 The Theory of the Cause of Earthquakes:
(A) Rock with stress acting on it.
(B) Stress has caused strain in the rock. Strain builds up over a long period of time.
(C) Rock breaks suddenly, releasing energy, with rock movement along a fault. Horizontal motion is shown; rocks can also move vertically.

- Ancient Faults

  Fewer than 1 per cent of all earthquakes occur away from plate boundaries, but some of these have caused great destruction to populated areas. Geologists believe that these devastating earthquakes may be related to a **renewal of ancient faults** that are deeply buried in the earth's crust.

Activity

1. What is an earthquake?
2. What effects do earthquakes have on the earth's crust when they are happening?
3. What causes an earthquake? Explain fully.

> Learn these four causes of earthquakes.

Categories of Earthquakes

There are three categories of earthquakes:

- shallow earthquakes
- intermediate earthquakes
- deep earthquakes.

Shallow-focus Earthquakes

Shallow earthquakes occur close to the surface along all plate boundaries.

At mid-ocean ridges **the crust is new and thin and splits easily.** This new rock is **not capable of storing strain** long enough to cause large earthquakes.

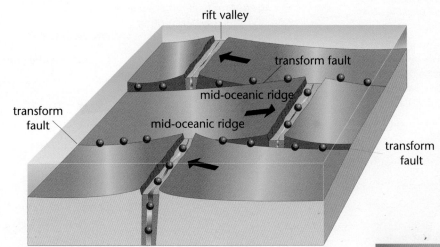

Fig. 1.40 Earthquakes occur along rift valleys and transform faults. Both of these appear at mid-ocean ridges.

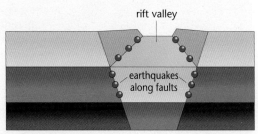

Fig. 1.41 Rift valleys are created where land collapses along parallel faults, such as along mid-ocean ridges and the African Great Rift Valley.

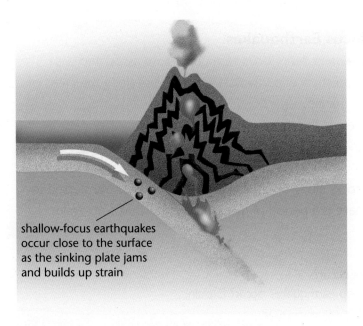

shallow-focus earthquakes occur close to the surface as the sinking plate jams and builds up strain

Fig. 1.42 Shallow earthquakes occur close to the surface where an ocean plate sinks into the mantle. This happens at zones of ocean-ocean convergence and ocean-continent convergence.

Earthquakes occur along the African Great Rift Valley. This is a constructive plate boundary where plates are separating and so create new crust along the valley floor.

Case Study: The San Andreas Fault in California, USA

The San Andreas Fault is the boundary between the North American and Pacific Plates. Both plates are moving in a north-west direction. However, the Pacific Plate moves faster than the North American Plate, giving the illusion that they are moving in opposite directions. When these plates jam together, they build up strain. Finally, they slip creating shallow-focus earthquakes. San Francisco and Los Angeles have suffered severely in recent decades from earthquake damage.

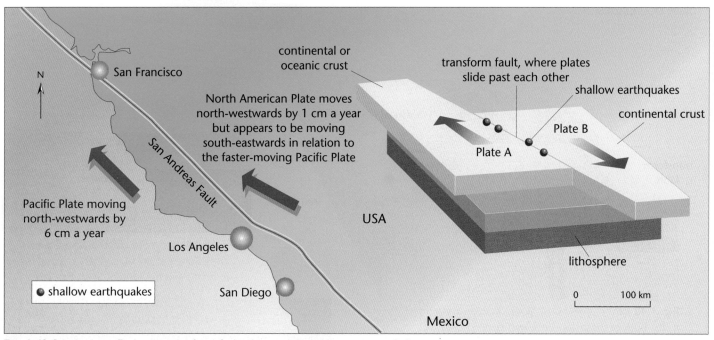

Fig. 1.43 San Andreas Fault — a transform fault where earthquakes occur regularly

Intermediate and Deep-focus Earthquakes

Virtually all the earth's intermediate and deep-focus earthquakes are associated with subduction zones. These create a pattern of earthquakes that occurs along the paths of ocean plates as they sink into the mantle.

Foreshocks usually come before the main event, as the rocks near the focus begin to crack. The main earthquake then arrives and can last from a few seconds to a few minutes.

Aftershocks follow as the rocks along the fault readjust and strain is transferred to the next jamming point. Then there is a period of quiet while strain builds up again.

> Shallow-focus earthquakes occur close to the earth's surface.

> All three types — shallow, intermediate and deep earthquakes — occur along the Pacific Ring of Fire at subduction zones.

Activity
1. Where do shallow earthquakes occur?
2. Where do intermediate and deep earthquakes occur? Explain.
3. Explain why all three types of earthquakes occur:
   a. along the west coast of South America?
   b. along the western edge of the Pacific Ocean? See Fig. 1.38 on page 27 and Fig. 1.4 on page 5.

Earthquakes occur along a descending plate as it sinks into the mantle.

- The earthquakes nearest the surface are called **shallow** earthquakes. They occur because the descending plate jams from time to time and builds up strain. When the strain is too much, the plate slips, causing an earthquake.
- As the plate descends (sinks), some of the plate melts to form magma. This melting creates **intermediate** earthquakes.
- **Deep** earthquakes occur when there are chemical changes and minerals within the rock change into other minerals.

About 40 per cent of the world's cities are located either on or near plate boundaries where earthquake activity has occurred. All of these cities have over two million inhabitants, and more than **600 million** people will live in these cities by **2035**. Since they live in areas of high risk, it is reasonable to assume that great destruction is likely to occur.

   In addition, many of these cities will be in developing countries where the vast majority of buildings have **no earthquake-proof design or materials**. Poorly built houses crumble and collapse on their occupants when earthquakes strike. This was the case in India and Iran in the past. Many new apartment buildings were constructed to cope with rapidly rising populations. These were often built with **low-quality concrete** and **badly designed joists**, and **lacked steel reinforcement**.

Why Earthquakes Occur in Central and Southern Italy

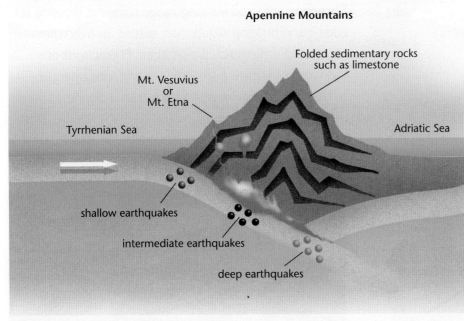

Fig. 1.45 Southern Italy is called the Mezzogiorno.

Fig. 1.44 Note that **intermediate and deep-focus earthquakes occur only** within the sinking slab of the ocean plate.

The floor of the Tyrrhenian Sea slips under the toe of Italy. Earthquakes occur along the path of this descending plate as it dips into the mantle. In addition, limestone sediment from the sea floor is squeezed and buckled up to form the Apennine fold mountains. This is why the land in southern Italy is steep. It is dry because any rain that falls on land quickly disappears through the limestone rock.

Some buildings sink into the ground during earthquakes.

How Earthquakes and Their Effects Can Be Predicted

Long-range earthquake forecasts are based on the idea that earthquakes are repetitive. As soon as one earthquake is over, the movement of the earth's plates builds strain until it is released by another quake along a fault line. This has led seismologists (scientists who study earthquakes) to study the history of earthquakes in an area and to search for patterns so that their occurrence might be predicted.

Slow tilting of the land surface and swarms of **foreshocks** indicate the possibility of an earthquake. However, predicting an earthquake is difficult. What would happen if the city of Los Angeles were evacuated? How can 10 million people be evacuated safely? What would happen if the predicted earthquake did not occur? Certainly, predicting an earthquake can be done. The difficulty is predicting exactly when it will occur. Studies of recurring earthquakes show a number of places where earthquakes are overdue and where strain is steadily increasing. These areas then become the places with the highest probability of earthquake activity (see Fig. 1.46).

Many geologists prefer to distinguish between a prediction and a forecast. A prediction specifies the time, location and magnitude of an event, whereas a forecast projects trends over a longer time. Each has its own purpose. **Forecasts** are used for long-range planning, drawing up zoning and building regulations, setting up evacuation routes and emergency procedures. **Predictions** are used for immediate preparations, evacuating people, turning off gas pipelines, stopping trains, closing off bridges.

Fig. 1.46 Probability of a major earthquake from 1988 to 2018 on the San Andreas Fault

Great earthquakes may cause even the best constructed buildings to collapse.

Activity

1. Look at Fig. 1.46. Which area in California is most likely to experience an earthquake in the future?

Seismic Gaps

Places along fault lines that have been 'quiet' for a long time are called seismic gaps. According to recent studies, quiet segments of a fault bordered by the places (epicentres) of recent earthquake activity are the **most likely places** to look for the next great earthquake.

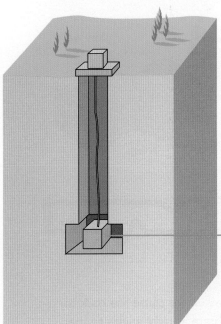

Dating

In order to forecast the future it is important to know the past pattern of earthquakes in an area. For example, it was found that there was an interval of 150 years between great earthquakes, and the last one occurred some 120 years ago, the probability of a great earthquake occurring within the next 30 years is high and even higher within the next 40 years and so on.

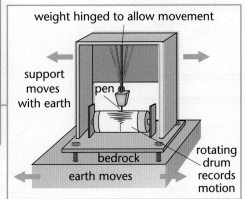

weight hinged to allow movement

support moves with earth

pen

bedrock

earth moves

rotating drum records motion

Fig. 1.47 A seismograph measures earth tremors.

Recording and Locating Earthquakes

Once it has been established where an earthquake has occurred and its magnitude (size), it is vital to estimate the damage created by an earthquake. For example, if an earthquake occurs in the middle of the Sahara desert, it is unlikely to cause any great damage or loss of life because very few people live in this area. But if the earthquake has occurred in a city in India, enormous damage and tens of thousands of deaths could have resulted. Locating and recording the size of an earthquake is vital to estimate potential damage and to arrange for emergency aid for the region. Local communications systems may be 'down' and there may be no way of contacting the affected population. The earlier help arrives, the greater the number of lives that may be saved.

Other Methods

Small changes can warn us if **strain is building up** and close to snapping. These include:

- **Increased uplift of land:** Land levels are recorded over a long time. If there is a noticeable change in movement of the surface level, it is a sign of increased stress on rocks. This stress can be measured using **creep meters**, **bore-hole strain meters** and **tiltmeters**.

- **Movement of rocks:** Lasers can measure the slightest movement of rocks across a fault line. Again this could indicate a build-up of strain in rocks on one or both sides of the fault.

- **Foreshocks:** Installing many **seismographs** in an area to record **foreshocks** (tiny earthquakes that occur before a great earthquake). It has been noticed that there is a pattern of numerous small quakes that occur over days, weeks or months before a major earthquake.

Activity

1. Identify four ways that earthquakes and their effects may be predicted.
2. Explain how people can estimate the damage created by an earthquake, even though they may be a long way from the earthquake site.

Earthquake Waves

An earthquake releases two classes of vibrations or seismic waves:

- **Body waves** that travel through the interior of the earth.
- **Surface waves** that travel mainly near the surface.

The **body waves** that travel through the interior of the earth are in turn divided into two types:

(a) **fast waves**

(b) **slow waves.**

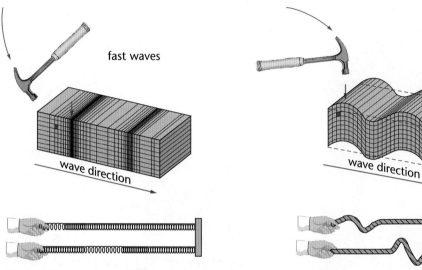

fast waves

wave direction

slow waves

wave direction

Fig. 1.48 Body or interior waves

Earthquake waves are also called seismic waves.

Fast waves alternately compress and expand the rocks they pass through in an accordion-like motion. These are the first waves to arrive at a recording station.

Fig. 1.49 The focus is the spot under the earth's crust where the earthquake starts. The epicentre is the spot on the earth's surface that is directly above the focus.

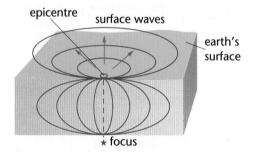

epicentre

surface waves

earth's surface

★ focus

Slow waves cause the rock to vibrate at right angles to the direction of the wave, much like what happens when you shake the free end of a rope tied to a pole. These waves arrive second, after fast waves.

Locating the Epicentre

The epicentre of an earthquake can be located by examining the arrival time of the body and surface waves from at least three recording stations. Their arrival times indicate the distance the epicentre is from the recording station. Intersecting circles from these stations then locate the epicentre.

Fig. 1.50 Typical earthquake vibrations on a seismograph. Note the time interval between the arrival of each wave type. Surface waves are the last to arrive because they take the longest route along the earth's surface.

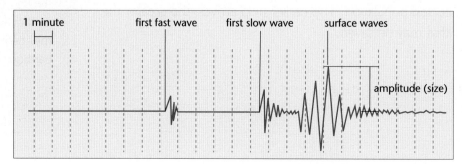

1 minute

first fast wave

first slow wave

surface waves

amplitude (size)

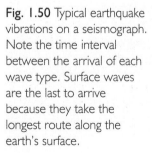

Locating the Focus

The greater the difference in arrival times of the shock waves, the deeper the focus. Once the epicentre and the focus are located, the effects of the earthquake can be established and emergency plans can be put into operation. The sooner this can be done, the greater the chance of saving lives.

Damage Caused by Earthquakes

The extent of the damage and loss of life caused by an individual earthquake depends on a number of factors:

- the magnitude (size) of earthquake
- the depth of the focus
- the types of rock and soil through which the waves travel
- how close the epicentre is to cities
- the buildings and utilities (water supply, gas pipes, etc.) affected
- the time it happens, i.e. day or night, rush hour, etc.

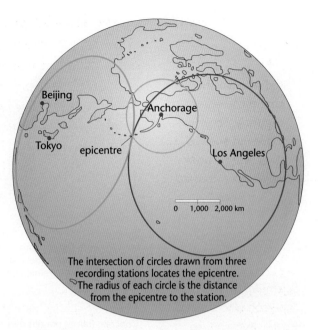

The intersection of circles drawn from three recording stations locates the epicentre. The radius of each circle is the distance from the epicentre to the station.

Fig. 1.51 Locating the earthquake focus

Estimating Damage

Two scales are used to estimate earthquake damage:

- The Richter scale is used to measure the earthquake size and the possible damage resulting from it.
- The Mercalli scale is used once the size and location of an earthquake are known.

Magnitude or Size

The Richter scale is an indication of the size, or magnitude, of an earthquake. A magnitude 2 is a mild quiver, undetectable by all but the most sensitive instruments. By contrast, a magnitude 7.0 is a major earthquake.

An earthquake's **size** and its **location** indicate the **potential damage** that an earthquake will cause. The size of an earthquake of 5 on the Richter scale is 10 times more powerful than one of 4 on the Richter scale and 10 times less powerful than one of magnitude 6. Earthquakes of magnitude 8 and above, which occur once every few years, are classed as great earthquakes.

The Mercalli scale measures earthquake damage on a 12-point scale: 1 means no damage, while 12 indicates complete devastation.

A Simplified Mercalli Scale		
Number on scale	**Type**	**Effect of earthquake**
1	Negligible	detected by seismographs only
3	Slight	vibration like the passing of a heavy truck; generally felt by many people indoors
5	Not very strong	felt by all except heavy sleepers; plaster cracks, windows break, unstable objects are overturned
8	Destructive	panic; chimneys, factory stacks and monuments fall; slight damage to well-designed buildings but heavy in poorly built structures
10	Disastrous	panic, many buildings collapse; large landslides; ground badly cracked; rails bent
12	Superpanic	damage nearly total: waves seen on the ground; objects thrown into the air

Fig. 1.52

Studies have shown that these effects regularly occur in buildings such as skyscrapers, brick and wooden-framed houses.

seismologist
A person who studies earthquake movements.

liquefaction
The transformation of normal solid sediment or soil to liquid when ground shaking causes the particles to lose contact with each other.

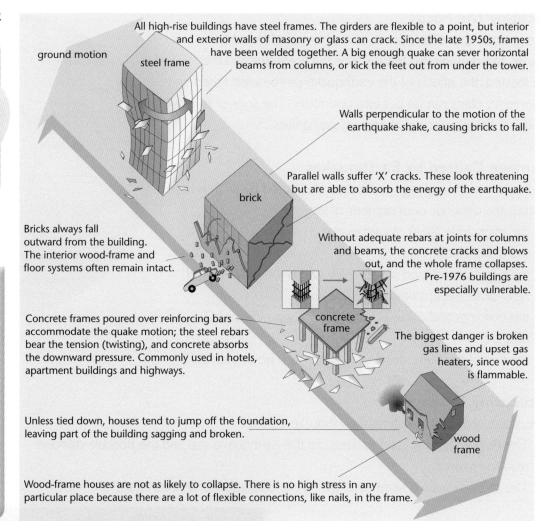

ground motion

steel frame

All high-rise buildings have steel frames. The girders are flexible to a point, but interior and exterior walls of masonry or glass can crack. Since the late 1950s, frames have been welded together. A big enough quake can sever horizontal beams from columns, or kick the feet out from under the tower.

Walls perpendicular to the motion of the earthquake shake, causing bricks to fall.

brick

Parallel walls suffer 'X' cracks. These look threatening but are able to absorb the energy of the earthquake.

Bricks always fall outward from the building. The interior wood-frame and floor systems often remain intact.

Without adequate rebars at joints for columns and beams, the concrete cracks and blows out, and the whole frame collapses. Pre-1976 buildings are especially vulnerable.

concrete frame

Concrete frames poured over reinforcing bars accommodate the quake motion; the steel rebars bear the tension (twisting), and concrete absorbs the downward pressure. Commonly used in hotels, apartment buildings and highways.

The biggest danger is broken gas lines and upset gas heaters, since wood is flammable.

Unless tied down, houses tend to jump off the foundation, leaving part of the building sagging and broken.

wood frame

Wood-frame houses are not as likely to collapse. There is no high stress in any particular place because there are a lot of flexible connections, like nails, in the frame.

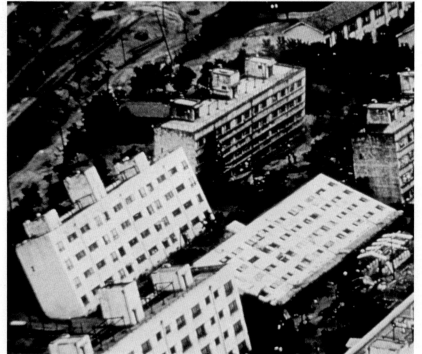

Liquefaction causes buildings to sink into the ground.

Liquefaction

Earthquakes can create a phenomenon called **liquefaction,** when a great thickness of silt or sand is saturated with water. Under these conditions, what had been a stable foundation soil turns into a thick liquid, like porridge, that is no longer able to support buildings. Underground objects, such as storage tanks and sewer pipes, may float up towards the surface of the ground, while multi-storey apartments may sink into the ground. Because Mexico City was built on an ancient lake bed, it is likely that some parts of the city will suffer from liquefaction during an earthquake. This type of knowledge also helps to estimate damage in earthquake-prone regions.

Tsunamis

Tsunami, a Japanese word, is the correct term for what is called a tidal wave. It can be any great event that causes a sudden large change in sea level, such as an earthquake on the ocean floor, an underwater volcanic eruption or a landslide. If the sea floor is suddenly uplifted five metres, a five-metre-high hump of excess water is created at the surface. Such a hump collapses to generate a series of waves that radiate outwards across the surface of the ocean and may cause damage and loss of life thousands of miles from their origin.

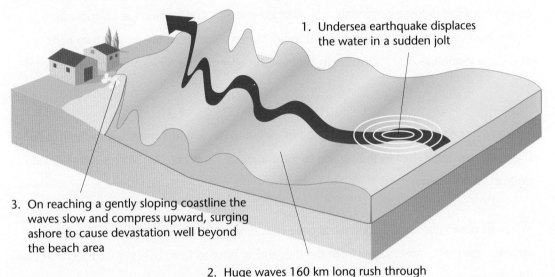

1. Undersea earthquake displaces the water in a sudden jolt

3. On reaching a gently sloping coastline the waves slow and compress upward, surging ashore to cause devastation well beyond the beach area

2. Huge waves 160 km long rush through the water at up to 1,000 km/h

> If the earthquake has occurred on the sea floor, it is likely to create a tidal wave. Early warning can save thousands of lives.

Fig. 1.53 Devastating tidal waves or tsunamis occur when an earthquake at sea combines with shallow coastal waters.

Think of a wave of 800 to 1,000 kilometres an hour, a metre high and 160 kilometres long rushing towards the shoreline. In the shallow water the front of the wave suddenly slows to about 30 kilometres per hour as 'it feels bottom', its wavelength shrinks to about 8 kilometres and the wave grows to about 5 metres in height. However, the back of the wave, still in deep ocean water, keeps rushing along at almost full speed. The wave races onto the beach without breaking and can devastate areas up to a kilometre inland.

Predicting a Tsunami

In the past, most of these tidal waves happened without warning. Today, with the immediate identification of an earthquake's epicentre on the sea floor and with the help of **satellite pictures**, it is possible to predict the arrival time of a tsunami on a coastline. With warning of potential destruction, people can evacuate low-lying coastal areas in the path of the tidal wave. Countries need a good radio and television network, good roads, and emergency plans to cope with such events.

In undeveloped countries, such as Bangladesh, these facilities may not be sufficiently well developed, and large-scale loss of life generally occurs. **Bangladesh** is in a low-lying delta area in the Bay of Bengal in the Indian Ocean. This **coastline narrows** towards Bangladesh and causes the tsunami to rise well above normal sea levels. Such waves regularly devastate coastal communities.

> A Pacific Tsunami Warning Centre in Ewa Beach, Hawaii, serves as the regional Tsunami Warning Centre for Hawaii and as an international warning centre for tsunamis that pose a threat for all countries that border the Pacific Ocean.
> Check for tsunami warning systems on the Internet. Use your search engine to look for **earthquakes**.

TEST YOURSELF AT

my-etest.com

Revision activity

Fill in the missing words to complete this text about processes on and within the earth's surface.

The planet Earth is about … … years old. Its lithosphere includes the continental crust, the ocean crust and the … … … . Continental drift is driven by … … that are located with the earth's mantle. At one time there was a single landmass called …, which was surrounded by a single ocean called … . About … … years ago this landmass broke up into many separate continents. One of these continents, … , crashed into Asia and formed the … mountains. These are the … mountains in the world today. When a continent breaks into two parts, a new … is formed. A … … forms at its centre. The edges of the new continents dip to form … … .

When two ocean plates approach each other, one plate is … and it melts within the mantle. Magma forms and it rises to the surface to form a … … . A deep … … forms along all such destructive boundaries.

When an ocean plate and a continental plate collide, the … plate is subducted. The layers of sediment on the … are scraped from the descending plate to form layers of … rock. Eventually these layers are … and … to form … … .

Volcanoes and earthquakes are located where plates … or … . Earthquakes only are found where plates … … … … .

As magma rises towards the surface at destructive boundaries trapped gases within the magma … dramatically. The volcanic mountain … and finally … , blasting ash, … and … into the air.

Sometimes volcanic eruptions result in mud flows, called … . On other occasions expanding clouds of poisonous gases, ash and rock particles rush down volcanic cones after an eruption. These clouds of ash, rock and gases are called … … .

The island of Ireland was formed about … … years ago when the … plate and the … plate collided. A high mountain range, called the … … mountains formed at the time.

SECTION 2 (CHAPTER 2)
HOW ROCKS ARE FORMED AND CHANGED

Why study rocks? For geologists, every rock contains clues about the environment in which it was formed. Rocks made up entirely of shell fragments tell us the rock came from a shallow sea environment. Other rocks contain clues showing that they formed from a volcanic eruption or deep in the earth's crust during mountain building. Geologists use the information they find in rocks to explain the settings where the rock formed and the history of the earth for thousands of millions of years.

The study of rocks also helps us to find and use natural resources, such as oil, iron and other minerals. This creates jobs, materials and energy supplies, allowing us to adapt our environment to suit our needs.

In your science course at Junior Certificate level you learned about atoms and elements, which are the building blocks of minerals. Minerals, in turn, are the building blocks of rocks. This section deals with the settings where igneous, sedimentary and metamorphic rocks form, the minerals they are made of and some ways that people interact with these resources:

●   Chapter 2   The Rock Cycle

Some rock, such as copper ores, has many colours.

Desert sand dunes may later form sandstone.

Coral reefs form limestone.

CHAPTER 2
THE ROCK CYCLE

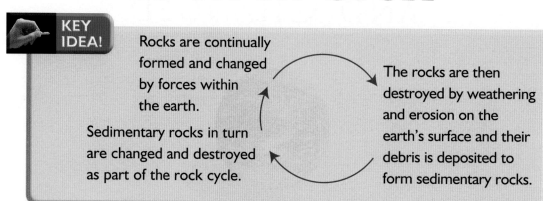

KEY IDEA!

Rocks are continually formed and changed by forces within the earth.

Sedimentary rocks in turn are changed and destroyed as part of the rock cycle.

The rocks are then destroyed by weathering and erosion on the earth's surface and their debris is deposited to form sedimentary rocks.

In your own words explain the processes that are involved in the rock cycle.

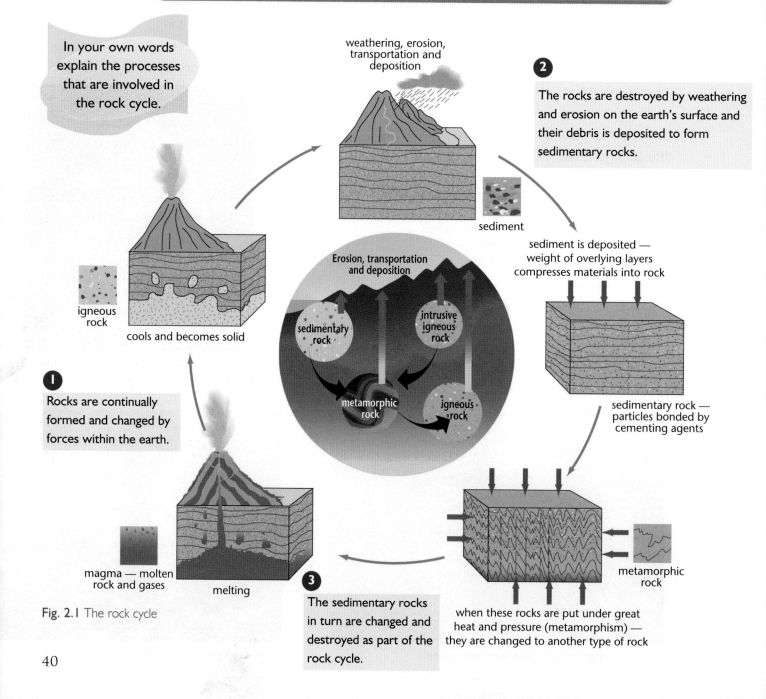

weathering, erosion, transportation and deposition

2 The rocks are destroyed by weathering and erosion on the earth's surface and their debris is deposited to form sedimentary rocks.

sediment

sediment is deposited — weight of overlying layers compresses materials into rock

igneous rock

cools and becomes solid

Erosion, transportation and deposition

sedimentary rock

intrusive igneous rock

metamorphic rock

igneous rock

sedimentary rock — particles bonded by cementing agents

1 Rocks are continually formed and changed by forces within the earth.

magma — molten rock and gases

melting

3 The sedimentary rocks in turn are changed and destroyed as part of the rock cycle.

metamorphic rock

when these rocks are put under great heat and pressure (metamorphism) — they are changed to another type of rock

Fig. 2.1 The rock cycle

SETTINGS WHERE IGNEOUS, SEDIMENTARY AND METAMORPHIC ROCKS FORM

KEY IDEA!

Rocks may be divided into three groups, depending on how they were formed.

Group	How formed	Examples
IGNEOUS	They were formed when hot, molten, **volcanic material cooled** and became solid.	granite, gabbro, basalt, lava, pyroclasts
SEDIMENTARY	They were formed from the **crushed-together remains** (sediments) of animals, plants and other rocks.	limestone, coal, sandstone, shale
METAMORPHIC	They were once igneous or sedimentary rocks, which were **changed by great heat or pressure**.	marble, quartzite, slate

Igneous Rocks of Ireland

Igneous rocks may be divided into **plutonic** and **volcanic** rocks.

Plutonic Rocks

Plutonic rocks (also called intrusive rocks) are formed when magma cooled within the earth. They have large crystals. The longer magma takes to cool the larger are its crystals. The most common of these is granite.

Granite has very large and colourful crystals.

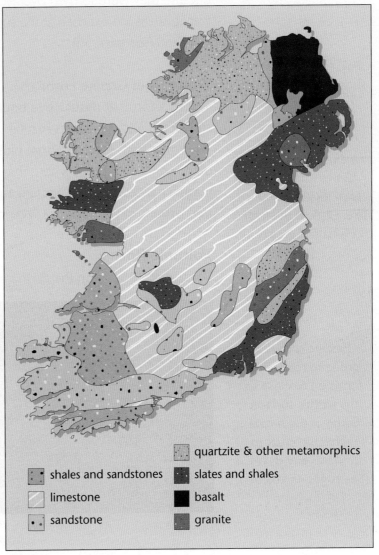

quartzite & other metamorphics
shales and sandstones
slates and shales
limestone
basalt
sandstone
granite

Fig. 2.2 Surface rock in Ireland

41

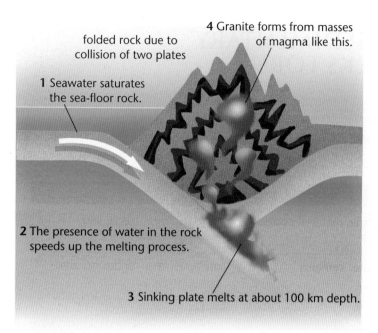

4 Granite forms from masses of magma like this.

folded rock due to collision of two plates

1 Seawater saturates the sea-floor rock.

2 The presence of water in the rock speeds up the melting process.

3 Sinking plate melts at about 100 km depth.

Fig. 2.3

Granite

Some magma **cooled very slowly** deep in the earth's crust to form granite. Granite is composed of three minerals, feldspar, mica and quartz. Feldspar and quartz (silica) form most of the rock. The quartz grains are clear and glassy, the feldspars vary from white to pink, and crystals of mica are black. The amounts of these minerals vary, creating granite rocks with a range of colours. Some may be black and white, something like a firelighter; others vary from pink to grey to black.

As the magma cooled slowly, **crystals were given time to develop and grow, so large crystals were formed**. This rock forms the core of most fold mountains.

Granite forms the core of fold mountains such as the **Caledonian Fold Mountains**. Because they were formed over 400 million years ago, they are greatly eroded and their granite cores are exposed at the surface in **Connemara**, **Mayo**, **Donegal** and **Wicklow** in Ireland (see page 50).

Where Does Granite Form?

This rock forms at **destructive boundaries** where the crust of the ocean floor is **subducted** into the earth's mantle. As the descending plate reaches a depth of about 100 km, it starts to melt. **Large blobs of magma rise into the buckled and folded rock** of the continent above, where they gather to form masses of magma. Because these magma masses are huge and are surrounded by solid rock that acts as an insulator, they take millions of years to cool. When they become solid they form granite.

Volcanic Rocks

Volcanic rocks form **on** the earth's surface. The most common volcanic rocks are:

- Lava
- Basalt
- Pyroclasts.

Lava

When magma pours out onto the earth's surface it is called lava.

> Ask your teacher to show you a sample of granite and basalt rock. Hold each sample and look carefully at each one. Get to know what each looks and feels like. Look at the large crystals of granite.

> Basaltic rock is a group of rocks that forms on or close to the earth's surface. Some of them cool within the crust to form sills and dykes. (See pages 43 and 61.)

Pahoehoe lava

Activity
1. Where and how does granite form?
2. Why does granite have large crystals?

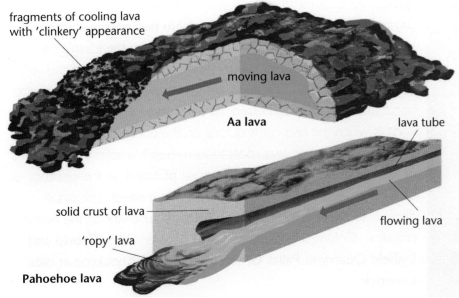

fragments of cooling lava with 'clinkery' appearance

moving lava

Aa lava

lava tube

solid crust of lava

'ropy' lava

flowing lava

Pahoehoe lava

Fig. 2.4 Aa lava flow (above) and Pahoehoe lava (below) flowing through a tube

A geologist takes samples of Aa lava to find out its chemical make-up.

Where Does Lava Form?

Lava flows out from the vent of a volcano and hardens either on the sides of a cone or on the land surrounding a fissure (crack in the ground). Sometimes lava bursts out through the side or base of a volcano. Lava flows are formed on each occasion. Sometimes it is runny and has a ropy appearance. On other occasions it has a clinkery appearance.

Pillow lava forms along cracks in a mid-ocean ridge or along fissures (cracks) in the seabed. Lava oozes out from the ocean floor, like toothpaste from a tube. It quickly hardens to form rounded blobs. As other blobs are fanned out from the same source, a pile of flattened pillow-shaped masses is formed.

When magma pours out on to the earth's surface it is called lava.

Basaltic Rock

Basaltic is the name given to a group of rocks that cooled and **crystallised quickly on** or **close** to the earth's surface. It is a dark green to black, heavy, hard rock composed of small crystals. It is formed from magma and lava that cooled quickly.

Where Do Some Basaltic Rocks Form?

As some magma rises towards the surface it forces itself into cracks in the surface and in between layers of rock such as limestone. As cracks in the crust and the bedding planes are narrow, the magma cools quickly, forming small crystals. These crystals are a little larger than those of basalt on the surface as the magma has cooled a little slower because it is surrounded by some rock layers.

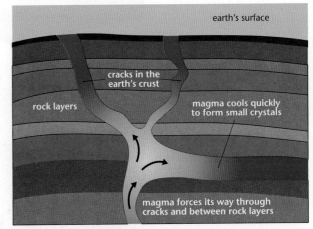

earth's surface

cracks in the earth's crust

rock layers

magma cools quickly to form small crystals

magma forces its way through cracks and between rock layers

Fig. 2.5 This magma cools quickly to form a basaltic rock, such as **gabbro** and **dolerite**. It is plutonic rock because it cooled within the earth's crust.

Basalt columns on the Antrim coastline in Northern Ireland

Basalt

Basalt is a volcanic rock and forms from lava on the surface. When magma flows out through **long cracks** in the earth's surface it is called lava. It does so **quietly**, without much violence and **spreads out evenly**. The flows are five to six metres thick and often occur after long intervals. Thick layers of lava form basalt with tiny crystals when the lava cools quickly on the earth's surface.

Regularly, when lava cools to form basalt, it splits into **columns of four, five or six sides**. It forms great **plateaus** on the sea floor or on land. An example of this is in **Antrim in Ireland**. This basalt displays six-sided columns at the **Giant's Causeway** on the Antrim coastline. Columns of basalt may also be seen at the **Grotto and Linfield Quarry at Pallas Green**, **Kilteely and Knockroe in east Limerick**.

Where Does Basalt Form?

Normally lava 'wells out' quietly from a crack **on the surface**, smothering the existing surface under a sheet of basalt. These sheets cover all humps and hollows and create a new level surface. They occur in areas where plates are being pulled apart. This pulling stretches the crust and long cracks appear through which the lava pours out. The eventual product is a plateau of basalt, often with **stepped sides**, as the later lava flows fail to travel as far as the earlier ones.

Fig. 2.6 Stages in the formation of a lava plateau

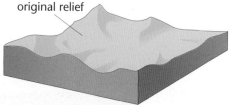
original relief

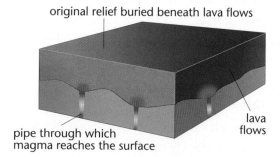
original relief buried beneath lava flows

pipe through which magma reaches the surface

lava flows

Magma cools quickly in the neck of a volcano to form a volcanic plug. This example is to be seen near Pallas Grean in County Limerick. Lichens now cover the rock, giving it a whitish colour.

Pyroclasts

Pyroclasts are ejected from all kinds of volcanoes. During an eruption, particles of rock and lava are blasted into the air. Some particles fall near the vent and form a volcanic cone. Others such as volcanic ash and pulverised rock may be carried great distances by the force of the eruption or by the wind or both. The particles produced by these processes are called **pyroclasts**, or **tephra**. The ejected lava fragments range in size from very fine dust to sand-sized volcanic ash to large volcanic bombs and blocks.

Where Do Pyroclasts Form?

Pyroclasts form **around the vent** of an active **volcano**. Small and large blobs of magma are blasted into the air, propelled by gases escaping from the magma. These blobs cool rapidly to form all kinds of pyroclastic rock. Some are so small they form light stones the size of peas. Other blobs are large and form rocks the size of turnips.

Some **large crystals** may be scattered within **pyroclastic rock**. Some pyroclasts have **no crystals** at all. These blobs of lava cooled instantly so that there was no time for crystals to form. This rock is called **glass**. **Obsidian** is a glassy black rock.

❷ Many volcanoes eject ash on some occasions and lavas on others. The result is a cone with alternating layers of pyroclasts and lava. Well-known examples are Vesuvius and Stromboli (Italy) and Etna (Sicily).

❸ Pyroclastic debris is also known as **tephra**.

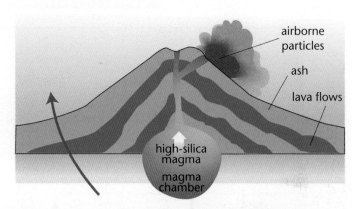

airborne particles

ash

lava flows

high-silica magma

magma chamber

❶ Magma commonly collects in a large reservoir, or magma chamber, a few kilometres or so beneath the surface. The rise of the magma from the chamber into the volcano proper is marked by earthquake tremors. They occur as the rising magma weakens fragments, melts the overlying rock, and moves through the newly created space.

Fig. 2.7 Pyroclastic rock being formed

A lava fountain displays pyroclasts being blown into the air.

Activity
1. Where do plutonic rocks form?
2. Name one type of plutonic rock and explain its crystal size.
3. Where do volcanic rocks form?
4. Name two types of volcanic rocks and explain their crystal size.
5. What crystal sizes would be found if a rock was cooling slowly deep within the earth's crust and then was suddenly blasted up a vent and into the air? Explain fully.
6. What is basaltic rock?
7. Where does it form?

Sedimentary Rocks of Ireland

KEY IDEA! When igneous, sedimentary and metamorphic rocks are exposed to weathering and erosion, their rock particles are carried by wind, water or ice and deposited elsewhere. Where these particles accumulate they are squeezed by their own weight and the weight of other overlying particles to form sedimentary rock.

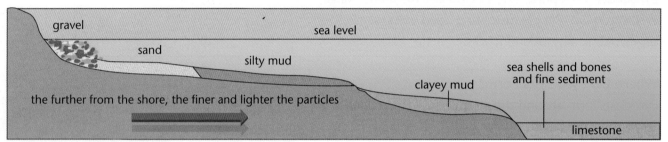

Fig. 2.8 The settings where some sedimentary rocks form

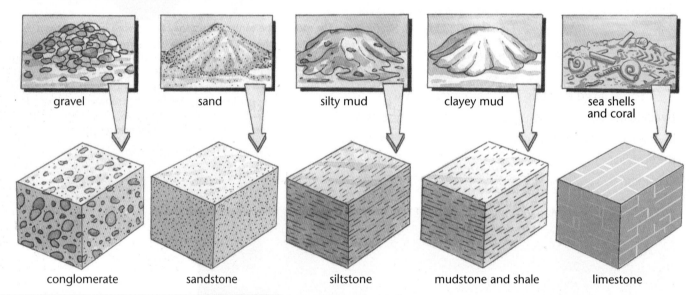

Fig. 2.9 Types of sedimentary rock

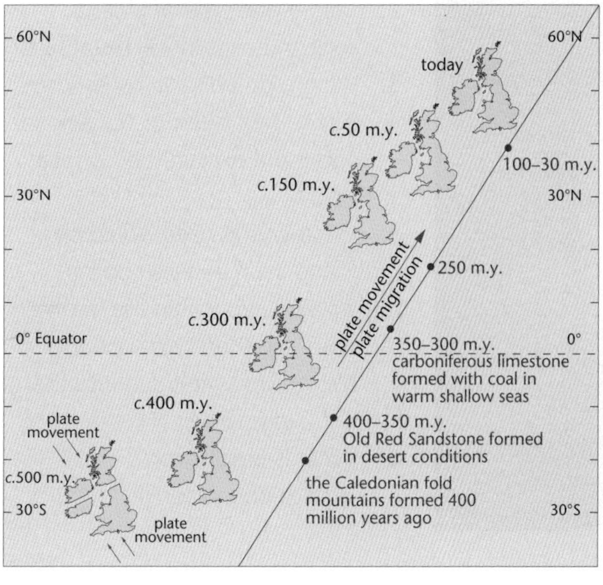

Ireland's sedimentary rocks were formed at various stages, as the European plate drifted north from its original location near the Antarctic about 500 million years ago. The climates it experienced on its northward journey and its position above or below sea level created the settings for its sedimentary rocks to form.

Activities

1. At which latitude was Ireland when the limestones formed?
2. At which latitude was Ireland when its Old Red Sandstones formed? Which deserts are located there today?

Fig. 2.10

Sandstone

The most common type of sandstone in Ireland is **Old Red Sandstone**. About 400–350 million years ago Ireland was located at about the same latitude as the Kalahari and Namib deserts in southern Africa and it had the same **hot desert climate** as they have today.

The Caledonian mountains of Galway, Mayo, Donegal and Wicklow stood tall and were subjected to **torrential downpours** from time to time. **Flash floods** from these downpours rushed down the mountains to lowland areas and the waters joined up to form **huge rivers**. Debris from the floods was spread out over much of the river **channels and floodplains** and along the seashore, in the form of **deltas**, and great sheets and **beaches of gravels and sand**.

These deposits were later cemented into conglomerates (from gravel) and sandstones (from sand). **Iron particles** in these deposits rusted and tinted them a **reddish colour**.

In other places, great **dunes of sand** were created and were moved backwards and forwards by the wind. These dunes were also compressed to sandstone.

Most of this sandstone was later covered by limestone deposits. However, it is exposed on the mountains of southern Ireland, such as the Macgillicuddy's Reeks, the Galtees, the Knockmealdowns, the Comeraghs and the Devils Bit.

Limestone

Limestone is composed of **calcium carbonate**, and is mostly formed of shells of sea creatures. It is mostly formed in warm seas within the tropics (near the Equator). It is formed by:

- **Calcium carbonate** from seawater collecting around tiny sand grains floating in shallow lagoons near the Equator.
- **Billions of shells** from tiny and large organisms, such as **corals**, that lived in tropical seas.

When shell creatures die, they may remain undamaged on the seabed or they may be subjected to wave action that breaks them up into tiny fragments or limey mud. More often than not, limestone is composed of both types. When great depths of these materials gather on the sea floor they are compressed by their own weight and the weight of later rocks to form solid limestone rock.

When sand dunes were compressed under layers of other rocks, they formed sandstone.

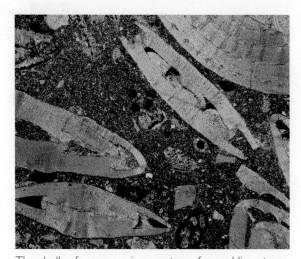

The shells of many marine creatures formed limestone.

Ask your teacher to show you samples of each of the rock types mentioned in the text. Hold each sample. Is it heavy or light? Rub your fingers across it to see if it's smooth or rough. What colour is it?

The Setting When Ireland's Limestones Were Formed

Most of Ireland was submerged beneath a warm, equatorial sea. The Caledonian mountain cores of Connemara, Mayo, Donegal, Down and Wicklow were exposed and stood as islands above the sea.

The great mass of Carboniferous rock that covers the plains of Ireland today must have been originally some thousands of metres thick.

The coalfields of Arigna, Castlecomer and Ballingary were laid down in swamp-filled depressions at this time.

Volcanic activities in the Carboniferous period produced the lavas and pyroclastic rocks of east Limerick on top of the limestone.

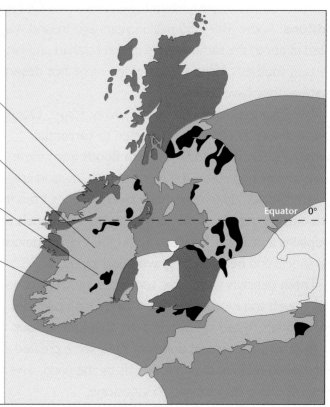

Equator 0°

	dry land
	mountains
	warm seas
	coal swamps

Fig. 2.11

Thin layers of shale break easily.

Irish limestone was formed when Ireland was **near the Equator** between **350 to 300 million** years ago. Corals were everywhere; shallow coral reefs and lagoons, as in the Caribbean today, surrounded the coastline, and the shells from billions of sea creatures and coral built up on the sea floor to form limestone.

Coal formed in some tropical swamps and so all the limestone rock formed at this time is called **Carboniferous limestone.**

Shale

Shale is composed of particles of silt and clay. It forms from fine sediments from rivers washed into the sea and carried by currents **away from** the coast. It also forms from river silt that builds up in **enclosed bays or estuaries**. When great thickness of this matter accumulates, it is compressed to shale. Shale is formed of very thin layers (strata) of rock that break easily.

Ireland's limestone was formed in a setting of coral reefs similar to this photograph.

Metamorphic Rocks of Ireland

Igneous and sedimentary rocks may change both in their **appearance** (physically) and in their **make-up** (chemically) as a consequence of heat or pressure or both. This process of changing is called **metamorphism**.

Factors that contribute to the end product include the **presence and amount of liquid** within the changing rock, the **length of time** a rock is subjected **to high temperature** or **high pressure**, and **whether** the changing rock is simply squeezed **(compressed)** or is **twisted**.

Masses of granite and metamorphic rock tend to be located next to each other. The nearer a rock is to the cooling granite magma, the more it is changed. The farther away it is, the less it is changed.

So three basic factors all contribute to metamorphism: **heat, compression** and the **presence of liquids**.

In a simple way you can think of metamorphism as baking. When you bake, what you get to eat depends on what you start with and on the cooking conditions. So too with rocks; the end product is controlled by the initial make-up of the rock and by the metamorphic conditions (baking ... the amount of heat).

The forces of heat and compression change sedimentary rocks to metamorphic rocks.

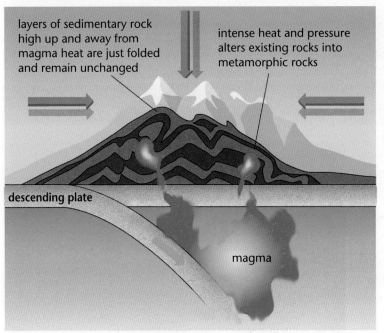

layers of sedimentary rock high up and away from magma heat are just folded and remain unchanged

intense heat and pressure alters existing rocks into metamorphic rocks

descending plate

magma

Fig. 2.12

Where Do Metamorphic Rocks Form?

Metamorphic rocks form **where plates** collide. In these places:

● Compression squeezes rock layers and they begin to heat and change.
● Rock layers come in contact with or are close to magma which heats them intensely causing change.
● Both compression and heat affect some rock layers causing change.

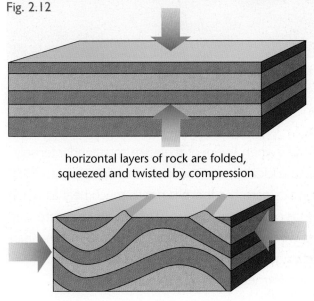

horizontal layers of rock are folded, squeezed and twisted by compression

Fig. 2.13

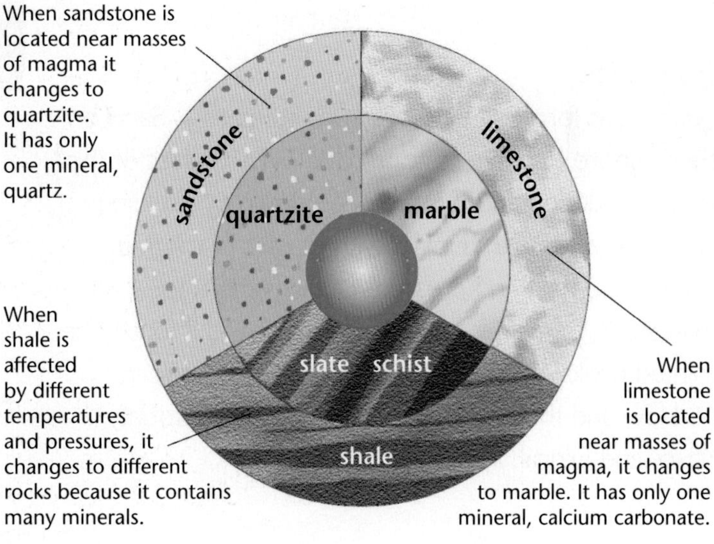

When sandstone is located near masses of magma it changes to quartzite. It has only one mineral, quartz.

When shale is affected by different temperatures and pressures, it changes to different rocks because it contains many minerals.

sandstone   limestone
quartzite   marble
slate   schist
shale

When limestone is located near masses of magma, it changes to marble. It has only one mineral, calcium carbonate.

Fig. 2.14

When Were Most of Ireland's Metamorphic Rocks Formed?

Irish marble, quartzite and slate formed about 400 million years ago, when the American and European plates collided and formed the Caledonian Fold Mountains. The descending ocean plate melted, producing magma that rose into the buckled rock, and its heat changed them to metamorphic rock. Since then, the tops of these mountains have been removed by erosion. The marble, quartzite and slate are now exposed on the surface next to the igneous rock, granite, the magma of which formed them originally.

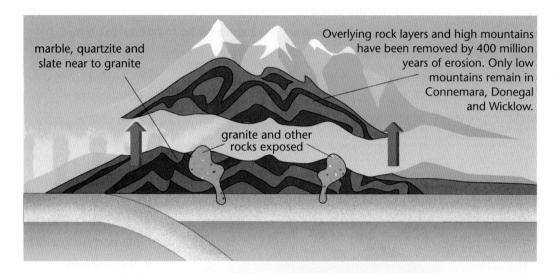

marble, quartzite and slate near to granite

Overlying rock layers and high mountains have been removed by 400 million years of erosion. Only low mountains remain in Connemara, Donegal and Wicklow.

granite and other rocks exposed

Fig. 2.15

Marble

Marble is formed when limestone is pushed down deep by the buckling of rock layers when plates collide at destructive boundaries. Magma created by the melting descending plate then rises to form huge masses of magma within the buckled rock layers. When the limestone layers come in close contact with this cooling magma, it changes to marble. Marble may vary in colour, depending on the impurities within the limestone.

Quartzite

Quartzite is formed in a similar way to marble. Sand on the seashore forms sandstone rock. When layers of this rock are buckled and pushed deep down by colliding plates, they come in contact with masses of magma. The intense heat and pressure changes them to quartzite. Quartzite is a **very hard rock** and it forms the pointed peaks of the Great and Little Sugar Loafs in Wicklow and the peaks of Croagh Patrick, in County Mayo, and Errigal, in County Donegal.

The Great Sugar Loaf in Wicklow is formed from quartzite. It is a hard rock.

Slate

Slate forms when layers of shale are squeezed intensely by folded rock as a consequence of colliding plates. Heat also plays its part, but there is not as much heat as when marble or quartzite is formed. This means that slate was formed when it was a farther distance from magma than marble or quartzite. When shale was closer to the magma, it formed schist rather than slate.

Activity

1. Explain when and where Ireland's limestones were formed.
2. Where do metamorphic rocks form?
3. Name the three factors that contribute to the formation of metamorphic rock.
4. How is quartzite formed?

Plates That Touch The North American Continental Plate

The most active plate boundary is where the North American Plate meets the Pacific Plate. The North American Plate forms a **natural region**. It forms a single continent that is almost completely surrounded by water and was formed by nature. It stretches from the Arctic Ocean to the Caribbean and from the Pacific Ocean to the Atlantic Ocean.

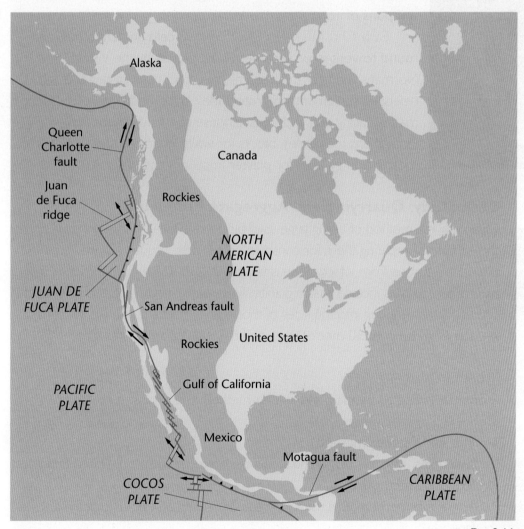

Fig. 2.16

Use *Our Dynamic World Workbook* to recap on the chapters so far.

Activity

Look at Fig. 2.16 and do the following:

1. Name the four plates that border the North American Plate:
2. Which mountain range was formed by the Pacific Plate and the North American Plate?

How People Interact with the Rock Cycle
Case Study: Extracting Building Materials

Stone masons and sculptors create designs by working stone.

Most **buildings** are built from rock, such as **limestone**, **sandstone** or **granite**, or rock compounds such as **concrete blocks** or **clay bricks**. Included in some compounds are metals, such as iron and steel to reinforce buildings or **pre-cast concrete** units.

Stone Age people – Paleolithic, Mesolithic or Neolithic as we now classify them – were so called because **tools** used by them were made from stone. **Iron Age** people (Celts) used stone as a foundation for their forts and lake-side crannog settlements and extracted metal from stone (smelting) to manufacture their **weapons** of iron.

Early Christian monks built beehive **cells** and **churches**, and **round towers** to protect them from attacks by the Vikings. The Normans and later the Irish chieftains built huge castles and defended settlements to protect their lands. Today stone is used for road surfacing and in domestic house construction, for filling, foundations (concrete), blocks for **walls**, concrete **tiles** or **slates** for roofing, and gypsum for **plaster** in ceilings and walls.

Case Study: Quarrying and Aggregate Products

Quarrying is a method of taking large solid blocks or broken masses of stone from the earth and preparing them for construction projects. A quarry is a large pit in the earth's surface from which stone is taken out (extracted). Some kinds of stone taken from quarries include basalt, granite, limestone, marble, sandstone and slate. Some quarries are dug into the sides of mountains. Most are open at the surface. A quarry may be over 30 metres deep and many times as wide as that.

Types of Quarrying

Stone is quarried by the plug and feather method, the explosive method or channelling by machinery.

- **Plug and Feather method**
  Drill holes, wedges (plugs) and steel rods are used to split rock into thin slabs.
- **Explosive method**
  The explosive method is used to break off huge masses of rock from a rock face.
- **Channelling by machinery**
  Huge slices of rock are cut off a rock edge by a large rotating disc. These slices are taken away for cutting into various sizes.

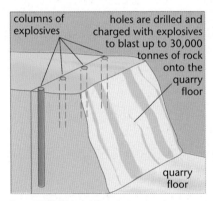

columns of explosives

holes are drilled and charged with explosives to blast up to 30,000 tonnes of rock onto the quarry floor

quarry floor

Fig. 2.17 Before blasting

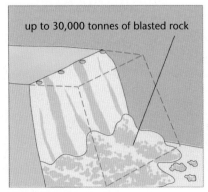

up to 30,000 tonnes of blasted rock

Fig. 2.18 After blasting

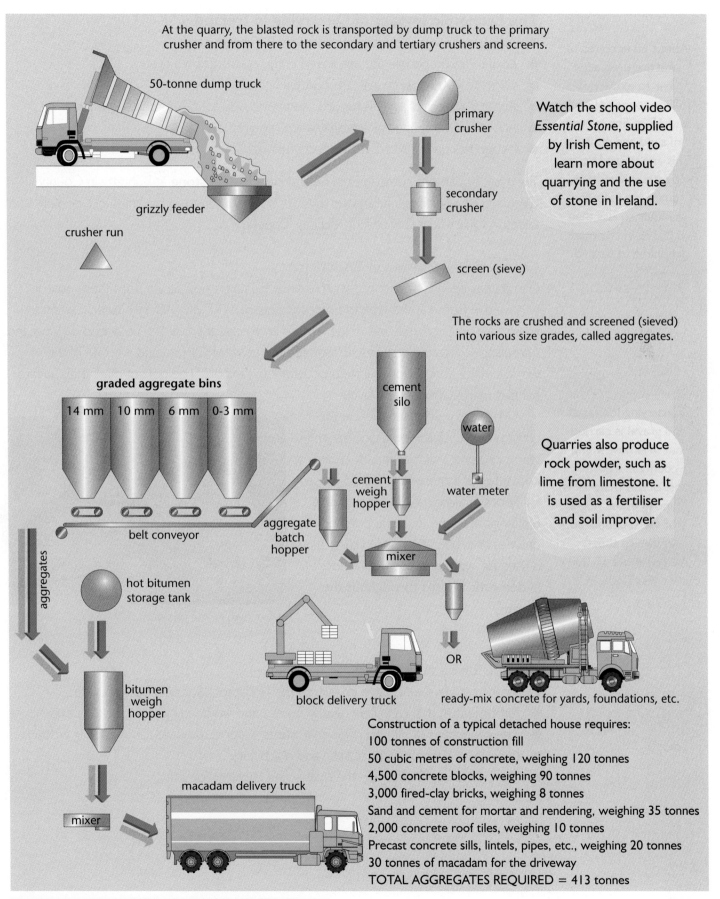

At the quarry, the blasted rock is transported by dump truck to the primary crusher and from there to the secondary and tertiary crushers and screens.

50-tonne dump truck

grizzly feeder

crusher run

primary crusher

secondary crusher

screen (sieve)

Watch the school video *Essential Stone*, supplied by Irish Cement, to learn more about quarrying and the use of stone in Ireland.

The rocks are crushed and screened (sieved) into various size grades, called aggregates.

graded aggregate bins

| 14 mm | 10 mm | 6 mm | 0-3 mm |

cement silo

water

cement weigh hopper

water meter

aggregate batch hopper

belt conveyor

mixer

Quarries also produce rock powder, such as lime from limestone. It is used as a fertiliser and soil improver.

aggregates

hot bitumen storage tank

bitumen weigh hopper

block delivery truck

OR

ready-mix concrete for yards, foundations, etc.

macadam delivery truck

mixer

Construction of a typical detached house requires:
100 tonnes of construction fill
50 cubic metres of concrete, weighing 120 tonnes
4,500 concrete blocks, weighing 90 tonnes
3,000 fired-clay bricks, weighing 8 tonnes
Sand and cement for mortar and rendering, weighing 35 tonnes
2,000 concrete roof tiles, weighing 10 tonnes
Precast concrete sills, lintels, pipes, etc., weighing 20 tonnes
30 tonnes of macadam for the driveway
TOTAL AGGREGATES REQUIRED = 413 tonnes

Fig. 2.19

Class activity
Look at Fig. 2.19. Examine the operation of a quarry as a system of inputs, processes and outputs.

The Economic Impact of Quarrying in Ireland

- Aggregates are an essential requirement for construction.
- About 90,000 people are employed in the construction industry.
- Over 40,000 housing units are built each year.
- About 7 tonnes of aggregates are used per 1,000 tonnes of building work.
- About 50,000 tonnes of aggregates are required each year.
- Ireland has over 200 active pits and quarries.

Two major quarrying companies in Ireland include **Roadstone** at Bunratty in County Clare and **Ready Mix** at Tullamore, in County Offaly. Private companies include Kelly and Gleeson Quarries at Donohill, in County Tipperary.

About 60 hectares of land are used each year to extract 35 million tonnes of rock and 15 million tonnes of sand and gravel. This annual land usage by the whole Irish quarrying industry amounts to less than 0.001% of the total land area of Ireland.

Carrara Marble Quarries in Tuscany, Italy

Carrara has been famous for its marble since Roman times. Stone from these quarries was used in Rome at the time of Emperor Augustus (27 BC–AD 14). Later Carrara's finest pure white marble was made famous by the great sculptors, Leonardo da Vinci and Michelangelo. Marble quarries surrounded the town of Carrara and it is one of the world's major centres for marble production and export. The port of Marina di Carrara handles marble almost exclusively.

Marble is used extensively in the construction of buildings, especially in warm countries, such as Italy. It creates a **cool interior** atmosphere and so is used for **floors in airports** and other **public buildings**. Because it can be polished at quarries to produce a smooth surface, it is used for **walls and bathroom floors in domestic houses throughout the world**.

Quarrying for sand and gravel is carried out in almost every county in Ireland. Most of this material is found in esker ridges that were deposited as the ice sheets melted about 10,000 years ago.

Carrara

- *How was marble formed?*
- *What are its uses today?*

Negative Effects of Quarrying

Quarrying can have a negative impact on the landscape. Some impacts include:

- Airborne dust that can affect nearby homes and farmland.
- The generation of silt into rivers that affects water quality and fish spawning grounds.
- Noise and vibration from blasting and machinery.
- Damage to roads between the quarry and construction sites.

CONSTRUCTION MATERIALS ARE PART OF OUR HERITAGE

Ireland has a substantial natural supply of building materials. These formed as Ireland migrated from the southern hemisphere to its present position and was subjected to earth movements, different climates and coastal settings along the way. Extracting these building materials creates work and saves the country money at the same time. Quarrying alone is an industry worth €2 billion a year to the Irish economy.

An ore is a rock that contains minerals, and these ores are used in manufacturing industry. Ireland's copper, lead and zinc ores are mined from limestone rock. Zinc is used as a weatherproof coating on iron, such as galvanize. Most of the ores are extracted by shaft mining. The major zinc mines in Ireland are at Lisheen in Co. Tipperary, Galmoy in Co. Kilkenny and Navan in Co. Meath.

Originally, these minerals were dissolved in super-hot water that came up through old faults or cracks from magma masses that were cooling deep down in the earth's crust. The hot, liquid minerals were seeped into the limestones near the surface, then cooled and became part of the rock.

Gypsum is a mineral quarried in open-cast mines at Kingscourt in Co. Cavan, with other deposits found in Co. Monaghan and Co. Meath. It is used in plaster for internal walls and ceiling slabs. The gypsum deposits formed by evaporation of water, in shallow coastal lagoons when Ireland was located just north of the Equator about 300 million years ago.

Gravels and sands are other materials quarried for use in constructing buildings and as raw materials in the manufacture of concrete, concrete blocks and roof tiles, as well as filling for farm passages, driveways and roads. These materials were deposited by rivers towards the end of the last ice age, which ended 10,000 years ago.

As limestone is the most common rock in Ireland, it is quarried in many parts of the country. It is broken down to small particles called aggregates. Because of high transport costs, limestone, sandstone and shale quarries need to be sited as close as possible to the point of use. A distance of more than 20 to 30 km is considered uneconomical. To avoid damage, dust and noise, quarries cannot be sited closer than 250 metres from the boundaries of a dwelling house. Because housing is so scattered across Ireland's countryside, it is becoming more and more difficult to open a quarry. This is one reason why planners try to direct new housing into village and town environments.

Activity

Read the article on page 55 and answer the following:

1. What is shaft mining?
2. What is an ore?
3. Name three different ores that are mined in Ireland.
4. Which ore is mined in large quantities?
5. How did these ores form?
6. Name the mineral that is mined at Kingscourt.
7. How was this mineral formed?
8. At what latitude was Ireland when this mineral formed?
9. What is this substance used for?
10. What other materials are quarried for the construction industry?
11. When and where did these minerals form?
12. Why is it necessary to locate quarries away from dwelling houses?
13. Why is it difficult to get planning permission for a quarry in Ireland today?

Some hydrothermal areas, such as geysers in Iceland, are used to generate geothermal electricity. Some geothermal areas in Ireland, such as near Mallow, are used to generate electricity.

Remember that oil and natural gas form in sedimentary rock. The sedimentary rocks of the North Sea and Celtic Sea have great deposits of oil and natural gas.

A volcanic landscape on the island of Lanzarote in the Canary Islands.

Class activity

1. How and why were the Canary Islands formed at that location? See Fig. 1.30 on page 21.
2. Suggest why these volcanoes are in a line.

TEST YOURSELF AT
my-etest.com

SECTION 3 (CHAPTERS 3–9)
HOW LANDFORMS ARE CREATED

For some people, mountains are sacred places; for others, they have spectacular scenery to enjoy. Valleys and plains are where most of the world's population lives, and people can grow and harvest food. The seas are used for leisure activities or transport routes for ships and ferries, against a backdrop of dramatic coastal scenery. Images of these natural features are shown in art and recorded in poems and in songs.

The ways that all of these natural areas have formed are called processes, and the features that are created by these processes are called landforms.

These natural processes are nature's ways of keeping the earth's crust in balance with the forces within the earth's mantle. Balance is rarely achieved. Erosion reduces weight in one area, while deposition increases weight in another, something like a seesaw effect.

This section explains how these natural processes work with each other to try and create a balance and how they lead to the creation of landforms. It also shows that people sometimes interact with processes and landforms with positive and negative impacts.

Coastal view of a basalt plateau

- Chapter 3   Landforms of Tectonic Activity
- Chapter 4   Understanding Ordnance Survey Maps
- Chapter 5   Understanding Photographs
- Chapter 6   Landforms Influenced by Rock Characteristics
- Chapter 7   Landforms of Denudation
- Chapter 8   Landforms of Isostasy
- Chapter 9   How People Interact with the Earth's Processes

A river flood plain is covered during very wet weather.

Front of an ice sheet on coastal waters

CHAPTER 3
LANDFORMS OF TECTONIC ACTIVITY

KEY IDEA! The development of landforms is influenced by structures that have been formed as a consequence of earth movements and deformation of the earth's crust.

SOME VOLCANIC AND PLUTONIC LANDFORMS

Some Intrusive and Extrusive Landforms

Volcanic means 'formed on the earth's surface'. Plutonic means 'formed within the earth's crust'. Both may now be on the surface after millions of years of weathering and erosion.

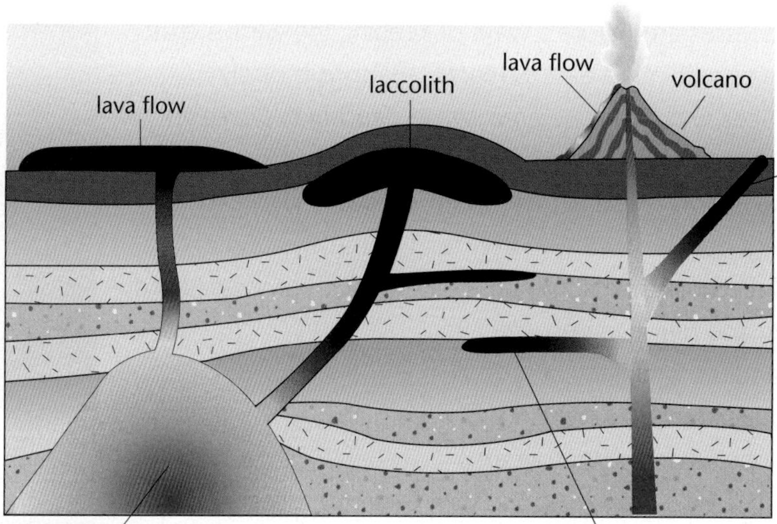

lava flow   laccolith   lava flow   volcano

Dyke
A vertical or sloping layer with horizontal cooling cracks. Cools rapidly on contact with surrounding colder rock. Cuts **across bedding planes**.

Batholith
Deep-seated landform and surrounded by rock. The magma cools slowly so that:
(a) large crystals form
(b) rocks in contact with batholith are **metamorphosed** (changed to other rocks due to extreme heat).

Sill
A horizontal or sloping layer **along** (between) **bedding planes** with vertical cooling cracks. Cools quickly on its outside, on contact with surrounding rocks — squeezes **between rock layers**.

Fig. 3.1

Extrusive means 'formed outside the earth's crust'. Intrusive means 'formed within the crust'. Volcanic rocks are extrusive and plutonic rocks are intrusive.

Extrusive Landforms in Antrim

During the **Tertiary period**, about **65 million years ago**, the American and European plates were pulling apart before the Atlantic Ocean formed. As they were stretched and separated, many cracks in the earth's crust allowed lava to pour out, red hot and liquid, onto the surface. Here repeated lava flows over a period of 2 million years built up to form the **Antrim Plateau**. Each time the lava cooled quickly to form layers of basalt rock.

Sometime after, part of the **plateau sagged** to form a shallow basin. This basin later filled with water to form **Lough Neagh**, the largest freshwater lake in Britain and Ireland.

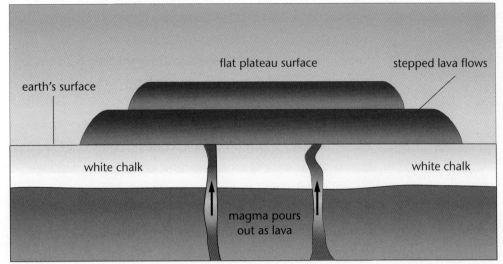

flat plateau surface

stepped lava flows

earth's surface

white chalk

white chalk

magma pours out as lava

Fig. 3.2

Landforms of the Antrim Plateau include:
- Antrim Plateau
- Lough Neagh
- Basalt columns
- Sills and dykes
- Volcanic cones.

For millions of years, the sea has eroded the seaward edge of the Antrim Plateau. The **force of water** from continual **pounding by ocean waves** has **undercut** the base of the plateau. This undercutting has led to **rock falls** and **landslides** and consequently created **high cliffs** along the coastline.

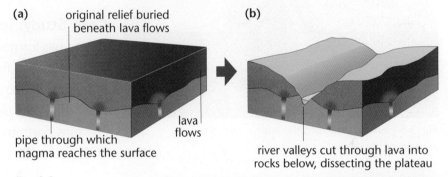

(a) original relief buried beneath lava flows

pipe through which magma reaches the surface

lava flows

(b) river valleys cut through lava into rocks below, dissecting the plateau

Fig. 3.3

Basalt columns and joints

If for some reason, the outpouring **lava is dammed up** forming 'lava lakes', such as in a blocked river valley, the basalt **cools** much **slower** than the thinner surface layers. In such places the slower cooling creates **five- and six-sided columns** of basalt rock. Spectacular examples of basalt columns can be seen along the seashore at the **Giant's Causeway, in County Antrim**.

The vertical cracks that separate each column from the next are called **joints**. The joints form for much the same reason that hot glass shatters when affected by cold water.

As basalt **cools slowly**, joints appear and form columns of basalt. Basalt columns are exposed at the Giant's Causeway. Sea erosion has worn away some of the columns.

Chalk cliffs are exposed in some places on the Antrim coast. This chalk covered Ireland before lava poured out to create the Antrim Plateau.

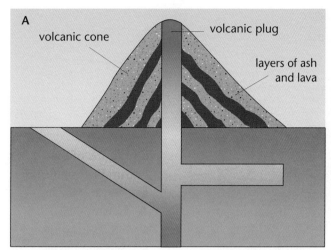

Fig. 3.4 Here **A** represents the volcanic cone which formed originally.

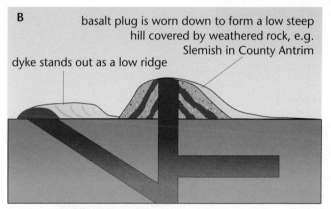

Fig. 3.5 Here **B** represents the worn remnants of the weathered cone.

Recent volcanic activity in Iceland

When lava cools in the vent pipe it forms a 'plug' of basalt rock. So volcanic plugs indicate the neck of the volcano through which the lava erupted originally.

During a violent eruption, lava is blown high into the air. Rocks, ash, cinders and volcanic bombs, called **pyroclasts, fall around the vent**. Lava pours out onto the layers of ash and flows downhill. All these materials build up to form a volcanic cone. Steep-sided cones are formed from thick lava. Gently sloping cones are formed of runny lava. When volcanic activity ceases, the lava in the vent pipe hardens to form a plug of basalt rock. Basalt is a hard rock and resists erosion.

Before, during and after the plateau formed violent volcanic activity created **volcanic cones** throughout County Antrim. As in Iceland today, volcanic cones formed along fissures (cracks) and formed chains of small volcanic cones. Most of the cones have since been weathered severely. These weathered **volcanic plugs form hills**, such as **Slemish**, near Ballymena, and **Scawt Hill**, near Ballygalley Head in County Antrim.

Case Study: Iceland on the Mid Atlantic Ridge

Iceland has formed at a hot spot on the Mid Atlantic Ridge. **Successive lava flows** and volcanic deposits **(pyroclasts)** have built up above sea level to form Iceland. Numerous small volcanoes also have formed in a chain along the fault that runs north to south through Iceland. Both Surtsey and Krafla are volcanic cones in Iceland.

Case Study: Hawaii at a Hot Spot

Hawaii is one of a group of volcanic islands formed at a hot spot, where a rising plume of magma forces its way through the earth's crust on the Pacific Ocean floor. Here numerous **lava flows** have built very gently sloping volcanic cones above sea level to form the Hawaiian Islands. Mauna Loa is a volcanic cone in Hawaii.

Hawaii is a **shield volcano**. This means that it is built up of runny lava (not explosive) flows and **little pyroclast materials**. Shield volcanoes are **very gently sloping** cones. The slope of the volcano sides varies from about 10 degrees at the summit (top) to only 2 degrees at its base on the ocean floor. Broad, gently sloping cones like these are the largest volcanoes on earth.

Intrusive Landforms in Antrim

Laccoliths, Sills and Dykes of Basaltic Rock

In some places the rising magma was unable to force its way to the surface and so it pushed its way into and along the bedding planes of sedimentary rocks, such as chalk, under the surface. Here it cooled to form laccoliths (see Fig. 3.6) or sills (see Fig. 3.7). In other places it cut across the bedding planes to form dykes. (See Fig. 3.8.)

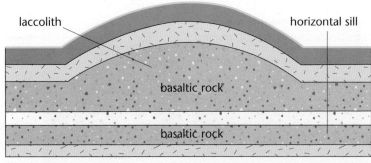
Fig. 3.6

● **Laccolith:** A laccolith is a small dome-shaped mass of igneous rock close to the surface. It forms when a tongue-shaped mass of magma forces the overlying layers of rock into a dome, producing a hill directly above it. (See Fig. 3.6.)

> When magma moves between bedding planes it forms a sill. When magma cuts across bedding planes it forms a dyke.

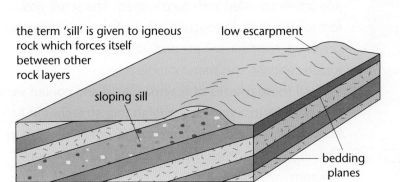
Fig. 3.7

● **Sill:** When a sheet of magma **lies along a bedding plane** it is called a sill. Some sills form horizontal layers, while others are sloping due to a tilt in the bedding planes.

● **Dyke:** When a sheet of magma **cuts across bedding planes** and forms a 'wall' of rock it is called a dyke. Dykes are formed when magma rises through vertical or near-vertical fissures (cracks) and cools to form igneous rock. So dykes may be vertical or sloping.

Laccoliths, **sills** and **dykes** have slightly larger crystals than basalt on the surface because they cooled a little slower. Because they are formed in the earth's crust they are **plutonic landforms**. They are formed of **gabbro** or **dolerite** rock.

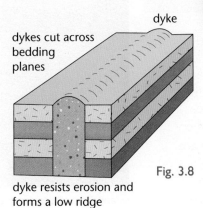
Fig. 3.8

dyke resists erosion and forms a low ridge

This dyke of basaltic rock is exposed in Antrim.

Activity

1. Explain how and why Antrim's Plateau formed.
2. Name two types of plutonic rock that form sills and dykes. See Fig. 2.5 on page 43.
3. Explain how a sill forms.

Case Study: Plutonic Landforms of the Leinster Mountains

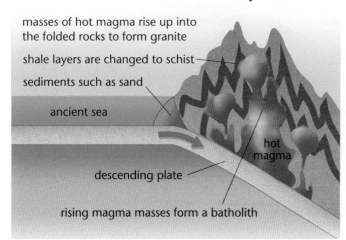

masses of hot magma rise up into the folded rocks to form granite

shale layers are changed to schist

sediments such as sand

ancient sea

hot magma

descending plate

rising magma masses form a batholith

Fig. 3.9

Remember the lava lamp. Similarly when magma masses rise they are trapped within the folded rock of the mountains where they cool slowly to form granite.

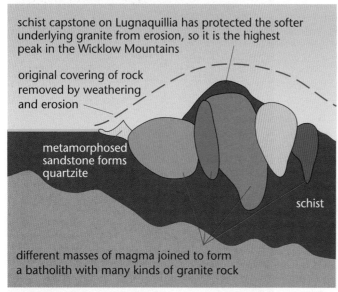

schist capstone on Lugnaquillia has protected the softer underlying granite from erosion, so it is the highest peak in the Wicklow Mountains

original covering of rock removed by weathering and erosion

metamorphosed sandstone forms quartzite

schist

different masses of magma joined to form a batholith with many kinds of granite rock

Fig. 3.10

Weathering and erosion exposes blocks of granite that were created by joints formed when magma cooled deep within the mountains originally. These may be seen on some mountain tops in Wicklow. These are called tors, see page 90.

The Leinster batholith consists of granite rock that formed from **magma masses** that **cooled very slowly,** deep in the earth's crust under the Wicklow Mountains. The Wicklow Mountains are part of the **Caledonian Fold Mountains** that formed when the American and European plates collided about 400 million years ago. (See page 25.)

After 400 million years of weathering and erosion most of the folded and metamorphosed overlying rock layers have been eroded, see Figs. 3.9 and 3.10. Most of the granite is exposed and its weathered rock forms rounded hilltops, such as Kippure and Two Rock. Others, such as Lugnaquillia, are still protected by hard **schist rock** and are steep-sided and more rugged. This schist was formed when **shale touched off the hot magma masses** under intense heat and pressure deep down under the folded rock and was metamorphosed.

All these masses of magma joined and cooled very slowly to form a granite batholith that stretches in a north-east to south-west direction from Sandycove in Dublin, through Wicklow to Thomastown in County Kilkenny.

As **batholith magma** collected deep within the mountains, it **came in contact** with coastal sandy deposits, such as **beaches and sand dunes**, that were intensely compressed and folded as the Eurasian and American continents collided. The **intense heat and pressure** of this location **metamorphosed** these sand deposits and changed them to a very hard rock called **quartzite**, as in the Great Sugar Loaf in County Wicklow.

Granite mountains produce poor wet soils suited only to sheep farming and forestry.

Case Study: The Devon and Cornwall Batholiths

The granite batholiths of Devon and Cornwall were formed from magma that cooled when it forced its way up into huge folds during the Armorican fold movement about 300 million years ago. The ridges and valleys of Munster were also formed at this time, however, folding was less severe in Munster and no magma was involved. Only buckling of the surface rocks took place in Munster to form ridges and valleys.

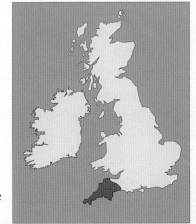

Fig. 3.11

Joints Formed by Cooling

As granite cools slowly, it naturally forms joints (cracks) that divide the granite batholith into regularly shaped blocks, something like an old-fashioned egg-box. Once they become **exposed or sufficiently close to the surface,** they are affected by the chemical weathering of **rainwater**. Rainwater is really a **weak acid** and it moves **along the joints** opening and enlarging them. The result looks like a series of stacked blocks of granite that may be exposed on a cliff face or on a mountain top. (See Fig. 3.12 and the photo.)

Joints Formed by Unloading

As overlying rock layers are removed by weathering and erosion the release of this weight-caused pressure allows the newly exposed granite batholith to expand, forming curved 'shells' of rock to pull away from the granite in a process known as **sheeting**.

This process produces a pattern of joints that **run** more or less **parallel to the surface** of the exposed batholith. Again chemical weathering acts on these joints to wear away the rock. So joints may run parallel, sloping or vertical to the surface rock.

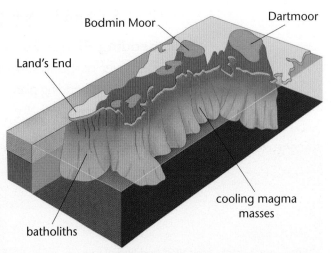

Fig. 3.12 Batholiths in Devon and Cornwall

Granite naturally forms joints as it cools slowly deep within a mountain.

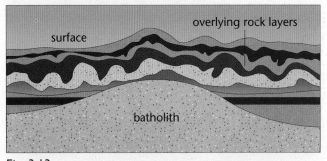

Fig. 3.13

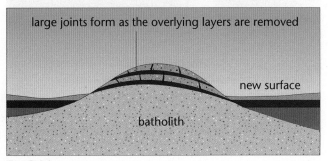

Fig. 3.14

63

SOME SEDIMENTARY LANDFORMS

Bedding Planes Formed by Deposition

Each layer of rock is separated from the next by a horizontal crack called a bedding plane. Each bedding plane indicates **where one stage of deposition has ended and another begins**.

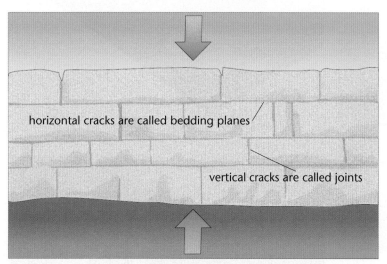

horizontal cracks are called bedding planes

vertical cracks are called joints

Fig. 3.15

Limestone is a well-jointed rock that allows water to seep through its joints.

The horizontal lines on these rocks indicate bedding planes that separate each flood deposit of gravels.

Joints Formed by Compression

As limestone is compressed by overlying layers, it shrinks and develops vertical cracks that split the rock into thick slabs. These hairline cracks are called joints. The joints and bedding planes in the limestone rock of the Dartry-Cuilcagh Uplands have been subjected to chemical weathering by the process of carbonation. Rainwater and ground water dissolve carbon dioxide to form carbonic acid. As water trickles downward, this acid dissolves limestone along the joints and bedding planes in a process called **solution**.

Once these joints and bedding planes are enlarged, they can accommodate more water from surface streams. When this happens, the load of the river erodes the limestone, creating even larger channels. So solution and erosion play their part in creating underground caverns and caves in limestone bedrock.

See Limestone Landforms, pages 83 to 89.

Solution by seeping rainwater and erosion by rivers created these caverns in the Marble Arch caves in County Fermanagh.

64

LANDFORMS OF TECTONIC ACTIVITY

...

Case Study: The Dartry–Cuilcagh Uplands

The landforms of the Dartry–Cuilcagh area are flat-topped mountain uplands. They have a **table-like shape**, like Benbulbin, with **steep sides** and a **flat top**. These were formed during the early Carboniferous period, when Ireland moved **close to the Equator** some 330 million years ago. It represents a time when earth movements raised and lowered Ireland's surface close to and below sea level, causing the surrounding **seas to become shallower and deeper** at different stages.

Formation of the Dartry-Cuilcagh Uplands

Ireland, then at the Equator, was covered by a warm sea. Standing out from the sea was the enormous chain of Caledonian mountains that included the Donegal, Mayo and Connemara mountains. Material was being washed into the sea from these mountains by huge rivers to form deltas and beaches of sand near the coast (sandstone), and silt and mud (shale) further out. Further still from the coast, limestone formed from shells and lime from the seawater. When the sea deepened, limestone was deposited on the delta and beach sand on the shale. When it became shallower again, sand and shale were deposited on the limestone, and coral reefs grew in clear silt-free shallow coastal areas. So alternate horizontal layers of limestone, sandstone and shale were deposited on top of the other.

Flat-topped uplands, such as Ben Bulbin and the Dartry-Cuilcagh Uplands, formed during the Carboniferous period.

bedding planes and joints allowed water to seep through the rock and dissolve the limestone

both sandstone and shale layers protect the limestone underneath from weathering and erosion

hard sandstones form flat tops, steep-sided ridges and cliffs

shale forms more gentle slopes than sandstone

cliffs of sandstone

when rivers meet the limestone layers, they disappear underground through sinkholes and form caverns

sinkhole

vertical cracks that split limestone into regular slabs are called joints

joints

sinkhole

bedding planes

springs

caverns

caverns

Fig. 3.16

> Gentle earth movements raised and lowered the land above and close to sea level to form these horizontal rock layers.

When the land was finally uplifted above the sea, the forces of weathering and erosion (frost, rivers and ice) attacked these rock layers. Since then, thousands of metres of rock have been worn away.

Because sandstone is harder than limestone (it resists weathering), in some places the sandstone and shale layers from delta and beach deposits have protected the limestone underneath from weathering and erosion, so these areas stand out as flat-topped table-like uplands, while the surrounding rock has worn away. These flat-topped mountains are the Dartry–Cuilcagh Uplands.

> Ground water, which is really carbonic acid, dissolved limestone bedrock to form sinkholes, caves and caverns, see pages 84 and 85.

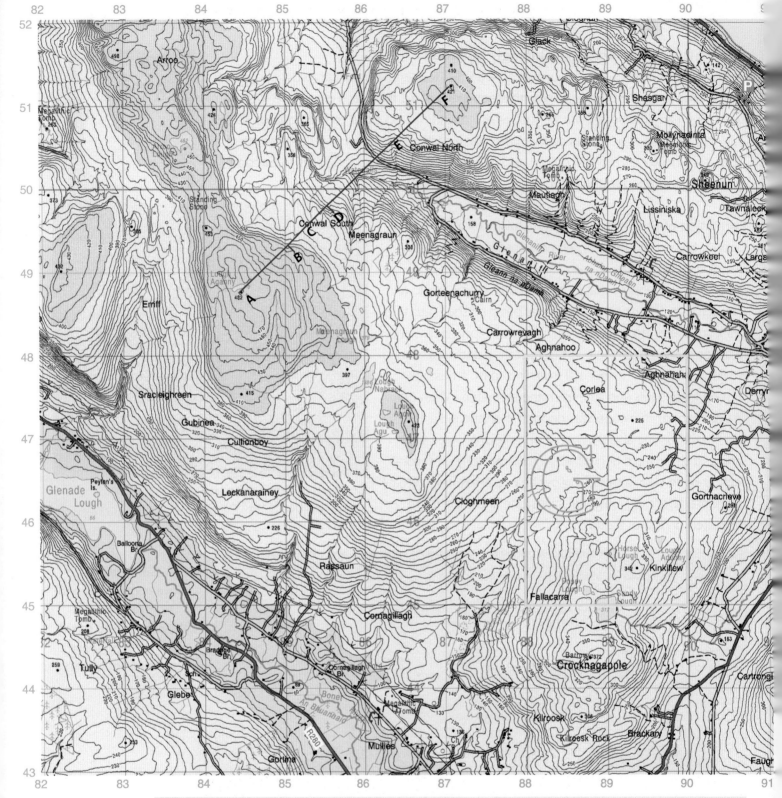

Activity

Carefully study the Ordnance Survey map of this upland region in Co. Leitrim.

1. Find the average height of all the hilltops over 400 metres. Compare this to the heights of the individual peaks. What does this tell you about the relief of this region before erosion took place?
2. Identify the angle of slope at the points marked A to F along the line drawn on the map.
   What does this tell you about the types of rock present at these locations? (See Fig. 3.16 on page 65.)
3. Explain why there is an absence of surface drainage in the area highlighted in yellow?
   Use evidence to support your answer.
4. Is there an absence of surface drainage anywhere else on the map? Explain.
5. Suggest how this upland region may have been formed?
6. Draw a cross section for the line A to F and label the alternate areas of steep and gentle slopes.

Escarpments of the Paris Basin

For millions of years sediments, such as sandstone and limestone, were laid down on a slowly sinking seabed. Then, about 30 million years ago when the Alpine earth movements uplifted these sedimentary layers, they were slightly wrinkled. Later, the rock layers sagged.

Both movements created a **dish-shaped basin**, lower in the centre at Paris and higher at its upturned edges in Burgundy to the east.

Since then, and especially since the last ice age, erosion has removed the younger rock layers from the upturned edges of the basin, exposing the older rock layers underneath. These layers form a series of **escarpments** that are like saucers stacked on top of each other, each one smaller than the last. Their rims form rings of sandstone, limestone and chalk hills, especially in the east of the basin. Because the rock layers dip (slope) gently towards the centre, there is a series of sharp dipping slopes, called scarps, facing east, such as the Côtes de Meuse.

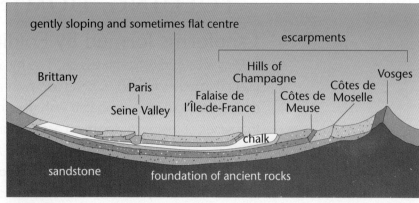

gently sloping and sometimes flat centre

escarpments

Brittany

Paris

Seine Valley

Falaise de l'Île-de-France

Hills of Champagne

Côtes de Meuse

Côtes de Moselle

Vosges

chalk

sandstone

foundation of ancient rocks

Fig. 3.17

What is a basin?
A basin is a dish-shaped circular structure with rock layers dipping towards the centre.

An escarpment has a steep slope on one side and a gentle slope on the other.

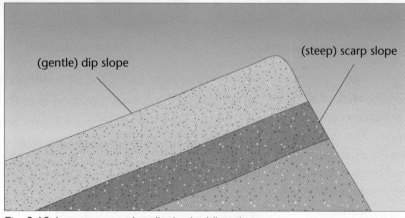

(gentle) dip slope

(steep) scarp slope

Fig. 3.18 An escarpment has dipping bedding planes.

The centre of the Paris Basin has rich soil on gently sloping and flat land.

The escarpments of the Paris Basin have been cut through in places by rivers, creating steep-sided gaps.

SOME LANDFORMS CREATED BY FOLDING, DOMING AND FAULTING

Landforms formed by Folding

Folding is caused by compression. This means that layers of sedimentary rocks are pushed together to buckle, bend and twist and are forced upwards into fold mountains, or uplands. Folding is associated with the closing of an ocean. On the ocean floor, thousands of metres of sediment are compressed by their own weight into solid rock. Once the ocean closes, these sedimentary rocks are crushed between the colliding continents. The **layers of sediments are compressed, folded and pushed up (and sometimes down) to form fold mountains.** The sedimentary rocks on the surface of the colliding continents are also compressed into folds to form ridges, called anticlines, and valleys, called synclines. The sides of anticlines are called **limbs.**

Fig. 3.19

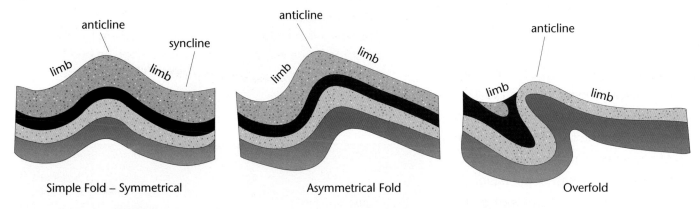

Simple Fold – Symmetrical   Asymmetrical Fold   Overfold

> The rock of an anticline cracks and opens. This allows the forces of weathering and erosion to attack and erode the anticline quickly.

- **Asymmetrical fold:** One limb steeper than the other.
- **Overfold:** One limb is pushed over the other limb.
- **Thrust fold:** When pressure is very great, a fracture occurs in the fold and one limb is pushed forward over the other limb.

When bedding planes run parallel, it indicates that all the rock layers were folded at the same time. It also indicates that the surface layers are younger than the lower layers. These layers are said to 'conform'.

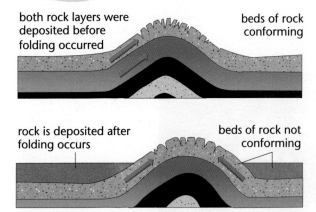

both rock layers were deposited before folding occurred

beds of rock conforming

rock is deposited after folding occurs

beds of rock not conforming

Fig. 3.20 When rock layers do not conform, it is clear in this case that folding has taken place before the horizontal surface layer was deposited.

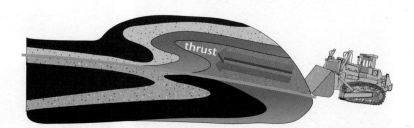

thrust

Fig. 3.21 A thrust fold occurs when rock layers are pushed up at a very low angle 'piggy-back' style on top of other layers. The surface layers may be pushed for some distance over the underlying rock layers.

Case Study: South of Ireland Ridge and Valley Region — A Natural Region

One of the best examples of folding in Ireland is in an area stretching from Waterford across Cork and Kerry. It is referred to as the 'Ridge and Valley Region'. This folding took place during the Armorican fold movement about 300 million years ago. This is now often called the **Variscan** fold movement.

Rocks of two basic types were involved in the folding:

- **Old Red Sandstone** (ORS), the older of the two and so the lowest layer.
- **Carboniferous limestone:** This rock was deposited during the Carboniferous period when Ireland was near the Equator.

The softer limestones were weathered and eroded faster than the harder Old Red Sandstone. So the sandstones stand out as ridges, while the limestones form valleys, such as the valleys of Rivers Lee, Bandon and Blackwater.

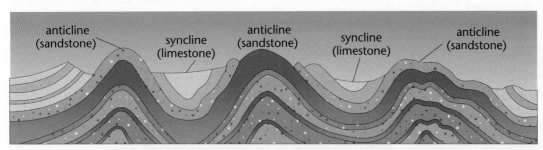

anticline (sandstone) — syncline (limestone) — anticline (sandstone) — syncline (limestone) — anticline (sandstone)

Fig. 3.22

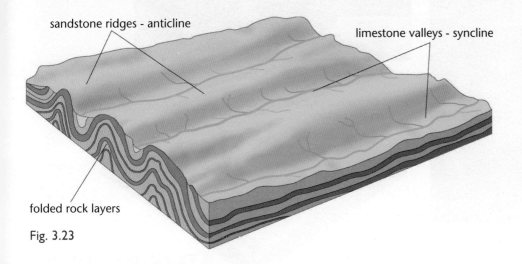

sandstone ridges - anticline

limestone valleys - syncline

folded rock layers

Fig. 3.23

Ireland's Ridge and Valley Region in Munster

Fig. 3.24

How Ridges and Valleys were Formed in Munster

At the end of the Carboniferous period the **African Plate** pushed into the **European Plate**. This movement **pushed from the south**, and mountains as high as the Alps were formed in Germany and Devon and Cornwall. This push, or thrust, from the south was losing force as it reached Ireland.

In Ireland the main effect was confined to **Munster**, where it caused extensive buckling of the crust. The surface Carboniferous rocks and the underlying Old Red Sandstones were folded into ridges and valleys that ran east-west.

In this mountain-building period all the mountains of the south and south west from Dungarvan in County Waterford to the sea in County Kerry were formed. They include the Comeraghs, Knockmealdowns, the Macgillicuddy's Reeks and the Galtees. The upland area of the Burren in County Clare was also raised.

Ireland's Ridge and Valley Region in Munster is a natural physical region. Its rock structure, land surface and trellised river pattern is different from those of all the surrounding areas.

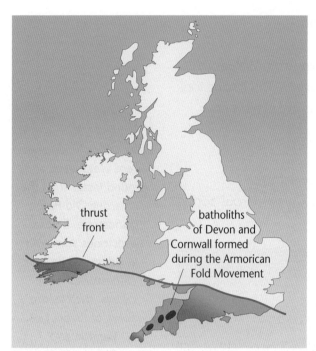

Fig. 3.25 The Armorican Fold landforms

The Macgillicuddy's Reeks run in an east-west direction due to folding.

Fig. 3.26

The Armorican Thrust Front

Folding does not continue forever. The folds tend to die out by becoming smaller and smaller wrinkles, in much the same way as ripples in a pond fade away. The main Armorican belt of **intensely folded rock layers** of Old Red Sandstone and Carboniferous limestone runs through southern England and southern Ireland. **Its northern margin, a line stretching from Dingle to Dungarvan, is called the Armorican Thrust Front or the Variscan Front.**

North of the Armorican Front, the same rocks deep in the ground are more gently folded in the same east-west direction as those to the south of the front.

The Weald region in southern England

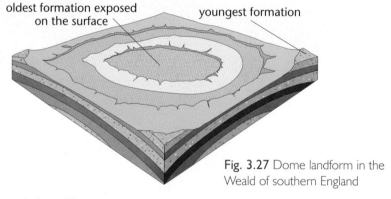

Fig. 3.27 Dome landform in the Weald of southern England

Landform Created by Doming

A dome is a structure in which the beds of rock dip or slope away from a central point. The folded rock layers are like a series of cereal bowls that are stacked inside each other. If the set of bowls is turned upside down, it is similar to the structure of a dome.

A dome is a large feature, up to 150 kilometres across, that has been uplifted a little more than the rest of the surrounding region. During the **Alpine fold movement**, the wide dome of the Weald in Sussex, southern England, was uplifted higher than the surrounding areas.

Weathering and erosion attack the uplifted rock. Over time rain, wind and ice combine to expose the older rock layers in the centre.

Landforms Created by Faulting

The following are some features that have been formed by vertical and horizontal rock movement.

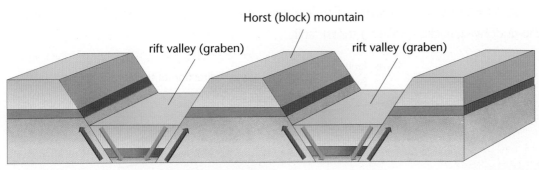

Fig. 3.28 Landforms created by vertical movement

Sometimes vertical movement may create high block mountains and deep rift valleys, e.g. the Rift Valley of Scotland.

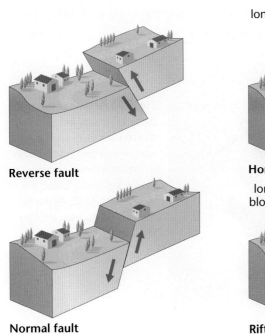

Reverse fault

Normal fault

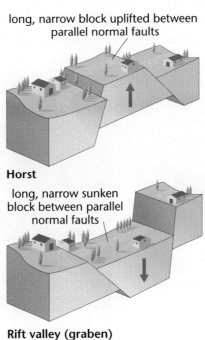

Horst

Rift valley (graben)

Fig. 3.29

The Victoria Falls in Zimbabwe are created by a fault line where the African Plate is being split apart. A rift valley has formed.

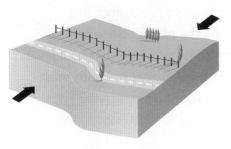

Fig. 3.30 Landform created by horizontal movement

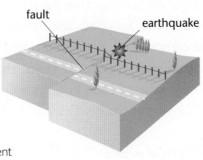

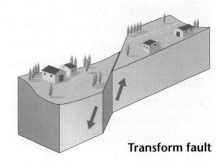

Transform fault

Thrust Fault

A thrust fault is formed when a thrust force (almost horizontal pressure) continues to build up and continues to deform a fold. The overturned rock layers may become so stretched that they eventually **break** (snap) and the overlying rock layers may be pushed forward for up to 40 kilometres. The line that separates the moved overlying rocks from the underlying rocks is called a thrust fault.

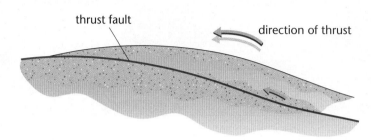

Fig. 3.31 Thrust faulting is created during fold mountain creation.

Tear Fault

When rock layers are wrenched sideways or horizontally along the edge of another plate the result is a tear fault. In this case there is little or no lifting of land on either side. The San Andreas is a tear fault.

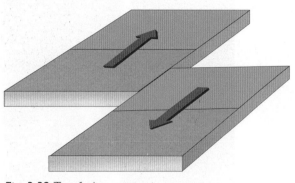

Fig. 3.32 Tear fault

Fig. 3.33 As the northern part of Donegal collided with the remainder of Donegal it was also wrenched sideways to create a thrust and tear fault. One fault is called the Gweebarra Fault. All the fault lines in the diagram indicate the lines of collision.

Case Study: A Donegal Thrust and Tear Fault

The great forces that created the Appalachians in North America and the other Caledonian Fold Mountains, such as the Derryveagh Mountains in County Donegal, scraped sediments and terranes (see page 17) from the ancient ocean floor that separated the American, European and African plates. **As the plates collided, these terranes were compressed (squeezed together) and some were wrenched sideways to form great fault lines, called tear faults, that run in a north-east to south-west direction.** The **Gweebarra Fault** in County Donegal is a thrust and tear fault. The Derryveagh Mountains in County Donegal were formed as a consequence of this collision.

Since then, **glacial erosion** has acted on these fault weaknesses, creating deep glacial valleys, such as **Glenveagh Valley in County Donegal**.

> The mountains and valleys of Donegal run north east to south west because of this wrenching sideways and the compressing of terranes as the continents collided.

Glenveagh Valley in County Donegal lies on a thrust and tear fault.

Class activity
1. Name two surface landforms created by lava.
2. Explain how each of these landforms was created.
3. Name three plutonic landforms created by magma.
4. Explain how each of these landforms was created.

The magma (batholith) that formed the Derryveagh Mountains was so hot that it metamorphosed all the rocks within a 3-km radius.

Class activity
1. Identify two natural regions, one in Ireland and one in Europe, created by folding and affected later by weathering and erosion.
2. Some landforms in Co. Cavan and Co. Fermanagh were formed due to rising and falling sea levels. Explain this statement fully.

Class activity
1. What is a rift valley?
2. Identify a rift valley in Africa and explain how it formed (see page 71).
3. Explain how thrust and tear faults have influenced the landscape in Co. Donegal.

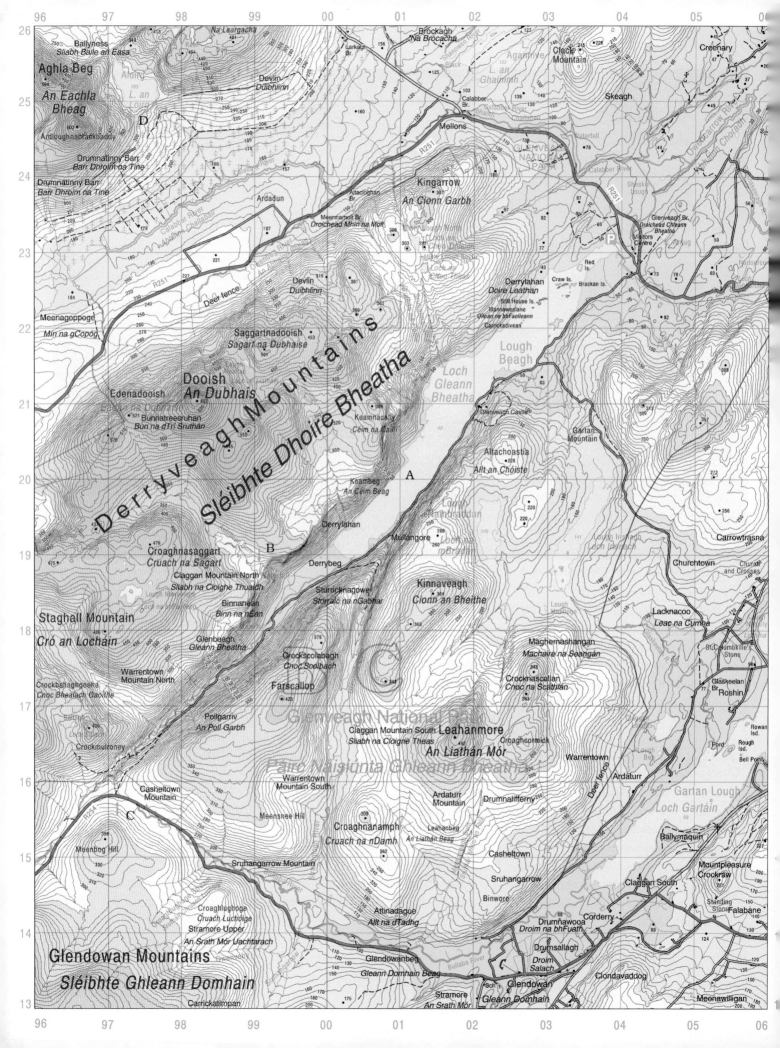

Activity

Carefully study the Ordnance Survey map of the Derryveagh Mountains in County Donegal on page 74. Then do the following:

1. What is the trend of the Derryveagh Mountains?
2. Why do these mountain ridges run in this direction?
3. What influence does this trend have on the:
   a. local river pattern?
   b. local routeways?
4. What processes were responsible for the creation of this mountainous landscape.
   In your answer refer to:
   a. internal forces.
   b. external forces.

Case Study: The Alps — A Fold Mountain System In Italy

The Alpine Fold Mountains are the **youngest** of all the fold mountains in Europe. They were formed about 37 million years ago. Before the mountains were formed, there was an ancient sea far wider than the present Mediterranean between the African Plate and the Eurasian Plate. For some reason the **African Plate moved towards the Eurasian Plate**.

As Africa advanced, **a small prong-shaped chunk of Africa**, that included present-day Italy, Yugoslavia (now Croatia, Bosnia-Herzegovina, Serbia, Montenegro, Macedonia), Albania and Greece, broke off and **collided with Eurasia** to **form the Alps**. The sedimentary rocks on the sea floor were buckled into folds, some simple and some complex like overthrust folds.

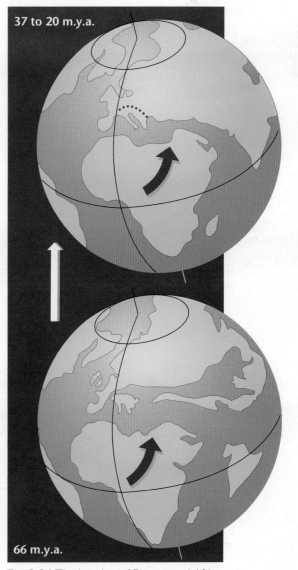

37 to 20 m.y.a.

66 m.y.a.

Fig. 3.34 The location of Europe and Africa

The Alps were formed between 37 to 20 million years ago.

Case Study: Formation of the Appalachians in North America

The Appalachian Mountains were **formed** as a result of not just one, but **two mountain-forming eras**.

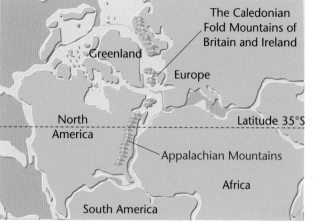
Fig. 3.35

The first mountain era was during the **Caledonian Foldings about 400 million** years ago when the **Eurasian and African plates** collided with the **North American Plate**. Before this collision, the continents were separated by an ancient ocean. As the plates moved towards each other, volcanic island arcs and other small areas of dry land, called terranes, were pushed up against the North American Plate. Finally the continents collided and the Appalachian fold mountains were formed. For the next 100 million years these mountains were eroded and lowered, and the eroded sediments were laid down on the surrounding lowlands.

The second mountain era was during the **Armorican Foldings** about **300 million years** ago. **America and Eurasia were still joined** at this time. Movements between these plates and the African plates raised and buckled the surface layers. This movement again raised the **Appalachian Mountains** that stretch along the **eastern edge of the United States**.

As with the fold mountains of Munster, **the folds formed low ridges and valleys** on the western part of the Appalachians, similar to the **Armorican Thrust Front in Munster**.

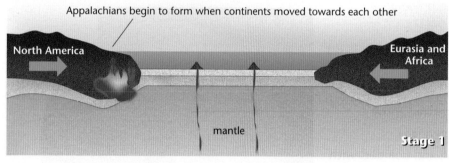
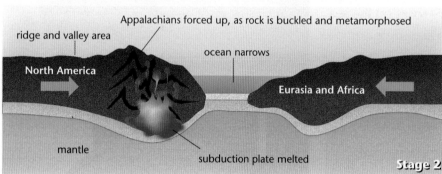
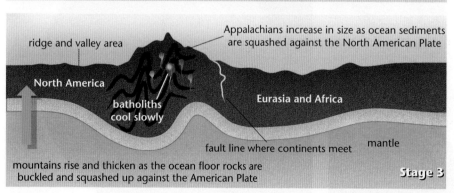
Fig. 3.36

CHAPTER 4
UNDERSTANDING ORDNANCE SURVEY MAPS

How to Locate Places on Ordnance Survey Maps

Can you remember how to locate a place on a map by a four-digit grid reference or a six-digit grid reference? Remember AT⌴AS – across the top, then along the side.

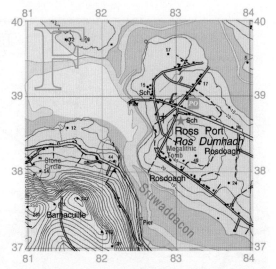

Activity
On the map extract use:
a. a four-digit grid reference
b. a six-digit grid reference to locate the post office.

The National Grid

A	B	C	D	E
F	G	H	J	K
L	M	N	O	P
Q	R	S	T	U
V	W	X	Y	Z

Fig. 4.1 Remember the national grid divides the whole country into 25 boxes, called sub-zones. Each sub-zone is identified by a letter of the alphabet.

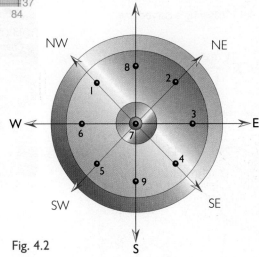

Fig. 4.2

Do this activity to recap on direction.

How to Find Direction on Ordnance Survey Maps

Activity
1. Use Fig. 4.2 and look at the example given in (a), then answer the following:
   a. The number 3 is _east_ of number 6.
   b. The number 2 is _____ of number 5.
   c. The number 8 is _____ of number 9.
   d. The number 7 is _____ of number 2.
   e. The number 1 is _____ of number 4.
   f. The number 7 is _____ of number 9.
2. In which direction would you travel when going from:
   a. 1 to 4?   b. 5 to 2?   c. 8 to 9?   d. 7 to 1?
   e. 7 to 3?   f. 7 to 6?   g. 9 to 3?   h. 6 to 8?

SCALE ON ORDNANCE SURVEY MAPS

Scale is the relationship between a distance on a map and its corresponding measurement on the ground. For example:

Remember what scale means. So what does 1:50 000 mean?

SCÁLA 1:50 000
SCALE 1:50 000

Fig. 4.3

2 ceintiméadar sa chiliméadar (taobh chearnóg eangal) 2 centimetres to 1 kilometre (grid square side)

Measuring Distance on a Map

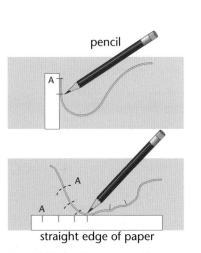

pencil

A

straight edge of paper

Fig. 4.4 Measuring a curved line

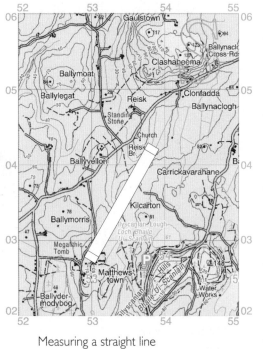

Measuring a straight line

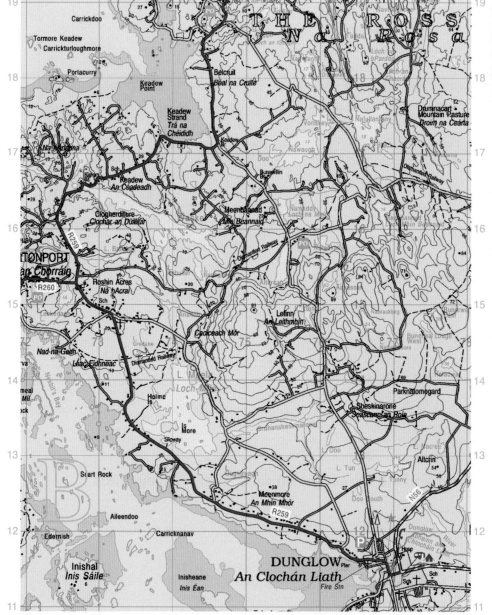

Activity

Find grid reference B 747 190 and measure the distance along the R259 between where the road enters the map at this point to where it meets the N56 at Dunglow. Then measure the distance between both places 'as the crow flies'. What is the difference in distance between these measurements?

Types of Slopes on Ordnance Survey Maps

Activity
Look at Fig. 4.5 and for A, B and C find the numbers and descriptions that go together.

Remember these types of slopes. Now do this activity.

Description:
- Concave
- Convex
- Stepped

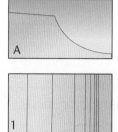
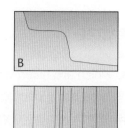
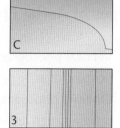

Fig. 4.5

Case Study: Cross Section

From spot height 397 m at grid reference T 012 730 to T 044 696 looking north east.

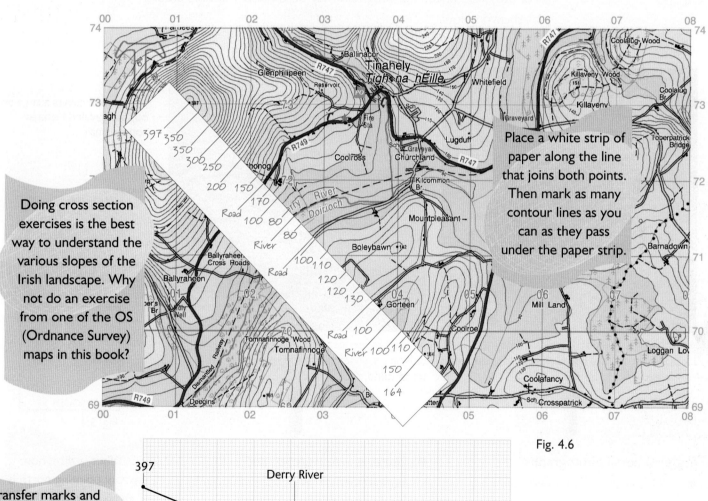

Doing cross section exercises is the best way to understand the various slopes of the Irish landscape. Why not do an exercise from one of the OS (Ordnance Survey) maps in this book?

Place a white strip of paper along the line that joins both points. Then mark as many contour lines as you can as they pass under the paper strip.

Fig. 4.6

Transfer marks and heights to graph paper. Then draw a cross section.

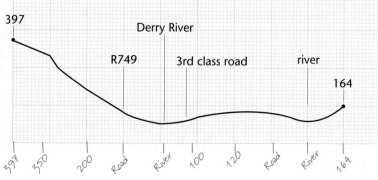

TEST YOURSELF AT

my-etest.com

CHAPTER 5
UNDERSTANDING PHOTOGRAPHS

Remember these few facts about aerial photographs.
- Scale
- The nine divisions on an oblique photo
- Direction

Types of Aerial Photograph

There are two types of aerial photograph:

- **Vertical photographs,** which are taken when the camera is pointing directly on the area being photographed.
- **Oblique photographs,** which are taken when the camera is pointing at an angle to the area being photographed.

Locating Places or Features on an Aerial Photograph

For easy reference, a photograph may be divided into nine areas, as shown below.

Vertical

Oblique

left   centre   right

background covers a large area but background features appear small

middle

foreground covers a small area but features appear large

A north sign is given on a vertical photograph, so locations, such as the **north west** or the **south east** or the **east,** should be used.

For easy reference on an oblique photograph, nine divisions, such as **right background** and **left foreground,** should be used.

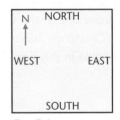

Fig. 5.1

Scale on aerial photographs

- All the features on a vertical photograph are in the same proportion to each other as they are on the ground.
  In other words scale remains true throughout the photograph.

- Features which are located in the background of an oblique photograph appear small because they are far from the camera.
- Features which are located in the foreground of an oblique photograph appear large because they are nearer the camera.

When a direction arrow pointing north is given, turn the photo until the arrow faces upwards. Then write 'north' at the top, 'south' at the bottom, 'west' on the left and 'east' on the right.

Finding Direction on Oblique Photographs

An arrow indicating north is sometimes printed on a photograph. From this arrow we can find other directions. If an arrow is not given, we can find direction if we have an Ordnance Survey map of the same area.

Aerial view showing Limerick city and the Shannon river.
- *In which direction was the camera lens pointing when this photograph was taken?*

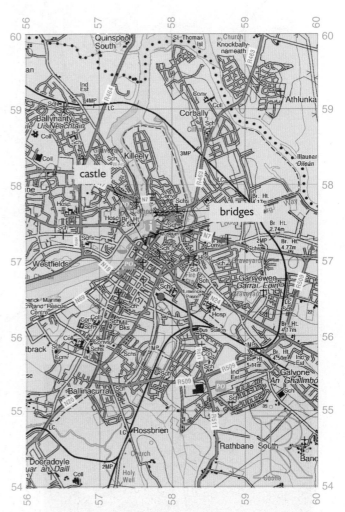

Finding Direction Using a Photograph and Map

Orientate your map or photograph

1. Draw a line through the centre of the photograph from the foreground to the background (from the bottom to the top). This line represents the direction the camera was pointing when the photograph was taken.
2. Identify some important features through or near which your line passes, such as a church, a railway or a road.
3. Identify these same features on the Ordnance Survey map. Then draw a line on the map that corresponds to the line you drew on the photograph.
4. On the line place an arrow near the feature on the map located in the background of your photograph.
5. Identify the direction of this line from the map. This represents the direction of the camera when the photograph was taken.

Match the features on the photograph with the ones marked on the map. Then find the direction the camera was pointing in.

Sketch Maps From Photographs and Maps

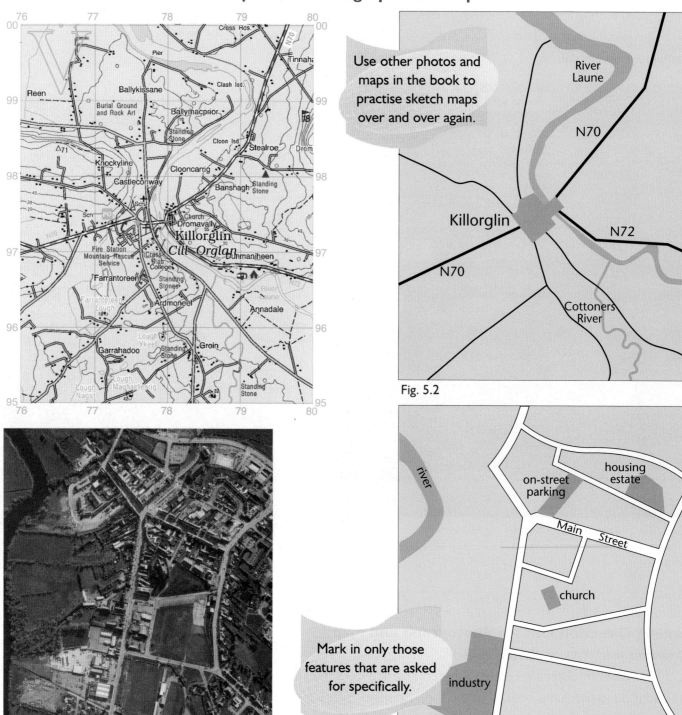

Use other photos and maps in the book to practise sketch maps over and over again.

Fig. 5.2

Roscommon Town

Mark in only those features that are asked for specifically.

Fig. 5.3

Class Activity

1. Draw a sketch map of the region shown on the Ordnance Survey map. On it mark and name the following:
   a. Killorglin Town
   b. two National Secondary roads
   c. five third-class roads
   d. a river.

2. Draw a sketch map of the region shown on the photograph. On it mark and name the following:
   a river; the street pattern; the main street; a housing estate; an area of on-street parking; a church; an industrial area.

TEST YOURSELF AT

my-etest.com

CHAPTER 6
LANDFORMS INFLUENCED BY ROCK CHARACTERISTICS

 **KEY IDEA!** The development of landforms is influenced by rock characteristics that have resulted from the way the rock cycle operates.

LANDFORMS ASSOCIATED WITH WEATHERED LIMESTONE ROCK

Karst Regions

Karst is a term used worldwide to describe the distinctive landforms that develop on limestone rock that is easily dissolved by water. Some Irish karst regions include:

- the Burren in County Clare
- Marble Arch upland in County Fermanagh
- Mask–Corrib Lowland in County Galway and County Mayo.

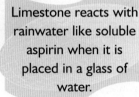
Limestone reacts with rainwater like soluble aspirin when it is placed in a glass of water.

Landform: Limestone Pavement in the Burren, County Clare

Process: Solution

Example: Near Black Head in County Clare

Limestone pavement forms over a very long time in areas where limestone rock is exposed at the surface. Its distinctive landscape forms for three main reasons:

1. Limestone is a rock which offers varied resistance to rainfall and surface water.
2. Limestone is pervious, which means that water is able to pass freely through its vertical joints and horizontal bedding planes.
3. Rain and ground water, as they trickle through the soil, dissolve carbon dioxide to form carbonic acid. This acid changes the limestone, which is calcium carbonate, to soluble bicarbonate and washes it away in solution. Put simply, water dissolves the rock.

Limestone pavement in the Burren

Because limestone is well jointed, it encourages water to flow along the path of least resistance through these joints, rather than percolating into the rock itself. Rainfall or carbonic acid acts upon these joints, enlarging them into long, parallel grooves called grikes. Between these grikes are narrow ridges of rock called clints. Such a surface resembles a paved or slabbed area and is called limestone pavement. See Fig. 6.1 and the photo above.

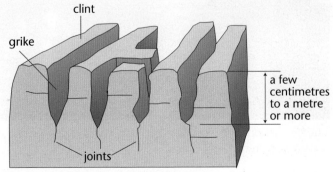
Fig. 6.1 Limestone pavement in the Burren

Landform: Sinkholes in the Mask-Corrib Lowlands
Processes: Solution and Gravity
Example: Pollnabunny in County Mayo

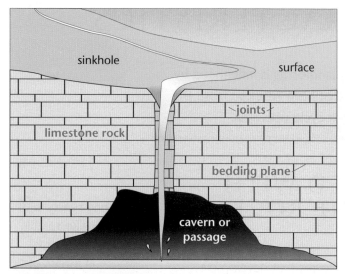

Fig. 6.2

A sinkhole is a surface landform.

A sinkhole is an opening in the bed of a river through which the river disappears underground in **karst** regions. It is also called a swallow hole, a slugga or a sink. Because water is a weak **acid, it dissolves the limestone** over which it flows. Limestone rock has many **joints** and bedding planes. The water seeps down through these cracks in the riverbed and widens them by the process of solution. As it flows, the weak carbonic acid **alters calcium carbonate in the limestone to soluble calcium bicarbonate**, and so widens the joints and bedding plane cracks. In other words, the water dissolves the limestone as it seeps through it underground.

The most impressive sinkholes occur in limestone regions where a local surface layer of **impermeable rock, such as shale, ends and the limestone begins**. This **concentrates** large volumes of rainwater into river channels where it can dissolve the limestone bedrock quickly. Such a **large volume** of water and its load of sand and pebbles quickly enlarges the joints to form an underground passage through which the river flows. If part of such a passage collapses, a hole may form on the **riverbed**, and the river disappears underground. This hole is called a sinkhole, for example the Cradle Hole in the Cuilcagh Uplands and Poll na gColm in the Burren. The plateau of Kentucky in the USA is said to have 60,000 sinkholes.

Some of the most remarkable sinkholes in Ireland are found between Lough Mask, in County Mayo, and Lough Corrib, in County Galway. **The waters from Lough Mask sink underground at many sinkholes on its southern shores**. Here, the surface rock has collapsed into underground caverns in many places. Some local names in the Mask-Corrib area begin with *poll,* the Irish word for 'hole'. Examples of these are Pollbeg and Pollnabunny, which suggests a sinkhole nearby.

Once a river disappears down a sinkhole, the remainder of the valley becomes dry and is called a **dry valley**. The river no longer flows through the valley, **unless** the underground passage fills during a long **wet spell** or a short **downpour**.

Sinkholes are openings on cavern roofs where rivers disappear underground from the surface.

Landform: Cavern in Marble Arch Upland, County Fermanagh

Examples: Marble Arch Cave in County Fermanagh
Mammoth Cave in Kentucky, USA

A cavern is a subsurface landform.

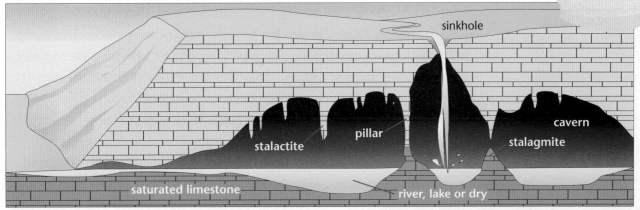

Fig. 6.3

The formation of most caverns takes place in the **zone of saturation**, at or below the water table. Some, such as the Marble Arch Caves in County Fermanagh, were formed by **flowing water** that came from the surface rivers.

Rainwater, which is a weak (dilute) carbonic acid, increases in strength as it seeps through the ground to reach the water table (the layer of rock that is always saturated with water below the surface).

As ground water follows lines of weakness (cracks in the limestone), it acts on these bedding planes and joints in the limestone bedrock. As time passes, the acid ground water dissolves the rock to create cavities and gradually enlarges them into caves. As joints in the limestone grow larger, some flowing water brings sand, soil and sometimes even boulders that enlarge the openings by abrasion.

Lastly, huge underground passages with caves are formed. An example of this is the **Mammoth Cave system in Kentucky, USA**.

Marble Arch Caves in County Fermanagh are part of a 6.5-km cave system and is one of the finest examples in Ireland. It was formed between 10 to 2 million years ago when the joints were sufficiently large to allow a flow of water (rather than seeping water) to dissolve the limestone on a large scale. During the melting of ice at the end of the last ice age, huge volumes of meltwater, sand and boulders flowed through the Marble Arch Caves. This increased flow and its load greatly enlarged the cavern to its present size. The Claddagh River forms in Marble Arch Caves from the waters of three rivers that join together there.

Mammoth Cave in Kentucky is one of the best-known caverns in the world.

Landform: Speleothems or Dripstone Formations
Examples: Marble Arch Caves in County Fermanagh
Mitchelstown Caves in County Tipperary

Stalagmites, stalactites and pillars develop in limestone caves in Guilin, China
● *Identify the landforms A to D.*

Dripstone deposits are a subsurface landform.

Rainwater is a weak acid, called carbonic acid, which forms as rainwater falling through the air joins with carbon dioxide. This water then soaks through the soil, picking up more carbon dioxide to make a stronger form of carbonic acid. This strong acid dissolves calcium carbonate, which is another name for limestone rock.

Dripstone is formed from **calcium carbonate** (calcite). **Evaporation** takes place as water seeps from limestone joints in cavern roofs. When this happens, some **carbon dioxide** is **released** from the 'water', which is no longer able to hold all the calcium carbonate that it dissolved as it seeped through joints in the limestone.

Tiny amounts are **left behind** on the ceiling or walls of the cavern as the water **drips** to the cave floor. The way it falls creates the various shapes of these deposits. All these calcium carbonate or calcite features are called **speleothems** or **dripstone formations**.

Dripstone features

Stalactites
Continuous seepage of water through cavern ceilings produces constant dripping and evaporation at specific locations. As drops of 'water' fall from the ceiling of a cavern, they leave behind a deposit of calcite. Deposition of the calcite is fastest at the circumference of the drop (outside of the drop). A hard ring of calcite develops and grows down to form a tube that eventually fills up to form a solid stalactite.

Calcite is a mineral formed from calcium carbonate and in its purest form it is white. However, seeping water contains impurities that discolour the calcite. These impurities are especially noticeable on stalagmites.

Stalagmites
If seeping water does not entirely evaporate on the ceiling, it drops to the cavern floor or to the sloping cavern sides. Here wider and shorter stumps or domes of calcite build up to form stalagmites. Their shape results from the dropping water splashing onto the floor, spreading out to form a wide base.

Columns or Pillars
As stalactites grow downward, they join with stalagmites growing upward. When they meet they form columns or pillars.

Curtains
As water seeps out of a continuous narrow crack or fissure on the cavern roof, a thin, winding sheet of calcite grows downward to form a curtain-shaped sheet of calcite.

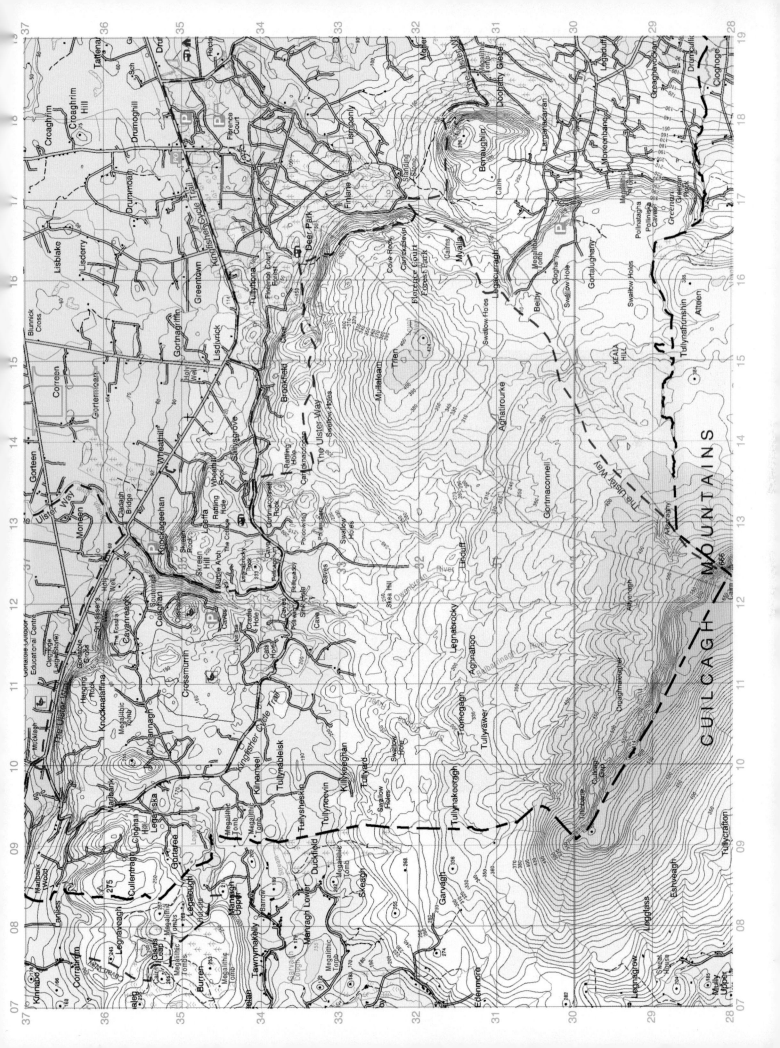

Activity

Carefully study the Ordnance Survey map of the Cuilcagh area on page 87. Then write short answers to each of the following:

1. What evidence on the map suggests that limestone is the bedrock over a large portion of this area.
2. Identify and locate some surface and subsurface (underground) landforms of limestone regions from evidence on the map.
3. Why have so many limestone surface landforms formed here? (Remember rivers and bedrock and the structure of bedrock.)
4. At what latitude was Ireland when its limestones were formed?
5. What tourist facilities are available in this area?
6. Explain how some limestone landforms influence tourism in this area.

Activity

Carefully study the photograph above. Then do the following:

1. Identify the landforms at A, B and C.
2. Explain why this upland has sloping sides and vertical cliffs at various levels.
3. Why does this upland have a flat top? See page 65.
4. Why has this upland not been eroded away like the surrounding countryside (marked D)?

Class Activity

1. When you have read page 89, explain the various geographical changes that would completely transform this region in China over time.

Landform: Tower Karst, Guangxi Province, South-West China

Example: Guangxi, in South-West China

Tower karst consists of isolated tower-like hills separated by flat areas of alluvium. Alluvium is fine sediment deposited by rivers when they are in flood. It is rich in mineral matter and is suited to all forms of agriculture.

Tower karst represents a late stage of weathering in a limestone region.

In its early stage, weathering and erosion wear away overlying bedrock until limestone is exposed. Joints and bedding planes are widened and surface streams flow through these joints and bedding planes, increasing them and forming passages and caverns under the surface. At this stage soil may be very thin as in the Mask-Corrib Lowlands.

Later, all surface drainage disappears through sinkholes into underground passages and caverns. The roofs of the caverns and passages collapse and large depressions called poljes develop, as in the Burren in County Clare. Towards the end of this stage, the surface level of the land between these collapsed features is worn down and tower-like hills of limestone, some up to 200 metres high, may remain.

Then, if sediment builds up in sinkholes and blocks drainage, the surface depressions including the sinkholes fill with sediment, and areas between the towers join to form a flat, alluvial surface (formed from alluvium) like a large river flood plain.

One of world's most famous tower karst landscapes is near **Guilin in south-western China**. This dramatic landscape has inspired many Chinese artists and photographers.

The heavy monsoon rain, sometimes exceeding 2000 mm, has led to rapid erosion by rivers, such as the Li Jiang (Li River). The availability of water together with the high subtropical temperatures encouraged highly active chemical weathering to create this unique landscape.

● At which stage of erosion is this limestone region in China?

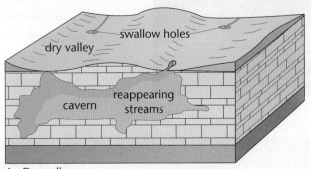

A   Dry valley

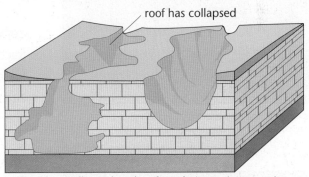

B   Roof has collapsed and surface drainage is non-existent.

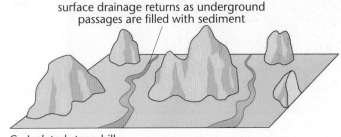

C   Isolated steep hills

Fig. 6.4 The stages of erosion that a limestone karst region passes through.

LANDFORMS ASSOCIATED WITH WEATHERED GRANITE ROCK

Remember acid in rain rots the feldspars, then the quartz and mica particles fall apart.

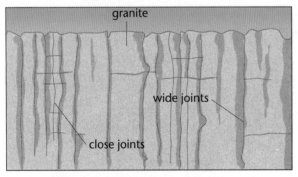

A tor in the Wicklow Mountains

Granite Regions
Landform: Tors
Examples: Wicklow Mountains
Land's End, Cornwall, UK
Bodmin in Dartmoor, UK

Tors are **blocks of granite,** one on top of the other, that are **separated** from the next by **joints** that have been enlarged by chemical weathering and unloading.

Cooling granite naturally forms **rectangular blocks,** separated by **fractures** called **joints**. These are affected by mechanical and chemical weathering.

When fold mountains are eroded severely, like the Wicklow Mountains, the **weight of overlying rock** layers no longer presses down on the batholiths **(weight removed)** that were once buried deep within the mountains. This removal of weight allows the granite to **expand**. This expansion causes fractures in the rock to widen, and these can be attacked by the forces of **weathering and erosion**.

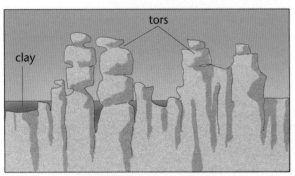

A. Joints widened by deep chemical weathering

B. Weathering creates rectangular blocks of granite with rounded edges.

Fig. 6.5

There are two theories how tors form.

● **Frost action** regularly occurs in upland and highland areas because they are cold places, especially in winter. This process was most active **close to ice sheets (periglacial conditions)** during the Ice Age. Water seeped into the rock fractures and joints during the day. At night it froze, and the frozen water expanded by about 9 per cent. This created stresses within the rock, causing it to shatter. In addition, gravity and rain transported the weathered material downslope to lowland areas, leaving the more weather-resistant, block-like granite rock piles exposed at the surface.

● The second theory suggests that joints in the granite were widened by **chemical weathering** under the surface by seeping **acid rainwater**. This weathering occurred during a very warm period from 4 to 2 million years ago. As the joints widened, roughly rectangular blocks or core stones were formed. The surrounding weathered material was then removed by rivers and gravity to leave the tors exposed. Tors formed only when the **spacing in the joints of the granite were far apart,** leaving these widely separated rock piles exposed at the surface.

Landform: Exfoliation Domes

Activity
1. What are karst regions?
2. Using an example, explain how regions of tower karst form.
3. What are tors and why do they form? (see also Dartmoor on page 92).

LANDSCAPE OR SCENERY INFLUENCED BY THE BEDROCK OF REGIONS

Some bedrock, such as granite and limestone, creates very different types of landscape or scenery, such as the flat limestone region of the Mask-Corrib Lowlands and the mountainous, granite, round-topped peaks of Co. Wicklow. The differences are often created by the resistance of these rocks to weathering and erosion and how the rocks were formed.

Case Study: Mask-Corrib Lowland Region

This is a lowland region surrounding the large solution lakes of Lough Corrib and Lough Mask, in the West of Ireland. Limestone is created in a sea (marine) environment. It forms from level deposits of calcium carbonate that fall to the sea floor and are levelled by the motion of the seawater.

Once the limestone is raised above the sea, it is attacked by the elements, especially rainwater. **Limestone** is **quickly destroyed** (dissolved) by chemical weathering in **warm, wet regions**. Limestone is formed of **one mineral**, called **calcium carbonate**. It is soluble in rainwater, which is a weak carbonic acid, and so it is removed by the action of flowing water. The more of it that is dissolved, the less of it remains in an area and over time the level of the land reduces. In addition, **limestone weathers evenly** and it creates level areas, such as the **Central Plain** and the **Mask-Corrib Lowlands**.

There is a clear boundary where the igneous rocks of the Connemara Mountains and the limestone plain of the Mask-Corrib Lowlands meet, see rock distribution in Ireland on page 41.

Limestone weathered evenly to create this extensive level lowland region.

Tors on Dartmoor create a distinctive granite landscape.

Case Study: Dartmoor in South-West England

Unlike limestone, granite is formed of three minerals, **mica**, **feldspar** and **quartz**. In addition, it is an igneous rock that formed deep within fold mountains. When granite is weathered in wet regions, the feldspars rot, and the mica and quartz particles are set free and the rock crumbles to form soil. Much of this soil is eroded from the mountain areas and deposited on lowlands. So granite areas have a thin soil cover.

Standing above this soil cover on hilltops and mountain tops are **tors**, blocks of granite rock standing one on top of the other and separated by joints that have been widened by chemical weathering and unloading (see page 90).

Bodmin Moor, in Dartmoor, is a distinctive region of smooth rounded hilltops and gentle slopes. The hilltops are covered with thin soils that support fields for cattle and sheep grazing. The farming areas are separated by extensive deciduous and mixed woodland. Standing above all of these are the tors, which add great character and individuality to granite landscapes. The Wicklow Mountains in Ireland also support a similar landscape. It differs greatly from the level lowlands of east Galway and Mayo, with their stone walls, limestone soils, grazing land and little forestry.

The pointed quartzite peak of the Errigal mountain in County Donegal.

Landform: Quartzite Region

Example: Great Sugar Loaf in County Wicklow

Quartzite sugar-loaf peaks, such as the Great Sugar Loaf in Wicklow, Croagh Patrick in Mayo and Errigal in Donegal, are always found near **granite areas**. They also are strikingly different in that they are steep-sided and pointed, while neighbouring granite highlands are generally round-topped with gentler slopes.

As **batholith magma** collected deep within fold mountains, it came **in contact with sandstone** formed from beaches and sand dunes that were intensely compressed and folded as continents collided. The **intense heat and pressure** of this magma-side location **metamorphosed** these **sandstones** and changed them to a very hard weather-resistant rock called **quartzite** (see page 50).

Once the overlying rock layers of fold mountains are removed by weathering and erosion, the quartzite becomes exposed to **frost action**, especially during ice ages. The frost action over time creates **pointed quartzite peaks**, such as the Twelve Bens in Connemara.

TEST YOURSELF AT
my-etest.com

Activity
1. Explain why quartzite regions are different from granite regions.
2. Explain how limestone regions are different from both quartzite and granite regions.

CHAPTER 7
LANDFORMS OF DENUDATION

KEY IDEA! The formation of landforms is influenced by surface processes, such as mass movement, and the processes of ice, river and sea. The intensity and frequency of these processes over time and from place to place also affect landform formation.

PROCESSES OF MASS MOVEMENT

The movement of debris, the loose material derived from the weathering of bedrock, down a slope as a result of the pull of gravity alone is known as mass movement. No transporting agency, such as running water, is necessary. The result is mass wasting.

Mass movement takes a variety of forms. Some movements are slow, almost impossible to notice, and continue over a long period of time. Others, usually on a large scale, act suddenly, rapidly and sometimes catastrophically. Some are caused as a result of weathering, others as a result of erosion. The more rapid movements may be set off by some influence that may be natural or man-made.

- Natural influences may be a strong downpour, snowmelt, an earthquake, or erosion by a river, such as undermining of a riverbank.
- Man-made influences include quarrying, dam collapse, the clearance of trees from a hillside or the vibrations caused by a loud noise or passing train.

Some of these processes include:

- Soil creep
- Mudflows (lahars)
- Rock falls
- Bog bursts.

In Chapter 7, students must study all the surface processes, i.e. pages 93, 98–99, 110–12, 126 and page 131. Then study only one of the following in detail:

- Mass movement, pages 93–7
- Ice, pages 98–109
- Rivers, pages 110–25
- Seas, pages 126–135

Avalanches occur mostly in spring when there is a thaw.

When rivers overflow their channels, bridges, roads and houses are in danger of being washed away.

93

Some Forms of Mass Movement
Soil Creep
Soil creep is a slow mass movement. Simply it is the slow descent of soil particles downslope due to the pull of gravity and the influence of frost action. Vegetation reduces this action by binding soil particles together and preventing the movement.

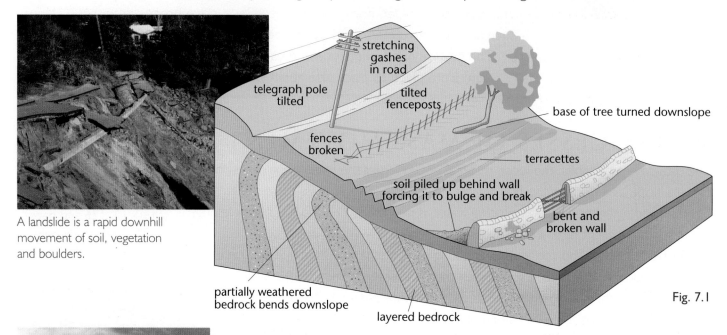

A landslide is a rapid downhill movement of soil, vegetation and boulders.

Fig. 7.1

Landslide, Avalanches and Rock Falls
Landslides and rock falls are very rapid slides of accumulated debris, such as scree, ice, rocks or snow. They may occur for the following reasons:
- The undercutting of a steep slope during road widening or by a river in flood.
- An earthquake or loud noise on a snow-covered mountainside (avalanche).
- A collapse of a cliff due to erosion of its base (undercutting).
- A rock fall due to frost action.

An avalanche is a rapid downslope movement of snow and ice.

Mudflows
Mudflows occur when soils with a high percentage of clay particles become saturated by water. The steeper the slope is, the higher the speed of the flow. Snow-capped volcanic peaks are particularly prone to a type of mudflow called a **lahar**. This occurs when hot magma is ejected from a volcano and lands on snow and ice nearby. This causes the snow or ice to melt, releasing vast quantities of water that saturate the soil, which moves downslope as a mudflow.

Any loose soil on a steep slope is likely to act in a similar way after a heavy downpour.

A mudflow is a rapid downslope movement of saturated soil that can devastate towns or villages.

Landforms of Mass Movement

Landslides

Landslides are very rapid slides of clay, rocks, gravel or other accumulated debris downslope. These may be caused by undermining activities by people, such as quarrying or road widening on a mountain or upland slope. These activities can make slopes unstable until they collapse, causing a landslide.

Rotational Slumping due to Erosion

Slumping involves both material falling downslope and a rotational movement of the falling material. It is especially common in cliffs of clay, which are under attack by waves or along the banks of rivers in their middle courses. This is particularly noticeable during times of flood.

Case Study: Rotational Slumping on the Antrim Coast

The Glenariff Valley is a spectacular example of a glaciated U-shaped valley. The steep sides and its U-shape were created by the erosive action of a glacier. The valley floor is formed of soft mudstone, while the valley sides are made of chalk at the base with basalt on top. Nearby at Garron Point, the same glaciers removed some of the mudstone and undermined the chalk. Consequently when the ice melted, the chalk and basalt cliffs here slumped as large blocks in a curved movement called rotational slumping.

In other places, the sea has undermined coastal cliffs creating landslides and rock falls along the coast.

> There are three activities relating to solifluction, Irish landslides and bog bursts in *Our Dynamic World Workbook*.

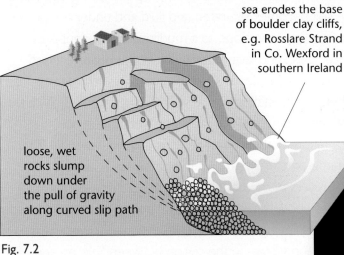

sea erodes the base of boulder clay cliffs, e.g. Rosslare Strand in Co. Wexford in southern Ireland

loose, wet rocks slump down under the pull of gravity along curved slip path

Fig. 7.2

Sloping cliffs due to slumping at Garron Point, County Antrim

Activity

1. What is mass movement?
2. Name five different types of mass movement.
3. What is slumping?
4. How does slumping affect some coastal areas?
5. In which part of a river valley is slumping most likely to occur? Explain.

Bog bursts can be slow or
fast depending on their
water content and the
slope of the land.

Bog Bursts

Earthflows occur in areas of frequent rainfall and areas
subjected to intense downpours. Where soils are deep on
sloping ground, they become mobile if saturated with water.
Then they may suddenly slip downslope. This action leaves
a curve-shaped scar (concave hollow) where the slip
occurred and a bulge where the landslide ended.

Blanket bogs are particularly prone to downslope
movement in places of high rainfall, such as in County
Donegal. This movement may be slow or fast. When it is
slow there is little or no danger to the public. But when it is
fast, loss of life and property may result. Peat has the ability
to absorb vast amounts of rainwater. If a saturated bogland
on a steep slope gets additional water, it is liable to flow.
The movements are called bog bursts.

In 2003, there were bog bursts in an area of impermeable rock at Derrybrien in
Co. Galway and Poulathomas in Co. Mayo. After a long dry period blanket bog dried
out and lost its grip on the bedrock underneath. When rain fell, the peat became
saturated, and the two-metre deep peat layer became fluid and moved downslope,
damaging houses, bridges and uprooting trees.

Rescue workers in a muddy
street in Sarno, near Naples

Case Study: Mudflows in Sarno in Italy

When torrential rain seeps into deep soil on a steep slope,
the soil becomes saturated and fluid and under the pull of
gravity slips downslope as a mudflow. Great depths of
volcanic ash and lava cover much of the region around
Sarno, near Naples in southern Italy. This ash became fluid
where deforestation and illegal building occurred. With
nothing to bind the soil particles together and no
vegetation to absorb some of the ground water, the full
volume of rainfall percolated into the soil making it fluid.

Rivers of mud burst into town centres, tearing apart
houses and bridges, swallowing cars and sending panicked
residents fleeing for their lives in the small towns, such as
Sarno, and villages in the region between Salerno and
Naples in the Mezzogiorno.

This region has experienced 631 landslides in the past seventy years. On Sunday,
10 May 1998, over a hundred people were buried in a special plot in the Sarno town
cemetery, as grief-stricken relatives looked on.

In southern Italy, from Naples southwards, the landscape is one of steep mountain
slopes, rock outcrops, coastal cliffs and terraced gardens and woodland. Dwellings and
towns are perched on cliffsides sometime formed of soft limestones or volcanic ash and
pyroclastic material. The landscape is steeply sloping, resulting in a severe shortage of

land to build on. With lax planning laws and uncontrolled construction, illegal and unplanned housing has been erected on these steep slopes over past decades. To allow for this development, woodland and other vegetation cover was removed from surrounding slopes. Each of these factors exposed mountainsides to erosion. Lack of control over construction was blamed on the corruption of government officials.

Landform: Lahar

Examples: Nevado del Ruiz in Colombia
Mount St Helens in Washington state, USA

See also **nuée ardente** on page 24.

Snow-capped volcanic peaks are particularly prone to a type of mudflow called a **lahar**. Steep volcanic peaks frequently contain thick layers of loose ash and rocks that were ejected from the volcano during an eruption or eruptions. Soils on such volcanic slopes have often become fluid.

In such instances, hot molten magma is ejected from the crater and may land on adjacent snowfields if the mountain is sufficiently high. This causes the snow or ice to melt, releasing vast quantities of water, which saturate the ground. At the same time, the shaking of the mountain loosens debris, which mixes with the flowing water. Huge volumes of liquid mud, called lahars, may run down the volcanic slopes at high speeds, often covering whole villages and towns.

Such lahars are common and deadly. On 13 November 1985, a lahar descended the 5,400-metre slope of Nevado del Ruiz in Colombia, in South America. Channelled within the valley of the Lagunilla River, the lahar was 15 metres high and travelling at 70 kilometres per hour by the time it reached the town of Armero, 48 kilometres from the summit of Nevado del Ruiz. The inhabitants of the town did not stand a chance. About 25,000 people were buried alive in the mud.

The lahars from Mount St Helens, in Washington state, in the USA, were the original cause of most of the death and destruction following the eruption there in 1980.

Nuée ardente

Lahars cause great devastation. Sometimes villages and towns may be completely covered by layers of mud.

GLACIAL PROCESSES, LANDFORMS AND PATTERNS

Remember do only
landforms of one of
these in detail:
● Mass movement
● Ice
● River
● Sea

During the last ice age that ended about **10,000 years ago**, highland and lowland areas were covered by a layer of ice some thousands of metres thick. Only some high **mountain peaks** were exposed and these were subjected to severe **frost action**. While ice increased in thickness in mountain areas, some moved down river valleys to form rivers of ice, called **glaciers**. As they moved, they eroded the landscape to form steep-sided **U-shaped valleys** and amphitheatre-shaped hollows, called **cirques**, **corries** or **cooms**. When the glaciers reached lowlands, they joined to form thick sheets of ice that completely blanketed the land. Glaciers still exist today in Iceland, the Alps, the Rockies and Himalayas. By studying these glaciers and **ice sheets** we can understand the various processes of ice action and how they create landforms of erosion and deposition.

Glacier are rivers of ice.

Processes of Ice Action
Erosion

Erosion involves **sliding and melting**. Ice melts under pressure and refreezes as soon as the pressure is released. This is the principle behind making a snowball. As glacier ice moves downhill, it alternately melts and refreezes in the downhill direction. Should the ice meet an obstacle in its path, it may melt along the uphill portion of the path where the ice is squeezed against the obstacle and refreeze downhill from the obstacle.

This melting supplies water on the valley floor and it mixes with the sand and gravel that is attached to the base of the glacier, creating a slippery slush. Like an oily skid, this slush allows the glacier to slide as a great mass downhill. This action is called **basal slip**. On occasion, some glaciers have been recorded moving downhill at up to 20 metres per day.

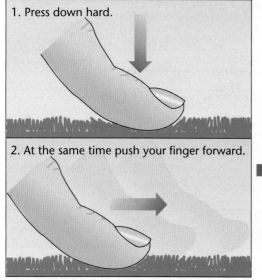

1. Press down hard.

2. At the same time push your finger forward.

Fig. **7.3** Pressure and motion increase temperature and cause melting at the base of a glacier.

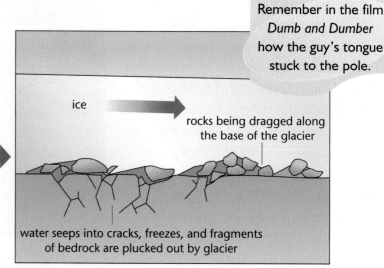

Remember in the film
Dumb and Dumber
how the guy's tongue
stuck to the pole.

ice

rocks being dragged along
the base of the glacier

water seeps into cracks, freezes, and fragments
of bedrock are plucked out by glacier

Fig. **7.4**

Plucking

Plucking occurs because of the drag created by moving ice on the rock with which it comes in contact. The base and sides of a glacier may melt into the ground due either to the pressure of the ice or the heat that was caused by the friction of moving ice.

Meltwater flows into the joints and cracks of nearby rocks. This water may then refreeze and cause the rock to stick to the glacier. When the glacier moves on, it plucks chunks of these rocks from the bottom and sides of the valley. This process is especially effective in places where the rock is already weakened because of jointing or freeze-thaw action.

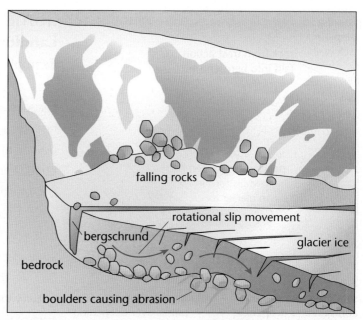

Fig. 7.5

Abrasion

The plucked rocks become part of the base and sides of the glacier. As the glacier moves, these rocks scour, polish and scrape the surface over which they pass (much as rough sandpaper acts on wood), leaving deep grooves and scratches called **striations** on the rock landscape.

Other Factors

The amount of plucking and abrasion often depends upon other factors.

- **The weight of ice:** Erosion increases with the weight of overlying ice. Glaciers were often over 600 metres thick in Ireland during the Ice Age.
- **Steep slopes:** Glaciers move faster on steep slopes, so increasing their power of erosion.
- **The hardness of rock:** The softer the rock, the greater the amount of erosion and the more rounded the upland peaks. Evidence of rounded hilltops and mountain tops may be seen in the uplands of southern Ireland, such as the Slieve Felim Mountains in County Tipperary.
- **Freeze-thaw:** Cracks in rock on high valley sides above ice level or on mountain peaks

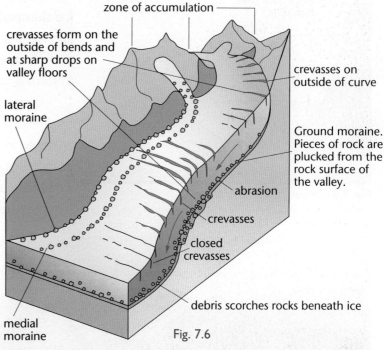

Fig. 7.6

regularly filled with water during the day. At night, when temperatures dropped, the water **froze and expanded**, breaking up the rock and causing rock falls onto the glacier sides below.

Crevasses generally are not deeper than about 35 metres, because at greater depths, where the ice is squeezed by its own weight, the ice acts like plastic and it bends and twists constantly. The squeezing is greatest at the head of the glacier where the ice is thickest. Restricted by the valley sides and floor, the **ice is forced to flow downhill like toothpaste squeezed out of an open tube**.

Learn these processes and include the relevant ones in your explanation of each landform.

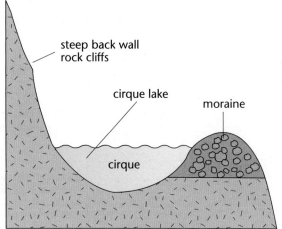

plucking steepens back wall

rock from frost action falls into bergschrund

bergschrund

firn

crevasses

heavily compacted snowfalls turn in to glacier ice

rotational slip

bedrock

shattered rock causes abrasion and deepening of cirque hollow

rotational movement of ice causes over-deepening of cirque

Fig. 7.7

steep back wall rock cliffs

cirque lake

moraine

cirque

Fig. 7.8 Cirques are regularly found in north-facing slopes.

Some Landforms of Glacial Erosion
Landform: Cirque

Example: Devil's Punch Bowl in the Macgillicuddy's Reeks

Cirques are deep **steep-sided, amphitheatre-shaped** (circular) hollows in mountain areas that were created by the erosive power of glaciers. They are also called **corries, cooms, cums** or **tarns**. Cirques began as slight hollows in mountain areas where snow gathered during the Ice Age. Each additional snowfall added weight so that the bottom snowflakes were squeezed to ice. Air that was trapped between the snowflakes was squeezed out and 'blue glacier ice' formed.

As the ice increased in thickness in these hollows, the pull of **gravity** created a deep crack, or crevasse, in the ice at the highest part of the hollow. This crack is called the **bergschrund**. Then, rocks shattered by frost action on higher ground fell into this crevasse. The movement of the ice used these rock fragments to erode and deepen the hollow by the process of **abrasion**.

As gravity forced the ice to pull away from the mountain, the **ice slumped** (much like the motion of a collapsing river bank), and the shattered rock fragments were dragged in a circular motion along the base of the hollow and deepened it by abrasion to form a cirque. This process is called **rotational slip**.

Cirques have steep, maybe even **vertical, rock walls** on all sides except that facing down the valley, and water often collected in the lowest part of the hollows to form a cirque lake. Sometimes these lakes exist because rubble was dropped by the ice when it melted at the end of the Ice Age. The rubble that dammed up the water within the hollow is called **moraine**.

Lakes with names beginning in *coum* or *coom* are cirque lakes.

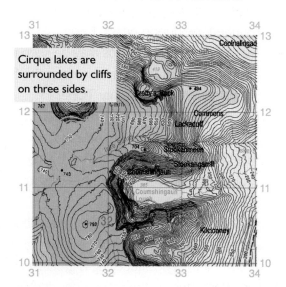

Cirque lakes are surrounded by cliffs on three sides.

100

Landform: U-shaped Valley
Example: Glendalough in County Wicklow

When glaciers moved downslope through preglacial river valleys, they changed their V shape into wide, steep-sided, U-shaped valleys. As the ice continued down the valley, it used material that it plucked away from the valley floor to increase its erosive power. In this way, gathered rubble was used to increase vertical and lateral erosion in the valley. These processes of **plucking** and **abrasion** changed the preglacial V-shaped valley to a U-shaped glaciated valley.

Most Irish mountain valleys were glaciated, e.g. Cummeenduff Glen in County Kerry and the Glenariff Valley in County Antrim.

A glacier is a solid mass of ice that moves down a valley. As it is solid, it may have difficulty in finding a route through a winding valley, which may also vary in width from place to place. However, a glacier overcomes this difficulty in a number of ways.

- **Pressure** is exerted on a glacier as it passes through a narrow neck in a valley. Squeezing produces heat, causing some ice to 'melt' and allowing the glacier to 'squeeze' through, only to freeze again when the pressure is released. Where obstacles occur in the glacier's path, local melting on the upstream side allows the glacier to move over or around these obstacles as it moves downhill.

- **Friction** between the base of the glacier and the valley floor causes melting, producing a thin film of meltwater which acts like oil or grease, so the glacier moves downslope.

Deep glaciated valleys are known as **glacial troughs**. Here, glacial erosion was intense due to the weight and pressure of a thick glacier. Deep glacial valleys display many landforms, such as **hanging valleys, ribbon lakes** and **truncated spurs**.

Hanging valleys are small, glaciated valleys that end abruptly on the sides of deeper valleys. These were formed by small glaciers, which had less erosive power than larger glaciers. Ribbon lakes were deep hollows on valley floors that were gouged out by large glaciers and later filled with water.

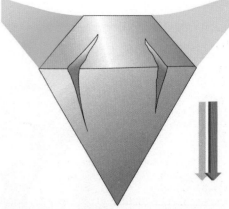

Fig. 7.9 V-shaped valley filled with ice

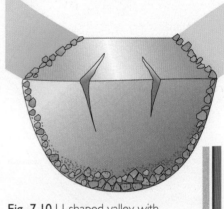

Fig. 7.10 U-shaped valley with moraine material

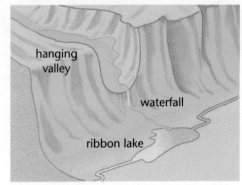

Fig. 7.11

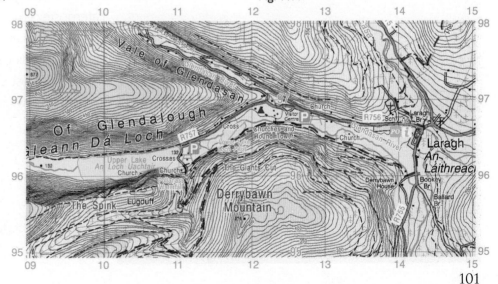

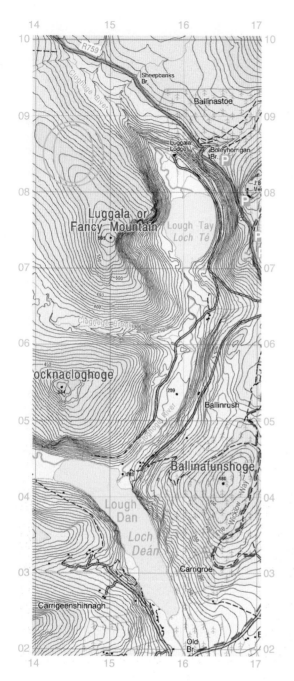

Landform: Ribbon and Paternoster Lakes
Example: Gap of Dunloe in County Kerry

'Rock steps' commonly occur where a tributary glacier joined the main valley, so the extra mass of ice was able to erode more vigorously. Over-deepened or unevenly scoured rock steps regularly contain small lakes that are joined by cascading waterfalls.

Long stretches of glacial valley floors may be scoured, creating deep rock hollows. Again these may be patches of soft rock or badly fractured rock due to ancient earth movements. When filled with water, these basins may be found in isolation and are called **ribbon lakes**. As with the 'rock step' lakes, if they are found in a string, they are called **pasternoster** lakes.

Lough Tay and Lough Dan (see the Ordnance Survey map extract) are ribbon lakes in County Wicklow, in Ireland.

As glaciers moved through valleys, they passed over the fractured or soft rock patches. During cold spells or at night they may have stopped moving. As such times the liquid created by friction at the base of the glacier freezes and attaches the glacier to the bedrock (see Fig. 7.4). Once the glacier moves again, chunks of shattered or soft rock are plucked from the valley floor creating hollows. These hollows increase in size as the glacier continues to erode the valley. When all the ice has melted from the landscape, these hollows fill to form lakes.

Glaciated valleys may have parts of their floors at **different heights**, much like a stairs. This may be caused by any or a combination of the following:

- Different **hardnesses** in the rock.
- Speed or **thickness** of the glacier.
- Patches of badly **fractured** bedrock.

Paternoster lakes are often found on the level parts of these steps and they are generally joined by a stream cascading over the steep steps between them. On most occasions, however, they are found in deep hollows on valley floors.

Lough Tay and Lough Dan in County Wicklow are ribbon lakes. They are large, long and deep lakes in the floor of the Cloghoge River Valley.

Landform: Glacial Spillway
Example: The Glen of the Downs in County Wicklow

Some mountain valleys were entirely **blocked by moraines or ice masses** lying across their former outlets. Meltwater from the ice and, in later times, rain-fed streams were **dammed up** within the valleys and formed lakes. These are called proglacial lakes. In time, the rising waters rose sufficiently high to flow over the lowest part of the moraine or the valley side, and **spillways** were cut by the escaping waters. The processes of **hydraulic action** and **abrasion** of the fast-escaping waters cut a V-shaped valley through one of the valley sides. So they are typically V-shaped.

In Ireland, examples of glacial spillways are found at the Scalp and Glen of the Downs in County Wicklow; at Keimaneigh, near Gouganebarra in County Cork: at Dundonald in County Down; at Galbally in County Limerick and at Clare Glens in County Tipperary.

Some of these spillways are so steep-sided that they have the character of a gorge. Clare Glens is an example of this. Many of these valleys became dry once the ice had disappeared from the landscape. Some however, still contain streams and display **features of young river valleys,** such as potholes, rapids, waterfalls and plunge pools.

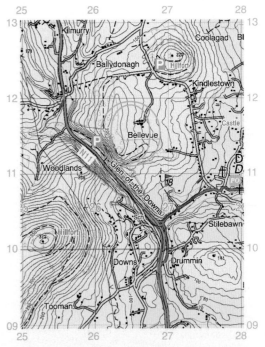

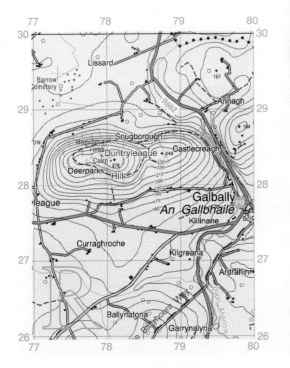

Glacial spillways are steep-sided, V-shaped valleys created by rivers during the Ice Age. Examples are Galbally in Co. Limerick and Glen of the Downs in Co. Wicklow.

Activity
Carefully study the Ordnance Survey map of the Derryveagh Mountains on page 74. Identify and explain the processes on the formation of the landforms at the following locations:
A. B 974 253
B. B 986 175
C. C 025 217
D. B 989 189.

Landform: Pyramidal Peak
Example: Carrauntoohil in County Kerry

A mountain in the shape of a pyramid is called a pyramidal peak. If three or more cirques erode back to back in a process called headwall recession, the surviving central rock mass becomes a pyramidal peak. This peak is made even more pyramidal (pointed) in shape by frost action.

Landform: Arête
Example: Above Curraghmore Lake near Carrauntoohil

An arête is a knife-edged ridge between two cirques or two valleys. When two cirques erode back to back, they may create a very narrow 'knife-edged' ridge between them. This ridge is an arête.

Activity
Carefully study the Ordnance Survey map and identify features A to D.

Landform: Fjords and Fjord Coastlines
Example: Sogne Fjord in Norway

Fjord coastlines are upland glaciated regions that have been drowned by the sea. When deep U-shaped valleys are flooded by the sea they are called fjords. The Norwegian coast is a fjord coastline. Sea levels rose after the Ice Age when the ice sheets that covered the northern continents melted to raise sea levels.

Carrauntoohil has a pyramidal shape because of frost action that eroded the back walls of its many cirques.

Norway has many fjords. Fjords are deep glacial valleys drowned by rising sea levels after the Ice Age.

Some Landforms of Glacial Deposition

The area where the ice melted and materials were deposited is called the **zone of ablation**. There are many landforms of deposition.

Drift is the term used to refer collectively to all glacial deposits. These deposits, which include boulders, gravels, sands and clays, may be **subdivided** into **till**, which includes all material deposited directly by ice, and **fluvioglacial material**, which is the debris deposited by meltwater streams. **Till** consists of **unsorted material**, whereas **fluvioglacial** deposits have been **sorted**. Deposition occurs both in upland valleys and across lowland areas.

In this section, till is divided into separate landforms:

- moraines
- boulder clay
- drumlins.

Landform: Moraine

Example: In the Gap of Dunloe in County Kerry

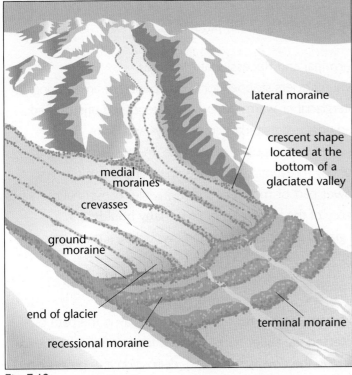

Fig. 7.12

Deposition

When world temperatures increased, glaciers and ice sheets melted. As they did so they deposited large amounts of material that they had eroded from highland areas on lowlands. This material is called **till or boulder clay**.

In addition, the water from the melting ice formed rivers under the lowland ice sheets and, as it flowed, it deposited huge amounts of sand and gravel in tunnels and on lowland areas in front of the ice sheets. This material is called **fluvioglacial deposits**.

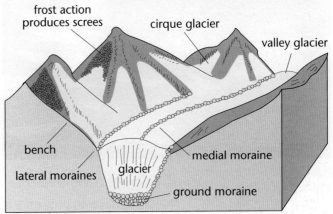

Fig. 7.13 Types of moraine

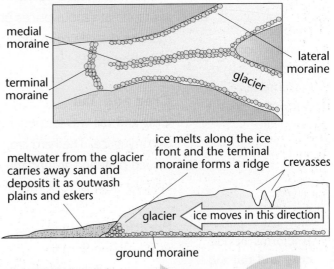

Fig. 7.14 Valley glacier

105

Unsorted material deposited by a glacier

A glacier melts at its snout and deposits its load.

Some less important landforms include **crag and tail** and **erratics**.

Lateral Moraine

Long, sloping ridges of material left along valley sides after a glacier has melted are called **lateral moraine**. Freeze-thaw action is active on the ridges (**benches**) above glaciers, and angular rocks of all sizes fall onto the glacier edges below. This material builds up to form lateral moraine. Vegetation may cover this material in time. It may now be recognisable only by having a lesser angle of slope than the valley walls or as a rocky, sloping surface along valley sides.

Medial Moraine

A **medial moraine** is formed from the material of two lateral moraines after a tributary glacier meets the main valley. These lateral moraines join and their material is carried down-valley by the main glacier. It is laid down as an uneven ridge of material along the centre of the main valley. There may be many medial moraines in a valley, the number varying according to the number of tributary glaciers (see Fig. 7.14, page 105).

Terminal and Recessional Moraines

When glaciers stopped for a long period of time during an interglacial or warm period, they deposited **unstratified** (not layered) and crescent-shaped ridges of material across valleys and plains. These deposits have an uneven surface and are composed of moraine. In some instances, they have caused lakes to form by blocking (preventing) drainage. In upland areas, terminal moraines are found across the lower part or mouth of a valley, while recessional moraines are found at various places up-valley of the terminal moraine. **Many boulders** in a moraine may be **rounded** from **glacial action,** much as they would be if they were waterborne.

Crag and Tail

Crag and tail was formed when a hard mass of rock called the **crag** lay in the path of oncoming ice. The hard crag protected the softer rocks in its lee from erosion, as the ice moved over and around the crag. On the downstream side, deposition also produced a tapering ridge of rock with glacial drift on the surface.

Erratics

As ice moved from the mountainous areas, large boulders were sometimes carried long distances and deposited as the ice melted. Sometimes, these boulders are perched in precarious positions and are referred to as **perched blocks**. In this way in Ireland, Mourne granite was carried as far as Dublin, Wexford and Cork. Galway granite was carried as far away as Mallow, while Scottish ice dropped erratics in Monaghan and Dublin.

Landform: Drumlins

Example: Hills in Cavan and
Islands in Clew Bay

Drumlins are mainly formed from boulder clay. They consist of **unsorted** material composed of rocks, pebbles, gravel, sand and clay all mixed up together. It represents the **ground moraine** of ice sheets that were stationary for some time. The materials that form drumlins mainly came from rocks that were plucked from the bedrock over which the ice passed and broken into clay and sand. Boulder clay deposits generally form undulating landscapes. In some regions boulder clay has been deposited in large heaps to form **swarms of rounded low hills**.

These hills are drumlins and range from small mounds just a few yards long to considerable hills a few kilometres or more in length and as much as one hundred metres high. Because drumlins are especially well developed in Ireland, the **Gaelic term 'drumlin'**, which means 'small hill', is given to them worldwide.

Generally, drumlins are **rounded, oval-shaped, egg-shaped or whale-back-shaped hills**. They usually occur in clusters or swarms forming 'basket of eggs' scenery. Their **long axis** lies in the **direction of the ice movement**. The steeper end represents the direction from which the ice came. They are the result of moving ice depositing each clay mound as it was unable to carry the sediment any further.

In some places, drumlins block the natural drainage of an area. Trapped water ranging from pools to oval-shaped lakes may form. Patches of marsh or turloughs may form in the other hollows due to waterlogging of the soil.

Drumlins in places such as Clew Bay in County Mayo and Strangford Lough in County Down were partly covered when sea levels rose at the end of the last ice age.

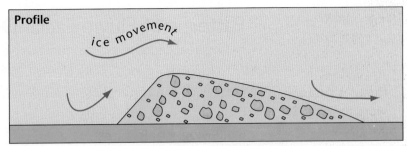

Profile

Fig. 7.15

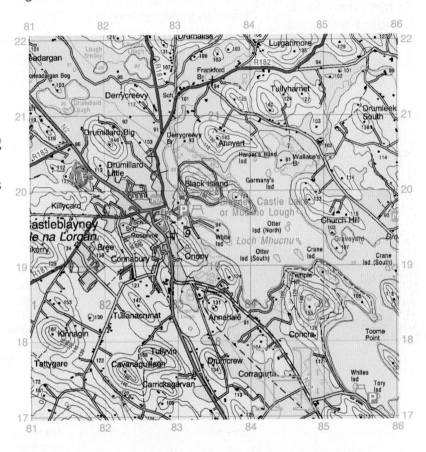

Activity

Carefully study the Ordnance Survey map extract above. Then do the following:

1. Look at the island in Muckno Lough at grid reference H 847 192. Is this a drumlin? Explain your answer.
2. In which direction did the ice pass over this area? Was it:
   a. north west to south east?
   b. south east to north west?
   c. neither?
   Explain you answer.
3. Have the drumlins in this area affected the shape of Castleblaney? Explain.

Patterns of Fluvioglacial Deposits

Fluvioglacial deposits include outwash plains and eskers.

> *Fluvius* is the Latin word for river. So fluvioglacial materials are those laid down by rivers that flowed under and from the front of ice sheets.

Towards the end of the Ice Age, vast amounts of meltwater were released from the melting ice as a result of rising temperatures. The many rivers that flowed from the melting glaciers carried large amounts of sands and gravels and deposited them to form the **fluvioglacial features**.

Irish ice generated a number of domes, or small ice sheets. One is in the west, based on a line between west Galway and north Tipperary; one is in the north, based on a line between Leitrim and Lough Neagh; and one is in the south west, based on the Kerry-Cork mountains. Small ice caps also developed in the Wicklow Mountains, in Corca Dhuibhne and in the Macgillicuddy's Reeks.

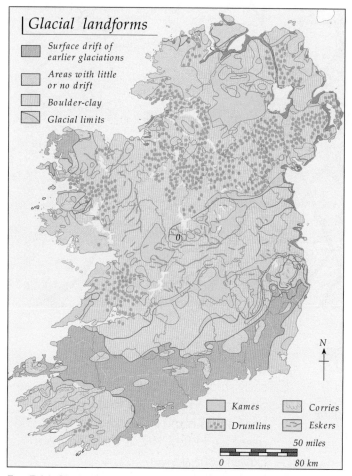

Fig. 7.16 Glaciers transported eroded material from highland and upland areas to the lowlands where it forms the widespread glacial drifts.

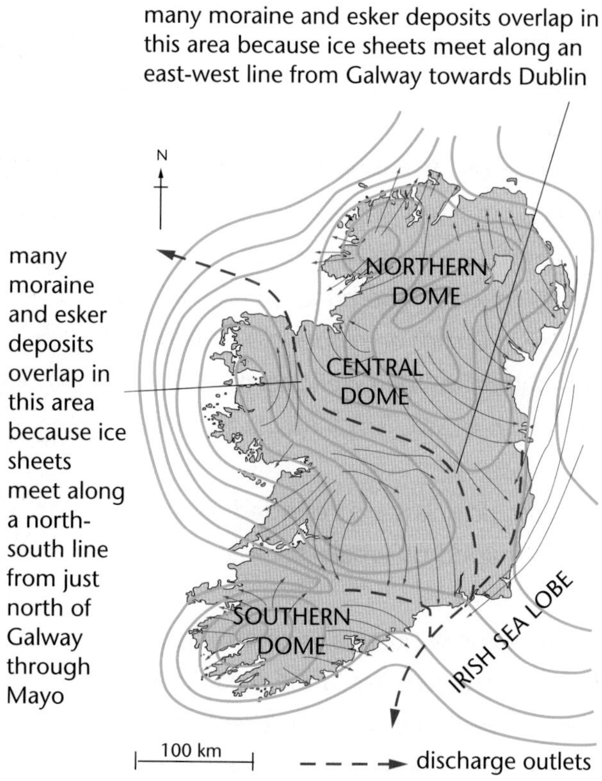

Glacial landforms

- Surface drift of earlier glaciations
- Areas with little or no drift
- Boulder-clay
- Glacial limits

Kames

Drumlins

Corries

Eskers

50 miles
0   80 km

many moraine and esker deposits overlap in this area because ice sheets meet along an east-west line from Galway towards Dublin

many moraine and esker deposits overlap in this area because ice sheets meet along a north-south line from just north of Galway through Mayo

NORTHERN DOME

CENTRAL DOME

SOUTHERN DOME

IRISH SEA LOBE

100 km

- - - → discharge outlets

Fig. 7.17 Domes

Outwash Plain

The melting ice sheet caused numerous rivers to flow from the front of the ice. This meltwater flushed sand, gravel and clay through the terminal moraine to form an **outwash plain**. The Curragh, in County Kildare in Ireland, is such a feature. Heavy deposits of coarse material are generally deposited near the ice, while thinner and finer deposits are deposited further away. During times of summer drought, in such areas the vegetation cover is inclined to scorch due to the coarse or stony nature of the soil.

Landform: Esker

Example: Eiscir Riada at Clonmacnoise, County Offaly

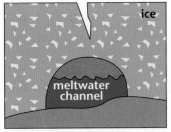
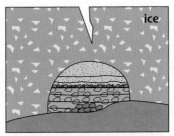
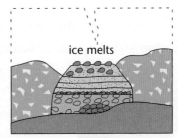
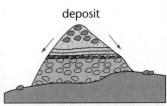

1. As ice melts, meltwater channels form under the ice.

2. Sand, gravel and boulders are deposited, depending on the speed of meltwater flow.

3. Meltwater channel fills with deposits as the ice melts.

4. After the ice has melted, esker slopes stabilise, leaving a ridge of sand, gravel and boulders.

Fig. 7.18

Eskers are long, low and winding ridges of sand and gravel, which are orientated in the general direction of ice movement. The word 'esker' comes from Gaelic – *eiscir* means 'ridge'.

Eskers show various layers of coarse and fine deposits, representing times of rapid and slow ice melts respectively. They represent the beds of former streams flowing in and under ice sheets.

Changes in stream channels sometimes led to a section of tunnel being abandoned by the main stream flow. It would then silt up with sand and gravel. When the ice finally disappeared, the tunnel fill would appear as an esker, a ridge running across the country for several kilometres and bearing no relation to the local landscape. Eskers were formed as ice sheets retreated rapidly (see above).

Most river processes were involved in the movement of material along the subglacial channel. Material was carried in suspension; more was dragged by traction and bounced by saltation (see page 110). Once the ice was gone, the newly exposed esker ridge was subjected to weathering processes such as slumping and gravity. Owing to the enclosed nature of the subglacial stream, water pressure was considerable, causing the flow of water to be fast, so these streams could carry a heavy load.

> Esker materials are often used for building construction. Can you suggest why they are suitable for this purpose?

Activity

1. Choose three glacial landforms and explain how the processes of erosion and deposition have formed them.

2. Where would you expect to find landforms of glacial erosion? Explain.

Esker ridges and moraines blocked to form shallow lakes where bogs developed in the Midlands of Ireland.

RIVER PROCESSES, LANDFORMS AND PATTERNS

Rivers perform three basic functions. They erode, transport and deposit material, so they are constantly changing the surface of their basins. The energy of a river depends on its **volume** and its **speed** or **velocity.**

Ashleagh Falls in the Erriff river valley

The material transported by a river is called its **load.** Most of the river's energy is used up in transporting this load. **As a river's volume increases, so does its load.**

A river carries its greatest load and its largest particles, such as rocks, when it is in flood after heavy rain. When in flood, a river's water turns brown due to the high content of soil particles that it carries in suspension. When a flood subsides and normal water levels occur once more, the brown colour disappears and only tiny particles can be moved.

Processes of Transportation

The river's load is carried in the following ways (see left):

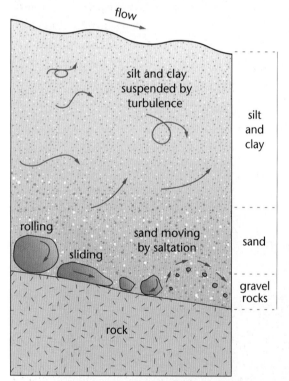

Fig. 7.19 Materials are moved along a river's course by processes of transportation.

* Suspended load
  Most particles, including fine clay and silt, are carried in suspension by a river. Water action may initially cause fine particles to be lifted from the riverbed, but once in suspension the turbulence of the water keeps them up and the particles are transported downstream.

* Solution
  Rivers that flow over soluble rock, such as limestone or chalk, will carry some matter in solution. Chalk streams, for instance, may appear to be carrying no load at all, whereas they may have large amounts of soluble minerals dissolved in their waters.

* Saltation
  Some particles are light enough to be bounced along the riverbed. They are lifted from the riverbed by **hydraulic action** (see page 111). Because they are too heavy to form part of the suspended load, they fall back onto the riverbed to be picked up once more. This process is repeated and so the pattern of bouncing stone is achieved.

* Traction (bedload)
  The volume and speed of a river is greatly increased during times of flood. Pebbles, large stones and sometimes huge boulders are rolled along the riverbed during these periods of high water. This process is often referred to as **bedload drag.**

Processes of River Erosion

Hydraulic Action

Hydraulic action is the force of moving water. By rushing into cracks, the force of moving water can sweep out loose material or help break up solid rock. Turbulent (very disturbed) and eddying (swirling) water may undermine (cut under) banks on the bend of a river. This process is called **bank caving**.

Erosion also occurs because of **cavitation**. Cavitation takes place when bubbles of air collapse and form tiny shock waves against the banks. These tiny explosions loosen soil particles and are particularly effective on banks of clay, sand or gravel.

Abrasion

Abrasion is the way the river uses its load to erode. The greater the volume and speed of a river, the greater its load and the greater is its power to erode. A river reaches its greatest erosive power during times of flood when riverbanks are most likely to collapse.

Abrasion is seen most effectively where rivers flow over layers of rock. Pebbles are whirled round by eddies in hollows in the riverbed. This action forms potholes (deep pools), which are regularly found in mountain streams.

Attrition

As a river carries its load, the particles are constantly in collision with each other and with the bed of the river. These particles get progressively smaller as they move downstream. Boulders and pebbles in a river are always rounded and smooth to touch.

Solution

Solution is chemical erosion. Rocks, such as limestone and chalk, dissolve when water flows across their surface. As rainwater seeps through soil it becomes more acid than rain. When it meets limestone or chalk, it reacts with them (it fizzes) and dissolves them. It then carries these dissolved particles away in solution.

Over time, hydraulic action breaks up solid rock.

A river undercuts a bank when it is in flood, causing bank caving and slumping.

Pebbles and rocks become rounded as they hit off each other on the riverbed.

The Long Profile of a River

A river's activity concentrates on the creation of a slope from source to mouth, a slope which will result in a speed that keeps erosion and deposition exactly in balance. At this stage the river is said to be **graded** and to have achieved a **profile of equilibrium**. Such a profile, however, is rarely if ever achieved. **Changes in volume, in the level of land or sea, or unequal resistance of underlying rocks all prevent a river from ever achieving a graded profile.** So landforms of erosion and deposition are constantly being formed and destroyed over time.

> Patches of hard bedrock are more resistant to erosion than soft rock. This causes uneven erosion in a riverbed.

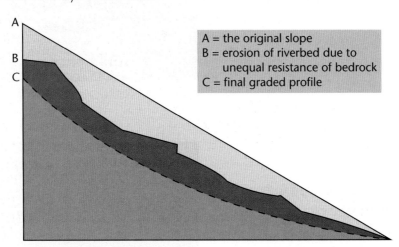

A = the original slope
B = erosion of riverbed due to unequal resistance of bedrock
C = final graded profile

Fig. 7.20 Typical river profile

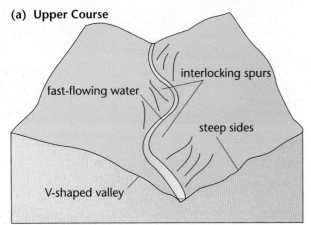

(a) Upper Course

interlocking spurs

fast-flowing water

steep sides

V-shaped valley

The river flows around the interlocking spurs.

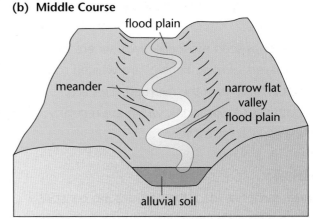

(b) Middle Course

flood plain

meander

narrow flat valley flood plain

alluvial soil

Interlocking spurs are cut away in the flood plain.

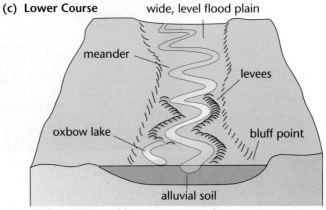

(c) Lower Course

wide, level flood plain

meander

levees

oxbow lake

bluff point

alluvial soil

Fig. 7.21 The three stages in the development of a river valley

Oxbow lakes and levees are created.

Some Landforms of River Erosion
Landform: V-Shaped Valley
Example: Devil's Glen, near Ashford in County Wicklow

Rivers follow a winding course as they flow downstream. This occurs for a number of reasons:

- Irregular patches of soft rock wear away easily, while patches of **hard**, more **resistant rock** push the stream to the side because it is forced to wind around the hard rock. This fast-moving water also tries to find the easiest route to lowland. Consequently, **it winds and twists** its way around obstacles. When this happens, the current tends to be strongest on the outside of a bend. As a result, erosion takes place and bends become more pronounced. This causes interlocking spurs to jut out from the side.

The Devil's Glen in Co. Wicklow has very steep sides created by erosion.

- Erosion is most effective in times of **heavy rain**. The volume of the river increases and so does the load of the river. The combination of these factors creates severe erosion and the riverbed is lowered faster than at times of low water.
- The fast-moving water carries eroded material and by **corrasion** (erosion of a rock surface by sand or rock particles in water or glacial ice) uses it to undermine land on the outside of bends. This process is called bank caving. Another process, **cavitation**, occurs as bubbles of air collapse and form shock waves against the river banks. As land is undermined, it slumps into the river channel. The rushing water **carries** this **material downstream**. The light material, such as silt and clay, is carried in **suspension**, and the sand, gravel and stones by **saltation** and **traction**.
- Many waterfalls and deep pools are formed in the riverbed by the process of hydraulic action and corrasion.

Activity
What evidence in this map indicates that the Devil's Glen is a deep V-shaped valley?

113

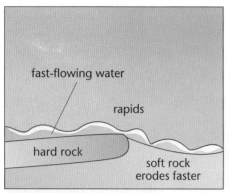

fast-flowing water

rapids

hard rock

soft rock
erodes faster

Fig. 7.22

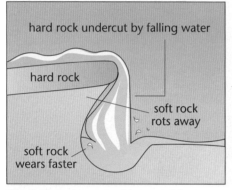

hard rock undercut by falling water

hard rock

soft rock
rots away

soft rock
wears faster

Fig. 7.23 A plunge pool is created by
the hydraulic action and abrasion of the
falling water.

Waterfalls create deep plunge pools
directly beneath the falls.

Landform: Waterfall

Examples: Torc Waterfall, near Killarney in County Kerry
Ashleagh Falls on the Erriff River in County Mayo
Falls on Inagh River at Ennistymon in County Clare

When a waterfall occurs in a river valley, it is usually located in the river's upper course or young stage. Its presence usually results from a layer of **hard bedrock lying across the river's course**. If this layer of rock is dipping gently downstream, it causes a series of rapids with much broken water. If, however, the layer of **rock is horizontal** or **sloping slightly upward**, it causes the water to fall vertically downward after a short time and create a waterfall. A waterfall is formed by the following processes:

● Because there is both hard and soft rock on the bed of the river, the soft rock erodes quickly and the hard rock, being **more resistant**, erodes at a slower rate. The **hydraulic force** of rushing water forces its way into cracks and weaknesses in the soft rock that lies downstream of the hard rock. As the water does so, it widens the cracks and after some time breaks some of the rock apart.

● The **eroding action** of the river's load erodes the soft rock quickly, while it finds the harder rock more difficult to remove. In this way, both the hydraulic action and abrasion of the river's load erodes the layer of softer rock creating an **overhang,** over which the river falls. The beginning stage of a waterfall is formed by this action.

● As the falling water strikes the soft rock on the riverbed, its erosive power gouges out a deep pool, called a **plunge pool**. This pool deepens gradually and the mist created by the falling water rots the soft rock underneath the hard rock cap. This soft rock gradually crumbles and the hard rock is **undermined**. Pieces of the hard rock layer break off from time to time and collapse into the plunge pool or gather at the base of the falls. This causes the falls to **retreat upstream**. A **gorge** is sometimes created downstream of the falls.

Landform: Flood Plain

Example: Blackwater Valley near Fermoy, County Cork

A **flood plain** is a level stretch of land along the edge of a river's channel. It is a **wide and flat valley floor** that is **often flooded** after heavy rain. As a river flows it carries away soil, sand and gravel particles downstream. It also swings from side to side and in doing so it erodes these particles from the sides of the valley and creates level land where it deposits sediment in areas of calm water. This level land is called a flood plain.

Processes of flood plain formation

A meandering river is one that swings from side to side across level land. A flood plain is created in this process and **each river loop is called a meander.** As water flows round a bend, it **erodes** most strongly on the **outside**, forming a river cliff. **Undercutting** of the bank occurs and parts of it collapse into the river. This is called **slumping** of the bank. This is lateral (sideways) erosion. Little erosion takes place on the inside of a bend, but there is often deposition, forming a gravel beach or a **point bar**. This entire process is called **divagation**.

This lateral erosion by a river **removes interlocking spurs** and lowers the slopes of the valley sides. Level land is also created on both sides of the river's channel. This level land is called its flood plain.

During times of heavy rain a river **overflows** its channel and spreads across the flood plain. Away from the river's channel, the floodwater is calm and it has lots of **fine sediment**, such as **silt and fine sand**, in suspension. This type of sediment is called **alluvium**.

The calm water is unable to support its load of alluvium and deposits it on the plain. This happens with each successive overflow of the river. Thousands of years of sediment deposited on the flood plain build up a thick 'blanket' to form extremely fertile, level land, suited to growing cereal or grazing cattle.

A flood plain is a landform of erosion and deposition.

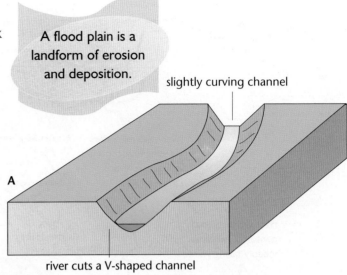

Fig. 7.24

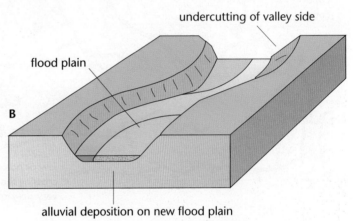

Fig. 7.25 A flood plain forms due to lateral erosion.

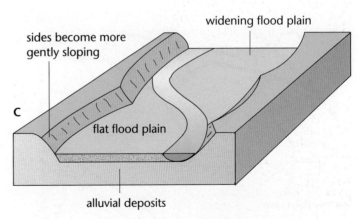

Fig. 7.26 A flood plain is fertile due to aggradation.

Practise these diagrams as often as possible. Make sure you can draw simple, clear diagrams with labels. They will help you remember information in your exam.

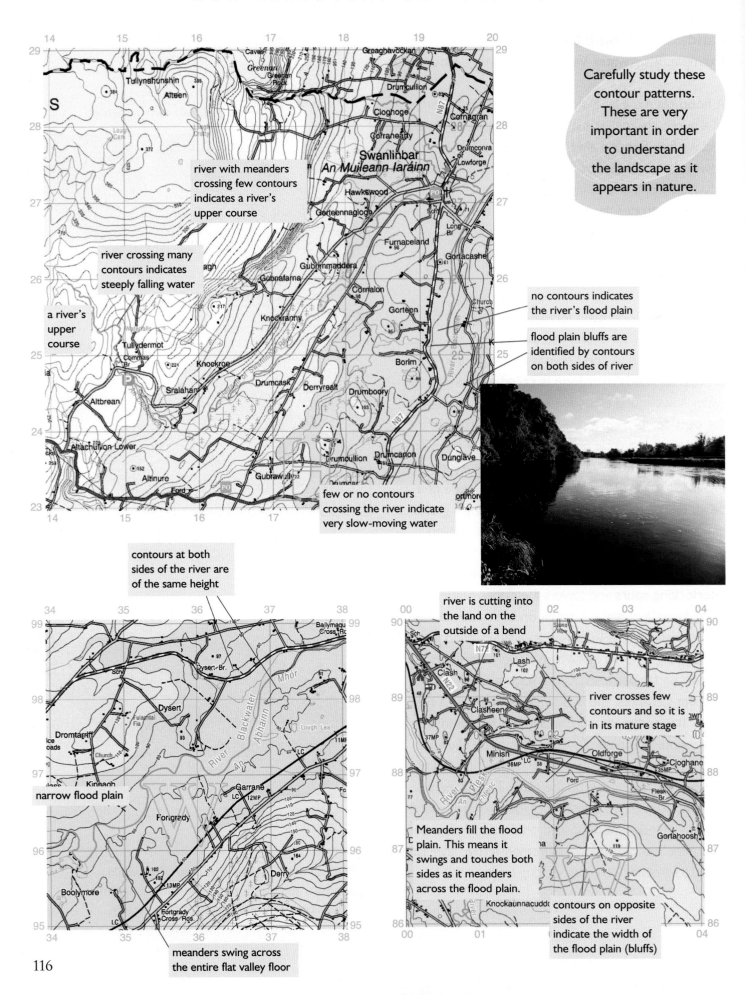

Carefully study these contour patterns. These are very important in order to understand the landscape as it appears in nature.

river with meanders crossing few contours indicates a river's upper course

river crossing many contours indicates steeply falling water

a river's upper course

no contours indicates the river's flood plain

flood plain bluffs are identified by contours on both sides of river

few or no contours crossing the river indicate very slow-moving water

contours at both sides of the river are of the same height

narrow flood plain

meanders swing across the entire flat valley floor

river is cutting into the land on the outside of a bend

river crosses few contours and so it is in its mature stage

Meanders fill the flood plain. This means it swings and touches both sides as it meanders across the flood plain.

contours on opposite sides of the river indicate the width of the flood plain (bluffs)

116

Landform: Oxbow Lake
Example: River Shannon at Leitrim Town

A river wanders over an extensive flat flood plain in a series of **looping meanders**. The edges of the flood plain are far from the river and they form low bluffs that have been reduced by weathering. Oxbow lakes form where the river makes huge sweeping or looping meanders. In fact these lakes are relics of looping meanders that have been cut off from the river and no longer hold the river's active channel.

- **Lateral erosion** of a river's channel causes meanders to move across its flood plain and to move downstream. Constant erosion on the **outside of a meander bend** leads to the formation of a sweeping loop in the river's course. This leads to the creation of a 'peninsula' of land with a **narrow neck** between two parts of the river's channel.

- As the river sweeps around this looping meander bend, the zone of highest speed swings towards the outer bank. There is great **water turbulence** where the river strikes the bank, which is formed of sediment already deposited by the river. The **abrasive action** of the river's load, the **collapsing of air bubbles** causing shock waves and the **hydraulic force** of the water combine to cause **undercutting** of this soft material. This undercutting causes slumping of the bank into the river.

- Meanwhile, along the inner (near) side of each meander loop, where water is shallow and slow-moving, coarse sediment such as gravel and sand accumulates to form a beach, called a **point bar**.

- Lastly, during flood, the river **cuts through the neck of land** and continues on a straighter and easier route, leaving the cut-off to one side. **Deposition** occurs at **both ends** of this 'cut-off' to form an oxbow lake. After a long time, the oxbows fill with silt from floodwater and they finally dry up. At this stage, they are called **meander scars** or **mort lakes**.

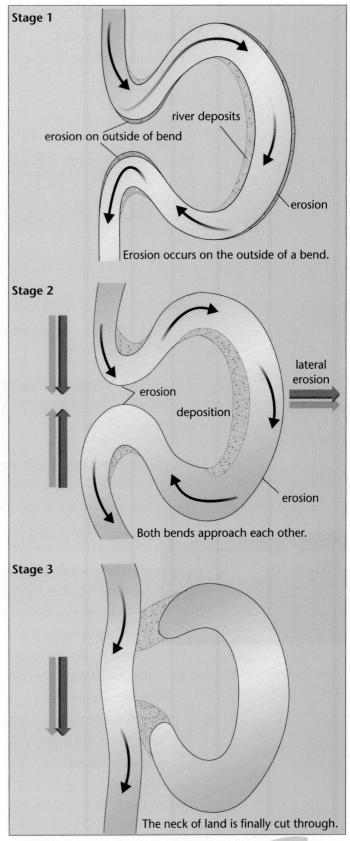

Fig. 7.27 Formation of an oxbow lake

Practise these drawings over and over again.

Some Landforms of River Deposition
Landform: Levees
Example: Mulkear River in County Limerick

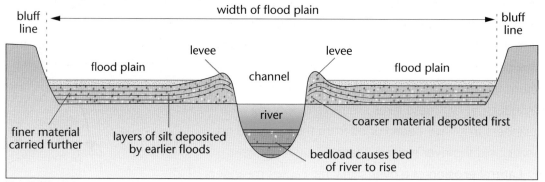

Fig. 7.28

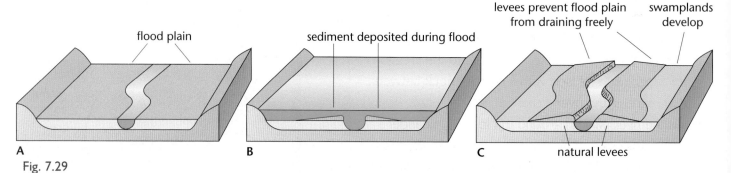

A
B
C

Fig. 7.29

Recent levee construction on the Mulkear River in County Limerick

There are **man-made levees** along the banks of the Mulkear River in County Limerick. These were created as part of a river drainage and reclamation scheme that was started in the 19th century and has been upgraded since 2000.

Levees are high banks along the river's edge and are raised above the flood-plain level. They were built to **retain the river's water** within a narrow channel, so as **to prevent flooding** of the surrounding farmland. Hundreds of miles of levees have been built along the Mississippi, in the USA, in order to control floodwater.

Levees can form naturally along the edges of large, silt-laden rivers as the rivers slowly wind their way across flat flood plains to the sea. The best-known natural levees are found along the **Yangtze Kiang** (Yangtze River) **in China**.

- A **natural levee** is a broad, low ridge of fine alluvium built up along the side of a channel by debris or silt-laden floodwater. As the sediment-laden floodwater flows out of its completely submerged channel during a flood, the depth, force and turbulence of the water decreases sharply at the channel margins (edges). The sharp decrease results in a sudden dropping of the coarser materials (usually fine sand and coarse silt) along the edges of the channel, building up a levee.

- As the levee increases in height it will eventually retain all floodwaters and prevent the river from spreading out onto its flood plain. Over hundreds of thousands of years, **deposition** builds up such a thick sediment blanket on the **riverbed** and **levee** that the riverbed may be well above the level of the surrounding flood plain.

- Villages are often built on these wide levees to avoid floodwater if it should ever spill over onto the flood plain.

Landform: Delta
Example: Cloghoge River Delta in Lough Tay, County Wicklow

When a river carries a heavy load into an area of calm water, such as an enclosed or sheltered sea area or lake, it deposits material at its mouth. The material builds up in layers called **beds** to form a **delta**. If it forms at a river estuary it is called a marine delta. If it forms in a lake, it is called a lacustrine delta.

The materials that build up to form a delta are composed of **alternate layers of coarse and fine deposits** that reflect times of high and low water levels respectively. These materials are classified into three categories:

1. Fine particles are carried out to sea and deposited in advance of the main delta. These are the **bottomset beds**.
2. Coarser materials form sloping layers over the bottomset beds and gradually build outwards, each one in front of and above the previous ones, causing the delta to advance. These are the **foreset beds**.
3. Sediment of various grain sizes, ranging from coarse channel deposits to finer sediment deposited between channels, is laid down and extends out at the level of the river's flood plain. These deposits are called the **topset beds**.

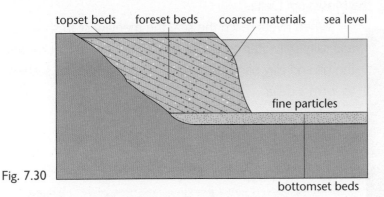

topset beds   foreset beds   coarser materials   sea level

fine particles

Fig. 7.30

bottomset beds

Lacustrine Delta
Mountain streams that flow into glacial lakes often build deltas within ribbon lakes that were formed by glacial erosion. This fills in the lake, reducing its length over time. If a mountain stream enters the lake from the side, it may divide the ribbon lake into two or more smaller ones. These deltas may occur at any stage of a river's course.

Fast-flowing rivers deposit their load when they enter the calm waters of glacial lakes.
● *Can you see the delta in the right foreground?*

Marine Delta
A marine delta has formed at the estuary of the Roughty River in Kenmare Bay, in County Kerry. If a river that is heavily laden with silt and fine sand enters a sheltered sea or bay, such as Kenmare Bay, it will deposit its load to form one of three types of delta. They are classified according to their overall shape.

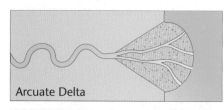

Arcuate Delta

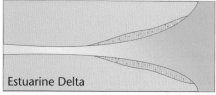

Estuarine Delta

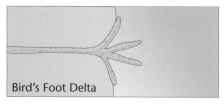

Bird's Foot Delta

Fig. 7.31 Marine deltas

There are three main types of marine deltas.

- **Arcuate**

  This type is triangular in shape, like the Greek letter 'delta'. The apex of the triangle points upstream. Arcuate deltas are composed of coarse sands and gravels. They are found where sea currents are relatively strong, which limits delta formation beyond the original estuary. This type of delta is constructed from porous deposits, e.g. the Nile Delta in Egypt.

- **Estuarine**

  Estuarine deltas form at the mouths of submerged rivers. The estuarine deposits form long, narrow fillings along both sides of the estuary, e.g. the Shannon Estuary.

- **Bird's Foot**

  These deltas form when rivers carry large quantities of fine material to the coast. These impermeable deposits cause the river to divide into a few, large distributaries. Levees develop along these distributaries, so long fingers project into the sea to form a delta shaped like to a bird's foot, e.g. the Mississippi Delta.

  When rivers reach the sea, the meeting of fresh water and salty seawater produces an electric charge that causes the silt and clay particles to '**clot**' and settle on the seabed to form a delta.

Egyptian farms till the rich soil of the Nile Delta and all the family members help to plant and harvest the crops.

Activity

Choose three river landforms and explain how the processes of erosion and deposition have formed them.

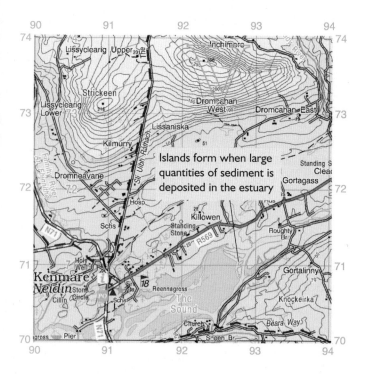

120

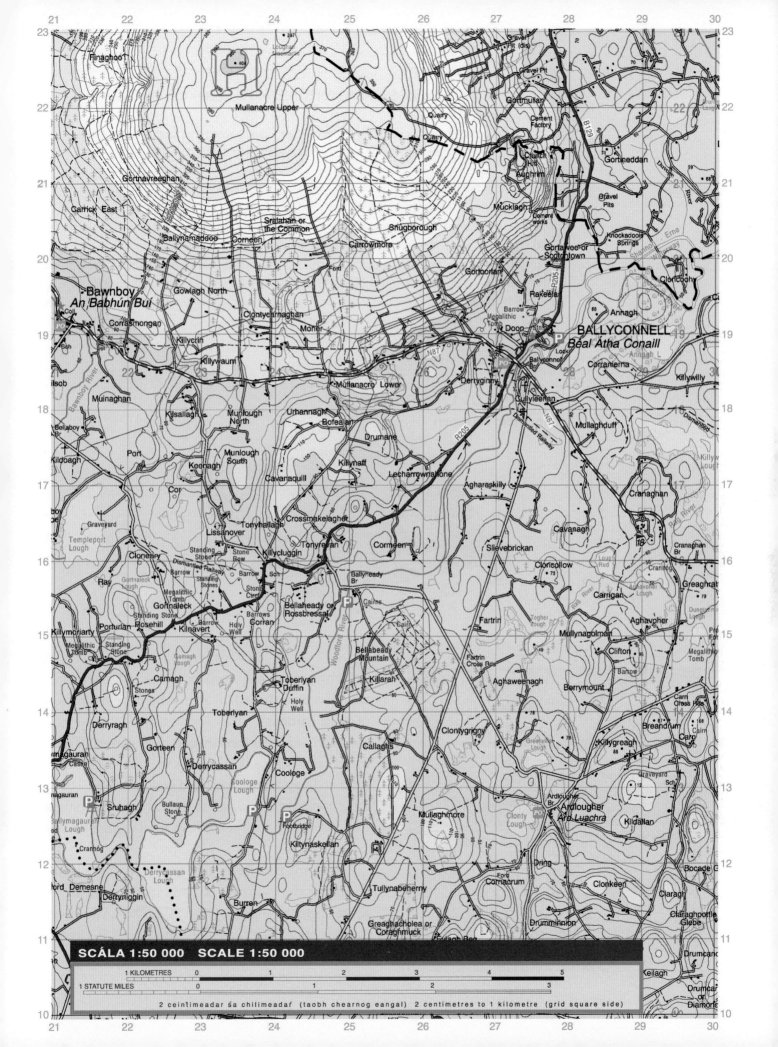

SCÁLA 1:50 000   SCALE 1:50 000

1 KILOMETRES   0   1   2   3   4   5

1 STATUTE MILES   0   1   2   3

2 ceintiméadar sá chiliméadaf (taobh chearnog eangal)   2 centimetres to 1 kilometre (grid square side)

Activity

Carefully study the Ordnance Survey map of Ballyconnell in County Cavan on page 121.
Then do the following:

1. River processes have affected this region in Co. Cavan over time. Using evidence from the map identify two landforms that have been created by these processes.
   In each case:
   a. Name the landform.
   b. Locate the landform on the map.
   c. Give another Irish example.
   d. Explain the processes that led to its formation.
2. Drumlins are low, rounded hills of boulder clay created by glacial deposition. An example of a drumlin is at grid reference H 235 172. The low-lying areas around these hills have a coating of clay, also deposited by the ice. Carefully study similar contour shapes on the map that indicate drumlin hills. Explain how these hills:
   a. were formed.
   b. have affected drainage on the map.

Patterns of Drainage
Dendritic Pattern

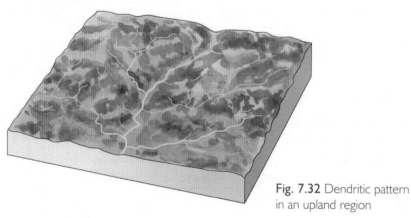

Fig. 7.32 Dendritic pattern in an upland region

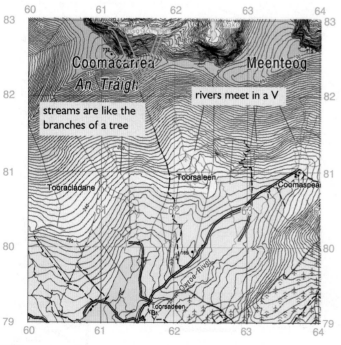

Dendros is the Greek word for 'a tree'. So a dendritic pattern is **tree-shaped**. In areas where the **bedrock** is of **equal hardness**, a river and its tributaries will erode evenly to provide a **tree-shaped river pattern**. The main river, because of its greater volume, will erode the most and so has the widest and deepest valley. The tributaries have less water, so their erosive power is less than the main river. Their valleys are therefore smaller and not as deep.

Each tributary **flows with the slope of the land** and meets the main river or other tributaries at an **acute angle** (an angle less than 90°). This is why every tributary appears to consist of a main trunk, fed from a variety of branches, each one running into a valley proportional to the river's size.

Trellised Pattern

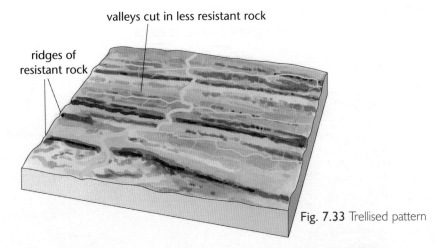

ridges of resistant rock

valleys cut in less resistant rock

Fig. 7.33 Trellised pattern

This trellised pattern formed in a steep-sided valley.

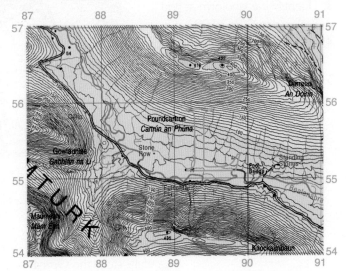

A trellised pattern forms when tributaries flow into the main river at right angles. This pattern forms when the bedrock of an area is of unequal hardness. Some areas have **soft rock** while other adjoining areas have **hard rock**. The hard rock is resistant to erosion, while the soft rock erodes quickly.

In Munster, for example, the bedrock consists of alternate parallel layers of sandstone, which is hard, and limestone, which is soft. The limestone has eroded quickly and forms valleys. The more resistant sandstone stands out as parallel ridges that separate the valleys (see page 69).

Trellised patterns develop also in **steep-sided valleys**, such as glaciated U-shaped valleys. Tributary water rushes down the steep slopes of the sides and enters the main river at **right angles**.

Radial Pattern

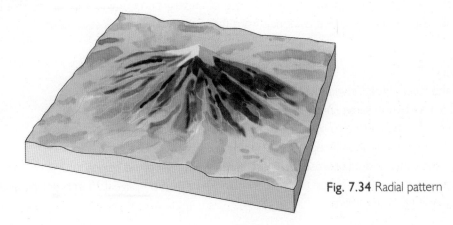

Fig. 7.34 Radial pattern

When rivers flow out and downslope from a mountaintop, they form a radial pattern. This is best seen in well-defined **circular or oval-shaped upland areas**. Some individual rivers may in fact display a different pattern from another, but together they may **radiate outwards** (north, south, east and west) from a central, elevated area. They all share a common watershed at their highest source streams.

Activity

Look at the OS map on the right.

1. Describe the variations in slopes along the sides of Tievebaun Mountain.
2. Explain why these variations might occur (see page 65).
3. Identify the landform at grid reference G 763 509.
4. Explain how this landform was formed?
5. Explain how this upland region formed? See page 65.

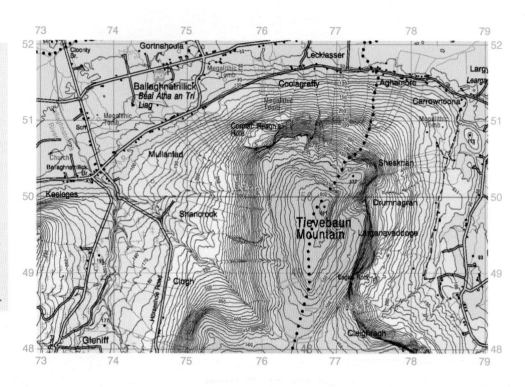

Activity

Carefully study the Ordnance Survey map extract of the Manorhamilton Region on page 125. Then do the following:

1. Identify two types of landforms that have been created by surface processes on this map extract. In each case explain:
   a. the processes involved in its formation.
   b. how rock characteristics may have influenced its formation.
2. Some uplands on the map display evidence of underground drainage similar to that in areas of limestone bedrock. Use evidence from the map to explain this statement.

Activity

Study the map of the Tievebaun Mountain region above and do the following:

1. Draw a box the same shape as this map.
2. Divide the box into two separate regions:
   a. one of them should represent a gently sloping lowland region.
   b. the other should represent a more steeply sloping upland region.
3. Use a sketch map to divide the map of Manorhamilton on page 125 into upland and lowland physical regions.

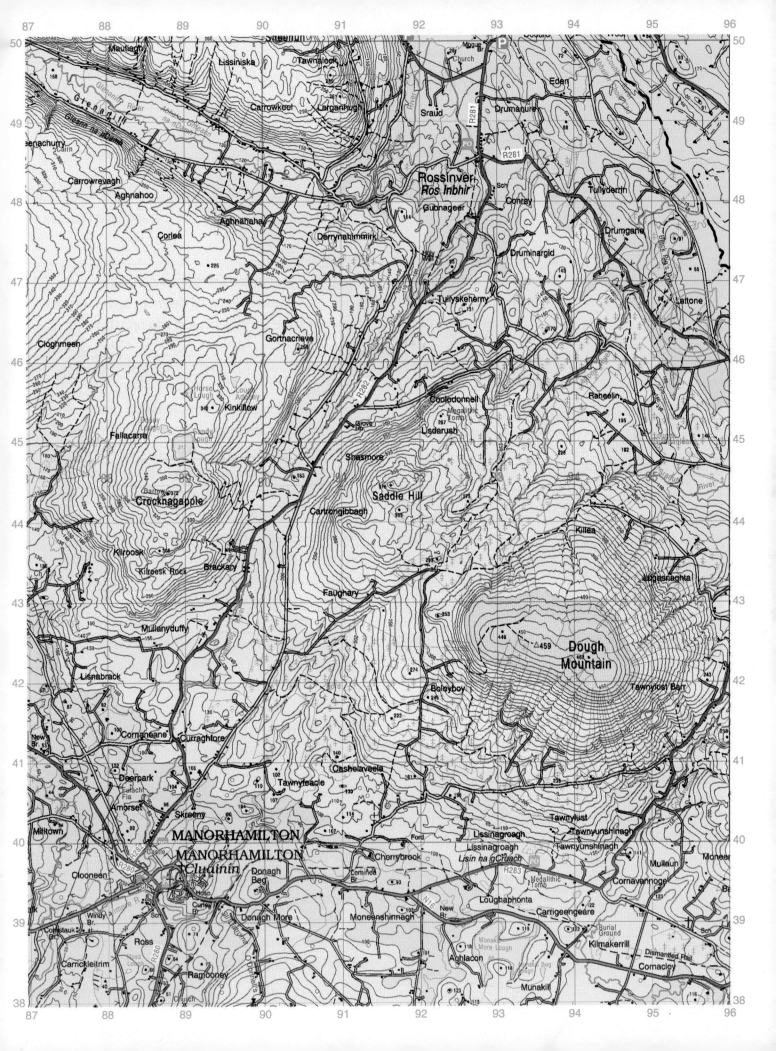

COASTAL PROCESSES, PATTERNS AND LANDFORMS

The character of any coastline depends on a number of factors. These include:

- The **work of waves, tides and currents**, which erode, transport and deposit materials.
- The **nature of the coastline**: whether the coastal rock is resistant or not; whether it is varied or even in character; type of coastline – highland or lowland, even straight or indented.
- The **changes** in the relative **levels** of land and sea.
- **Human interference**: the dredging of estuaries, the creation of ports, the reclamation of coastal marshes, the construction of coastal defences against erosion such as groynes, dykes and breakwaters: the building of piers and promenades.

Factors That Aid Erosion
Natural wall (soil)

Destructive Waves

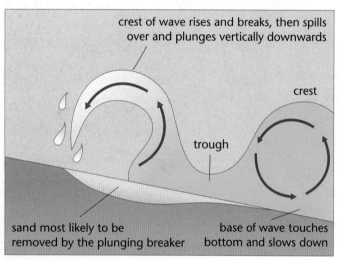

crest of wave rises and breaks, then spills over and plunges vertically downwards

crest

trough

base of wave touches bottom and slows down

sand most likely to be removed by the plunging breaker

Fig. 7.35 Process of a destructive wave

The power and size of a wave depends on the speed of the wind and the **fetch**. The fetch is the length of open water over which the wind blows. The stronger the wind and the longer the fetch, the stronger the waves will be and the greater their erosive power.

Destructive breakers that pound a coastline have their greatest effect during storms. Because of the frequency (twelve per minute) and because of the vertical plunge of the breakers (breaking waves), the backwash (when waves move back) is much more powerful than the swash (when water rushes onto the beach). So these destructive waves dig up beach material and carry it seaward or pick up loose material near a cliff and bash it against the cliff face.

Refraction

The speed of waves is reduced when waves approach the shore. The depth of water varies on shorelines that have promontories and bays. In such cases, the water is shallower in front of the promontory, or headland, than in the bay. As waves approach the shore, the shallower water off the promontory causes the waves to bend towards the headland, so increasing erosion there. This wave **refraction**, or bending, also occurs when waves pass the end of an obstacle such as a spit, creating a hook. So the process of refraction is involved in both erosion and deposition along a coastline.

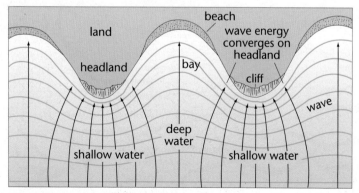

land

beach

wave energy converges on headland

headland

bay

cliff

wave

deep water

shallow water

shallow water

Fig. 7.36 Waves are deflected and are pulled towards shallow water along headlands.

waves can change direction

Processes of Coastal Erosion

These processes include:

- Hydraulic action
- Compression
- Abrasion
- Attrition

Fig. 7.37 Hydraulic action

Hydraulic Action

When strong waves crash against a coast, they have a shattering effect as they pound the rocks. Waves crashing against the base of a cliff force rocks apart, making them more prone to erosion. Cliffs of boulder clay are particularly affected, as loosened soil and rocks are washed away.

Compression

Air filters into joints, cracks and bedding planes in cliff faces. This air is trapped as incoming waves lash against the coast. The trapped air is compressed by the waves squeezing their way into the air-filled cavities. When the wave retreats, it results in a rapid expansion of the compressed air creating an explosive effect that widens the cracks (fissures) and shatters the rock face.

Abrasion

When boulders, pebbles and sand are pounded against the foot of a cliff by waves, fragments of rock are broken off and undercutting of the cliff takes place. The amount of abrasion depends on the ability of the waves to pick up rock fragments from the shore. Abrasion is most active during storms and at high tide, when incoming waves throw water and suspended rock material high up the cliff face and sometimes onto the cliff edge.

Attrition

Fragments that are pounded by the sea against the cliff and against each other are themselves worn down by attrition, creating sand and shingle.

The ability of waves to pick up rocks and lash them against a coast is many, many times greater than waves during periods of calm weather.

Rocks that are bashed against a coast knock chunks of rock from a cliff face during storms. These rocks are also reduced in size as they shatter on hitting the cliff face.

Fig. 7.38 Compression

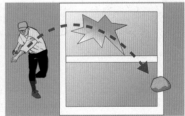

Fig. 7.39 An explosive effect, shattering

Water-rolled rocks are rounded and smoothed as they roll back and forth on top of each other.

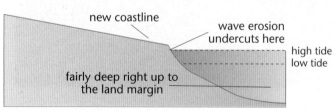

Cliffs occur where contour lines meet the coast.

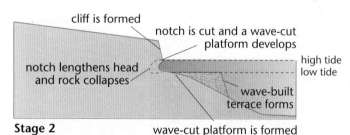

Stage 1

new coastline
wave erosion undercuts here
high tide
low tide
fairly deep right up to the land margin

Stage 2

cliff is formed
notch is cut and a wave-cut platform develops
notch lengthens head and rock collapses
high tide
low tide
wave-built terrace forms
wave-cut platform is formed

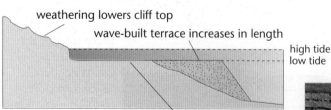

Stage 3

weathering lowers cliff top
wave-built terrace increases in length
high tide
low tide
wave-cut platform increases in length

Fig. 7.40 Stages in the formation of a wave-cut platform

Some Landforms of Sea Erosion
Landform: Cliff
Example: Cliffs of Moher in County Clare

When waves crash against a coastline, air is forced into cracks, joints and bedding planes in rock layers. The air is trapped and compressed by the force of incoming waves. When each wave retreats, the air instantly expands and its 'explosive' expansion enlarges the cracks and eventually shatters the rock face.

The **hydraulic action** of waves over time helps to erode a cliff face, especially at just above sea level where waves are constantly pounding against the shore. In addition when boulders, pebbles and sand are thrown by waves against the shore, a high rock slope is created along the coastline. This process is called **abrasion**. The high rock slope may be vertical or slope steeply to sea level. It is called a cliff.

A cliff increases in height as its base is worn away by the abrasive action of rocks and stones. Undercutting takes place creating a **notch**. Above the notch, an **overhanging ledge** is formed that eventually collapses into the sea, as erosion continues to wear away the base of the cliff. Abrasion is most active during storms.

As a cliff face 'retreats', a **wave-cut platform** is formed at the base. This is a level stretch of rock that is often exposed at low tide. It may have occasional pools of water, such as the Pollock Holes at Kilkee; shells and seaweed attached to the rock surface, while sea urchins, shrimp and small fish may be found in the rock pools. A boulder beach may form in the backshore.

Generally, the wider a wave-cut platform, the less the erosive power of waves, as shallow water reduces wave action, so the rate of coastal erosion slows down. Wave-cut platforms and cliffs occur above the present sea level in some parts of the country, such as at Dun Quin, in County Kerry, and Annalong, in County Down.

The sea cuts a notch to create a cliff and wave-cut platform.

Landform: Sea Stack

Example: Sea Stacks off Saddle Head, Achill Island in County Mayo

Stage 1: Cave

Caves form in areas of active erosion, where there is some **local weakness**. A jointed or faulted zone or weak or soft rock may be visible at a cave entrance. The sea erodes more effectively at such places. Air filters into cracks and joints, and bedding planes. The air is trapped as incoming waves lash against the coast. The trapped air is **compressed** until its pressure is equal to that exerted by the incoming wave. When the wave retreats, the resulting instant expansion of the compressed air has an **explosive effect**, enlarging cracks and shattering the rock face, so lengthening the cave. Also aiding this process is the **hydraulic force** of the wave itself. This force erodes material from the cave just as a power hose does during a car wash.

Stage 2: Sea Arch

In addition, boulders, rocks and pebbles are pounded by waves against the coastline, especially during storms. This material also enlarges and lengthens a cave as it is bashed by the waves against the cave roof and sides. This process is called **abrasion** and is most active at high tide or during storms. In this way, a cave retreats into a promontory until it reaches the other side, so forming a sea arch.

Stage 3: Sea Stack

These processes continue until the **arch roof** becomes too wide and finally **collapses** into the sea. Part of the promontory is therefore cut off from the coastline and it stands alone as a sea stack.

A sea arch may be seen at the Bridges of Ross in County Clare.

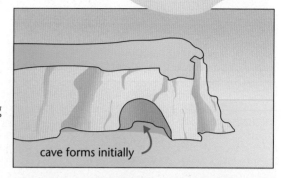
cave forms initially

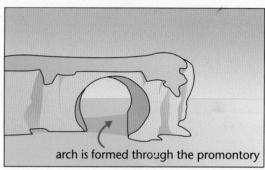
arch is formed through the promontory

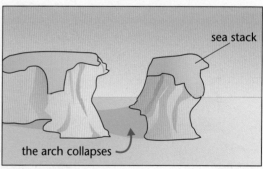
sea stack
the arch collapses

Fig. 7.41 Stages in the formation of a sea stack

Tiny islands called Carricknalicka in Achill are sea stacks that were cut off from the coast. Other tiny islands, such as those at F 565 080, are also sea stacks.

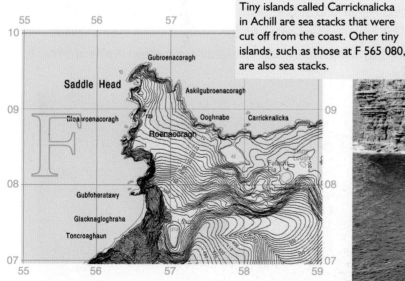

A sea arch near Kilkee in Co. Clare

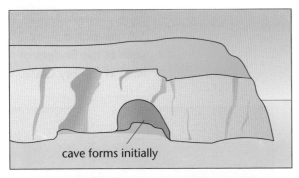

cave forms initially

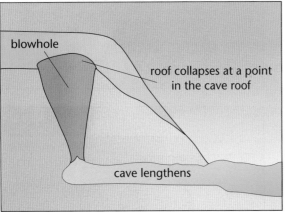

blowhole

roof collapses at a point in the cave roof

cave lengthens

Fig. 7.42

Landform: Blowholes
Example: Bridges of Ross in County Clare

Blowholes form at weak points or faults in coastal rock along the coastline. They form in wave-cut platforms or on cliff edges directly above caves. They are formed by the combined forces of **hydraulic action**, **compression** and **abrasion**.

Stage 1

The hydraulic action of destructive waves pound coastal rock surfaces either on a cliff face or on a wave-cut platform. The force of the waves erode weak rock areas or act on **fault lines** in rock surfaces, much like a power-hose acts on dirt when a car is being cleaned. As waves crash against coastal rock, air is forced into **cracks**, **fault lines**, **joints** and **bedding planes**. This air is trapped and is compressed by the force of the incoming waves. When each wave retreats, the air instantly expands and the **explosive expansion** enlarges the cracks, eventually shattering the rock face. This is especially severe where rock is weak or is faulted. Caves usually form at these weak points.

Stage 2

Loose **rock fragments** gather at the end of the cave and also on the cave floor under the water. These rocks are bashed against the cave sides and roof and make the cave larger and longer. This process is called **abrasion**.

Stage 3

As the cave is lengthened under the cliff face the roof of the cave gets higher and at one point may **collapse** into the cave beneath. This creates an **opening to the surface** a few metres inland through which foam and sea spray are ejected during storms.

A weakness is eroded on the wave-cut platform and a cave forms underneath a cliff edge.

An opening to the surface forms in the cave roof to create a blowhole.

Blowholes often form in wave-cut platforms when a slab of rock collapses into a cave.

Processes of Coastal Transport and Deposition

These processes include:

● Longshore drift
● Wind action.

Longshore Drift

Longshore drift refers to the movement of material, such as sand and shingle, along a shore. When waves break obliquely onto a beach, pebbles and sand are moved up the beach by the **swash**, at the same angle as the waves. The **backwash** drags the material down the beach at right angles to the coast, only to meet another incoming wave and the process is repeated. In this way, material is moved along the shore in a zigzag way.

Wind Action

As beaches dry at low tide, some dry sand is blown up the beach. Here it gathers above high tide level in large heaps or tiny hills that get more extensive over time. These hills are called sand dunes.

Breaking Waves and Surf

On reaching a shore, waves are said to **break**. The way this happens is of fundamental importance to coastal processes. Shallow water causes incoming waves to steepen, the crest spills over and the wave collapses. The turbulent water created by breaking waves is called **surf**. In the landward margin of the **surf zone**, the water rushing up the beach is called the **swash**; water returning down the beach is the **backwash**. The swash moves material up the beach and the backwash **may** carry it down again.

As well as destructive waves, there are **constructive waves**. They break slowly, and more material is left on the beach.

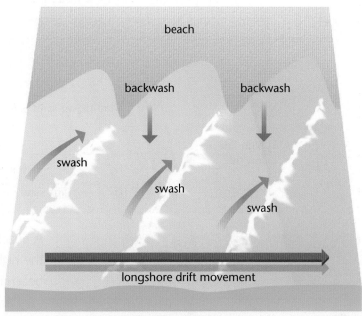

Fig. 7.43 The process of longshore drift

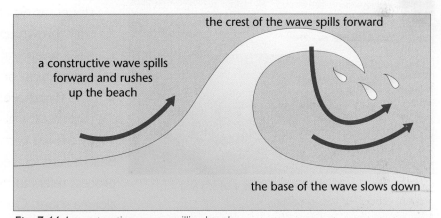

Fig. 7.44 A constructive wave: spilling breaker

Waves break as they approach a shore.

Landform: Beach
Example: Tramore Beach in County Waterford

Fig. 7.45 The profile of a beach

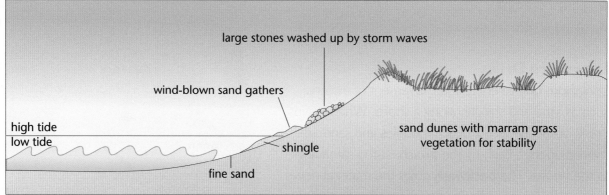

large stones washed up by storm waves

wind-blown sand gathers

high tide
low tide

shingle

fine sand

sand dunes with marram grass vegetation for stability

Groynes are sometimes built to create a beach and prevent erosion of the coastline.

yellow indicates a beach

A beach is the build-up of material between low tide level and the highest point reached by storm waves. The most typical beach is one which slopes gently to the sea.

An ideal beach profile has two main parts:

- **The backshore**: This is composed of rounded rocks and stones, as well as broken shells, pieces of driftwood and litter thrown up by storm waves. This part of the beach has a steep gradient and is reached by the sea during the highest tides or during storms.

- **The foreshore**: This is composed of sand and small shell particles. It has a gentle gradient and is covered regularly by the sea each day.

Beaches are formed by the process of longshore drift. This process refers to the movement of material (sand and shingle) along a shore. On reaching a shore, waves break. Shallow water causes incoming waves to steepen, the crest spills over and the wave collapses.

When constructive waves break, they are called spilling breakers. They break slowly, and their ability to move material reduces. The **spilling breaker** has a **powerful swash**, which rushes obliquely up the beach. It spreads over a large area, and drops most of its load as the water seeps through the sand. Little water returns down the beach as the backwash. The backwash drags the remainder of its load down the beach at right angles to the shore. There is a net gain of material up the beach, so these are called **constructive waves**.

The swash and backwash create a **zigzag** movement of material **along the shore**. This movement is called **longshore drift**.

On an upland coast, a beach may be just a loose mass of boulders and shingle under a cliff, while a bay between headlands generally has a crescent-shaped beach and is called a bayhead beach or a pocket beach. Many such beaches are found on the west coast of Ireland, as well as on the east and south coasts.

Landform: Sand Spit
Example: Inch Strand in County Kerry

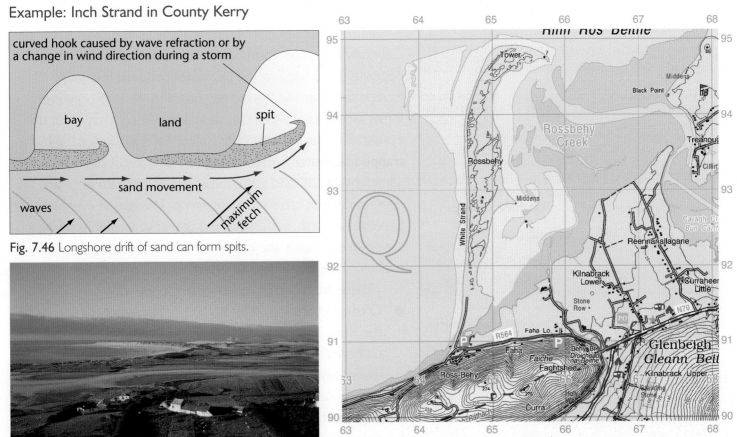

curved hook caused by wave refraction or by a change in wind direction during a storm

bay

land

spit

sand movement

waves

maximum fetch

Fig. 7.46 Longshore drift of sand can form spits.

A sand spit projects into a bay at Gotahork, Co. Donegal.

A spit forms when beach material builds out into a bay or across a river estuary with **one end attached to the land**. Spits generally develop where a **coastline changes direction sharply**, and longshore drift is unable to continue its zigzag movement of sediment along the shore. When this happens, the sediment, sand and shingle are deposited (dropped) on the seabed and they build up to sea level, so creating the first stages of a sand spit. The sand spit continues to add material to its seaward end, making it longer and extending out into the bay.

Besides getting longer, a spit gets wider from deposition by longshore drift. Swash from spilling breakers carries material, sand and shingle, up the beach. Here, it deposits most of its load as the water seeps through the sand. The backwash drags the remainder of its load down the beach at right angles to the shore, only to be brought back up the beach by the next incoming wave. In this way, the swash and backwash create a zigzag movement of material along the shore, building up the beach and making the beach wider. In addition, storm waves sometimes throw large rounded rocks at the back of the beach, forming a **storm beach**.

Beach sand dries when it is exposed at low tide. The sea breeze blows this dry sand behind the storm beach to form low hills of sand called sand dunes on the landward side of the spit. Once **marram grass** (a coarse grass with many long roots) becomes established on these dunes they are stabilised and can **resist wind erosion** from the strong coastal breezes.

Activity

1. Look at the Ordnance Survey map above. What human activities in this region relate directly to the natural processes at work here? Explain using evidence from the map.

2. Choose two coastal landforms and explain how the processes of erosion and/or deposition have formed them.

133

Landform: Sand Bars and Lagoons

Example: Lady's Island Lake and Sand Bar in County Wexford

Generally a sand bar forms when a sand spit extends to the opposite shore trapping the bay water between the newly formed sand bar and the old bay coastline. As longshore drift forms sand spits, it also forms sand bars. When a bay is cut off from the sea, as it is with Lady's Island Lake in Wexford, the **trapped seawater is called a lagoon**. In times of storm, waves sometimes wash sand and pebbles into its seaward edge and rivers and winds carry sediment into it. The lagoon eventually becomes a marsh, with reeds and coarse vegetation growing in the sediment. Finally the combined forces of waves, wind and rivers turn the marsh into an extensive area of sand dunes.

There are two main types of sand bars:

● **Offshore bars** are ridges of sand or glacial till lying parallel to the shore and some distance out to sea. Sometimes these offshore bars are pushed along in front of the waves until finally they may lie across a bay to form a baymouth bar (see **A** below). Bartragh Island in Killala Bay is an offshore bar.

● **Baymouth bars** form from offshore bars as mentioned above, but generally they form when sand spits grow across a bay to the far shore. In this way they cut off the original bay from the sea to form a lagoon.

waves build an offshore bar

height of offshore bar increases — lagoon — material fills up enclosed lagoon

offshore bar — salt marsh develops

eventually the sand dunes move over the salt marsh — sand dunes — finally the marsh becomes an area of sand dunes

Fig. 7.47 The lifecycle of a lagoon

A baymouth bar cuts off Lady's Island Lake from the sea in Wexford.

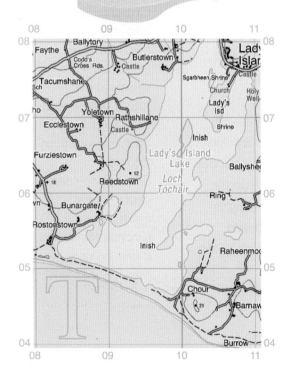

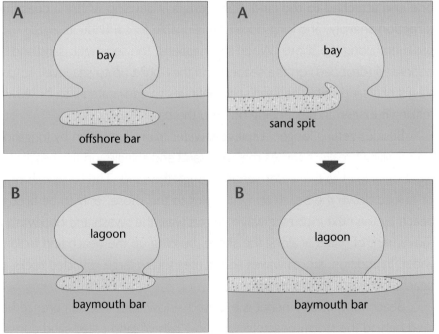

Fig. 7.48 Stages in the formation of a lagoon

Landform: Tombolo

Example: Tramore Strand and Inishkeel, near Portnoo

This landform is created when either a spit or a bar links an island or a sea stack to the mainland. The Sutton tombolo in Dublin, the narrow neck of land which links Howth to the mainland, is such a feature.

If two tombolos join an island from opposite directions, they may enclose seawater between them and create a lagoon. Tombolos are regularly formed along rugged coastlines, such as the west coast of Ireland.

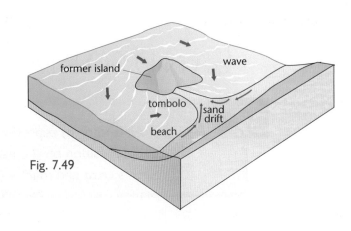

Fig. 7.49

Tramore Strand joins Inishkeel Island to the mainland in Co. Donegal. The beach is exposed at low tide.

Activity

Carefully study the photograph and map above. Then do the following:

1. What natural processes in relation to the sea allow these people to make this journey?
2. Identify any two other coastal landforms, locate them and explain the processes involved in their formation.

TEST YOURSELF AT
my-etest.com

CHAPTER 8
LANDFORMS OF ISOSTASY

All landforms represent a balance between forces of erosion and deposition on the earth's surface and other forces within the earth's crust and mantle. From time to time, this balance changes.

ISOSTASY

The theory of isostasy explains why vertical and horizontal movements take place in the earth's crust. From this theory we know that gravity plays an important role in determining the elevation, or height of the land.

Let's compare the continents with a series of wooden blocks of different heights floating in water. Notice that the thicker wooden blocks float higher in the water than the thinner blocks. Their bases also extend deeper into the water than those of the thinner blocks.

In this way the wooden blocks and the water are in perfect balance. Any reduction in the timber blocks (reduced weight) will cause a corresponding fall in the water level. Extra weight on the timber blocks will cause a rise in the water level. **Similarly, mountain belts stand higher above the surface and also extend further into the supporting material below.**

The earth's crust is composed of rocks of different weights. The continents are composed of **light rocks**. The **ocean floors** and the

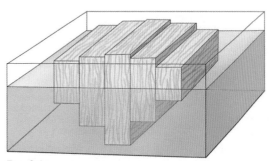

Fig. 8.1

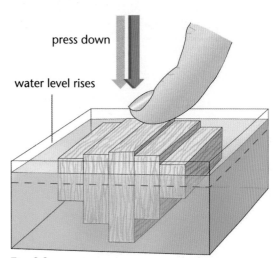

press down

water level rises

Fig. 8.2

Press down and the water level rises (land sinks and water rises). Lift the pressure off and the water level falls (land rises and water level drops).

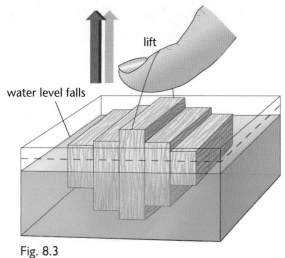

lift

water level falls

Fig. 8.3

materials that the **continents 'float on'** are heavy. A continent is regarded as 'floating' on the underlying rock because its weight is lighter and because the underlying rock is thought to be in a semi-liquid state (like thick jelly).

When highlands are lowered by erosion, the eroded material is deposited on the surrounding lowlands and in the seas, under the pull of gravity. As the mountains are worn down by weathering and erosion, their weight reduces. With less weight, they now float lighter and their bases rise, but the eroded sediments build up on surrounding lowland and the seafloor. These areas are now heavier than before and press down with more force on the sima and mantle underneath. The adjustment of balance appears on the surface as a levelling of the landscape. New earth movements, however, may raise land levels again during this process, and the cycle is repeated.

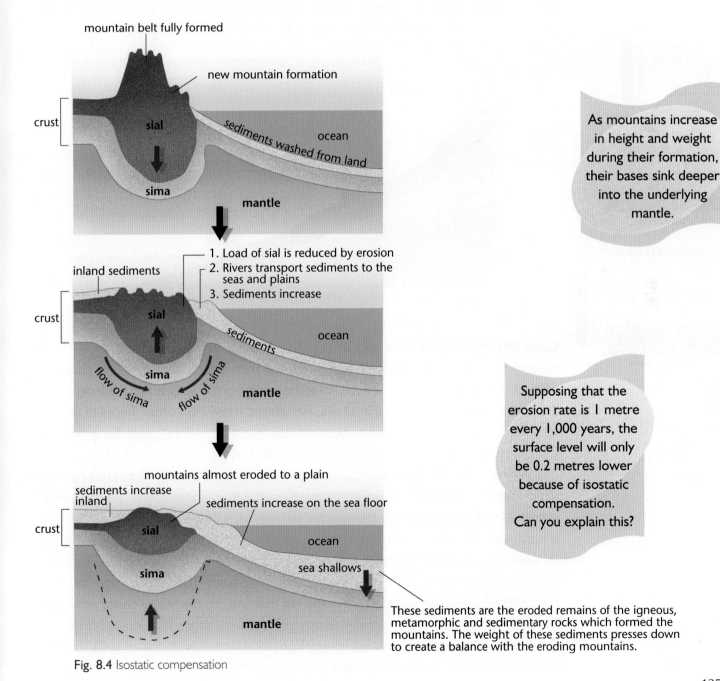

As mountains increase in height and weight during their formation, their bases sink deeper into the underlying mantle.

Supposing that the erosion rate is 1 metre every 1,000 years, the surface level will only be 0.2 metres lower because of isostatic compensation. Can you explain this?

These sediments are the eroded remains of the igneous, metamorphic and sedimentary rocks which formed the mountains. The weight of these sediments presses down to create a balance with the eroding mountains.

Fig. 8.4 Isostatic compensation

137

ADJUSTING TO BASE LEVEL

KEY IDEA!

When earth movements raise land, the rivers in that region will erode to create a new graded profile. This can also happen if sea levels fall. This process is called adjusting to base level.

The Long Profile of a River

A river's activity concentrates on creating a slope from source to mouth, which will result in a river speed that keeps erosion and deposition exactly in balance. At this stage the river is said to be **graded** and to have achieved a **profile of equilibrium**. Such a profile is rarely if ever achieved. Changes in volume, rising or falling sea level or unequal resistance of rocks all prevent a river from ever achieving a graded profile.

press down

squeezed

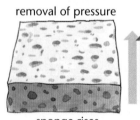

removal of pressure

sponge rises

Fig. 8.5

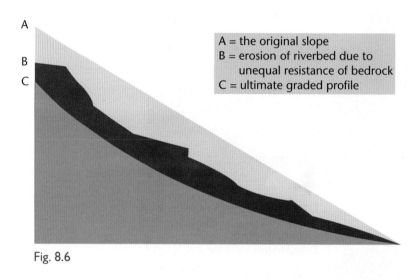

A = the original slope
B = erosion of riverbed due to unequal resistance of bedrock
C = ultimate graded profile

Fig. 8.6

Case Study: The Rivers of Donegal in North-West Ireland

Land on the rim of a continent or of a continental shelf is particularly prone to **changes of level**. There is evidence that even since the ending of the last ice age the level of the land in Ireland, relative to that of sea, has altered more than once. Traces of old shorelines, sometimes called raised beaches, are found around the coast (for example in Co. Donegal) some metres above present high-tide levels.

When raising of shorelines occurs, rivers that had once slowly meandered their way across their flat flood plains now find themselves, due to isostatic change, **pouring over waterfalls** or **flowing through steep-sided valleys** before they enter the sea. Donegal, in north-west Ireland, had a cover in excess of a thousand metres of **ice**, pressing down on the land and '**squeezing**' it like weight on a sponge, during the last ice age. The absence of this weight since the ending of the Ice Age some 10,000 years ago has allowed the land to rise and the rivers now cut their way to the sea to create new river channels.

Streams that receive renewed energy from local land movements of uplift, or fall in sea level, are said to be **rejuvenated**. For a meandering stream that flows on a flood plain and has just been rejuvenated, the method of achieving its new profile is to cut deeply into the thick flood plain sediment of its old valley.

When sea levels fall, the river begins to cut upstream from its mouth. This produces a new curve, or profile of erosion, that intersects with the old curve at the **knickpoint**. The knickpoint is identified by a clear break of slope, and may be marked by rapids or a waterfall. The **knickpoint moves up upstream** at a rate that depends on the resistance of the bedrocks and the river's volume.

The **Gweedore River** is one of the many rivers in County Donegal that has been rejuvenated.

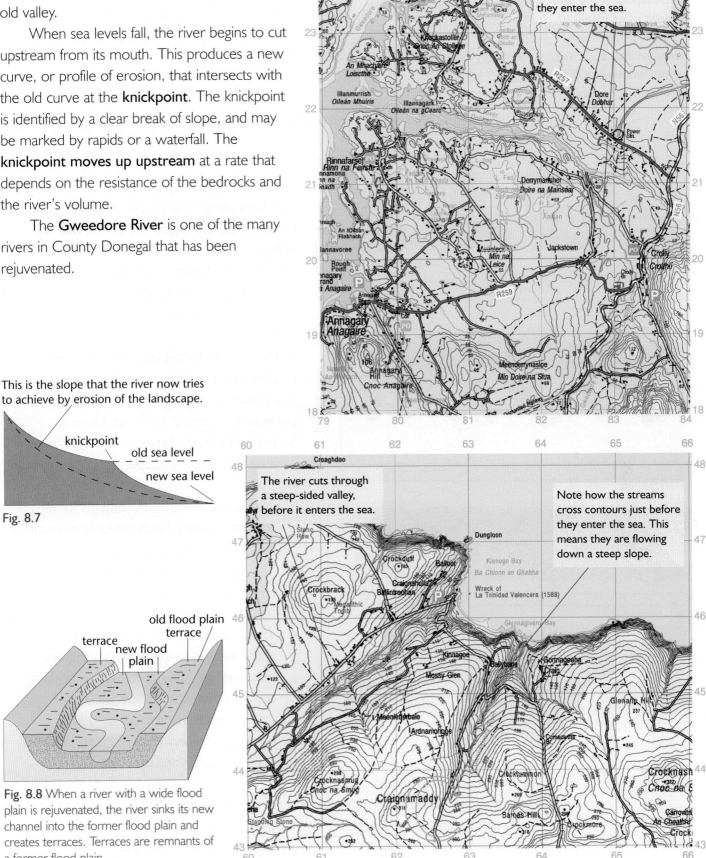

This is the slope that the river now tries to achieve by erosion of the landscape.

knickpoint
old sea level
new sea level

Fig. 8.7

old flood plain terrace
terrace
new flood plain

Fig. 8.8 When a river with a wide flood plain is rejuvenated, the river sinks its new channel into the former flood plain and creates terraces. Terraces are remnants of a former flood plain.

Note how the streams cross contours just before they enter the sea.

The river cuts through a steep-sided valley, before it enters the sea.

Note how the streams cross contours just before they enter the sea. This means they are flowing down a steep slope.

Cycle of Landscape Evolution

While streams are cutting their valleys they are really sculpturing the land. To describe this unending process, we have to visualise a beginning. For this let us think of a relatively flat upland area with a wet climate such as Ireland's. Within this landscape, lakes and ponds will occupy any hollows that exist. As streams form and cut their valleys, they will eventually drain the lakes or fill them with sediment.

> A peneplain is the end result of an idealised cycle of landscape erosion that ends in a gently undulating plain almost at sea level.

Early Stage

During the early stage the landscape retains its **relatively flat surface**, interrupted only by narrow stream valleys.

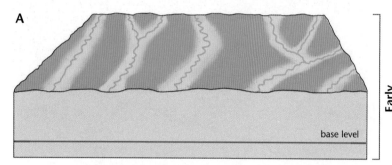

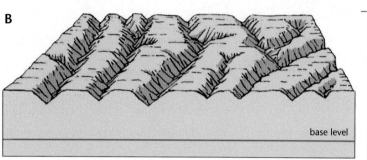

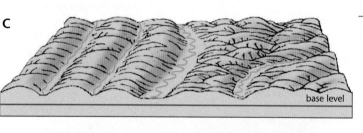

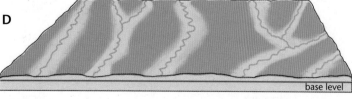

Fig. 8.9 How landscape evolves

Middle Stage

As downcutting continues, relief increases and the flat landscape is changed into one of **hills and valleys**. This is the middle stage. Eventually, some of the streams will approach base level and downcutting will be replaced by lateral erosion.

Later Stage

As the cycle nears the later stage, the effects of flooding, mass movement, and lateral erosion and deposition by rivers will reduce the land to a **peneplain** (an almost extensive flat area).

Such a simple cycle, however, rarely occurs because it could only happen if:

- The region was not affected by any additional local or global earth movements for tens of millions of years. Earth movements regularly occur over short periods of time.
- The climate remained constant for millions of years, but climates are always changing and sometimes rapidly.
- The underlying rock layers had similar characteristics to the upper rock layers, so that drainage patterns remained constant over millions of years. We know that different rock characteristics, such as hardness and permeability, create different rates of erosion and drainage patterns.
- No ice age occurred to:
  - reduce sea levels or for rivers to cut to new base levels.
  - erode highlands and deposit materials on lowland.
  - squeeze the land during glaciation and create uplift after glaciation.

Case Study: Planation Surfaces in Munster

It is believed that in Munster there was a **peneplain** that sloped southwards to the sea. This sloping surface may represent an old marine-eroded sea floor or one formed by weathering and erosion on dry land. Since then a combination of falling sea levels or earth movements has over the past three million years caused the Rivers Blackwater, Lee and Bandon to cut into this peneplain to form a landscape of **parallel ridges and valleys** with a **trellised drainage** pattern.

The tributaries of these rivers have in some places divided the peneplain into **isolated hills** of more or less even height separated by small river valleys. In some places, rivers such as the River Blackwater in County Cork have cut steep-sided gorges as they flowed southwards to the sea.

The sloping sides of the valley of the River Blackwater indicate that it is flowing along a narrow flood plain.

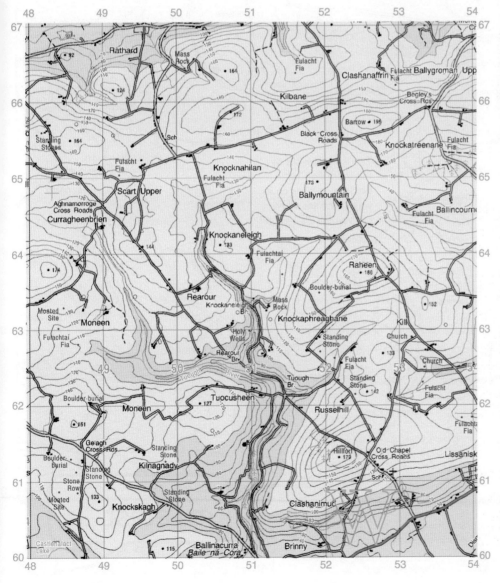

Activity

In the map on the left identify the heights of any six hilltops. Then find their average height. Now find how much each hilltop height differs from the average height.

Activity

Study the Ordnance Survey map of the River Blackwater on page 142. Then do the following:

1. What evidence on the map suggests that the River Blackwater has eroded its valley into a landscape that at one time was a south-sloping even surface? (See hilltops.)
2. What pattern of drainage is displayed by the River Blackwater and its tributaries?
3. What evidence on the map indicates that the rivers of south Munster flow through parallel east-west river valleys?

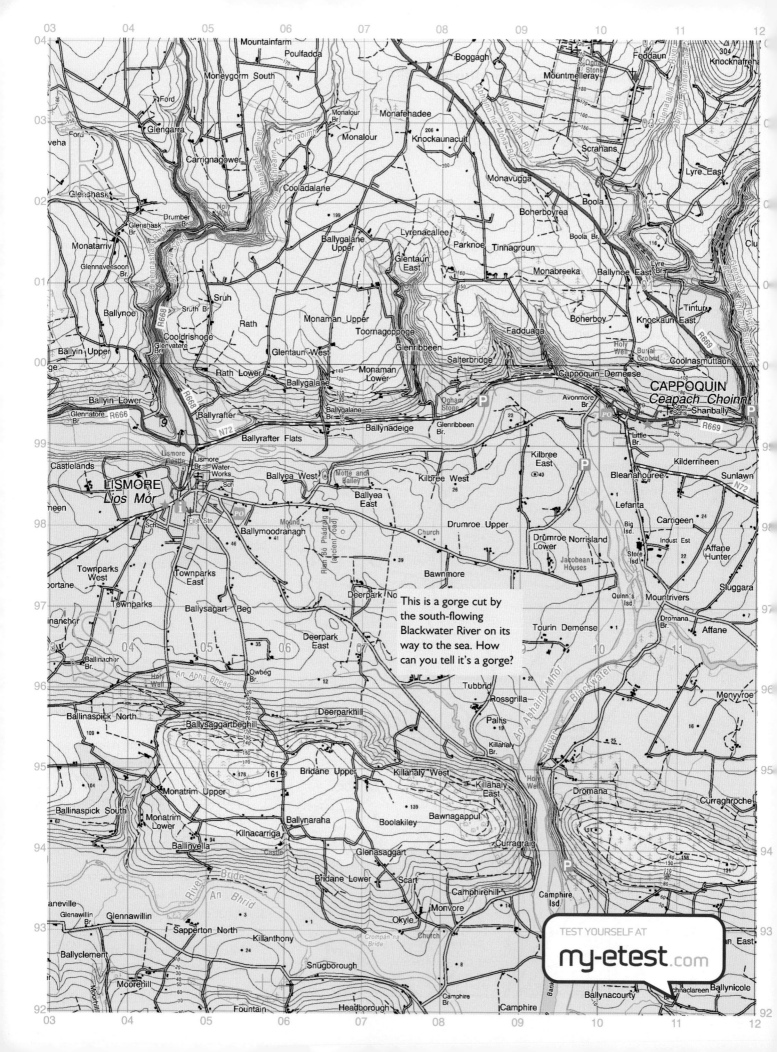

This is a gorge cut by the south-flowing Blackwater River on its way to the sea. How can you tell it's a gorge?

CHAPTER 9
HOW PEOPLE INTERACT WITH THE EARTH'S PROCESSES

 **KEY IDEA!**

People's activities can affect the process of mass movement.

MASS MOVEMENT

The Impact of Overgrazing

At moderate densities as farm animals graze land, they encourage plants to grow by manuring the soil and clipping off the tops of plants, just as pruning encourages new growth on fruit trees or roses. With a high density of animals, the vegetation is eaten faster than it can grow, plant cover is reduced and soil may be washed away or blown away by the wind.

The number of cattle, for example, that can be supported on farmland varies from region to region. In areas with moderate to high rainfall evenly distributed throughout the year, such as Ireland, cattle can be maintained at high densities (about three cattle per hectare). For arid and semi-arid regions, the density drops greatly. In Arizona, on range land, it takes between 17 to 25 hectares to support one animal.

Over the past few hundred years throughout peninsular Italy, sheep and goats have overgrazed the slopes of the Apennines. Soils that once supported these animals were exposed to summer thunderstorms and winter rains that washed downslope into rivers, where they clogged the water channels, and swamps and marshes were created. An example of this is the Pontine Marshes, south of Rome. Malarial mosquitoes bred in these warm swamplands leading to widespread malaria among rural families and working conditions that made farming uneconomic. In a huge project starting in 1928, the Pontine Marshes were drained to create fertile farmland.

Students need study only ONE of the following:
People's activities and their impact on:
- Mass movement processes
- River processes
- Coastal processes.

Overgrazing by too many sheep has led to severe soil erosion in the Galtee Mountains.

Severe gully erosion of the sides of a canyon due to overgrazing by cattle in British Columbia, Canada. Only conifer trees now remain on the canyon sides.

Erosion of Irish Mountainsides

There was overgrazing of some Irish mountainsides between 1990 and 2000. Two examples include the Galtee Mountains, in Tipperary, and the Mweelrea Mountains, in Mayo. Overgrazing by sheep has been the main cause of this problem. Farm subsidies for sheep led to a rapid increase in sheep numbers on mountainsides. The land became overstocked, and the grasses and heather were overgrazed. Mountain soil was exposed to heavy rains and localised landslides became commonplace (see the photo of the Galtees on page 143).

The Impact of Overcropping

One of the worst examples of overcropping occurred in the **Dust Bowl** region of North America between 1934 and 1936. The worst affected areas were parts of **western Kansas, Nebraska, Oklahoma** and **Texas.** It happened when wheat was planted in semi-arid grazing areas, because grain was fetching high prices and the region appeared to be moist enough to produce crops. Then the years of sufficient rain were followed by several years of very low rainfall. The tilled soil was exposed to the strong winds of these level lands and was literally blown away, leaving only sand and gravel particles. Some of the lightest particles were carried as far as the Atlantic east coast, where city skies were darkened by the migrating soil of the west.

Many **farmers abandoned their farms and their homes** and headed west with their belongings. They went to California to become the penniless fruitpickers who were immortalised in John Steinbeck's novel, *The Grapes of Wrath*.

Bangladesh suffers from severe flooding that has increased due to deforestation in the nearby mountains.

The Impact of Deforestation

When agriculture was introduced into Ireland in Prehistoric times, the first farmers cleared land for cattle grazing. This practice happened throughout the world and on every continent. Today, deforestation continues in the areas where forests remain. Most of these forests are in the tropics, in mountain regions or in high latitudes, areas that were up to now less hospitable and offered difficult working environments. The problem of deforestation is especially severe in the **tropics,** where population numbers are increasing rapidly.

Forests are a **global resource**, so cutting forests in one country may severely affect another. For example, **Nepal in the Himalayas**, one of the most mountainous countries in the world, lost more than half its forest cover between 1950 and 1980. Today, little forest land remains in Nepal. Cutting down forests removes the foliage (leaves) that protects the soil as well as killing the tree roots that bind the soil particles together. This exposes the soil to heavy monsoon rains that increase the rate of landslides. Large quantities of topsoil are washed downhill into streams and rivers that flow into India and Bangladesh, causing death and destruction on delta lowland due to flooding.

Other reasons for felling trees include the sale of timber for construction and paper pulp. Slightly more than half of all wood used in the world is used for firewood. In developed countries, firewood provides less than 1 per cent of total energy needs. But it provides a quarter of the energy in developing countries and more than half the energy in Africa. As human population grows, firewood use increases.

Combined Effects of Overgrazing, Overcropping and Deforestation

Case Study: The Sahel in North Africa

The Sahel region of North Africa is located between the Sahara Desert and the equatorial rainforest. The natural vegetation of the Sahel region is savannah grassland and scrub. Traditionally it is a cattle-grazing region on a nomadic basis. This means that traditional herdsmen, such as the Fulani, the Tuareg and the Masai, moved in their own traditional areas with their herds of cattle in search of fresh pasture. For some of these tribes cattle numbers are a status symbol, and therefore numbers rather than cattle quality are the priority. From 1950 to 1970 the annual rainfall on the southern fringe of the Sahara was greater than average and the resulting increase in the supply of pasture allowed for:

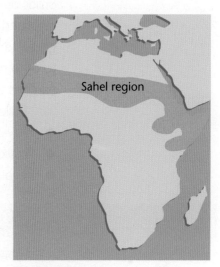

Fig. 9.1 Sahel region

- **A substantial increase in the numbers of cattle** owned by these herdsmen. This led to livestock overgrazing these marginal lands. Land that used to be green pasture during short wet spells turned into desert after four years without rain.
- **An invasion of tillage farmers,** who clear the land to plant crops in what had been a pastoral area. In Niger, for example, farmers pushed northwards, planting fields of millet and groundnuts in the area traditionally occupied by nomadic herdsmen.

To pay taxes farmers planted special crops to sell for money rather than to eat themselves or feed animals. This cash cropping and agricultural demands led to the clearance of natural vegetation. Over the past thirty years the woods that covered the Sahel have been reduced by felling.

As firewood is the main source of energy in underdeveloped countries, many people whose income had suffered as a consequence of soil erosion supplemented their income by cutting and selling firewood in cities and towns. The disappearance of tree cover leads to wind erosion of the soil. Run-off (where some rainwater runs into streams as surface water rather than being absorbed by the soil) accelerates, ground water is no longer replaced, water tables drop and **wind erosion** attacks the soil, robbing it of its small particles and its fertility.

Activity
Explain the ways that farming activities can seriously damage the environment and so lower living standards.

The Impact of Hydro-electric Dams

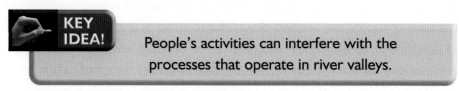

KEY IDEA!

People's activities can interfere with the processes that operate in river valleys.

Examples: Ardnacrusha on the River Shannon
Pollaphuca Dam on the River Liffey

Dams are constructed across a river's channel to generate hydro-electric power. The dams interrupt the natural flow of rivers and reduce the ability of rivers to carry sediment from their upper valleys to their flood plains and their estuaries in lowland areas.

Hydro-electric dams are designed to block and use the flow of rivers. Water builds up behind the dams to form lakes, called **reservoirs**. The depth of a reservoir is regulated by allowing some water to flow through pipes in the dam, called penstocks, to generate **hydro-power**. As reservoirs are calm water areas, they cause inflowing streams to drop not just their load of heavy particles but also some of their finest and mineral-rich particles that are normally deposited on the flood plain below.

Building hydro-electric dams may have some **positive results**. These include:

● Providing over 6 per cent of the world's energy needs.
● Providing reservoirs for irrigation and water supply.
● Regulating floodwaters to reduce flooding in lowland areas.

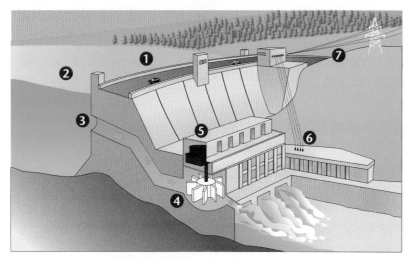

Fig. 9.2
1. The water is held back by a dam.
2. The water has potential energy.
3. The water flows downhill through penstocks to a power station.
4. The flowing water turns wheels called turbines.
5. The turbines turn the generators.
6. The generators change the energy of moving water into electrical energy.
7. The electricity is carried to houses and factories by cables on pylons.

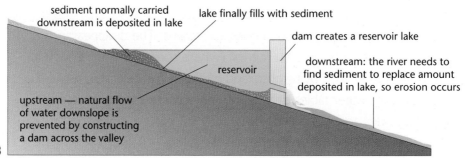

sediment normally carried downstream is deposited in lake

lake finally fills with sediment

dam creates a reservoir lake

reservoir

downstream: the river needs to find sediment to replace amount deposited in lake, so erosion occurs

upstream — natural flow of water downslope is prevented by constructing a dam across the valley

Fig. 9.3

The way dams interfere with rivers' natural processes has **some negative effects**. These include:

The Laggin Dam in Scotland has affected river processes in the valley.

● **Loss of soil fertility**

The annual flooding of the Nile in autumn allowed floodwater to cover the flood plain, where it remained trapped until it had deposited its silt. This silt enriched the land with minerals carried in tiny grains of soil. The building of the Aswan High Dam, which controlled the waters of the Nile, prevents this from happening today. This has led to additional fertiliser costs for Egyptian farmers.

● **Submerging farmland and settlements**

Damming water for hydro-power may involve submerging farmland and settlements on the upstream side of the dam. If people live in the areas to be submerged, they have to be evacuated and relocated elsewhere. More often than not, this causes great upset to the people involved. The submerged farmland is lost.

● **Limited lifespan**

Although water power is considered a renewable resource, the reservoirs created to provide hydro-electricity have a limited lifespan. All rivers carry sediment. This sediment accumulates in the reservoirs behind the dams. Eventually the sediment will fill the reservoir. So each hydro-electric dam has a limited lifespan. Egypt's huge Aswan High Dam reservoir, which was completed in the 1960s, will have half its volume filled with sediment by the year 2025.

● **Erosion of deltas**

When a river that once entered the sea in a delta is dammed for producing hydro-electric power, its load is reduced. This reduction may lead to erosion of its delta because the reduced river load may not be sufficient to balance coastal erosion along the delta shoreline. This has happened in the delta of the Nile due to the construction of the Aswan High Dam. Egypt relies on its Nile Delta for living space and especially for the production of food. The loss of sediment created by deposition in Lake Nasser above the dam has led to erosion of the Nile Delta coastline.

Activity
Explain how dam construction may devastate the number of migratory fish in a river.

● **Loss of natural vegetation and wildlife**

The rise in water levels behind hydro-electric dams also wipes out wildlife that once frequented the area. The flooding of habitats forces animals or birds to move or drown when trapped by rising waters behind the dam.

Natural vegetation, such as tropical forest, is cut down and removed or left to rot where it stands, often bare of its vegetation after chemical sprays (defoliants) have been used over vast areas, such as behind the **Tucurui Dam** in south-east **Brazil**.

Case Study: Three Gorges Dam in China

Positive Aspects

Midway between its icy source in Tibet and the fertile delta at its mouth in Shanghai 6,300 kilometres to the east, China's Yangtze Kiang (Yangtze River) rushes through a series of vertical-sided channels, known as the Three Gorges. The Chinese government is using these gorges to build the world's largest hydro-electric dam.

Villages like this have been submerged in the Three Gorges section of the Yangtze River.

Activity
'The construction of the Three Gorges Dam is essential for the future development of economic activities in China.' Explain one point for and one point against this statement.

- Chinese government leaders argue that the Three Gorges scheme is vital to their country's future and will be good for the environment as a whole. They say it will prevent the periodic flooding of the Yangtze Kiang that claimed 500,000 lives in the 20th century.

- More importantly, the production of clean hydro-electric power will reduce China's reliance on coal, the dirtiest of all fossil fuels, which now supplies 75 per cent of the country's needs. At present, the burning of coal has helped make lung disease the nation's leading cause of death.

Negative Aspects

- Besides being a major waterway, the Yangtze may be compared to a human artery. The river supports huge numbers of settlements that have grown up along its banks, even within the gorge sections. All of these settlements will disappear, once the dams are built and the settlements are flooded. People are being rehoused in new settlements on raised land above the gorges. This great upheaval will include the loss of the waterside sites and the traditional character of the river's settlements that has evolved over generations.

- The dams may lead to a dangerous build-up of silts in some parts of the river, creating new obstacles to navigation.

The Impact of Canalisation

Food Supply

Case Study: The Aral Sea

The waters of the two largest rivers, the Amu Darya (Amu River) and Syr Darya (Syr River), which provide water for the freshwater Aral Sea, were diverted through canals to irrigate seven million hectares of cotton, rice and melons for the markets of the former Soviet Union. The water was diverted to increase agricultural production.

Before Canalisation

In the 1950s, the Aral Sea supported mixed agriculture around its shores and a flourishing fishing industry. The Aral Sea has no outlet. The rivers' water simply evaporated and kept a local ecosystem and its dependent population of 30 million people in balance with the second largest inland body of water in Asia.

After Canalisation

Canalisation has had the following effects:

● The immediate effect is that the Aral Sea has been greatly reduced in size. Some ships that once transported goods on the Aral Sea and others that fished its waters are now beached on dry seabed some 80 kilometres from its present shoreline.

● The salt content of the sea has increased from its original 10 per cent to 40 per cent. This has changed the sea from being a freshwater lake to a saltwater lake.

● Many fish species have been wiped out.

● Summer temperatures near the lake have increased (up to 45°C) and winter temperatures have become colder.

Water Supply

In many parts of the world, demands are being made on rivers to supply water to agricultural and urban areas. This is not a new trend. Ancient civilisations, including the **Romans** and **Native Americans**, constructed canals and aqueducts to transport water from distant rivers to where it was needed. In our modern civilisation, as in the past, water is often moved long distances from areas with abundant rainfall or snow to areas of high usage (usually agricultural areas). In California, two-thirds of the state's surface water (run-off) occurs north of San Francisco in the valley of the Sacramento River where there is a surplus of water. Two-thirds of the water use occurs south of San Francisco, in the valley of the San Joaquin River, where there is a water shortage. The canals of the California Water Project have moved vast amounts of water from the northern to the southern part of the state.

Transporting water by canal from the north to the south of California has **improved agricultural production** and has supplied towns and cities, such as Los Angeles, with badly needed **drinking water**, but the **salt content** of the soils where the water has been used for irrigation has increased. As irrigation water evaporates quickly in hot climates, the naturally dissolved minerals of the fresh river water remain on the surface and the salt content of the irrigated soils increases. This increased amount of salt can poison the soils.

> The Aral Sea has been shrinking for the past 30 years because of canalisation.

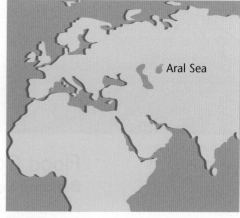

Fig. 9.4

Fig. 9.5 This sketch shows that the Aral Sea is shrinking.

Activity

Explain how canal building in the Aral Sea area has affected the:

a. fresh water supply in the Aral Sea.
b. local living standards.
c. natural wildlife of the area.

Irrigation has increased food production in Southern California.

When the flow of some rivers is reduced, the outflow is no longer able to maintain freshwater marshlands along coastal estuaries. This has happened along the San Joaquin and Sacramento river estuary in California.

Activity
Explain how canal construction in California:
a. improved food supplies.
b. damaged soils.

Flood Control Measures
Building Levees
Example: Mulcair River in County Limerick

Levee comes from the French word *lever*, which means 'to raise'. In the United States of America, the term is used to describe walls or dykes built along the southern part of the Mississippi River. The levees on the Mississippi are over ten metres high.

A river and its nearby flat flood plain together make up a natural system. In most untouched natural river valleys the water flows over the riverbanks and on to the flood plain every year or so. There are a number of natural processes that occur because of this flooding:

- Water and nutrients are stored on the flood plain.
- Silt deposits on the flood plain increase the mineral content of the soil.
- Wetlands on the flood plain provide a natural habitat for many birds, animals, plants and other living organisms.
- The flood plain acts as a green belt and helps provide diversity of flora and fauna.

Natural flooding is not a problem until people choose to build homes and other structures on flood plains. These structures are prone to damage and loss when flooded. People have chosen to build on so many flood plains that flooding is the most universal natural hazard in the world. The 1993 flood of the Mississippi took over 50 lives and caused over US $10 billion in damages. About 70 per cent of the levees failed. They simply were not designed to withstand a flood that lasted over two months.

Flooding in Bangladesh in 1970 and 1991 killed more than half a million people. Today people try to tame nature by building dykes and levees to retain floodwaters. Vast areas of existing farmland, towns and cities lie below water when rivers are in flood.

Local people build a levee from sandbags to stop floodwaters from the Mississippi River.

Fig. 9.6

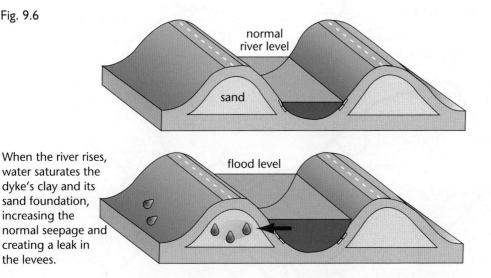

normal river level

sand

When the river rises, water saturates the dyke's clay and its sand foundation, increasing the normal seepage and creating a leak in the levees.

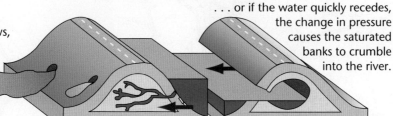

flood level

Activity
Explain how levee construction can:
a. prevent regular flooding of the area.
b. improve farming output.
c. devastate an urban area.
d. damage wildlife habitats

As the leakage grows, the outflow carries away eroding base materials, turning muddy and threatening stability. . .

. . . or if the water quickly recedes, the change in pressure causes the saturated banks to crumble into the river.

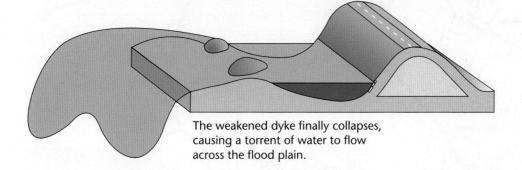

The weakened dyke finally collapses, causing a torrent of water to flow across the flood plain.

Dam Construction

Dams are an efficient way to control floodwaters. The building of the Aswan High Dam prevented annual flooding on the Nile downstream and allowed farmers to produce many crops in a single season.

Activity
Carefully study the Ordnance Survey map extract of Blessington Lake on page 152.
Then do the following:
1. Give one fully-developed reason for the presence of this lake in this area.
2. Identify and explain how this lake has interfered with the processes of river action that operated in this area before the lake existed.
3. Identify the reasons for the siting of the power stations.
4. Identify one way the building of the power stations has affected:
   a. the people who lived in this area before the power stations were built.
   b. the people who live here now.
   c. the tourist industry.

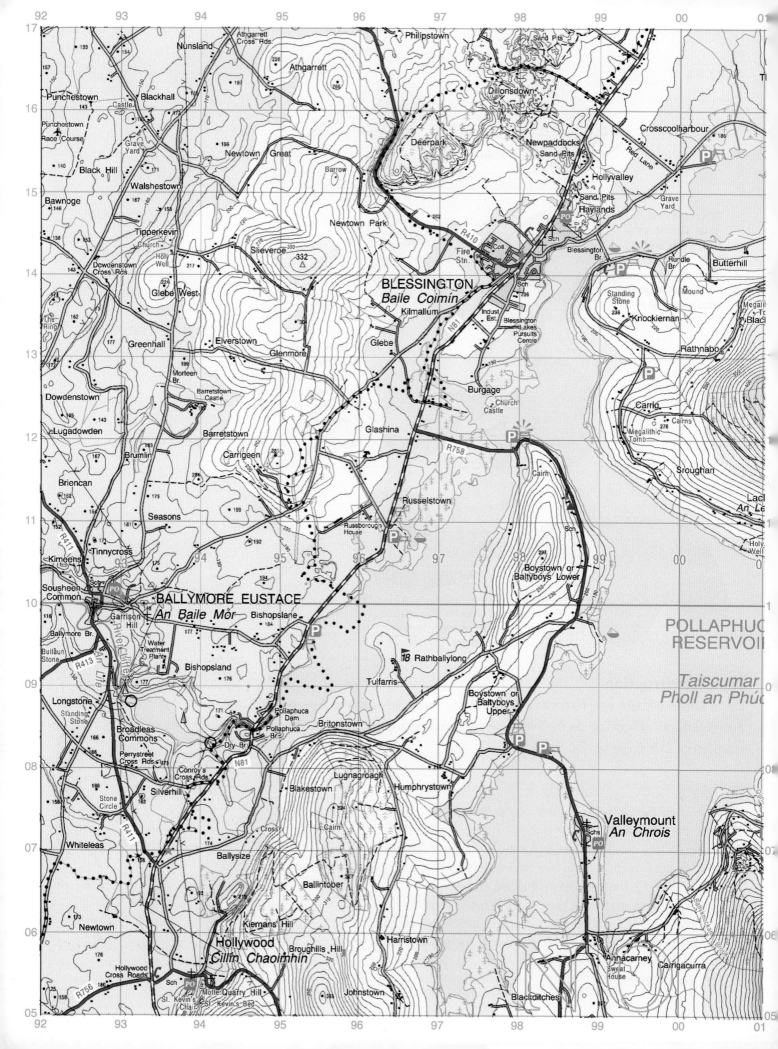

The Impact of Recreation

KEY IDEA! People's activities can interfere with coastal processes. As populations and living standards rise, fragile coastal areas are subjected to ever increasing pressure from recreation. In some areas this interference may lead to erosion, pollution or loss of lands, while in other areas it may lead to deposition and the creation of new land and wildlife habitats.

Coastal Buildings

When towns, seaside resorts or individual dwellings are constructed in low-lying coastal areas on offshore bars or sand spits, it increases pressures on local governments to maintain and protect these areas from attack by the sea. These places are not ideal sites for urban construction as they are low-lying coastal areas that are especially vulnerable to storm waves. In addition, sand-dune hills on these bars or spits may be levelled and destroyed for house construction or the covering of marram grass may be damaged from overuse by tourists.

Long lines of hotels have been built along the shoreline throughout the Mediterranean region. In many instances these hotels prevent public access to the shore, which is developed with swimming pools, restaurants and bars reserved for hotel guests only. This is especially true along the Costa Blanca, Costa Brava and Costa del Sol in Spain.

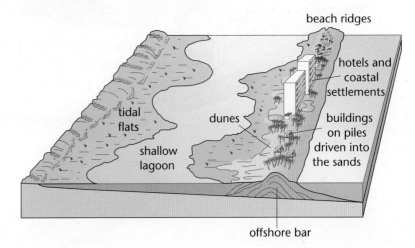

Fig. 9.7 Offshore barrier island bars are developed as coastal resorts, with hotels and holiday complexes along much of the east coast of the United States.

Water Quality

The expansion and development of coastal settlements has increased the likelihood of coastal pollution in many areas. This is especially true of Mediterranean resort areas, such as the Costa Blanca and Costa Brava, and Italian and Greek coastal waters where large-scale resort development has taken place over the past thirty years. Ireland's coastal waters also have suffered pollution, until recent EU environmental laws forced local councils to treat and monitor their sewage discharges. As settlements grow, their sewage discharges increase dramatically especially during the summer months of July and August.

High-rise hotels and apartment blocks line the coast in many Spanish coastal regions.

153

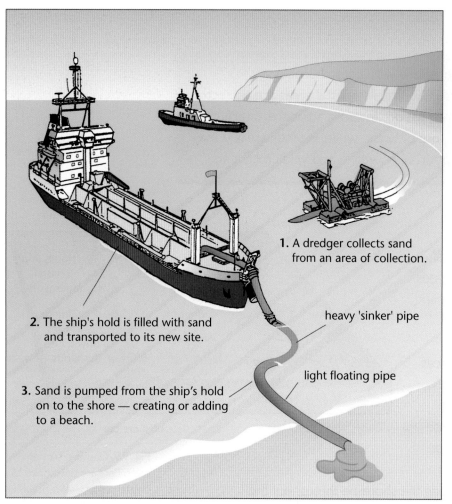

1. A dredger collects sand from an area of collection.

2. The ship's hold is filled with sand and transported to its new site.

heavy 'sinker' pipe

light floating pipe

3. Sand is pumped from the ship's hold on to the shore — creating or adding to a beach.

Fig. 9.8

Beach Nourishment

Beach nourishment is simply the pumping of sand into an eroded beach to change wave movement, so as to increase deposition. This additional sand is normally obtained by offshore dredging, although in certain cases sand quarries are used for small schemes. Great **care** is taken in choosing **sand-grain size** and its distribution, so it suits the site.

This practice is regularly carried out along the Mediterranean coast, such as Majorca, where there is a need for beach facilities for children and tourists. What often causes the loss of sand is storm waves removing the sand and leaving only bare rock or gravel. To replace it, sand is brought from another location in a large ship and pumped from the ship onto the affected beach.

A beach-nourishment project was undertaken in Rosslare Strand from October 1994 to January 1995. Over a quarter of a million cubic metres of sand was dredged from a site 6 km offshore and pumped onto the beach. A rock groyne system helps to retain sand on the beach. In this case, beach nourishment was carried out for coastal defence work as well as for recreational use.

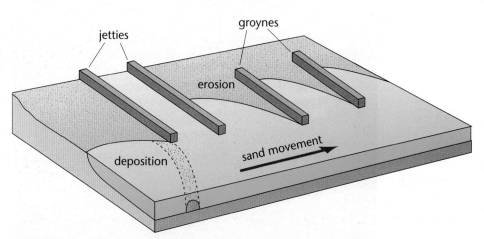

Fig. 9.9 Jetties, groynes and breakwaters interrupt the movement of sand by beach drift and longshore currents. **Beach erosion** often results **down current** from the site of the structure.

The Impact of Coastal Defence Work
Coastal Erosion and Building Groynes

Longshore drift is the process that carries material from areas of erosion to areas of deposition. Any interference with this natural process in an area may lead to either increased erosion or increased deposition.

The location and spacing of groynes must be studied carefully

154

to make sure that the correct level of sediment retention is achieved and to provide a balance between the need for protection of the area and the requirements of the zones further along the coast. After careful monitoring, these groynes may be adjusted if erosion further along the coast is too great.

Breakwaters

Offshore breakwaters are **long parallel mounds of rubble or rock, which are built parallel to the shore to reduce erosive wave action**. Like groynes, breakwaters are designed to suit each individual site of coastal erosion. The effect of wave change around the breakwater is to set up new currents that trap sediment in the sheltered side of the structure. The sediment deposited in the lee of the breakwater may result in either an increase in the beach width at the shoreline or a sandbar reaching to the breakwater in the form of a tombolo. The formation of the tombolo will depend on local factors, such as tidal current, storm frequency or the shape of breakwater.

Breakwaters are sometimes attached to the shore. These include long walls built across a harbour to protect fishing trawlers and ferries that are moored to a quayside. However, leisure craft are sometimes moored apart from industrial port areas and also need the protection of breakwaters from storm waves.

Groynes and artificial honeycomb rocks are used to reduce wave action.

Activity
Explain how people's activities in coastal area can:
a. improve local environments.
b. damage local environments.

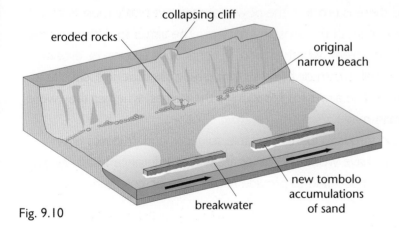

collapsing cliff
eroded rocks
original narrow beach
breakwater
new tombolo accumulations of sand

Fig. 9.10

Conservation and Management Measures

In recent decades it has been recognised that a coastline is a valuable natural resource that needs careful and sensitive management. This is especially so in the case of Ireland where our shores are subjected to severe storm waves from the Atlantic every year and human interference by the recent rapid developments of golf courses and coastal holiday homes and mobile home sites.

A code of practice for coastal management and conservation has been established on the basis of pilot projects and gathering expert knowledge of coastal areas.

Leisure craft, such as sailing boats, are often protected by breakwaters in coastal areas.

155

This code of practice is called **ECOPRO – Environmentally Friendly Coastal Protection**. The objectives of ECOPRO are:

- To develop monitoring methods suited to various types of coastline.
- To develop a sensitivity index to grade a coastline's susceptibility to erosion.
- To present an evaluation of various coastal protection and management methods.
- To present case histories of some of these methods.

Straw bales and jute matting placed behind rocks to protect beach sand from erosion

Beach Management

The principle behind the code of practice is the need to maintain as far as possible the protection created by the natural features of the coast. For example, a beach is nature's way of reducing the energy of sea action. The objective should be to keep beaches in place. Beaches and sand dunes are valuable coastal resources and where human activities may lead to their destruction or deterioration, coastal management will be needed.

Because the depth of sand on beaches may naturally fluctuate (increase or decrease) from season to season, the beach must be allowed to do this without interference. The dunes at the back of beaches form an integral part of the system and so also must be allowed to fulfil their function. While dune systems are valuable for leisure activities, it is necessary to regulate their use. It is important to note that a valuable resource may be easily and permanently destroyed by allowing an inappropriate management structure or protection solution.

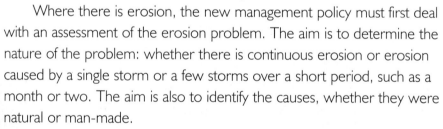

Where there is erosion, the new management policy must first deal with an assessment of the erosion problem. The aim is to determine the nature of the problem: whether there is continuous erosion or erosion caused by a single storm or a few storms over a short period, such as a month or two. The aim is also to identify the causes, whether they were natural or man-made.

The next step is to identify suitable solutions and to assess how these solutions have worked in other areas with reference to liability and environmental impact and to provide information on cost-benefit analysis.

Marram grass planted to stabilise sand dunes

Causes of Erosion

Coastlines are constantly receding because they are being worn away by the forces of nature. The many causes of erosion may be classified into two groups:

- Erosion caused by people
- Erosion caused by nature.

Erosion Caused by People

Human interference includes removing sand directly (for buildings and other uses) or indirectly by interfering with natural processes such as longshore drift.

The coastal engineer must aim to strike a balance between preventing erosion and interference with natural processes that may destabilise the coastline.

Erosion Caused by Nature

Natural causes include the erosion-deposition balance, which may be affected by climatic change (such as increased storm frequency); rise or fall of sea level due to earth movements, and natural changes of sediment supply.

Sand Dune Management

Recreational activities, such as pedestrian traffic, cars, caravan parks, horse riding and scrambling, can seriously damage dune vegetation and increase the rate of sand loss through wind erosion. This loss of sand could directly affect the amount of sand on the beach and the size of the sand dunes.

Some Effects of Recreational Activities

- The trampling of vegetation due to pedestrian traffic is the most widespread form of damage to sand dunes by people. This occurs where human activity is concentrated in small areas to form a fan-shaped network of paths and tracks developing from caravan parks, car parks and other areas of public access to the coast. As vegetation is damaged, erosion begins and the wind attacks the exposed sand, eventually forming gullies and gaps called blow-outs. Paths across the tops of dunes are most at risk, as wind speeds are greater there and path slopes are often steeper. Gullies created in cliffs of boulder clay can lead to cliff slumping.
- Ideally vehicles, horse riding and motorbike scrambling should be banned from beach areas as they can devastate sand-dune systems. The passage of 200 vehicles per year over sand dunes can reduce vegetation cover by 50 per cent. Where these activities are allowed on dunes, their paths should run perpendicular to the direction of the prevailing winds.

> **Activity**
> 1. Why are beaches important for controlling coastal processes?
> 2. Explain why evaluating and recording natural coastal processes is essential for balanced human interaction in coastal areas

Protection of Natural Wildlife Habitats

Sandflats and **mudflats** in tidal areas, such as river estuaries, hold dense populations of marine worms, shellfish and other invertebrate life. These are the foods that attract large numbers of wintering migrant birds. Some of these birds include the oystercatcher, curlew, redshank and ducks such as teal, waders and geese. **Salt marsh areas** attract birds to hatch and rear their young. One of the best-known wildlife habitats is in Dublin Bay, off **Dollymount Strand**. Usually the greatest abundance of life is close to land and so is under constant threat of pollution and habitat destruction. Careless dredging, dumping of waste or coastal defences could pollute these areas or remove them due to changes in coastal currents. To protect these areas, some inshore areas are designated as **Natural Heritage Areas**.

A wildlife habitat on the coast

TEST YOURSELF AT
my-etest.com

Revision activity

Fill in the missing words to complete this text.

There are three types of rock, … , sedimentary and … . Rocks that are changed due to heat or pressure are called … rocks. Rocks that form from magma within the earth are called … rocks. Two examples of this rock type are … and … . Rocks that form from magma on the surface are called … rocks. Two examples of this rock type are … and … . Gabro and … are examples of … rock. They form in … and … , as magma forces its way towards the surface.

Sandstone forms from b… and sand … . Limestone was formed from c… and s… in an … environment. Ireland's limestones were formed when Ireland was near … … .

Three factors contribute to metamorphism. They are … … and the presence of … . Slate forms from … .

When masses of magma cool within buckled rock, they form … , which are formed of … rock. This type of rock is found in places such as … and … in Ireland. More masses of this rock are found in … and … in southern England.

The … foldings in Cork and Kerry created … and … about … million years ago. Examples of these uplands include the … and the … … mountains.

When limestone weathers, it generally forms a l… l… area. When granite weathers, it forms … hilltops. Standing on top of these hilltops are … formed from weathered … rock.

Large areas of … rock are found near granite regions. This rock type forms pointed peaks called …s.

SECTION 4 (CHAPTERS 10-17)
REGIONS

The word **geography** comes from the Greek words **'geo'** (meaning 'earth') and **'graphia'** (meaning 'to describe'). Geography is a subject that aims to describe and understand the earth.

   To understand the earth's different environments and how they act with each other, geographers use the concept of a region. They have divided up the earth's surface into smaller areas or **regions**.

   This has given rise to **regional geography**. By looking at regions, geographers are better able to study the complex patterns of physical and human activities on the earth's surface.

   There are many **different types of region** that we can study. This section introduces some of these types of region.

Mountainous region: Scandinavia

Urban region: London

CHAPTER 10
WHAT IS A REGION?

The Concept of a Region

By the start of the twenty-first century, a large number and variety of natural and human environments existed on the earth. These are due not only to processes of natural change, such as erosion and earth movements, but also to the growing and more intensive ways that people interact with their natural environments. To understand better the earth's different environments and their complex inter-relationships geographers use the concept of a **region**.

Regions and Differences of Scale

There are many sizes of region. Some such as the subcontinent of India are huge, while others such as the Gaeltacht regions in the West of Ireland are small. The size of a region and **scale** of map used to define a region depend on the reason for studying it.

Figs. 10.1 and 10.2 show this with maps of two regions drawn at different scales. The first map, in Fig. 10.1, is drawn at a large scale to show the region of Europe. Not much detailed information can be shown at this scale. In contrast, Fig. 10.2 is drawn at a much smaller scale and allows for more detailed study of the Greater Cork Area.

So what is a region?
A region is an area of the earth's surface that has human and/or physical characteristics that give it an identity and makes it different from all the areas around it.

Cultural region: Connemara Gaeltacht

Fig. 10.1 The countries of Europe

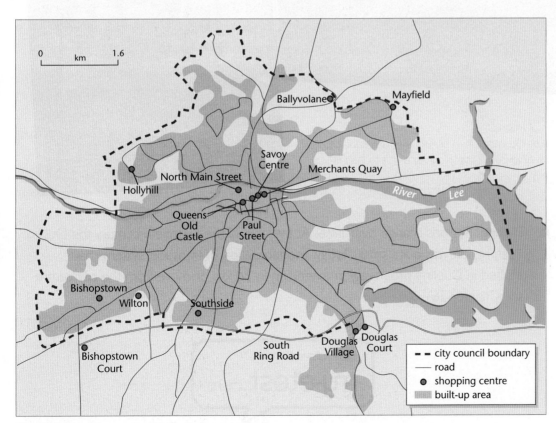

Fig. 10.2 Shopping centres in Cork city and suburbs

161

General Characteristics of a Region

Although regions can be defined in different ways, some factors are the same for all regions:

- **Area:** Regions occupy an area of the earth's surface that can be identified as being different from surrounding areas.
- **Boundaries:** Regions are enclosed by boundaries that separate them from surrounding regions. Some boundaries are easily identified on the earth's surface, such as the crest of a mountain range or the course of a river. Most boundaries used by people, however, are not so easily recognised in the landscape, for example local government boundaries.
- **Image:** For most people mentioning the name of a region often creates for them a perception or image of that region. These images are usually based on someone knowing about or being familiar with a region.

Different images of Ireland.
- *Which would be the image for a person living in Ireland as opposed to an American tourist planning a visit to Ireland?*

- **Change:** Regions change over time. At the start of the twentieth century the Dublin urban region was quite small. Today, modernisation of transport systems has resulted in Dublin's urban region extending to 80 km or more from the city centre (see Chapter 26).

TEST YOURSELF AT
my-etest.com

CHAPTER 11
CLIMATIC REGIONS

KEY IDEA!
A climatic region is an area with an identity that comes from regular weather patterns over a long period of time. These weather patterns affect vegetation and soils in a region.

Climatic regions are areas that have their own distinct climate and are separated from each other by boundaries. In some areas these boundaries are sharply defined, while in others they are not as well defined because one climate area blends into another. Within a climate region the unique weather system and its temperature, precipitation, seasons, soil and vegetation make it completely different from all the surrounding regions.

Some climate regions are huge, for example the equatorial climate region that includes the Amazon Basin in South America, the Congo Basin in Africa and the Indonesian islands.

Remember from your Junior Certificate how climate affects soil. Cold boreal climate areas have **podzol** soils and hot climates have **laterite** soils.

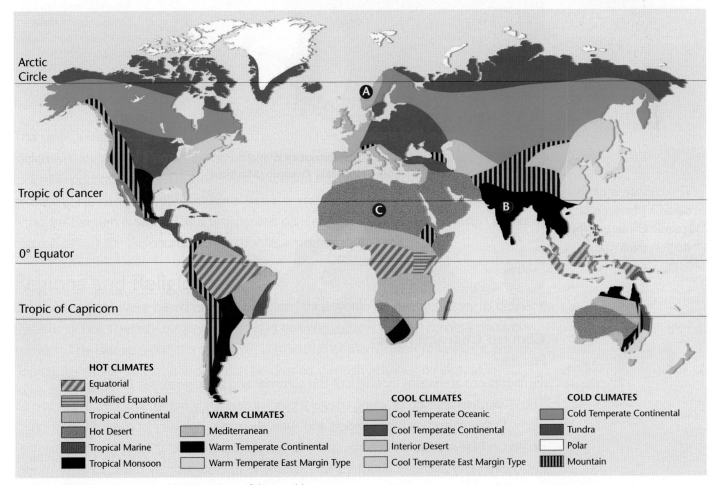

HOT CLIMATES
- Equatorial
- Modified Equatorial
- Tropical Continental
- Hot Desert
- Tropical Marine
- Tropical Monsoon

WARM CLIMATES
- Mediterranean
- Warm Temperate Continental
- Warm Temperate East Margin Type

COOL CLIMATES
- Cool Temperate Oceanic
- Cool Temperate Continental
- Interior Desert
- Cool Temperate East Margin Type

COLD CLIMATES
- Cold Temperate Continental
- Tundra
- Polar
- Mountain

Fig. 11.1 These are the main climate regions of the world.
- *Identify the climates at A, B and C.*

Other climate regions are tiny. These are called **microclimates**. The physical presence of a city affects the local climate, and as a city changes so does its climate. The bigger the city becomes, the more polluted the air is and the warmer its temperature. Buildings absorb and release heat while the dust in the air traps and reflects heat back into the city, making the urban area warmer than its surrounding areas. This is called an urban microclimate. Microclimates may vary from one side of a rock to another, or from one side of a tree to another.

Every island has its own microclimate. The islands off the coastline in County Kerry have different climates from those of the Aran Islands off the Clare coastline.

- *What evidence on this photograph suggests that the Skellig Rocks off the Kerry coast have their own microclimate?*

This climate is often called a Maritime or Oceanic Climate. Why do you think this is?

Case Study: Climate of North-West Europe
Cool Temperate Oceanic Climate

The region with this climate includes the west coast of Scandinavia, the whole of Britain and Ireland, Denmark, Belgium, the western half of France and north-west Spain.

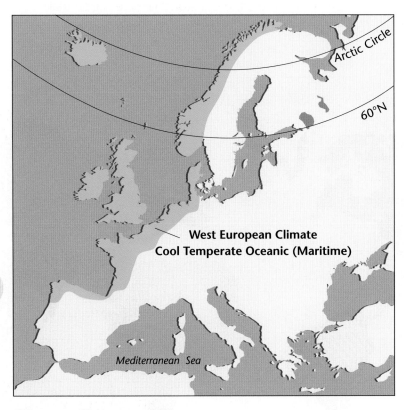

West European Climate Cool Temperate Oceanic (Maritime)

Mediterranean Sea

Fig. 11.2 Cool Temperate Oceanic climate in north-west Europe
- *Name the countries on this map which have coastal edges with a Cool Temperate Oceanic climate.*

Climate Characteristics
Summer

Temperatures are warm throughout the summer and average about **15°C to 17°C**. The lower averages occur along coastal areas, while slightly higher averages occur in places further inland such as London and Paris. Averages also vary from south to north. Bergen in Norway has an average summer temperature of about **14.5°C,** while Valentia in County Kerry averages about **15°C**. Daytime temperatures may reach **23°C** or more on hot days.

Winter

Temperatures are mild through winter months and January temperatures may average about **4°C to 5°C**. The warm North Atlantic Drift that flows from the Gulf of Mexico to the west coast of Europe influences all the sea areas. Blowing over this warm water surface are the South West Anti-Trade Winds that bring warm air to coastal areas throughout the year. This is most noticeable during winter as temperatures are generally above **4°C** and so make the weather mild and moist.

Precipitation

The one certainty about precipitation (rainfall) in this climatic area is that it may fall at any time of year. Most rain, however, falls in winter. It is mostly associated with depressions or cyclones that travel from a south-west to north-east direction across the North Atlantic and bring changeable weather to this coastal region.

Relief rain also occurs, and highland and upland areas, such as the mountains of the West of Ireland, the Scottish Highlands and the Scandinavian Highlands receive more rain than lowland areas. Some precipitation falls as snow. The total rainfall can vary from as little as 500 millimetres (mm) in lowland areas to 2,500 mm in highland areas.

The Climate of Ireland

Ireland is located in north-west Europe and so has a Cool Temperate Oceanic or Maritime climate. Its prevailing winds are the South West Anti-Trades that blow from the Atlantic Ocean. These winds and the presence of mountains along Ireland's coastline cause Ireland to be divided into **two climatic regions**. They are the wetter West of Ireland and the drier eastern Ireland.

Class Activity

Look at Fig. 11.3 and answer the following:
1. Using a diagram explain why Ireland's heaviest rainfall occurs along the western coast.
2. Explain why the Dublin region in the east of the country has the least rainfall. Think about: relief rain and rain shadow.

TEST YOURSELF AT
my-etest.com

▪ over 2000 mm	▪ 1000-1200 mm
▪ 1600-2000 mm	▪ 800-1000 mm
▪ 1400-1600 mm	▪ less than 800 mm

Fig. 11.3

CHAPTER 12
PHYSICAL REGIONS

A physical region is an area with an identity that comes from its surface characteristics being different from all its surrounding areas.

Physical regions have surface characteristics that make them different from all the areas around them. The physical differences may be due to height and relief, the rock types, drainage pattern or internal rock structure, or a combination of these factors.

Karst Landscapes

Karst landscapes are regions formed by chemical weathering.

Case Study: The Burren in County Clare

The Burren is an upland, terraced limestone region in County Clare. The beds of rock dip gently to the south. In some places the limestone is covered by shale. Some of the soil cover was eroded by glaciers, and by early farmers tilling the land that left the remaining soil exposed to strong coastal winds.

Most of the Burren today has no soil cover and weathering has created a karst landscape. Large expanses of limestone pavement with grikes and clints dominate the area. There are few surface streams. Most disappear underground through sinkholes (swallow holes) and flow through underground passages and caverns.

Karst landscapes occur in many areas in Ireland, such as the Dartry-Cuilcagh Uplands in County Fermanagh and Cavan (see Chapter 6, pages 83, 87 and 88). The best example in Ireland is the Burren in County Clare.

Formation

The Burren was formed when the African and European plates collided. This collision also formed a huge mountain chain across Europe of which the Galtees, the Macgullicuddy's Reeks and the ridges of Munster are remnants.

> Remember how landforms of karst landscapes were explained in Chapter 6, page 83.

● *What evidence in the photograph suggests that the Burren in Co. Clare is a karst region?*

Munster Ridge and Valley Region

This natural region is explained in Chapter 3, page 69.

The North European Plain Region

The North European Plain is a lowland region that covers Britain and Ireland, Poland, northern Germany, southern Sweden and Finland, Latvia, Estonia and Lithuania, Belgium, the Netherlands, northern and western France, Romania and the Bulgarian and Hungarian plains (see Fig. 12.1).

Formation

The forces that created the ridge and valley region of Munster and the Burren Upland in County Clare also rippled the seafloor that now forms the foundation of the North European Plain. Later, after the Alps and surrounding uplands were formed, sediments were washed down or blown by wind onto the plain from the weathered and eroded mountains and levelled it. The final result was the North European Plain. Slight warpings have made it undulating rather than flat.

Remember isostasy in Chapter 8 on page 136.

During the last great ice age an enormous ice sheet squeezed down this lowland region of north-west Europe. When the ice melted and raised the level of the sea, much of the land that had subsided was submerged beneath the North and Baltic Seas. In this way, Britain and Ireland were cut off from mainland Europe. Rivers flowed northwards and formed deltas along the Netherlands, Belgium and northern Germany. The land started to rise again as the great weight of ice was removed. This process continues today and is noticeable in the raised beaches found along the coast of Northern Ireland, Scotland and the Baltic coastline.

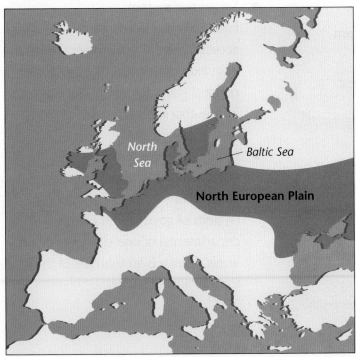

The North and Baltic Seas are shallow because their floors were once part of the North European Plain.

Fig. 12.1 The North European Plain

TEST YOURSELF AT
my-etest.com

CHAPTER 13
ADMINISTRATIVE REGIONS

KEY IDEA!

There are many types and sizes of administrative regions.

ADMINISTRATIVE REGIONS AT DIFFERENT SCALES

One of the most basic forms of region are administrative units such as county and city councils. A government divides its national space into a hierarchy of local and regional areas to manage development better. It has to decide on the **scale**, or size, of the administrative units and how to link the various levels of administration.

Why do communities prefer small and more localised forms of administration?

The **scale** of administrative units generally depends on the type of service to be provided and the objectives of the government. Administrative areas need to be **large** enough to allow for providing services efficiently; an example of this is the Health Board Region. The areas also need to be **small** enough to work effectively and reflect community interests, for example local school districts. In general, central governments prefer the efficiency of working with a small number of large administrative units, whereas communities prefer smaller-scale, localised units.

The links between various levels of administration generally take one of two forms (see Figs. 13.1 and 13.2).

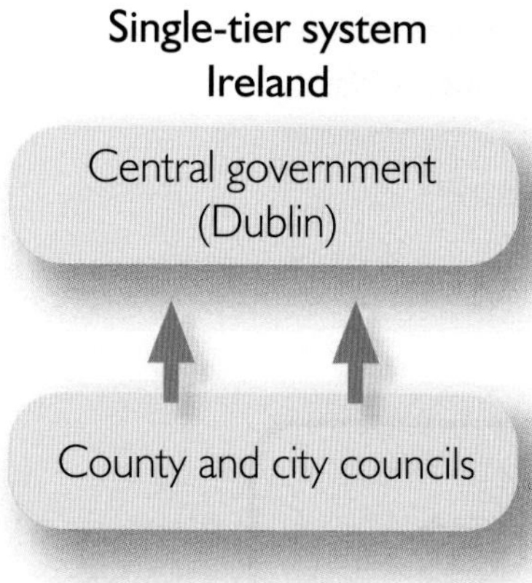

- **Single-tier system:**
  Each administration area has direct access to central government. Ireland is an example of this. As no effective regional government has developed, local authorities have direct links to central government.

- **Multiple-tier system:**
  Local authorities work with central government through a bureaucracy (system of government officials and departments) of one or more regional levels. France is an example of this form of administration.

**Multiple-tier system
France**

Central government
(Paris)

↑

22 regional governments

↑

92 *départements*
(local government)

**Single-tier system
Ireland**

Central government
(Dublin)

↑ ↑

County and city councils

Fig. 13.1 A single-tier system of government

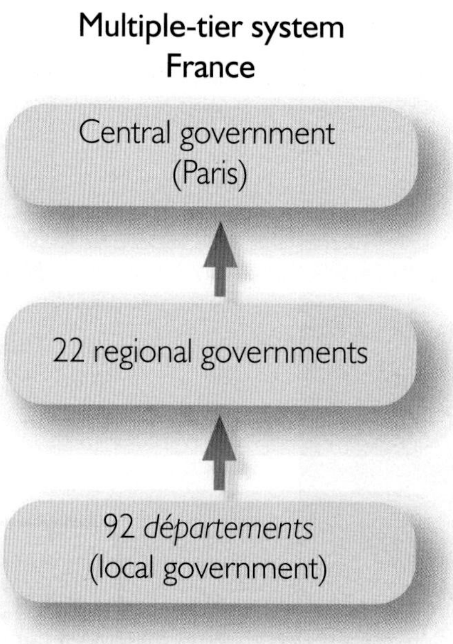

Fig. 13.2 A multiple-tier system of government

Major hospitals offering specialised services are usually located in large cities. Why?

Schools for young children are generally provided at a local level. Why?

ADMINISTRATIVE UNITS IN IRELAND

The Counties of Ireland

Most of Ireland's administrative units go back as far as the Anglo-Norman invasion of 1169. The Anglo-Normans introduced new forms of administration, or adapted existing forms, to allow them to control the territory they conquered in Ireland. The **county** was the central part of this system.

By the mid-thirteenth century, the settled parts of Ireland had been divided into eight counties: Cork, Dublin, Kerry, Limerick, Louth, Tipperary, Waterford and Connaught, which was later subdivided. As Anglo-Norman influence extended over the country, so did the county system, which was completed in 1606 when Co. Wicklow

> What counties make up present-day Connaught?

● *While the landscape may not change dramatically when moving from one county to another, would you feel you were entering a different part of Ireland? Why?*

was set up. So the twenty-six counties that made up the Republic of Ireland until 1994 have a long history (see Fig. 13.3).

Many counties were defined by major physical features such as the River Shannon or mountain ranges such as the Blackstairs Mountains. Counties also bring to mind powerful images of distinctive cultural and physical landscapes. What images do you have of the underdeveloped counties of western Ireland compared with the counties that form Dublin's urban region?

People identify strongly with their county and relate to being, say, a Dubliner or from Mayo. They have a pride in and loyalty to their county, as well as the special characteristics associated with different counties. This is often expressed by the support and intense rivalries generated at GAA matches at county level and between neighbouring counties, such as Cork-Kerry, Dublin-Meath, Tipperary-Kilkenny.

> In 1994, County Dublin was subdivided into three new counties – Dublin, Fingal and Rathdown – to reflect the complexity of this capital-city region.

Urban-based Administrative Units

With the growing role of urbanisation in Ireland, three types of administrative units are based around urban centres:

- city councils
- borough councils
- town councils.

City Councils

There are city councils for the **five** most populous and important cities: Dublin, Cork, Limerick, Waterford and Galway (Fig 13.3). These cities have played an important role in the development of the state and especially in their hinterlands (surrounding areas). This is linked directly to these cities' roles as ports and stresses the importance of trade for an island economy.

One of the major problems for all city councils is that their administrative areas have not expanded enough to take account of suburbanisation (how new suburbs have been built and the population has spread beyond their historic city boundaries). Modern growth now occurs mainly outside town boundaries and in areas of neighbouring county councils.

An example of this is in Limerick. When the city tried to extend its administrative boundaries into nearby County Clare, this was strongly resisted, showing the great commitment to county identity. This highlights the need for greater cooperation in planning between county and city council administrations.

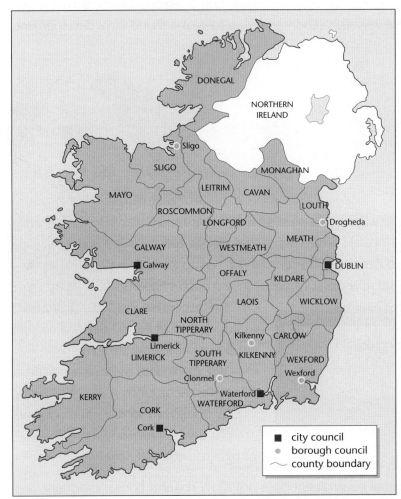

Fig. 13.3 Counties, city councils and borough councils in Ireland

Why should Ireland's five largest urban areas be ports?

Limerick City council offices and the River Shannon

Borough and Town Councils

Borough councils administer the five medium-sized towns which come below the city councils in Ireland's urban hierarchy, for example Kilkenny.

The 75 councils that make up the third type of urban-based administrative unit have their roots in the nineteenth century. They are based on historic rather than present patterns and functions of towns in Ireland. While they have some planning powers, they do not play a vital role in the administrative framework of modern Ireland.

Fig. 13.4 Regional Authority Areas and two new planning regions for European Union (EU) funding

Regional Administration

There is no effective regional level of administration in Ireland. From the 1960s, some efforts have been made to set up regional administration units to help planning within the state. Different types of regional authority areas relating to issues of public concern have been created, for example for regional development and health (see Figs. 13.4 and 13.5). Regions were created by grouping neighbouring counties, but there was no common basis for planning the regions. For example, health board regions cover different areas to the regional authorities set up to deal with industrial development.

Fig. 13.5 Health Board Regions

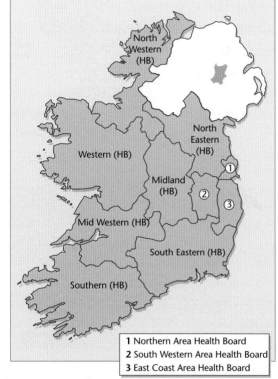

Activity

Look at Figs. 13.4 and 13.5 and answer the following:

1. Which health board regions differ most from the areas covered by regional authority areas?
2. Can you suggest problems that these differences may cause for effective planning?

The state recognises that local government is important as a forum for representing local communities democratically and in carrying out at a local level powers and functions given by law. Through government initiatives, the state also promotes the interests of these communities (according to the *Constitution of Ireland, Article 28A*).

As regional authorities cover different areas, such as health and industrial development, and the central government does not allow regional bodies important decision-making powers, regional administrative units within Ireland are not as important as in other countries. This was difficult for the Irish Government when it was negotiating for structural funding from the European Union to help finance the country's Third National Plan, 2000–2006 (see Chapter 15).

Local Government in Ireland

There are over a hundred local authorities in Ireland. They form the country's system of local government. The present system can be traced back to the Local Government (Ireland) Act of 1898, which set up the principles of democracy and efficiency in local government. Almost a century later, the 28th amendment to the Constitution confirmed that local government had an essential role for the state and emphasised the idea of dealing with local issues at a local level.

County Development Plans

As well as providing the community with essential services, such as sewerage services and housing, local authorities have also taken on a development role. Local authorities have to draw up strategic County Development Plans to meet the development needs of their areas. These must be updated every five years and are key documents in shaping transport, industry and housing developments in local authority areas.

Activity
Access the development plan of your local authority area. What are the main features of the plan for your community?

Local planning operates under **three** key principles:
- **Subsidiarity**: Decision-making should allow people to have a major role in governing their own affairs. This encourages self-reliance rather than depending on outside organisations to encourage development.
- **Appropriateness**: Services and administration should be provided as close to the people as possible. This emphasises, where practical, local rather than regional or national levels of government.
- **Partnership**: This encourages local people to take part in government.

> The principle of **subsidiarity** also operates in the EU to bring decision-making closer to people.

Local Government in Ireland
There are:
● 114 local authorities
● 29 county councils
● 5 city councils
● 5 borough councils
● 75 town councils
● There are over 1,600 elected members and elections occur every five years
● Local authorities employ over 30,000 people and spend approximately €4 billion every year. This has significant multiplier effects in local communities.

Table 13.1

Services Provided by Local Authorities
● Housing
● Urban renewal
● Road transport and safety
● Water supply and sewerage
● Refuse collection and environmental protection
● Recreation and amenities
● Development incentives and controls
● Education, health and welfare
● Miscellaneous services

Table 13.2

- *What is meant by 'multiplier effect'? Give two examples of how large-scale spending by local authorities can help development in local communities.*

The range of services and facilities provided by local authorities is important for the state to function efficiently. They are also essential for a high quality of life for the communities living in local authority areas. Some of the more important services are listed in Table 13.2.

> Why have local authorities built so many houses in Ireland?

For example, making sure enough housing is available is one of the great challenges for local authorities. Since Ireland's local authority system was set up at the end of the nineteenth century, local authorities have provided over 350,000 houses for people who otherwise could not have afforded a house of their own.

The *Départements* of France

France is one of Europe's largest countries with a surface area of 551,000 km², a population of 58 million and a wide variety of human and physical landscapes. Despite its size and diversity, government is centralised on Paris, although by the late twentieth century regional administrations had a stronger role.

Fig. 13.6 The regions and *départements* of France

Class activity

Which French region in Fig. 13.6:

1. is linked most to Celtic culture?
2. produces high-quality sparkling wine?
3. includes the capital of France?
4. includes the country's largest port?
5. is the location of the EU Parliament?

Much of the present regional administration in France can be traced to the French Revolution of 1789. After the Revolution, a new pattern of local government was based on the *département*. These were designed to be approximately the same size and with the same number of people and, where possible, with some special cultural feature. There are 92 *départements* in present-day France (see Fig. 13.6).

The *départements* are responsible for a number of functions, including social services and coordinating urban and regional planning in their areas. The central government in Paris still has a powerful role and influence on local administration because it appoints the key administrative officer, known as the *préfet,* for each *département*. As local administration was centred on the main town in each *département*, no regional centres developed enough in size and function to rival the dominance of Paris.

After the Second World War, there was some administrative reform and 22 regions were created in 1955 (see Fig. 13.6). These were, however, little more than a collection of *départements* and had little authority. Pressure to decentralise (spread out) power from Paris increased in the 1970s, and a 1982 law gave the regions a new status.

French regions now have responsibilities for economic and cultural activities, such as job creation, tourism and heritage. They have become effective planning bodies, and coordinate initiatives put forward by the *départements*. The state finances this. People vote in direct elections to new regional assemblies, so they are represented there.

As each region is a large size and has a greater range of planning functions, some regional centres have now become more important. These include Lyons-St. Étienne-Grenoble, Toulouse and Bordeaux. This is important to counterbalance the dominance of Paris.

Do you remember the importance of the French Revolution in history from your Junior Certificate?

Départements are the equivalent of counties in Ireland.
Why did the fact of local government being based on a large number of towns in France limit the growth of major regional centres?

The *départements* centred on Bordeaux have been linked to the production of high-quality wine for centuries.
● *In which ways would the wine industry have helped the growth of Bordeaux as an important regional centre?*

TEST YOURSELF AT
my-etest.com

CHAPTER 14
CULTURAL REGIONS

KEY IDEA!

Language and religion are two major factors that are used to define culture regions.

Defining a Culture Region

In constructing regions based on human rather than physical factors, **culture** is the most fundamental factor. Yet culture is a difficult concept to define. It involves many features such as behaviour, attitude, learning and knowledge, and how these are passed on from one generation to the next.

These values, however, have an impact on the landscape. This can be through the ways in which people organise and adapt to their resources. In farming it could be building stone walls and the field patterns in County Galway, or in a city it might be its special architecture and street layout.

Three different cultural landscapes from Ireland, Italy and India

By mapping cultural features, geographers create **culture regions.** Identifying culture is complex, but **two key factors** are often used to map cultural regions. These factors are language and religion.

Language Regions

Language is central to cultural identity, as it is the main way of knowledge and ideas passing between people. It is seen as a powerful symbol of cultural identity, and many cultures strongly resist outside pressures to reduce the vitality of 'their' language.

Language as a symbol of cultural identity operates at various levels. Although France is a powerful state and French an important international language, the French are concerned with the growing importance of English as the dominant world language. In many national territories, there are often strong passions about keeping minority regional languages, such as the Basques in Spain and Bretons in France. Yet there are also many cases in which different language groups can co-exist with little sign of stress.

In Switzerland there are four official languages: French, German, Italian and Romansch. This causes little or no problem for the Swiss.

Supporters of the Welsh language frequently object to the dominance of English in Wales.

Case Study: Ireland and the Gaeltacht

In the Republic of Ireland, the Irish language has an important role in expressing Irish culture and identity. In the 2002 Census, 1.57 million people (40 per cent) in the Republic claimed some ability to speak and understand Irish. This is almost three times the number of people who claimed this ability when the Free State was set up, reflecting the efforts of government and voluntary bodies to promote the Irish language, especially within the education system.

How is Irish promoted as a language in the Irish education system? Is this a success?

Although more people claim to have some knowledge of Irish, Irish is used in everyday life only in relatively small and peripheral parts of the country. These are the **Gaeltacht regions,** and are the heartland of the Irish language and culture (see Fig. 14.1).

The Gaeltacht was defined in 1925 by a Commission for Irish-Speaking Districts. To qualify as an Irish-speaking district *(Fíor Gaeltacht)*, 80 per cent of the population had to speak Irish. Partly Irish-speaking districts *(Breac Gaeltacht)* were defined as areas where 25 to 79 per cent of the population spoke Irish. Using District Electoral Divisions as a basic area for analysis, the Commission was able to create distinctive cultural regions based on the Irish language (see Fig. 25.2 on page 288).

At the start of the twenty-first century, the Gaeltacht is composed of a number of relatively small areas scattered along the west and south coast of the country from Donegal to Waterford. The total population of the Gaeltacht in 2002 was about 86,500. Of this total, about 61,150 people over the age of three years spoke Irish. Although these Gaeltacht areas are small and have peripheral locations, they have a special importance for the Irish people and are strongly supported by government grants and incentives (see Chapter 25).

In 2002, what percentage of the population of the Gaeltacht spoke Irish?

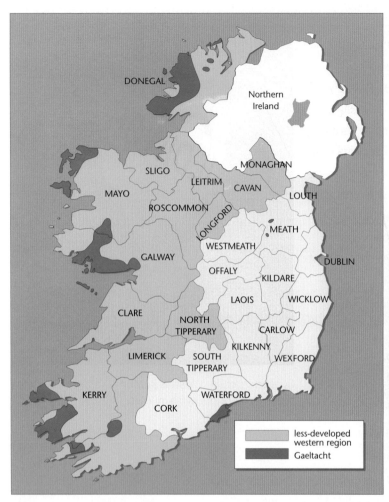

Fig. 14.1 The Gaeltacht areas

Activity

Look at Fig. 14.1 and answer the following:

1. In which counties are the Gaeltacht areas?
2. Why do you think the Gaeltacht is confined mainly to the less developed West?
3. Why are there few Gaeltacht areas in the eastern half of the country?

A welcome sign for visitors to the Aran Islands in the Galway Gaeltacht. Locate these islands on Fig. 14.1.

Belgium and its Language Regions

Belgium was created as an independent state in 1830, following a revolution which led to this area separating from the Netherlands. Despite Belgium's relatively small size (30.5 million km², which is less than half the area of Ireland), the country has **three** official languages: Flemish, French and German (see Fig. 14.2). The Flemish language is a type of Dutch.

Since the 1960s, tensions between the two main language-based communities (Flemish and French) have increased. Although Flanders has a majority of the national population and has attracted a lot of growth industries to become one of the EU's most prosperous regions, its Flemish-speaking community feels under threat from the more dominant international language of French. Evidence of this appears in bilingual Brussels, where French-speaking communities are increasing at the expense of Flemish communities.

As tensions grew and the different communities wanted to gain more autonomy (control) over their own affairs, fundamental reforms have been made to Belgium's constitution. There is now a federal-style government, which recognises three separate regions based mainly on language. These regions are Flanders, the Brussels-Capital Region and Wallonia (which is French speaking but includes a small German-speaking community).

> If you were going to live in Brussels would you choose to learn French or Flemish? Explain your answer.

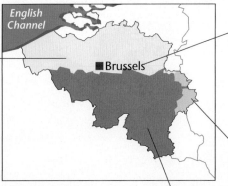

This Flemish-speaking area is culturally linked to the Netherlands. Historically, this was a poor region that lived from farming. Since the 1960s, this region has become more prosperous, attracting industries to places such as the port of Antwerp and its hinterland.

Brussels is the capital of Belgium. It is a bilingual city where French and Flemish are given the same status.

This small enclave of German-speakers is territory ceded to Belgium by Germany after the First World War.

Fig. 14.2 The language regions of Belgium

The southern part of Belgium is mainly French-speaking because it is near France. During the 1800s, this region became prosperous, based on heavy industries that developed in the Sambre-Meuse and Liège coalfields. The collapse of these industries has seen the prosperity of Wallonia decline sharply.

Two Belgian students at a protest, highlighting the bilingual nature of the country

The new political-cultural regionalisation has highlighted divisions within Belgium. The 'defensive' attitude of Flemish communities about French-speaking culture spreading led to a new political party called *Vlams Blok*. Based in Flanders, the party is committed to protecting Flemish culture, with more extreme elements seeking an independent state. Although Belgium is viewed as a prosperous core state within Europe, language tensions make it difficult for the country to function as a single national unit.

Regions and Religion

If cultural regions were based only on language, they would be relatively easy to define. Systems of belief, which are key elements in defining culture, can cut across language barriers. The Islamic world, for example, is made up of many different language groups. Sometimes similar language groups can be divided through religious conflict, as in Northern Ireland.

Each of the world's major religions has a distinctive geography (see Fig. 14.3) and has had a key role in shaping individual and group identities. These include aspects such as attitudes to women, birth control, the environment and diet.

For example, in some traditional Islamic societies, women generally play an inferior role to men in daily life. A large number may be uneducated.

179

Fig. 14.3 The world's major religions

Traditional Chinese religions

	A
	B
	C
	D
	E

Much of sub-Saharan Africa is dominated by traditional religions.

Which two religious groups clash in Palestine and Kashmir?

Most religions wish to convert non-believers to their faith. As a result, boundaries that define religions change through time and for varying reasons, such as the work of Christian missionaries. The passion of some religious groups is so strong that conflict zones occur along boundaries between different religions. Present-day examples include Israel and the neighbouring Arab countries; Islamic Pakistan and Hindu-dominated India, especially in Kashmir; Christian and Islamic communities in countries formed when Yugoslavia broke up in the Balkans.

Two examples we shall look at are regions associated with religion but on very different scales:
- Northern Ireland
- the Islamic world.

Cows are regarded as holy creatures in the Hindu faith. They cannot be killed or mistreated.
- *What problems could this create?*

In the middle of Rome is the Vatican City. It is the centre of the Roman Catholic Church, where the Pope lives.
- *What regions of the world are dominated by the Christian faith?*

How does gender inequality affect development in Islamic countries? (Think about: employment and population growth.)

Religious Divide in Northern Ireland

The Irish Free State set up in 1921 did not cover the whole island of Ireland. After a referendum, six counties in north-east Ireland chose to stay as part of the United Kingdom. This decision was associated with British colonial rule when large numbers of English and Scottish Protestant communities had been settled there. In contrast, the rest of the island was, and remains, dominated by the Catholic faith. Northern Ireland emerged as a distinctive cultural region based around its majority Protestant population.

Despite many changes in the Protestant and Catholic populations in Northern Ireland, the political divide separating the region from the Republic has not changed. In Northern Ireland, however, Catholic and Protestant communities became increasingly segregated, especially after the outbreak of violence in the region in 1968. Generally, the Catholic population tends to form the majority in more rural areas, while Protestants dominate in the larger urban centres. At the start of the twenty-first century, approximately 55 per cent of Northern Ireland's population was Protestant.

> Which six counties make up Northern Ireland?

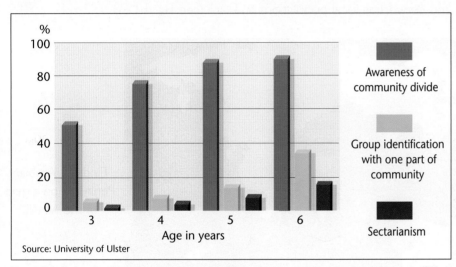

Source: University of Ulster

Awareness of community divide

Group identification with one part of community

Sectarianism

Fig. 14.4 Cultural and political awareness of 3 to 6 year olds in Northern Irelands (%)

● *What does this image and Figure 14.4 suggest about the cultural divide in Northern Ireland?*

Within Belfast there is religious segregation. After the outbreak of civil disorder in 1968, minorities of both religions who had chosen to live in a different majority community often had to retreat into their own communities. The result was Catholic-only and Protestant-only ghettos and a divided city.

A geographer named Paul Doherty drew up an interesting map of the Belfast urban area to show religious segregation in 1981 (Fig. 14.5). Using one-kilometre squares, Doherty shows that only 19 of 157 squares had a Catholic majority (for example, in the Falls Road). In contrast, there are large areas with a majority of Protestant residents (for example, in the Shankill Road).

> What is a ghetto? Use a dictionary to find out.

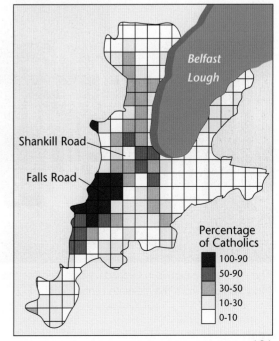

Fig. 14.5 Belfast Urban Area, 1981

Percentage of Catholics
100-90
50-90
30-50
10-30
0-10

The Islamic World

Islam is one of the world's great religions, with more than a billion believers. It is a religion that is expanding its number of converts and the areas of the world in which it is practised.

The Islamic religion traces its origin to the prophet Muhammad (Mohammed), who was born at Mecca in the Arabian Peninsula in AD 571. Muhammad received revelations from Allah (God) and committed his life to teaching these divine revelations. At first there was opposition, but his teachings quickly became accepted in Arab society. After his death in AD 632, the Islamic religion, its teachings and cultural landscapes spread quickly from its source area in the Arabian Peninsula (its cultural hearth) to the surrounding regions.

Islam was spread by powerful, conquering armies that invaded other parts of the Middle East and North Africa, Spain and the Balkans. Arab traders travelled to distant markets such as the Indian subcontinent and the islands of South East Asia, taking their faith with them and converting local populations to Islam (see Fig. 14.6).

Fig. 14.6 Where Islam spread around the world

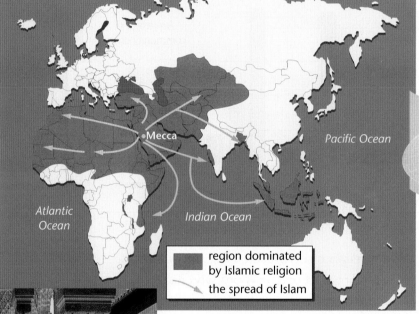

Find the Arabian Peninsula on a map of the world.

region dominated by Islamic religion
the spread of Islam

The Alhambra palace is in Granada, which became the capital of Moorish Spain from the eleventh century until 1492.

Today the global region of Islam occupies most of North Africa and south-west Asia, with important outlying areas in the densely populated islands of South East Asia, such as Indonesia. In these regions, religion is still a powerful influence on the lives of people and in shaping distinctive cultural landscapes, such as the design of towns, palaces, gardens and mosques, and in the role of women in society.

Even in areas that were under the influence of Islam centuries ago, there are still impressions of the past in the present-day landscape, as in the case of **southern Spain**. When the Moors invaded Spain in 711, they spread the

Islamic faith there. They were finally pushed out of Spain in 1492, but palaces like the Alhambra, in Granada, are a reminder of nearly eight hundred years of Moorish presence in Spain.

Islam continues to expand as a global religion. For some, this is seen as a threat associated with **Islamic fundamentalism,** and conflict zones have emerged in places such as the Balkans and Kashmir. Yet Islam also expands along more peaceful avenues, often associated with migration into countries of the developed world. An increasing number of major cities in Western Europe, such as London, Paris, Amsterdam, and also in North America, now have mosques, reflecting their growing population of converts to Islam.

Mecca is the most sacred city in Islam. Up to 750,000 Muslims can gather to pray together at the Kaaba, or Sacred Mosque of Islam.
● *In which country is Mecca?*

What do you know about Islamic fundamentalism? What is it?

For Muslims, making a pilgrimage to Mecca is one of the five pillars (or duties) of Islam.

CHAPTER 15
SOCIO-ECONOMIC REGIONS 1: CORES AND PERIPHERIES

There are major differences in levels of development between regions, especially between cores and peripheries.

A core is a centre point, while peripheries are out on the edge.

Why are some regions rich, while others remain poor?

Economic development does not affect all areas in the same way. Some regions develop strongly because there is a good combination of factors, including what raw materials are available or being a strategic location for trade. In contrast, regions without enough resources, unfavourable environments and poor access to trade routes and market centres usually fail to develop prosperous communities.

It is important to note that less-developed regions can occur **within** countries that are prosperous. In this case, the status of these regions is relative to the more prosperous regions in that country. For example, the West of Ireland is less developed compared to the eastern region centred on Dublin.

The core-periphery model is a simple model that divides an area into **two** types:
- core
- periphery.

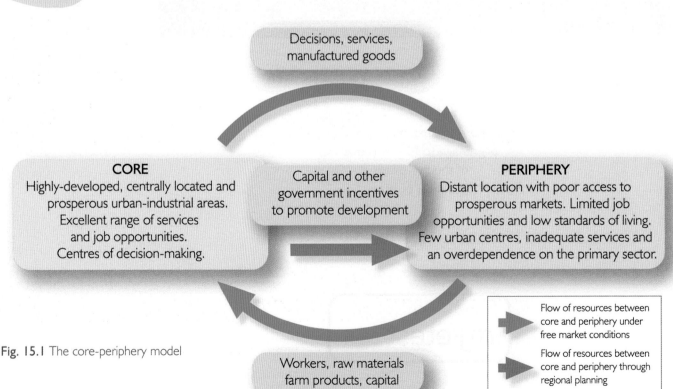

Decisions, services, manufactured goods

CORE
Highly-developed, centrally located and prosperous urban-industrial areas. Excellent range of services and job opportunities. Centres of decision-making.

Capital and other government incentives to promote development

PERIPHERY
Distant location with poor access to prosperous markets. Limited job opportunities and low standards of living. Few urban centres, inadequate services and an overdependence on the primary sector.

Flow of resources between core and periphery under free market conditions

Flow of resources between core and periphery through regional planning

Workers, raw materials farm products, capital

Fig. 15.1 The core-periphery model

The difference between the core and periphery encourages resources to flow in a way that benefits the core, e.g. migration of young people. Some recent trends, however, have encouraged development in the periphery, but are linked directly to the flow of resources from the core: industrial investment, tourism and government incentives through regional planning. This is seen between the core region of northern Italy and the Mezzogiorno in southern Italy (see Chapter 19).

National Cores

All countries have a **national core,** which is the most important area for national development. Most national cores are centred on capital cities and have had a historic as well as a present-day role as core regions, for example London or Paris. Some important national cores, however, have evolved away from political capitals such as the North West region of Italy.

Core areas are economically strong and usually create growth in neighbouring areas. These regions are well connected to the core by well-developed transport systems, such as good road, rail and air links. This is seen in Greater Paris, South East England and the expanding Dublin urban region.

Dublin is Ireland's national core. It is the country's capital, its largest centre of population and services and has well-developed transport and communication systems. In Fig. 15.2 see how the Dublin core region has attracted most foreign investment. Over a third of all full-time jobs in foreign-owned manufacturing and financial services are in Dublin.

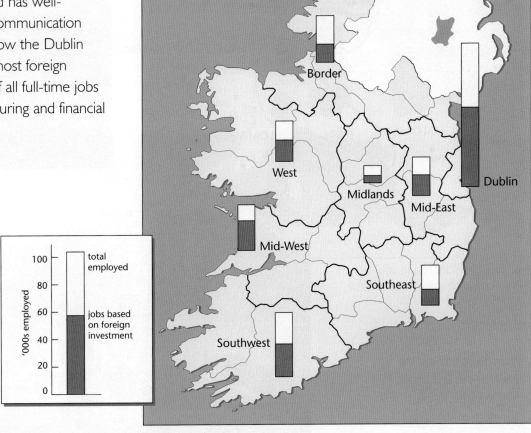

Fig. 15.2 Total industrial employment and dependence on foreign investment by region

An International Core in Western Europe

An international core has emerged in Western Europe as a number of national cores and growth regions have combined. They are usually located next to each other and are well connected through a variety of links. These links have become stronger throughout the last half of the twentieth century, as the European Union has encouraged more international trade between its member states.

Fig. 15.3 shows the international core of the European Union, which has been given a variety of names, including European 'Dogleg' and the 'Hot Banana'. It also includes the four regions considered to be the 'motors' of the European Union. This is because of their powerful economies and their increasing role within the EU's single market.

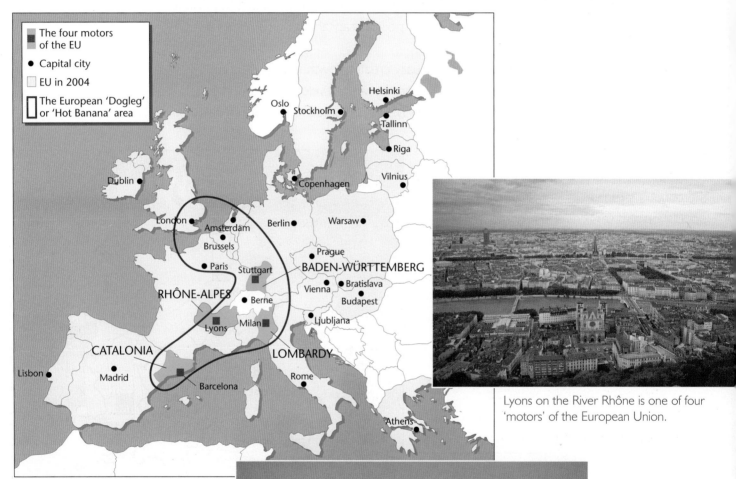

Fig. 15.3 The core region of the European Union

Lyons on the River Rhône is one of four 'motors' of the European Union.

> Why do you think the core of the EU been given the name 'dogleg' or 'banana'?

A village in the Meseta of Central Spain.

- *What evidence suggests that this is part of Europe's periphery?*

186

Peripheral Regions

Although core areas have socio-economic problems such as congestion, high land values and inner-city decline, regions with the greatest development problems are in peripheries. There are a variety of problem regions, but two types can be highlighted:

● **Rural underdeveloped,** such as the **West of Ireland** and the **Mezzogiorno**.
● **Regions of industrial decline,** such as the coalfields of the **Sambre-Meuse Valley** in Belgium.

Class Activity

Use the following factors to highlight the problems faced in peripheral economies:
● Environmental conditions
● Dominant economic activity
● Any alternative growth industries
● Unemployment levels
● Migration
● Urban base
● Location and accessibility.

Ireland's Problem Region

In Ireland, the main problem region has long been associated with rural underdevelopment. This was officially recognised by the State in 1952 when the Undeveloped Areas Act was passed. Under the Act, large areas of the West of Ireland were recognised as needing government support to help with their problems and promote investment in this less developed 'half' of the country (see Fig. 14.1).

This east-west division in Ireland has been adjusted more recently by the government, so it could access structural funds from the EU for the period 2000-2006. The new Border, Midland and West (BMW) region has been created to define Ireland's most problematic region and has retained an Objective 1 status in the EU (see Fig. 15.4).

Activity

Look at Fig. 15.4 and answer the following:
1. Name the Objective 1 regions marked on the map as A, B, C, D and E.
2. Why would these regions want to have access to structural funds?

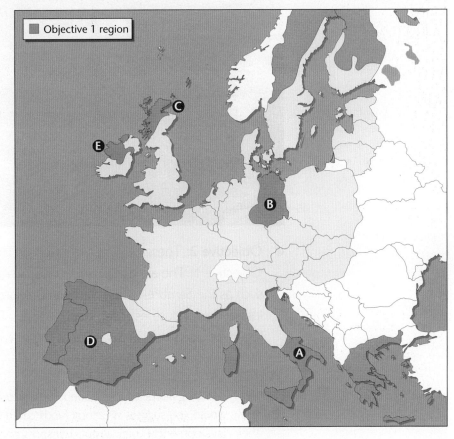

Fig. 15.4 Objective 1 areas for structural funding, 2000-2006

Objective 1 region

Problem Regions in the European Union

In 1988, the EU's Common Regional Policy (CRP) was reformed to deal with problems of increasing inequality between richer and poorer regions. More money to deal with this was made available through structural funds. This money has to be spent in achieving common objectives. There were six objectives at first, but they were reduced to three in the 2000-2006 programme for structural funds.

Structural funds are used by the EU to assist development in problem regions and to help disadvantaged communities throughout the EU, e.g. youth unemployment. The best known is the European Regional Development Fund (ERDF).

> GDP (Gross Domestic Product) measures the wealth of a country or region. If you divide this by the population of that area, this gives the average wealth per person. This is a key indicator for measuring development.

- **Objective 1:** To make economic adjustments in regions where the economies lag behind the rest of the EU. They are generally defined as having a GDP (Gross Domestic Product) per capita (per person) of less than 75 per cent of the EU average. They are EU regions with most problems and need most support from structural funds. Objective 1 also includes regions of Northern Sweden and Finland, where the main problem relates to the very low population density (see Fig. 15.4).

- *Do you think building new roads such as this in Spain is a good way to spend structural funds in Objective 1 regions?*

- **Objective 2:** These regions are based on much smaller areas and populations than Objective 1. The aim is to help economically depressed urban-industrial regions, such as the Sambre-Meuse Valley in Belgium and Lorraine in France, to adjust to the loss of their industries (coal, steel, textiles). Funding also helps to attract industries to less-developed rural areas, such as the Massif Central in France.

Activity
1. Why is funding needed to upgrade infrastructure in Objective 2 areas?
2. How would you suggest structural funds could be spent in Objective 2 regions to assist their development? (Think about: transport improvements, alternative industries.)

- **Objective 3:** Objective 3 applies throughout the EU. It is aimed at helping more marginal groups of people to become better integrated into society and the economy. These groups include ethnic minorities, the handicapped or unemployed young people.

Plans to enlarge the EU will add to the problems of regional development in Europe. More structural funds will be needed (and have been allocated) for this in the 2000-2006 Plan. Competition for this funding will be strong between the existing Objective 1 and 2 regions and problem regions in the proposed new member states. In Ireland, the South and East region has already lost its Objective 1 status (see Chapter 18).

- *Why is new international investment so important for depressed industrial regions such as Lorraine in north-eastern France?*

- *Why is training or education so important for marginal groups?*

CHAPTER 16
SOCIO-ECONOMIC REGIONS 2: REGIONS OF INDUSTRIAL DECLINE

KEY IDEA!

Once prosperous regions based on coalmining and heavy industries have declined and face major problems.

The Industrial Revolution started in Western Europe during the late eighteenth century. This led to a new regional pattern of industrial development, based around **coalfields**. These became the growth regions of the nineteenth and early twentieth centuries.

> For well over a hundred years, coalfield areas were the growth regions of Western Europe.

Case Study: The Sambre-Meuse Coalfields

The Sambre-Meuse coalfields stretch about 150 km from the French border to Liège along the Sambre-Meuse Valley in Belgium (see Fig. 16.1). It was one of the first regions of continental Europe to experience large-scale industrialisation at the start of the nineteenth century. The region's development depended on reserves of coal, a location central to the major urban-industrial markets of north-west Europe, and well-developed canal and railway networks.

The Sambre-Meuse coalfields are located at the core of Wallonia. Rising levels of prosperity and jobs in coal mining and heavy industries, such as iron, steel, engineering and chemicals, attracted large numbers of migrants, especially from Flanders. This made Wallonia the dominant cultural and economic region in Belgium.

After the 1950s, the economy of the Sambre-Meuse coalfields declined. This was due to a number of factors:

- There were alternatives to coal as a **source of energy.**
- **Costs of production** were high and the industries were less competitive in world trade.
- **Cheaper imports** especially from less developed economies.
- **Alternative products** became available, for example plastics replaced metals.
- **New technologies** reduced the number of jobs available for people in these industries.
- **New plants** were built to replace older units, but these were often in different regional locations such as coastal sites rather than inland coalfields, e.g. the modern steelworks at Zelzate.

As the heavy industries declined, so did the regions that depended on them. There were huge job losses and high levels of unemployment, out-migration and economic depression in these once proud and prosperous communities.

Deindustrialisation is the term used to describe a large-scale decline in the industrial base.

Steelworks at Charleroi surrounded by old, working-class housing for its labour force.

By 1984, the last colliery in the Sambre-Meuse coalfields had closed (Fig. 16.2). This left many mining communities with a high level of unemployment and a scarred landscape, which was not attractive to modern industries.

The decline of the heavy industrial base meant that the coalfields and Wallonia emerged as major problem regions. Out-migration increased from these economically depressed communities to more dynamic growth centres, such as Brussels, and Antwerp and Ghent in Flanders. Flemish-speaking Flanders replaced French-speaking Wallonia as the economic core of Belgium.

Government and EU support has been essential for promoting development in this declining industrial region. It is an Objective 2 region in the EU.

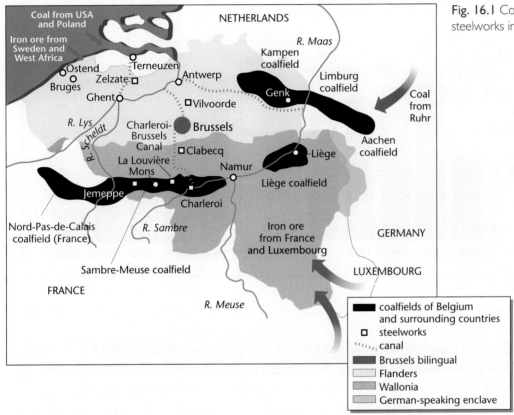

Fig. 16.1 Coalfields and steelworks in Belgium

Which languages are spoken in Wallonia and Flanders? See Chapter 14.

Activity

Look at the map in Fig. 16.1 and answer the following:

1. In which Belgian region are the Sambre-Meuse coalfields?

2. Do you think rivers and canals have been an important factor influencing the location of Belgium's steelworks? Explain your answer.

3. How does the Belgian steel industry source its main raw material inputs even though the country produces no coal or iron ore?

4. Is this a disadvantage for steelworks in the Sambre-Meuse area compared with Zelzate? Explain your answer.

Collieries such as this once had a dominant role in the landscape and economy of the Sambre Meuse.
What impact did their closure have for this region's economy and quality of environment?

Fig. 16.2 Whereas the coal industry of the Sambre-Meuse Valley ended in 1984, investment in the region's steel industry allowed for increased productivity.

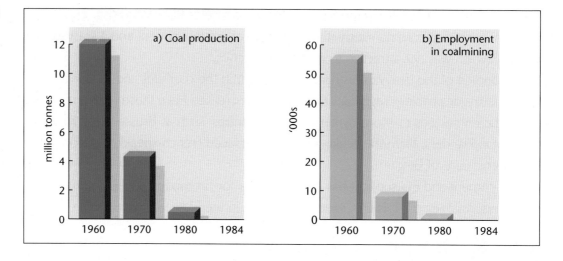

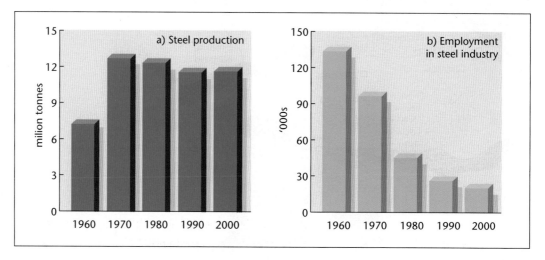

Activity

Look at Fig. 16.2 and study the caption to answer the following:
1. What is the trend for employment and coal production from 1960 to 1984?
2. Why is the loss of jobs in mining an important problem for the Sambre-Meuse Valley?
3. Contrast the trends for steel production and employment from 1960 to 2000. Explain these different trends.

This Objective 2 region has had a large amount of investment to change its image and make it more attractive for private investment. Of special importance have been:
- Investment in transport infrastructure and especially new motorways that link the region to neighbouring growth regions (see Fig. 16.3).
- New industrial estates located along the motorways and near larger urban centres such as Charleroi and La Louvière.
- Upgrading the airport at Charleroi, mainly for Ryanair, to improve international access.
- Cleaning up the derelict landscape to improve the image of the local environment and take away an impression of economic depression.

The results have been quite good, and a large number of new industries, such as Caterpillar at Charleroi and Ford at La Louvière, have attracted different types of industry to the region. Despite this, the Sambre-Meuse area remains a problem region in Belgium and has a long way to go before it becomes as prosperous as it was in the early twentieth century.

Activity

Look at the map in Fig. 16.3 and answer the following:

1. Name some growth regions in neighbouring countries that can now be easily accessed by road from the Sambre-Meuse Valley area?

2. Why are motorways seen as a key factor in the modern development of the Sambre-Meuse Valley?

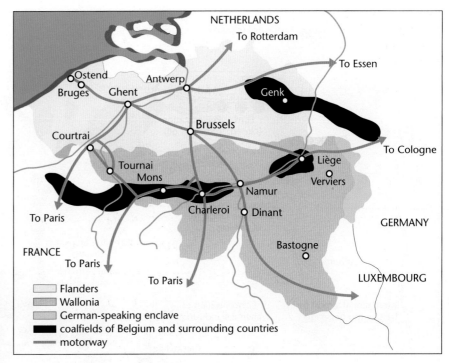

Fig. 16.3 Motorways in Belgium

Case Study: The Greater Cork Area

When Ireland joined the European Union in 1973, Cork was the country's dominant centre for large-scale, port-related industries. These included Ireland's only:

● steelworks (Irish Steel)
● shipyard (Verholme)
● oil refinery (Irish Refining)
● car assembly plant (Ford).

Cork also had a number of large chemical plants and a range of more traditional Irish industries, such as food processing, clothing and textiles.

These industries had been attracted to Cork by a combination of location factors linked to the city and its main physical asset: Cork Harbour (see Fig. 16.4).

Up to the 1980s, these industries provided the Greater Cork area with good employment prospects. Cork was considered a **growth centre** for the national economy (see Chapter 26).

At the start of the 1980s, an international recession and growing competition in European and world markets caused major problems for Cork's industrial base. The local industrial plants were mostly small, relatively inefficient and high-cost producers by

Before the 1980s, Cork had built its economy around a limited number of large but slow-growing or declining industries.

Cork outer harbour is an ideal location for a growing number of port-related industries, especially chemicals.

193

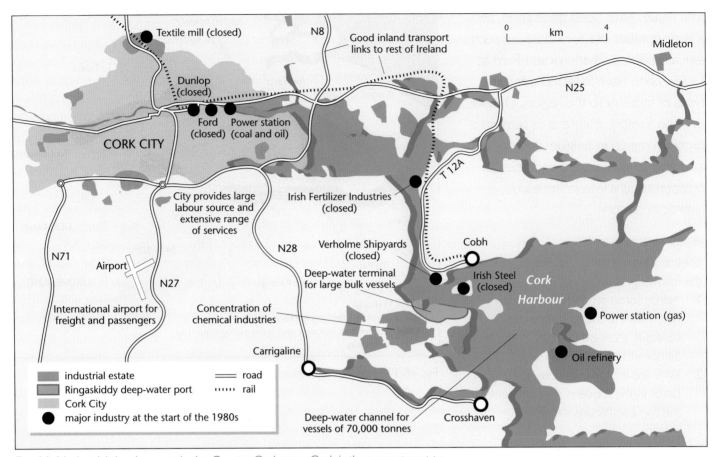

Fig. 16.4 Industrial development in the Greater Cork area. Cork is the nearest port to continental Europe. This and access to shipping routes are important for import/export.

> **How many jobs in manufacturing did Cork lose from 1980 to 1985? Note that this was almost a third of the industrial base.**

international standards. Decisions were taken to close or run down most of Cork's long-established industries.

By 1985, the shipyards, Ford and Dunlop had been closed, with a loss of about 3,000 jobs. Cutbacks at other plants added another 2,500 job losses. Most of these jobs had been thought of as well paid and secure. Losing these jobs led to huge social problems for communities that had depended heavily on these industries. Cork had experienced **deindustrialisation,** becoming a region of industrial decline and a 'blackspot' for national unemployment.

During the 1990s, Cork's industrial economy was revived, and a large number of new growth sectors were attracted to the city region.

- Chemical and pharmaceutical companies have located, mainly around Cork's Outer Harbour and especially near the deep-water terminal at Ringaskiddy (see Fig. 16.4). This is now regarded as the 'chemical capital of Ireland'.
- A growing number of electrical and IT (information technology) firms have set up in the 'necklace' of industrial estates that have been set up around the edge of the city.

Government and regional planning have been vital in achieving this change of fortune for Cork. A large investment has been made in modernising the region's infrastructure, including education institutions, port facilities, airport, roads and urban renewal. This has changed the image and attractiveness of the region for growth industries.

At the start of the twenty-first century, Cork can no longer be described as a region of industrial decline. The change was not easy to achieve but shows the importance of effective national and regional planning. In spite of this, the effects of global recession have caused unemployment to rise from the low levels of 2000. It also shows the problem of depending too heavily on foreign investment.

The inner quays of Cork were the site of early industrial development in the city.

- *Do you think these areas remain attractive for manufacturing?*

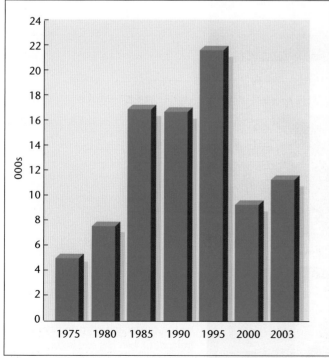

Fig. 16.5 Unemployment in the Greater Cork area, 1975-2003

Activity

Look at the chart in Fig. 16.5 and answer the following:

1. What were the years of lowest and highest unemployment?
2. Do the figures support the idea that unemployment became a major problem in the early 1980s?
3. Do trends for the late 1990s suggest that Cork benefited from a significant increase in new jobs?

TEST YOURSELF AT
my-etest.com

195

CHAPTER 17
URBAN REGIONS

KEY IDEA! Urban regions (regions centred on urban areas) have become more important in modern development.

An **urban region** is an area that surrounds a human settlement and is linked to it by interactions, such as shopping, the journey to work and supplying farm produce.
The area linked to the urban centre is called the **hinterland** of that centre.

What is an Urban Region?

Geographers use different types of regions to study patterns and processes of change, but one regional type has become much more important. This is the **nodal** or **city region**, also called the **urban region**. In this chapter, the term **urban region** will be used.

Urban regions are important because:

- More and more of the world's population lives in towns and cities. In Western Europe, it is 80 per cent of people, Britain (87 per cent) and Ireland (60 per cent).
- The lives of people are increasingly organised by an urban-based environment.
- Urban areas can be seen easily in the landscape. These built-up areas can be easily mapped.

As the capital and primate city of Ireland, Dublin has expanded greatly from its original site on the River Liffey.

Ireland's Urban Regions

Ireland is one of the least urbanised societies in Western Europe. This reflects its past as a colony, its underdeveloped economy, its peripheral location in Europe and its dependence on the primary sector. By 2000, 60 per cent of the country's population lived in urban centres.

In Ireland, the eastern and southern parts of the country are the most urbanised. More market towns grew up on the richer agricultural land. The southern and eastern ports were also developed to trade with Britain. In contrast, the West of Ireland was in a more peripheral location and had difficult environmental conditions for productive farming, so there were fewer towns, which were more spread out across the region (see Fig. 17.1). In the Southern and Eastern (S & E) Region, almost 75 per cent of the population lives in urban areas (areas with a population larger than 1,500), while the Border, Midland and Western (BMW) Region has only a third of its population in towns and cities.

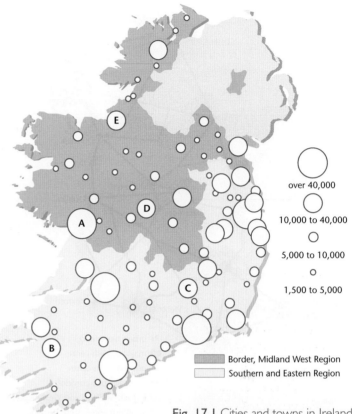

over 40,000

10,000 to 40,000

5,000 to 10,000

1,500 to 5,000

Border, Midland West Region
Southern and Eastern Region

Fig. 17.1 Cities and towns in Ireland by the size of population

Activity

Look at Fig. 17.1 and answer the following:
1. Name the towns marked A, B, C, D and E on the map.
2. Why are there so few towns in Connaught?
3. Why are there so many ports along the east and south coast?

As well as Ireland's unbalanced regional pattern of urbanisation, it also has a **primate** urban structure. This happens when a very large part of a country's population is concentrated in a single city. The Greater Dublin Area with a population of 1.3 million (35 per cent of the national total) is a primate city.

Other primate cities in Europe include London, Paris and Athens.

Galway is the main city of the West of Ireland and has grown significantly since the 1960s, as both an industrial and services centre.

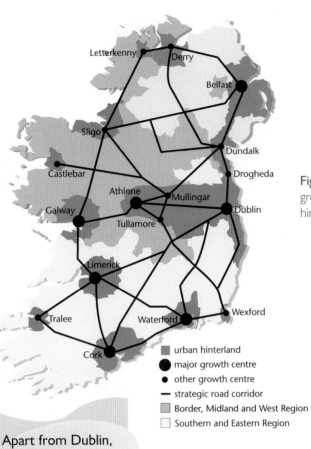

Fig. 17.2 Ireland's regional growth centres and their hinterlands

urban hinterland
major growth centre
other growth centre
strategic road corridor
Border, Midland and West Region
Southern and Eastern Region

Fig. 17.2 shows the hinterlands of Irish cities and towns suggested by planners as growth centres for national development. It also highlights the large area influenced by Dublin. This stretches both north to south and east to west.

A growth centre is a town that is chosen for development, so that growth will spread out into its hinterland.

The north-south coastal corridor that links Dublin to Belfast is becoming an important area for economic development. To the west, Dublin's influence goes as far as Athlone. This leaves only a narrow strip of more rural space separating Dublin's hinterland from Galway, the main urban centre of the West of Ireland.

Apart from Dublin, what are Ireland's four other cities?

Apart from Dublin, you can see the important urban hinterlands of the other four main cities, which also have roles as regional centres. These cities supply a wide range of services and have improved transport links to their well-populated hinterlands.

What is a hinterland?

The smaller urban centres are, the fewer the services they offer and the smaller their hinterlands are. Tralee, in County Kerry, and Castlebar, in County Mayo, are examples of reduced hinterland areas of smaller market towns in rural Ireland (Fig. 17.2).

Kilkenny (left) and Clifden, Co. Galway (right), are examples of smaller urban centres that have developed in different physical environments.
● *Do these photographs suggest ways in which their locations influenced the scale and nature of their development?*

European City Regions

One of the outstanding features of Western Europe's human geography is the large number of urban centres across the region. By the start of the twenty-first century, about 80 per cent of the region's population was living in towns or cities.

The well-developed countries that border the North Sea have the highest levels of urbanisation. In Belgium, 95 per cent of the population lives in urban centres (Netherlands 89 per cent and Britain 87 per cent). Peripheral countries with underdeveloped economies usually have lower levels of urbanisation. In Portugal 30 per cent of the population lives in towns and cities (Ireland 60 per cent). The least urbanised area of Western Europe is in Northern Scandinavia, where extreme climate conditions discourage people from settling there.

Fig. 17.3 shows that there are **three** major zones of urban settlement in Western Europe:

- Manchester-Milan axis
- Paris-Berlin axis
- coastline of Western Europe.

Manchester-Milan Axis

The Manchester-Milan axis is the most important area of concentrated urban development in Europe and includes many major cities. It is based on a historic trading corridor that links the North Sea lowlands and the Mediterranean.

What are the extreme climate conditions in North Scandinavia?

What is the river that forms this trade corridor?

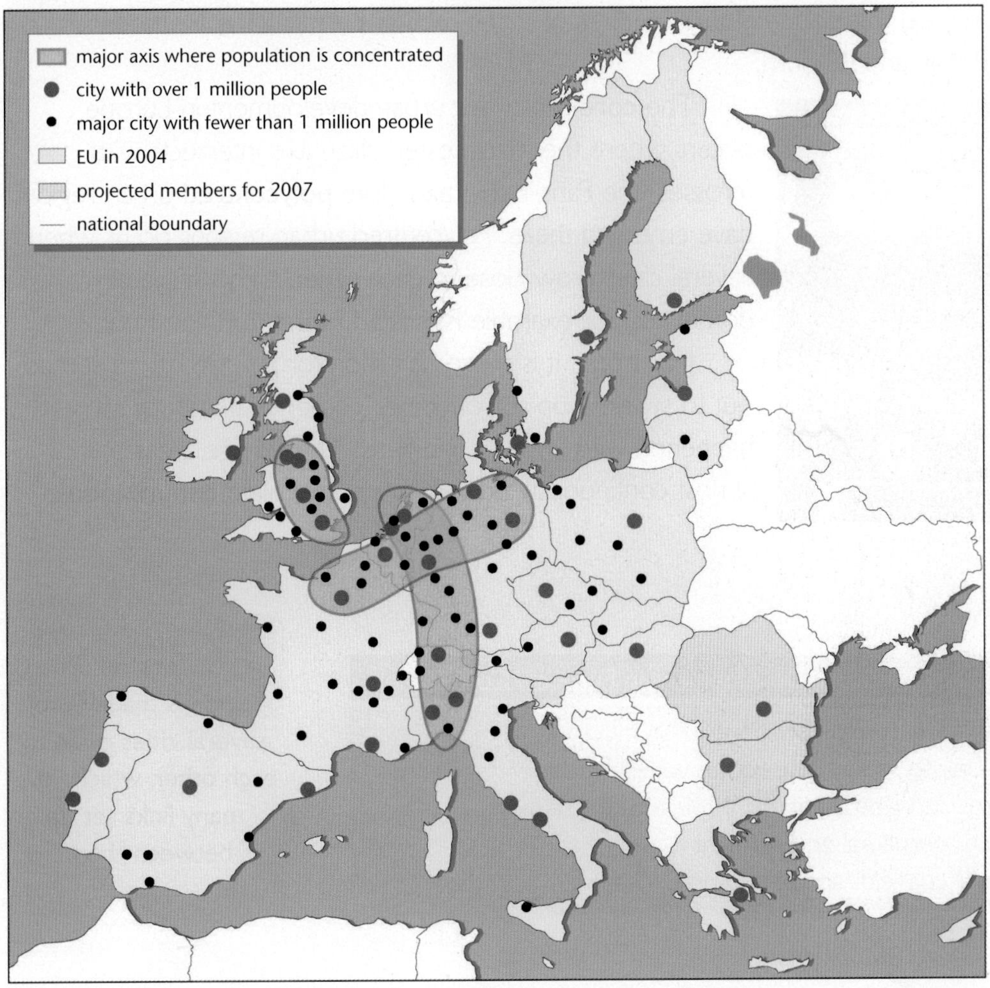

Fig. 17.3 Major urban centres and axes where population is concentrated in the Europe Union.

legend:
- major axis where population is concentrated
- city with over 1 million people
- major city with fewer than 1 million people
- EU in 2004
- projected members for 2007
- national boundary

Activity
Look at Fig. 17.3 and answer the following:
1. Through which countries does the Manchester-Milan axis pass?
2. Why did the Alps **not** cause a major problem for trade along the Manchester-Milan axis?
3. What modern growth industry is helping to promote urban growth along the Mediterranean coast? Explain you answer.

Köln (Cologne) on the River Rhine has long been a major trade and religious centre.
- *What evidence in the photo supports this statement?*

Paris-Berlin Axis

The Hellweg is a lowland route made up of rich glacial soil (loess). These factors helped the growth of cities. Why?

The Paris-Berlin axis links the capitals of France and Germany. It follows an east-west lowland corridor called the Hellweg. This links the coastal areas of north-west Europe to the Baltic Sea and more continental parts of Europe.

Coastline of Western Europe

Many of Europe's largest cities are ports. This is linked to Europe's long tradition of maritime (sea) trade and colonial empires of states such as Portugal, the Netherlands, Spain, Britain and Belgium.

Barcelona is one of the four 'motors' of the EU. Its prosperity is due mainly to its historic and present role as a major port.

The **core** region for urban development in Europe occurs where the Manchester-Milan axis intersects with (crosses) the Paris-Berlin axis. Two **polycentred** urban regions have emerged there. Polycentred urban regions occur when several cities grow close to each other, so no single city dominates, for example Randstad Holland, Rhine-Ruhr.

In Europe, it is more common for a single city to spread out to swallow up surrounding, smaller settlements, as happened with London and Paris. These large areas of almost continuously built-up areas are called **conurbations**.

A polycentred urban region is made up of several cities close to each other, which have many links set up between them.

Advantages for Urban Development in Europe's Core Region
• Centrality (central position)
• Access to major trade routes within Europe
• Access to global markets through major seaports
• Rich agricultural environment
• Near coalfields and early industrialisation

Table 17.1

Case Study: The Paris City Region

France has one dominant city – Paris. Since the first settlement over 2,000 years ago, it has grown into a sprawling urban region, which covers an area of approximately 100 km in diameter. Paris is a primate city of about 10 million people, and is located at the heart of the Paris Basin, the core region of France.

The growth of this urban region can be related to:

- **Site:** The original settlement was on an island (Ile de la Cité) near the confluence (where two rivers meet) of the rivers Marne and Seine. As an important point for crossing the rivers, Paris has a long tradition as a trade, administrative and military centre.

Cereal farming in the Paris Basin.
- *Why does the rich agriculture of the Paris Basin add to the growth of Paris?*

> Remember what a **primate city** and **core region** are.

> What is the difference between **site** and **situation?**

- **Situation:** Paris is located at the centre of the rich Paris Basin, with river valleys (Seine, Marne, Oise) providing natural routes to reach a large hinterland. It is the hub of France's national and international transport systems, which connect the city to a global market.
- **Capital city:** Paris has been France's capital for over a thousand years. Many of the national government and administration offices are based there, as well as other key services such as finance and the headquarters of international firms.
- **Agriculture:** The Paris Basin is the richest farming region in France, and Paris became the major market centre for its prosperous agricultural hinterland.
- **Industry:** The wealth, centrality (central position) and labour force of the Paris city region attract a diversified (varied) range of industries, for example manufacturing vehicles and chemicals, and financial services and tourism.

Paris is one of the world's most important cities.
- *Locate and describe from the photograph the original site of Paris.*

Growth on the scale that happened in Paris brought not only wealth but also **problems** for the city region. This required careful planning to sort out problems in the city and in its hinterland.

La Défense was the first and largest of the suburban nodes planned to revitalise Paris. Today it is a modern and important centre for offices.

Problems Linked to Urban Growth in Paris	
In the City	**In the Paris Region**
• Inner-city housing is old, but is expensive due to high demand. • Overcrowded conditions and not enough recreation space • Severe traffic congestion linked to commuting • Pollution • Inner-city population is getting smaller and suburbs are growing.	• Dominance of Paris has restricted development in other places in the region. • Regional centres are comparatively small and have limited functions. • Urban area spreading out

Table 17.2

Are these problems also found in Dublin?

• *Can you suggest any reason why Disney chose a location near Paris?*

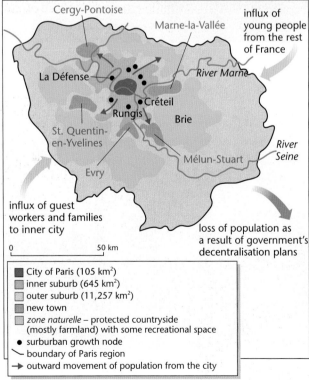

influx of young people from the rest of France

Cergy-Pontoise

Marne-la-Vallée

La Défense

River Marne

Créteil

Rungis

Brie

St. Quentin-en-Yvelines

River Seine

Mélun-Stuart

Evry

influx of guest workers and families to inner city

loss of population as a result of government's decentralisation plans

0 _____ 50 km

■ City of Paris (105 km²)
▨ inner suburb (645 km²)
▢ outer suburb (11,257 km²)
▨ new town
▨ *zone naturelle* – protected countryside (mostly farmland) with some recreational space
• surburban growth node
⌐ boundary of Paris region
→ outward movement of population from the city

Fig. 17.4 New towns around Paris

In Paris, there are **two** principal approaches to planning:
• **Promotion of major suburban nodes:** Large-scale investment has been made at **eight suburban nodes** to upgrade housing and services and create jobs. This helps accommodate population growth within the city, improves the quality of life for the citizens and reduces commuting distances.
• **New towns:** To help control the way that population spreads out from Paris, **five new towns** were created along two axes to the north and south of the Seine (see Fig. 17.4). Since 1975, these towns have grown, until each has over 100,000 people. The fact that Euro Disneyland was built east of the new town of Marne-la-Vallée highlights the growth in this part of the Paris conurbation.

To offset the dominance of Paris in its region, planners have encouraged growth around a number of other cities in the Paris Basin. These include Rouen, Orléans and Reims. Transport links between these cities and the capital have been improved, and they have been revitalised as centres for employment, services and culture. This is important because a more balanced urban structure reduces the pressure on Paris, while raising living standards throughout the Paris Basin.

Explain why a more balanced urban structure helps development in the Paris urban regions.

202

SECTION 5 (CHAPTERS 18–21)
THE DYNAMICS OF A REGION

In the section Regions you saw how regions were described by using different physical and human processes. Regions were defined using one major aspect.

To discover more about regions, it is important to realise that within any region there is a complex range of processes that act on each other. Physical aspects affect what humans do. Mountains or rivers may influence the crops people grow or where they build a town or city. This has an impact on the way people live and the cultures that develop. In turn, what humans do can have a strong effect on the physical environment around them.

This section shows how the economic, human and physical processes work together to give a region its identity. Examples of four regions are used to help you understand how these processes interact.

- Chapter 18   Ireland: Contrasts Between East and West
- Chapter 19   The Mezzogiorno
- Chapter 20   Norrland
- Chapter 21   India

A busy street in Dublin

Forest in Norrland

Dry mountain area in the Mezzogiorno

Street traffic in India

CHAPTER 18
IRELAND: CONTRASTS BETWEEN EAST AND WEST

KEY IDEA!

The way human and physical processes interact gives rise to major contrasts between the east and west of Ireland.

Ireland is a relatively small island economy off the west coast of continental Europe. It forms part of the European Union's underdeveloped Atlantic periphery (see Chapter 15).

Even in a country as small as the Republic of Ireland (70,000 km²) there are many different landscapes, cultures and levels of development. Traditionally, there have been strong differences between a more prosperous eastern part of Ireland and the more marginalised western regions.

Why do you think the Southern and Eastern Region lost its Objective 1 status?

Under Ireland's National Development Plan 2000-06, the country's regional divisions have been redefined to help receive structural funding from the EU. The new Border, Midland and West (BMW) Region is for the less developed economy of western Ireland, which needs to keep its Objective 1 status. This contrasts with the more prosperous Southern and Eastern (S & E) Region, which has lost its Objective 1 status.

PHYSICAL PROCESSES

The relief, climate, soils and drainage of Ireland have a strong impact on the country's economic development and patterns of human activities, such as urban settlement.

If you look at the **relief,** it is something like a saucer shape: a broad central lowland area surrounded by a broken rim of higher land (see Fig. 18.1).

The **climate** is influenced mainly by its island location and onshore south-westerly winds, which bring mild temperatures all year round and annual precipitation (rainfall) that is well distributed around the country. There is a dense drainage pattern of lakes and rivers, together with a wide variety of soil types. While these patterns are general to Ireland, there are important differences between the western and eastern regions.

Glacially eroded mountains in Connemara.
● *Do such areas provide a good basis for farming?*

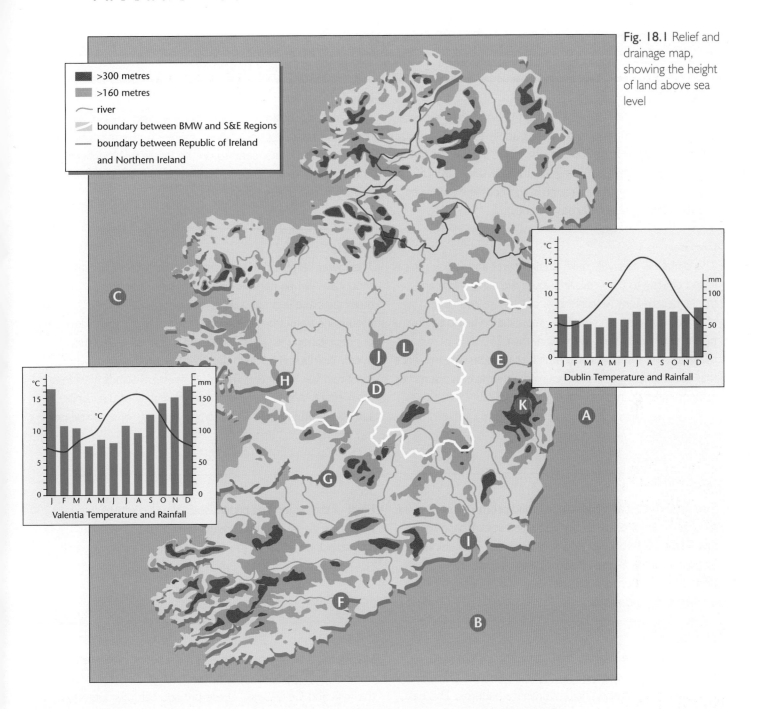

Fig. 18.1 Relief and drainage map, showing the height of land above sea level

Legend:
- >300 metres
- >160 metres
- river
- boundary between BMW and S&E Regions
- boundary between Republic of Ireland and Northern Ireland

Dublin Temperature and Rainfall

Valentia Temperature and Rainfall

Class Activity

Look at the map in Fig. 18.1 and and answer the following:

1. Name the:
   a. sea areas A, B and C.
   b. rivers D and E.
   c. towns F, G, H, I and J.
   d. upland area K.
   e. lowland area L.
2. Why is 'saucer shape' a useful way to describe Ireland's physical relief?
3. Why is drainage so poor in the Central Lowlands?
4. Look at the climographs for Dublin and Valentia. Does Dublin have a greater temperature range than Valentia? Explain your answer.
5. Why does Valentia have higher levels of rainfall than Dublin? Explain your answer.

205

Relief, Climate, Soil and Drainage	
Border, Midland and West Region	**Southern and Eastern Region**
Relief Much of the region has bleak, rugged upland areas, especially along the western seaboard where glacially-eroded mountain ranges rise higher than 300 metres. Inland areas form the western part of the undulating Central Lowlands (50-150 m). In general, the region has a submerged coastline that gives rise to a deeply indented coastal zone.	**Relief** The Central Lowlands generally have a larger area of low-lying and undulating landscapes. There is a mountainous area in the Leinster chain, centred on the Wicklow Mountains. The coastline tends to be less indented (jagged) and is more low-lying than the west coast.
Climate The climate is relatively mild, but very wet and windy. This is linked directly to the prevailing south-westerly winds and frontal depressions, which are forced to rise over the mountainous western coastline. Precipitation levels can be higher than 1,500 mm, with more than 250 days of rain in the year. The North Atlantic Drift has a moderating influence that keeps winter temperatures mild, while average summer temperatures do not rise much above 15°C.	**Climate** The lower relief and the rainshadow effect of the western mountains (when rain-bearing winds blow towards mountains and less rain falls on the other side of the mountains away from the wind) result in much lower levels of precipitation (less than 1,000 mm). Rainfall is also more evenly distributed through the year than in the West where most rain falls in winter. The south-westerly winds have less of an effect. Winter temperatures are slightly colder, while summer temperatures and average amounts of sunshine per day are higher.
Soils The upland relief and high, year-round precipitation give rise to large areas of peaty and waterlogged soils. These have low fertility, with blanket bog in many areas. The unique landscape of the Burren in Co. Clare is where the underlying Carboniferous Limestone of the Central Lowlands is exposed.	**Soils** Most of the region has brown soils, derived mostly from the limestone glacial drift that covers the Central Lowlands. These include some of the most fertile soils in the country.
Drainage Large areas of the West of Ireland have poor drainage. As well as upland bogs, glacial deposition on the Central Lowlands has disturbed natural drainage patterns. This has given rise to many lakes and poorly drained river flood plains, leading, for example, to flooding along the Shannon River. Apart from the Shannon, few major rivers reach the west coast.	**Drainage** In general, drainage patterns are much better, as there are a number of large rivers, which flow through the region into the Irish and Celtic Seas. These provide natural routeways and, at their mouths, important urban centres and ports have developed, e.g. Dublin, Waterford and Cork.

Table 18.1

ECONOMIC PROCESSES

The Industrial Revolution had little impact on Ireland, and its economy depended on the primary sector for much longer than most countries in Western Europe. During the 1960s, the country began its own industrial revolution based mainly on attracting a lot of foreign industries. This has been a key factor in the success of the Celtic Tiger economy in the 1990s. Employment in services has also grown rapidly (see Fig. 18.2), although the level of development varies between the west and east of Ireland.

Why should the growth of industries also encourage growth in services?

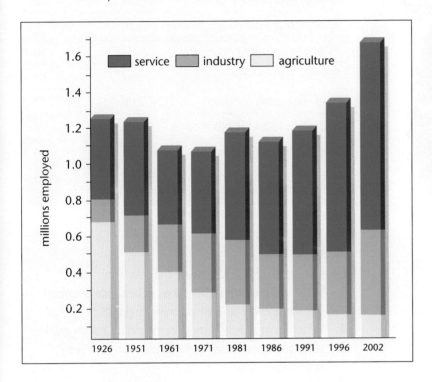

Activity

Look at Fig. 18.2 and answer the following:
1. What was the most important sector in 1926?
2. What has been the trend for this sector since 1926?
3. Which sector is most important for employment in 2002?
4. Why has this sector grown so strongly since the 1960s?

Fig. 18.2 Ireland's employment structure, 1926-2002

The Primary Sector
Agriculture

'Agriculture is the most important single industry in the economy in the Republic of Ireland. The agri-food sector generates about one-third of the Republic's net foreign earnings and employs one out of every eight people in the workforce. On the total land area of approximately 7 million hectares, almost 5 million hectares are used for agricultural purposes, including forestry. Historically, the fortunes of the Irish people have been closely linked to life on the land. Furthermore, in the present context of the Republic's participation in the European Union, the implications for its agricultural economy are a major consideration in the way Ireland negotiates its international trading relationships.'

Irish Agriculture in Transition, 1999

Although agriculture is very important for Ireland, the trends and types of farming vary within the country. The way land is used highlights how physical factors can shape the agricultural geography of Ireland (see Fig. 18.3). The differences between the west and east of the country can also be seen from data for the West and Mid-East planning regions (see Table 18.2).

207

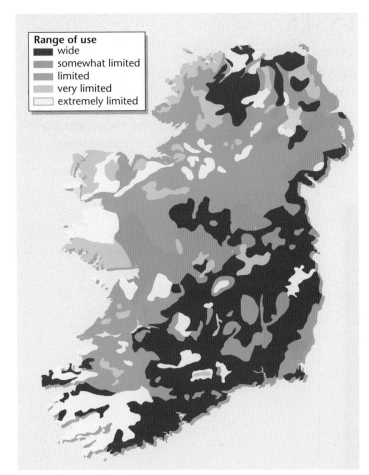

Range of use
- wide
- somewhat limited
- limited
- very limited
- extremely limited

Fig. 18.3 Land-use capability in Ireland

- *Which regions in general can support the widest choice and most productive farming?*

Key Agricultural Indicators in the West and the Mid-East Planning Regions of Ireland		
	West	Mid-East
Number of farms	38,960	11,630
Average farm size (ha)	18.4	36.0
% farmers over 65 years	29	21
% farm land under pasture	54	52
% farmland under rough grazing	20	6
% farmland under crops	1	18
Tractors per 10 farms	6.7	10.4
% of state totals for dairy	6	7
% of state totals for other cattle	16	9
% of state totals for sheep	25	14
% of state totals for wheat	0.2	33

Table 18.2

Activity

Look at Table 18.2 and answer the following:
1. What are the main differences in land use between the West and Mid-East planning regions?
2. Which farm activity is most common on rough grazing?
3. Why are there more older farmers in the West? Is this a problem?
4. Which region has larger, more mechanised farms?

Traditional farming in the West of Ireland provides only low income to most farmers. This contrasts with intensive farming in eastern Ireland.

- *Do the photographs support this contrast?*

Agriculture in Western and Eastern Ireland	
Border, Midland and West Region	Southern and Eastern Region
• Difficult environmental conditions limit how productive the land can be for agriculture (see Fig. 18.3 on page 208). Despite this, 63 per cent of Irish farms are located in the BMW region. • The average farm size is small, levels of mechanisation low and a high proportion of farmers are older. • Tillage is not suitable for most of the region. Grazing is dominant, with beef cattle and sheep rearing. • Farming is widespread, but income levels are low. Poor prospects in the sector add to problems of rural depopulation and underdevelopment. • Average farm income is only 50 per cent that of the eastern region, and only 14 per cent of farms can be considered viable, full-time units.	• A favourable natural environment encourages a wide range of productive agriculture. • Although the region is more urbanised, farming remains an important economic activity. • To be competitive, farms are more mechanised, larger and have a higher percentage of younger, more innovative farmers. • Highly productive arable and pastoral activities occur throughout the region. Sheep and cattle reared in the West are often fattened on these lowland pastures. • Farming is intensive and specialised, giving better income levels and prospects for rural communities. • Average farm income is 40 per cent above the national level.

Table 18.3

Activity

Look at Table 18.3 and answer the following:
1. What causes income levels to be so low in the West of Ireland?
2. Why is average income so high in eastern Ireland?

Why is the West of Ireland not suitable for arable farming?

What is the difference between intensive and extensive farming?

Forestry

About 50 per cent of Ireland's land can be classified as marginal for agriculture, but environmental conditions are more suitable for forestry. A long growing season, well-distributed rainfall and mild temperatures give an average growth rate of trees estimated at three to five times as high as in continental Europe.

Despite this favourable environment, less than 10 per cent of the country is forested. The reasons for this are:
- Irish farms are generally small.
- In the past, farmers have not been keen to give up land for trees.
- Forestry involves high costs at first and requires a long-term view while trees are growing.

Since the 1980s, both state and private interests in forestry have increased. This has been aided by the EU, which sees forestry as a profitable, alternative enterprise for farmers, especially in more marginal agricultural areas. The environmental benefits of forestry (including drainage control, wildlife habitat, scenic qualities) have also been highlighted to help promote a stronger 'tree culture' within Ireland. State policy is to have 15 per cent of land under forestry, with most of the extra areas planted to be in the western regions.

209

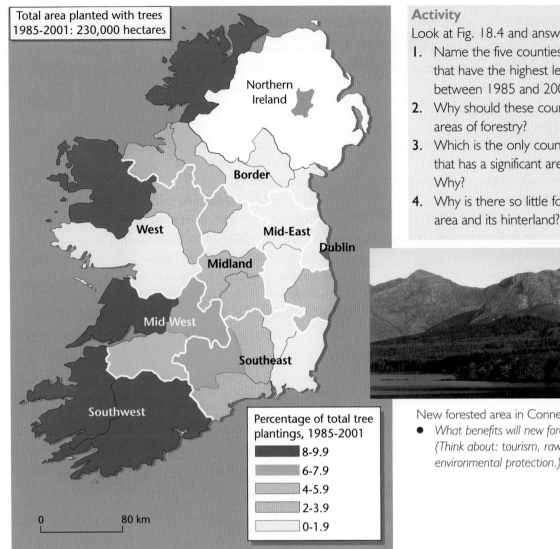

Total area planted with trees
1985-2001: 230,000 hectares

Percentage of total tree
plantings, 1985-2001

- 8-9.9
- 6-7.9
- 4-5.9
- 2-3.9
- 0-1.9

0   80 km

Fig. 18.4 Tree planting distribution in Ireland, 1985-2001, as a percentage of the total

Activity

Look at Fig. 18.4 and answer the following:

1. Name the five counties in the west and south that have the highest levels of forestry planted between 1985 and 2001.
2. Why should these counties be suitable for large areas of forestry?
3. Which is the only county along the east coast that has a significant area given over to forestry? Why?
4. Why is there so little forestry in the Dublin area and its hinterland?

New forested area in Connemara.
- *What benefits will new forest areas like this have? (Think about: tourism, raw materials, jobs and environmental protection.)*

Fishing

Although the continental shelf around Ireland is an extremely rich fishing area, the country's fishing industry is underdeveloped. Part of the reason for this is the historic fact that Irish people have tended to look more to the land than the sea for their identity and for earning a living. The fishing industry has, therefore, been small-scale and spread around a large number of small harbours.

The importance of fishing as an industry that creates jobs and wealth for regional development has increased recently with the growing market demand for fish products. Unfortunately, problems of overfishing, and restrictions under the EU Common Fisheries Policy have reduced the opportunities for large-scale development of this industry in Ireland.

Despite problems of overfishing and EU fishing quotas, the number of full-time fishermen and the quantity of fish landed at Irish ports have increased. There is also more aquaculture (fish and seafood farming) around Ireland's coastline, bringing more jobs and income from the fishing industry.

In Norway, people turned to the sea because the land is mountainous and the climate is difficult for farming. Contrast this pattern with Ireland.

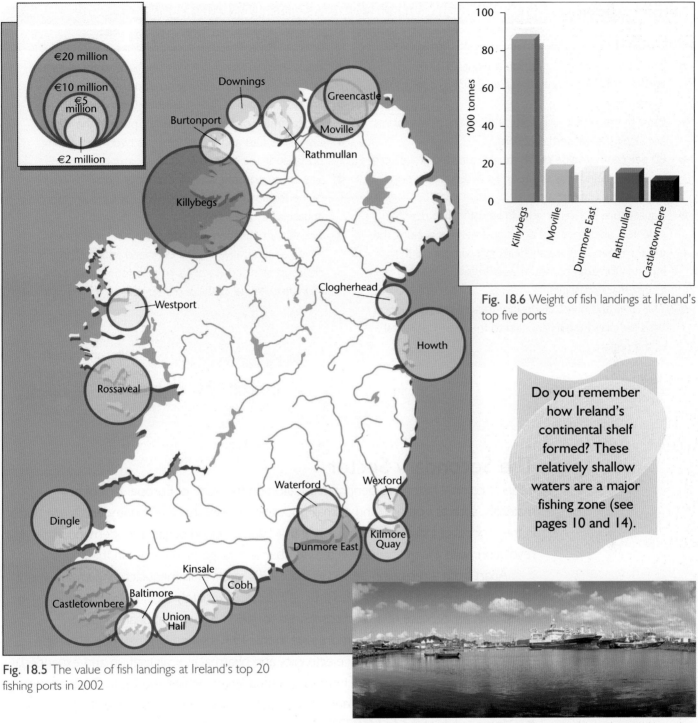

Fig. 18.6 Weight of fish landings at Ireland's top five ports

Fig. 18.5 The value of fish landings at Ireland's top 20 fishing ports in 2002

Do you remember how Ireland's continental shelf formed? These relatively shallow waters are a major fishing zone (see pages 10 and 14).

Modern fishing vessels in Killybegs, Ireland's largest port

Activity

Look at Figs. 18.5 and 18.6 and answer the following:

1. Which is Ireland's most important fishing port?
2. How many of the top 20 fishing ports by value of fishing catch are on the west and south-west coast?
3. Why is the fishing industry concentrated along the western rather than the eastern coast of Ireland?
4. Can you suggest any reasons why the top five fishing ports by weight are not the same as the top five ports measured by value of fish landed?

Why are the South West and Connemara coasts ideal for aquaculture?

Fishing in the Border, Midland and West and Southern and Eastern Regions

Border, Midland and West Region	Southern and Eastern Region
• The deeply indented coastline provides sheltered harbours and faces onto the large fishing grounds of the North Atlantic. • Most of Ireland's fishing ports and fish processing plants are along the western seaboard. • 80 per cent by value of fish caught is landed at western ports. Killybegs is, by far, Ireland's largest fishing port, followed by Castletownbere. • Aquaculture is a major growth industry. The deeply indented, sheltered and pollution-free waters along the western seaboard are an ideal environment for this industry, for example south west Ireland and the Connemara coastline. • The lakes and rivers of western Ireland provide a good basis for inland fishing and add to the tourist potential of the region.	• Boats from ports on the Irish Sea have to travel further to access deepwater fishing grounds. • Smaller number of fishing ports as the industry concentrates on larger, specialised ports in the West. • Dunmore East and Howth are the two major fishing ports along the eastern seaboard. • The more polluted waters, especially along the coastline of the Irish Sea, limit opportunities for large-scale aquaculture. • Greater urbanisation and pollution along major rivers have had a negative impact on inland fishing. The clean-up of inland waters is helping to improve the tourism potential of these resources.

Table 18.4

Why are eastern waters more polluted than western coastal waters?

The Secondary Sector

Ireland's colonial history, its peripheral location on the edge of Europe, lack of raw materials, such as iron ore, and a small population meant that the country was a late starter in the process of industrialisation. During the 1960s, Ireland began a modern industrial revolution, with a large increase in the number and range of industries in the country.

Apart from a recession period in the 1980s, growth in manufacturing employment has been impressive (see Fig. 18.7). By 2002, approximately 228,000 were working in this sector, an increase of a third compared to 1961. By international standards, developments were especially impressive in the 1990s when large numbers of high-technology industries (especially electronics and pharmaceuticals) set up and expanded production facilities in Ireland. This was a central factor behind the Celtic Tiger economy. The factors that account for Ireland's successful programme of industrialisation are:

● Membership of the EU (1973).

● Improved transport and communication systems.

● Larger and developing urban areas provide a better range of essential services, e.g. banking, education and marketing.

● A growing and well-educated labour force.

● Government policy.

Government policy has been very important. Generous incentives, especially low levels of corporation (business profits) tax have encouraged a large number of foreign companies to come to Ireland. These include many high-growth, high-technology industries, such as Intel, Dell, Pfizer, and are essential to Ireland's economic well-being.

By 2002, almost 50 per cent of the country's manufacturing employment was foreign-owned.

Although Ireland has benefited from these trends, there are large differences between the west and east.

The large Intel plant at Leixlip, Co. Kildare, is one of many high-tech industries attracted to Ireland.

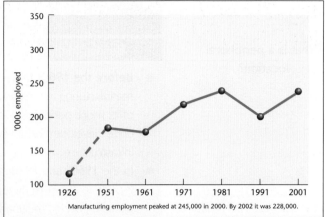

Manufacturing employment peaked at 245,000 in 2000. By 2002 it was 228,000.

Fig. 18.7 Employment trends in Ireland's manufacturing Industries, 1926-2001

Activity

Look at Fig. 18.7 and answer the following:
1. Estimate the total of people working in manufacturing in Ireland in 1926. Compare this with 2002.
2. Was there growth in manufacturing employment throughout the period from 1926 to 2002?
3. Do the 1990 figures justify Ireland being called the Celtic Tiger economy?

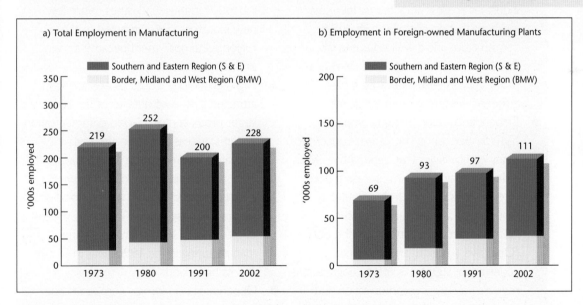

Fig. 18.8 Regional trends in manufacturing employment, 1973–2002

Activity

Look at Fig. 18.8 and answer the following:
1. Which of the two regions is most important for manufacturing?
2. What percentage of jobs is in foreign-owned industries in Ireland in 1973 and in 2002? Why is this a concern for Ireland?
3. What differences do you note between the two regions between 1980 and 1991. Explain your answer.
4. Why should the S & E region gain many more jobs than the BMW region in the 1990s?

Look back to Fig. 18.1 on page 205 to see the areas of Ireland covered by these two regions.

213

Employment in Manufacturing in Border, Midland and West Region and Southern and Eastern Region	
Border, Midland and West Region	**Southern and Eastern Region**
• **Before the 1960s** there was very little manufacturing in western Ireland because of its more peripheral location and underdeveloped urban system and infrastructure. • In the **1960s** and **1970s** there was rapid growth in industrial development. Branch plants of foreign multinationals chose to locate factories in rural areas because of cheaper costs of land and labour. Government incentives also encouraged firms to locate in the western regions. • **During the 1980s**, jobs in manufacturing were created at a much slower rate. While there were still government incentives to attract new industries, many uncompetitive branch plants closed or reduced their workforce. • This region benefited less from **the Celtic Tiger economy**. High-technology industries are less attracted by low-cost locations that do not offer high quality infrastructure and a well-educated labour force. The university city of Galway is a major growth centre because it has attracted modern growth industries. • Dependence upon foreign companies is high (51 per cent). This causes concern for many communities that depend heavily on a single foreign company, in case it decides to close or run down Irish operations when global competition increases. • Access to structural funds from the EU (Objective 1 region) and continued government support is vital to upgrade this region's transport, communication and general urban facilities to make it more attractive for modern growth industries.	• Most of the country's limited industry was in major urban centres such as Dublin and Cork, with large population, infrastructure and access to ports for trade. **By 1961**, over half of the country's manufacturing was in the East region centred on Dublin. • The higher costs of locating in larger urban areas, together with government policy to spread development away from the more prosperous eastern regions, led to lower growth in manufacturing activity in the 1970s. The East region, however, remained dominant with almost 40 per cent of the country's employment in manufacturing. • The **1980s** was a very difficult decade for the region. Older traditional industries, such as textiles and clothing, were concentrated in large urban centres, especially Dublin. There were very large job losses in these industries, while few new industries were attracted to the region. Unemployment became a major problem. • High-technology industries are strongly attracted by the advantages of the country's larger urban centres. Good communication systems, access to universities and educated workers, international transport links, such as airports and ferry services, and recreational facilities are key locational factors for these growth industries. Almost 60 per cent of Ireland's net growth in manufacturing in the **1990s** was in Dublin and its hinterland. • Dependence on foreign companies has increased to more than in the western region. This leaves the region open to potential problems if there is a global or US recession. • The future prospects for continued industrial development are good. The higher value aspects of modern industries, such as research and development, must be promoted better.

What is a peripheral location?

What is a branch factory?

Have any industries closed in your area? What impact did this have?

Why should Galway emerge as a good location for modern industry?

What does 'dependence' mean?

Table 18.5

The Tertiary Sector

The tertiary sector is made up of activities that provide services rather than producing goods. Since the Second World War (1939-1945), the service sector has become more important and now forms the main economic activity in all developed economies.

Growth in Ireland's service sector has been slower than in most other developed economies. This was linked to the country's underdeveloped economy and having many people with low income levels, which reduced the demand for services. Since the 1960s, however, Ireland's successful economic take-off and the higher living standards of a growing population have encouraged rapid growth in services. In 1981, Ireland became defined as a service economy when, for the first time, more than half the working population was employed in the tertiary sector. By 2002, approximately 70 per cent of all employment was in services, and during the 1990s four out of every five jobs created was in this sector.

Developments in services have been different depending on the region. Service industries prefer major urban centres, which have good access to large and prosperous markets. The country's western regions have therefore benefited less than the more urbanised eastern regions in developments within the service sector.

> Ireland became a service economy in 1981.

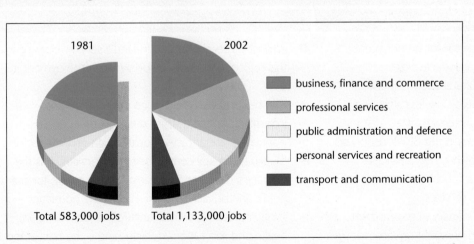

1981   2002

- business, finance and commerce
- professional services
- public administration and defence
- personal services and recreation
- transport and communication

Total 583,000 jobs   Total 1,133,000 jobs

Fig.18.9 Changes in Ireland's service sector, 1981–2002

> Why are service industries located mostly in larger towns and cities?

Activity
Look at Fig. 18.9 and answer the following:
1. Calculate the growth of jobs in services between 1981 and 2002.
2. Which service sector has the most jobs in 1981 and in 2002?
3. Why are business, finance, commercial and professional services so important for a modern economy?
4. Why do you think that there has been a large increase in the number of people working in personal services and recreation?

Since its development in the 1980s, the IFSC (International Financial Services Centre) has become a major employer and landmark of inner-city Dublin.

Although the capital has problems, do you think it is easy to get civil servants to leave Dublin and relocate to the West of Ireland? Explain your answer.

The growth potential of services was recognised by Ireland's government in 1981. Eleven service industries were identified as having excellent prospects in international trade and were given the full range of state incentives.

The three most important of these **internationally traded services (ITS)** are:

- computer software development
- data processing (including telesales)
- international financial services.

Each of these sectors has received large inflows of foreign money. By 2002, some 56,500 jobs were available in ITS. This was an increase of almost six times in 10 years. Ireland has also emerged as second only to the US in exporting computer software.

Greater Dublin has benefited most from ITS. Its well-developed communication systems have been vital in attracting data-processing operations, while the concentration of third-level education facilities has attracted computer-software companies. One of the most notable new developments in Dublin has been the **International Financial Services Centre**, which has helped to rejuvenate Dublin's inner city.

Outside Dublin, other regional centres such as Cork, Limerick and Galway have also experienced growth in ITS.

Services in the Border, Midland and West and Southern and Eastern Regions	
Border, Midland and West Region	**Southern and Eastern Region**
• Dependence on the service sector for employment (60 per cent) is less than the national average. • The more rural society, agricultural economy and lower average levels of prosperity are less attractive for large-scale developments in services. • Apart from Galway, most towns in the BMW region do not provide a good range of high-quality services. Many people commute to cities such as Cork, Limerick and Dublin to access services. • Decentralising service jobs, especially in government departments, has aided growth in some regional centres, e.g. moving the Department of Education to Athlone. • The underdeveloped service sector is an important factor for future development. Improving quality of life for the region's population requires easier access to essential services.	• Almost three-quarters of Ireland's service jobs are in this region. Dependence on service employment is over 70 per cent. • The region's well-developed urban areas and infrastructure and a large, relatively prosperous population are attractive for this high-growth sector. • Dublin is the key centre for many services. It is the country's capital and decision-making centre for many public and private enterprises. It is the dominant shopping centre, with a range of major education, health and recreational facilities and is the hub of the country's transport system. • Planners have tried to decentralise service jobs from Dublin because of problems of higher costs and traffic congestion. In spite of this, the attractions of the capital-city region mean it is still growing quickly. • The service economy of regional centres and larger market towns must be built up to act as more effective counter-poles to Dublin.

Table 18.6

Tourism

Tourism is part of the service sector and is one of Ireland's main growth industries. In 2002:

- 5.9 million foreign tourists visited Ireland.
- There were also 5.9 million trips by Irish tourists.
- Total foreign earnings were €3.9 billion.
- Total tourist revenue was €4.9 billion.
- Tourism provided the equivalent of 141,000 full-time jobs.

Over 60 per cent of tourist revenue is spent in **the Southern and Eastern region**. This is linked to air access (93 per cent of the scheduled air flights to Ireland go to Dublin), and all ferry port access is in this region. Dublin benefits from this gateway function, and together with its cultural and historic attractions accounts for a quarter of all tourist revenue.

The Border, Midland and West (BMW) region has many advantages for tourism: scenic landscapes, historic monuments and cultural tradition. Despite this, the industry remains underdeveloped and grew less in the 1990s than the Southern and Eastern region. While the BMW region has 52 per cent of tourist bed capacity, it generates less than 40 per cent of the country's tourist revenue.

There are **two** problems for tourism in the **BMW region:**

- Direct **access** to the region for foreign visitors is limited and more expensive than for the S & E region.
- While **seasonality** of tourism in Ireland is high, it is especially strong in the BMW region. Most visitors come in July and August.

Major efforts are needed to improve access to the BMW region and provide facilities for tourists that would generate a greater year-round industry, for example, conferences, leisure activities (golf, fishing) and cultural events.

> What is meant by seasonality? Why is it high in the BMW region?

- *Use this photo to suggest why tourists are attracted to the West of Ireland, and what benefits they might bring to the local economy.*

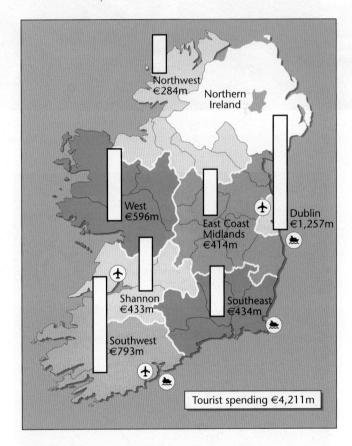

Fig. 18.10 Tourist revenue in Ireland by Bord Fáilte planning regions (in euros)

Activity

Look at Fig. 18.10 and answer the following:

1. Which region generates the most revenue from tourism? Why?
2. What advantages does the West of Ireland have for tourism?
3. Why should the tourism revenue be so low in the north west?

217

The M50 ring road and the Blanchardstown interchange in Dublin.
- *Use the photo to suggest how such road improvements have assisted the development and expansion of the city.*

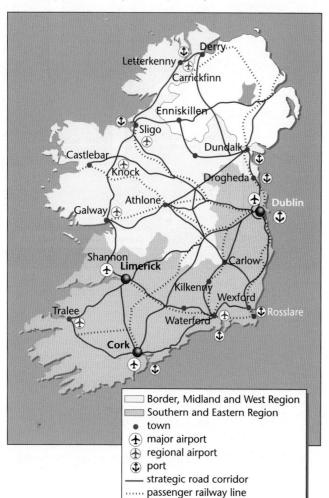

Border, Midland and West Region
Southern and Eastern Region
● town
⊕ major airport
⊕ regional airport
⚓ port
— strategic road corridor
····· passenger railway line

Transport

Successful socio-economic development depends, to a large extent, on an efficient transport system. Until the 1980s, Ireland's internal and external transport infrastructures were poorly developed. This added greatly to the country's problems of being a periphery and its difficulty in accessing EU and world markets. With the help of structural funds from the EU, the country's transport systems have been improved.

The transport system will be further improved under the country's National Development Plan 2000-2006. This allocates €10 billion, mainly to upgrade the country's national road system. Strategic road corridors across the country will allow for more effective links between regions. Improved port facilities will be important for more efficient import and export of goods.

The Southern and Eastern region has more developed transport systems than the BMW region (see Fig. 18.11):

- Apart from the Shannon Estuary, it has all of the country's major ports.
- It has two of the three major international airports
- National rail network converges on Dublin.
- The national road network and strategic corridors focus on Dublin.
- Despite severe congestion in Dublin's transport system, the S & E region has a greater choice, a lower cost and more efficient transport system than operates over most of the BMW region.

Fig. 18.11 Transport in Ireland

218

Human Processes

The human geography of the island of Ireland varies greatly. One clear regional difference is the political-cultural divide that exists between Northern Ireland and the Republic. There are also many contrasts between the west and east of the Republic. These are linked to the physical and economic processes already outlined in this chapter. These differences can also be seen in population dynamics, the rural-urban divide and the level of development (see Tables 18.7 and 18.8 and Fig. 18.12).

Human Factors in the Border, Midland and West and Southern and Eastern Regions	
Border, Midland and West Region	Southern and Eastern Region
• The population has gone down for most of the twentieth century because of underdevelopment and the problematic environment of the region. Recent growth is less than in eastern regions.	• Throughout the twentieth century the region has increased its share of national population (see Fig. 18.12).
• Although it covers 60 per cent of the country, it has only a third of the country's population.	• A densely settled region: the density of population is three times that of the BMW region.
• There are few large towns. Two-thirds of the population live in rural areas.	• It has a well-developed and more balanced distribution of urban centres. Almost three-quarters of people live in urban areas.
• Galway is the only urban centre, with more than 50,000 people. It is the region's dominant town.	• Dublin is the country's major city, with 1.3m people. Cork, Limerick and Waterford are important regional centres, all with populations over 50,000.
• A lot of people have migrated from the region to the rest of Ireland and abroad. With the better circumstances in the 1990s, there has been a net inflow (more arriving than leaving) of migrants and retirees, especially to Galway City and its hinterland.	• It has received a lot of migrants from the rest of the country, who were attracted by the job opportunities in Dublin.
• Only one of Ireland's seven universities is in the region. Most students have to leave for further education, and only 13 per cent of students graduating find a job in the region. This could be called a **brain drain** and is an important problem for the West of Ireland.	• An estimated 86 per cent of Ireland's third-level places are in the region. Almost all students wishing to enter further education can find a place in their home region. A variety of good quality jobs also means that almost 90 per cent of graduates find employment in the Southern and Eastern Region.
• Problems of migration are linked to the region having more older people in the population. Over 18 per thousand of the population in Connaught are aged over 60 years. Death rates are 10.8 per thousand.	• The population is younger, with only 14 per cent aged over 60 years. Birth rates in Leinster (14.4 per thousand) are higher than in Connaught (12.9 per thousand), while death rates are lower (7.8 per thousand).
• The value of output created in the region is only a quarter that of the rest of Ireland.	• The concentration of high value-added (where processing adds to the price manufacturers get for their products) industries and services allows this region to be the largest contributor to national output. It provides an above average income level for its population.
• The BMW region is an Objective 1 region in the EU because it is underdeveloped. Structural funding will continue to be needed to support development in the region.	• The rapid economic growth in the 1990s has given this region prosperity levels above the EU average. As a result, the region lost its Objective 1 status in 2000 and will receive less financial support from the EU.
• The region is the heartland of Irish culture, with most of the Gaeltacht areas located in the region (see Chapter 14, Fig. 14.1).	• A much more cosmopolitan society and culture shows more openness to outside influences.

Table 18.7

Selected Indicators for:		
	Border, Midland and West Region	Southern and Eastern Region
Population (000)	1,038	2,879
Area (sq km)	40,873	28,715
Population per sq km	25	100
% population in urban areas	33	74
% population change 1996-2002	7.5	8.2
Natural increase 1996-2002	24,137	114,045
Output (billion euros)	14.7	45.75

Table 18.8

Where do all the students in your class plan to study or work after leaving school? Find out the main reasons for their choices.

Trinity College, Dublin, is one of several third-level educational institutions in the east of Ireland.
- *How does this benefit Dublin and the east of Ireland?*

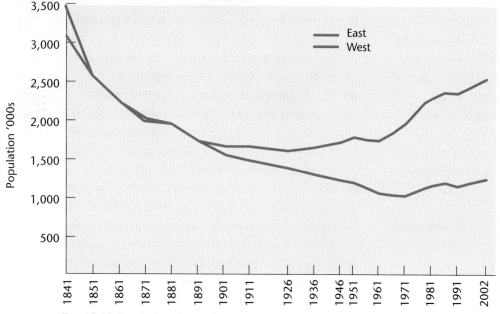

Fig. 18.12 Population changes in eastern and western Ireland, 1841–2002

Activity
Look at Table 18.8 and answer the following:
1. Although the west is a larger area than the east of Ireland, why are its population totals and densities lower?
2. What factors affect population change? Use these factors to explain why natural increase is higher in the east than in the west.
3. Calculate the per capita income for the two regions. Explain the large difference in per capita incomes between the two regions.

Why have so many young people left the West? What influence does this have on economic development?

Class Activity
Look at Fig. 18.12 and answer the following:
1. Before the Famine, which region had the most population?
2. Contrast the trends for both regions before and after 1926.
3. Briefly explain these different trends.

TEST YOURSELF AT

my-etest.com

CHAPTER 19
THE MEZZOGIORNO

KEY IDEA!

The Mezzogiorno is one of the least developed regions in the EU.

Italy is a long peninsula, shaped something like a leg and a foot that stretches down into the middle of the Mediterranean, with the island of Sicily off the southern tip. This large country has 58 million people.

Separated from the wealthy core of north-western Europe by the Alps, Italy was more or less bypassed by the Industrial Revolution in the nineteenth century. Since the Second World War (1939-1945), however, national development has been impressive. Italy became a founder-member state of the EU and is now one of the world's largest industrial economies.

Italy is a country of great contrasts. Some of Europe's most prosperous areas – centred on the cities of Milan, Turin and Genoa – are in North West Italy (see Fig. 19.1). Since the 1960s, growth has spilled over into nearby regions. The result has been a surge in prosperity and optimism in the North East and Centre region, for example, Veneto, Emilia-Romagna and Tuscany. The south of Italy is one of the poorest regions of the EU: the Mezzogiorno.

The Mezzogiorno, or 'land of the midday sun', is the part of the Italian peninsula south of Rome (see Fig. 19.1), and includes the islands of Sicily and Sardinia. This region has a long history of widespread poverty and underdevelopment and contrasts strongly with North West Italy.

Fig. 19.1 Italy's three main regions (The Three Italies)

Activity
Look at the map of Italy in Fig. 19.1 and name the:
a. neighbouring countries A, B, C and D.
b. major mountain range along Italy's northern border.
c. cities E, F, G, H, and I.
d. two islands J and K that are part of the Mezzogiorno.

PHYSICAL PROCESSES

Relief, Drainage and Soils

Southern Italy is dominated by the steep slopes of the Apennines, the mountain chain that stretches 1,050 km down the Italian peninsula. About 40 per cent of the land in the Mezzogiorno is mountainous and too steep for crops to be grown. Another 45 per cent is hilly and there are problems with soil erosion. The hilly soils have few nutrients.

The rich, fertile soils are mostly on narrow, coastal plains and valley floodplains that follow rivers flowing down from the Apennines to the coast. These include alluvial soils from river deposition and rich volcanic soils from weathered lava. Calabria, in the 'toe' of Italy, is mostly granite plateaus with poor quality soils.

The largest river is the Tiber, which enters the sea south of Rome. The remaining rivers are small, fast-flowing streams from the Apennines that often reach the sea through narrow, gorge-like channels, especially in the west. To the east, along the Plain of Apulia, there are few rivers. The bedrock is porous limestone that allows little surface drainage. The high Apennines and some other uplands are karst landscapes, as in the Burren in County Clare, where no rivers flow on the surface. Where there are rivers, water levels can be very low during the hot, dry summers in June, July and August.

Goats grazing on the poor and relatively arid landscape of the Apennines.
- *Would you describe this as subsistence farming?*

The Mezzogiorno
• 40 per cent of Italy's territory
• 36 per cent of the country's population
• 25 per cent of its GDP (Gross Domestic Product)
• 50 per cent of Italy's agricultural employment
but it has only:
• 17 per cent of industrial employment
• 70 per cent of average GDP per person

Table 19.1

Climate

Summer

High pressure dominates in summer. Winds are hot and dry, and blow as north-easterly winds from the continent of Europe. These winds blowing off the land bring drought in June, July, August and September. Temperatures are high, with averages of between 28°C and 30°C throughout the summer. This causes drought-like conditions, with intense evaporation for up to five months. Any summer rain usually falls in heavy downpours. This runs off the steep, sun-baked slopes, causing problems of gully, soil erosion and mud flows.

Winter

Winters are mild, about 17°C, and moist. South-westerly winds that blow from the Atlantic and across the Mediterranean sea bring moisture that falls as relief rain over the Apennines. Amounts vary from 900 mm to 500 mm. The lower amounts fall along the Adriatic coast because it is in the rain shadow of the Apennines.

While high summer temperatures give the region an advantage for growing specialised crops such as citrus fruits, not having enough rain is a disadvantage. This can be overcome by using irrigation, but there are problems with this. In summer, many rivers dry up, and drilling for water and transferring it over distances are expensive.

Get to know the Mezzogiorno by learning the features of southern Italy on the map. Look at your atlas as well.

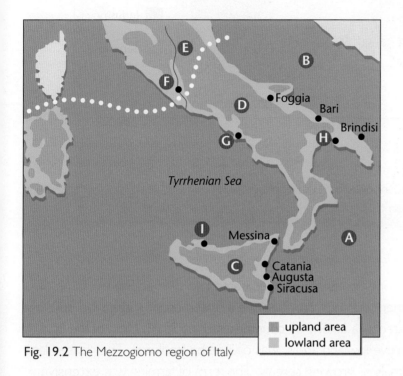

Fig. 19.2 The Mezzogiorno region of Italy

Activity

Look at Fig. 19.2 and use an atlas to identify:

a. where the main lowland areas are located.
b. sea areas A and B.
c. island C.
d. mountains D.
e. river E.
f. cities F to I.

Activity

Look at Fig. 19.3 and answer the following:

1. Which months have less than 25 mm of rain?
2. What is the temperature of the hottest month?
3. Contrast the climograph of Palermo with the one for Valentia (see Fig. 18.1, Chapter 18, page 205).
4. Explain the reasons for the differences.

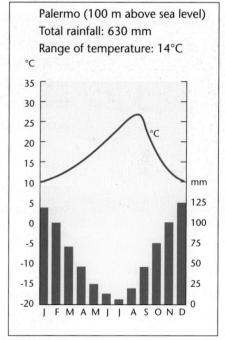

Fig. 19.3 Temperature and rainfall in Palermo, Sicily

ECONOMIC PROCESSES

The Primary Sector

By the start of the 1950s the Mezzogiorno was something like an underdeveloped country. Because people depended on a primary sector which was weak and in a difficult environment, most of the population was poor. There were some small-scale fishing activities around the coastal areas, but the once extensive forests of the Mezzogiorno had been cleared for farming and provided few prospects for jobs. Agriculture dominated the economic and social life of the Mezzogiorno (see Fig. 19.4).

223

Fig. 19.4 Employment by sector in the Mezzogiorno, 1950-2002

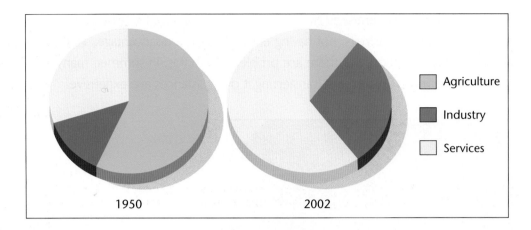

1950   2002

Agriculture

Industry

Services

Activity

Look at Fig. 19.4.

1. In which sector of the economy did most people work in 1950?
2. What have been the main changes in the Mezzogiorno economy since 1950?

Agriculture

For centuries, Italy was not one country; it was separated into different states, some of which were colonies of other countries. Italy became a united country again in 1860.

The South was exploited as a colony by countries such as Spain. Most of the land, especially the more productive lowland areas, was owned by landlords. They leased land to peasants for grazing animals or growing cereals. The form of farming was **extensive farming**, where a lot of land is used but the yield is low. It was very inefficient and provided low income for the people. This system of land use is called **latifundia.**

Latifundia are large estates owned by landlords who had little interest in investing in their land and often did not live in the area. Farming was extensive, with low-yielding cereal crops (especially wheat). Every year, farmers left some land fallow (when the land was not used for crops) to help the soil get back its productive capacity. Sheep and cattle also grazed on the estates.

To work the estates, large numbers of peasants were hired as day workers or were sharecroppers. Sharecropping is a farming system where tenant farmers pay their rent with a share of the crop. This was the main system in the South until after the Second World War.

The peasant farmers mostly lived in large, overcrowded hilltop villages. From here, many travelled to work on the latifundia, since almost half of agricultural workers owned no land. Even for the 25 per cent who owned some land, families were large and there was not enough land so holdings were often subdivided. By 1950, 70 per cent of land holdings were smaller than 3 hectares in size.

To support large families, these tiny plots of land had to be worked intensively by the peasants and their families. This often led to overgrazing and over-cultivation of the hillsides, causing soil erosion and less fertile soil. This system of farming, called **minifundia** because the plots are very small, increased the poverty of farming and the people in the Mezzogiorno.

'At the local level of individual communes, hundreds of villages were discovered (in a 1940 report) where virtually all the worthwhile farmland was in the hands of a single noble family, on whom the entire village population was ... dependent. In one village, for example, two large landholdings accounted for 97.6% of the commune's agricultural area, the remaining 311 ha being divided among 387 properties, an average of only 0.8 ha each.'
Italy, Russell King

A hilltop village in the Mezzogiorno. Note the scarcity of suitable farmland near the village to support the rural population.

Problems for Modernising Farming in the Mezzogiorno

- Difficult physical environment, often made worse by over-cultivation and overgrazing.
- Land hunger: 45 per cent of peasants owned no land.
- 25 per cent of peasants were sharecroppers, who paid up to 60 per cent of their crops in rent.
- Most of the land was in latifundia estates.
- Uneducated, traditional-minded farm population.
- Poor market outlets and transport systems.
- Low-yielding and extensive forms of farming, involving cereals, olive trees and sheep.

Table 19.2

By 1950, the Italian government realised that it was necessary to try and deal with the many problems in the Mezzogiorno's primary sector and its underdevelopment. To promote development in the Mezzogiorno the Italian government introduced the *Cassa per il Mezzogiorno* (Fund for the South). This was also supported by the European Union. At first, about 80 per cent of funding went to modernise farming, and this had some success.

Solutions to the Agricultural Problems

To introduce a more productive and intensive form of farming, **land reform** was necessary. Most of the large estates were bought by the state and the land redistributed to landless peasants. New holdings of approximately 5 hectares were created in the lowlands, but larger units (up to 50 hectares) were formed in the upland.

On the new, family-owned farms, farmers were trained to use more intensive farm methods. This involved both growing **new cash crops**, such as citrus fruits and vegetables, and producing **traditional crops more intensively**. These traditional crops included olives, vines and cereals.

The success of this **transformation** of farming depended on three related factors.

- **Irrigation:** The success of intensive farming in the region depends on a regular supply of water to compensate for summer droughts. Large amounts of money were spent on developing reservoirs, wells and irrigation systems.
- **Transport:** Improved transport, such as the *autostrada* (motorway) system, was needed to allow high value but more perishable crops to gain access to major markets such as North West Italy and Germany.

The *Cassa per il Mezzogiorno* operated until 1984. After that the Mezzogiorno received structural funds as an Objective 1 Region of the EU.

Why would upland farms need to be larger?

225

- **New towns:** When the new, family farms were created in the lowlands, many people moved from hilltop villages down to new farmhouses or villages, which were built to act as new service centres. These villages had schools, health care, leisure facilities and other services, which helped raise the **quality of life** for people living in the countryside. Processing and packaging factories were built in larger towns, which brought more jobs.

What is quality of life? Why is it important for regional development?

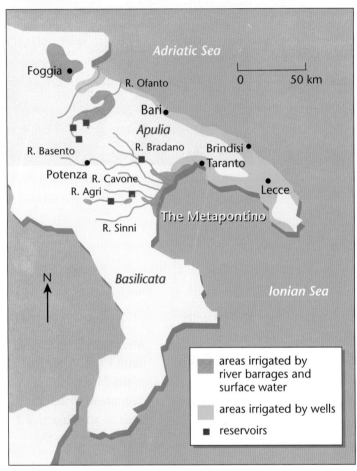

Fig. 19.5 Irrigation in Apulia and Basilicata

Land Reform in the Metapontino

The Metapontino is a coastal strip, which was originally a badly drained, malarial coastal plain. As part of the Apulia Land Reform Agency, irrigation and drainage were improved. Using the five rivers that cross the area for irrigation, a wide range of cash crops, including citrus fruits, peaches, table grapes, strawberries, flowers, salad crops and vegetables are grown.

In all, 5,000 families were settled here on farms with an average size of 6 hectares. The land is now ten times more productive than the extensive wheat and olive farming practised before. Today, this area is called Italy's 'Little California'.

Activity

Look at Fig. 19.5 and the text above and answer the following:

1. Why are rivers so important for the Metapontino?
2. What types of crops are grown in the Metapontino?
3. How many families were resettled?
4. Would you describe farming in Italy's 'Little California' as:
   a. extensive or intensive?
   b. subsistence or commercial?
   Explain your choice.

Why is irrigation essential for farming in the Mezzogiorno?

One of many new villages built in lowland areas of the Mezzogiorno as a basis for more productive agriculture.

- *Contrast this photograph with the one on page 225 in terms of the opportunities for farming.*

● *Why were the small lowland farms in the Mezzogiorno able to support more intensive agriculture, such as citrus fruit growing, and provide a better standard of living for the farmer?*

Land Reform in the Apulia and Basilicata Regions
● 200,000 hectares of land expropriated (taken legally) from 1,500 landowners and assigned (given) to 31,000 families.
● 15,000 new farmhouses were built.
● 50 service centres and new villages were built.
● 1,700 km of new roads and 7,500 new wells.

Table 19.3

Find the regions of Apulia and Basilicata in the Mezzogiorno on Fig. 19.1.

Present-day Farming Activities

Dependence on agriculture has gone down dramatically. Today, only one in ten of the region's workforce works in farming. The move to more intensive farming has also increased rural prosperity. The Mezzogiorno is a now a major supplier of citrus fruits, vegetables and olives to European markets.

The successful transformation of farming in the South happened mainly in the coastal lowlands and river valleys, where irrigation is available. In the mountain areas inland, less successful traditional and extensive forms of farming are still used. Low incomes and continued out-migration from the region are typical of the more difficult conditions in Europe's most problematic farming regions.

Why has it been more difficult to change farming in the Apennines? (Think about: environment and location.)

The Secondary Sector
Industry

By the early 1950s, only 17 per cent of Italy's industrial workforce and output were located in the Mezzogiorno. This was due to:

● Few sources of raw materials and energy supplies.
● Peripheral position and high transport costs.
● Unskilled and poorly educated labour force.
● A large but poor rural population.
● Few large towns to provide services such as banking, legal services.

Explain why **each of** these factors limits the development of industry.

227

As with agriculture, government intervention was needed to encourage the industrial take-off. From the 1960s, there was help from the *Cassa per il Mezzogiorno* and EU funding. Among the key incentives for promoting industrial growth in the South were:

● Generous grants and tax relief.

● Major improvements to the physical infrastructure, such as building an *autostrada* (motorway) system (see Fig. 19.6) and modernising key ports, such as Naples, Taranto, Siracusa.

● State-controlled companies had to make 80 per cent of new investment in the South.

● Across the South, a number of industrial development areas were created to act as a basis for regional growth.

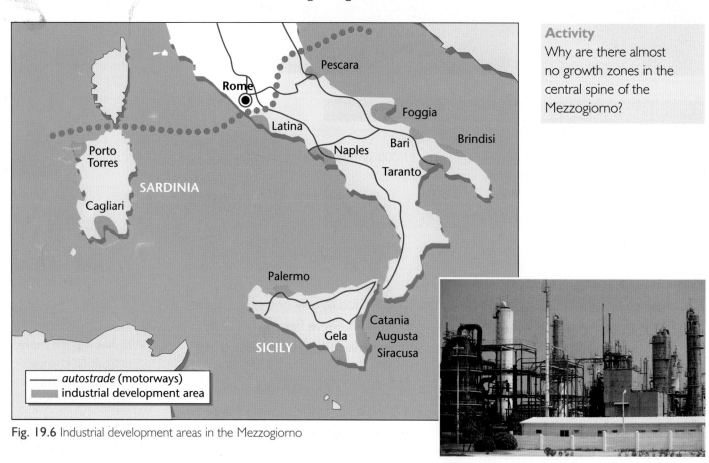

Fig. 19.6 Industrial development areas in the Mezzogiorno

Activity
Why are there almost no growth zones in the central spine of the Mezzogiorno?

Capital intensive projects such as this petrol-chemical plant at Siracusa were the basis for economic development in the Mezzogiorno.
● *Do you think these 'cathedrals in the sun' were successful in developing the problem region?*

Industrial development in the Mezzogiorno has had successes and failures. A large number of new jobs has been created. Between 1960 and 2000, the region's industrial workforce almost tripled to 1.4 million. This has reduced dependence on agriculture and encouraged growth in the service sector. Overall, the region's economy became more diversified. Despite this, unemployment is still well above the national average, while the region is poorer than the rest of Italy.

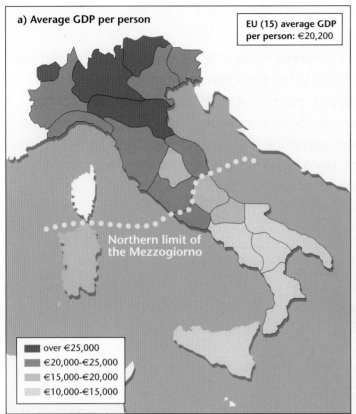
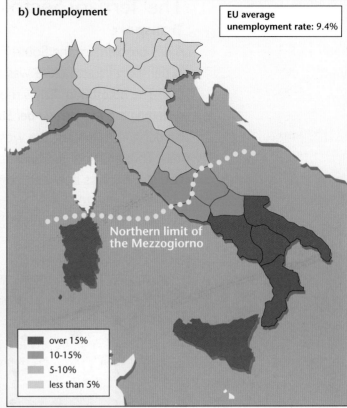

Fig. 19.7 Average GDP (gross domestic product) and unemployment levels in Italy

Class activity

Look at the two maps in Fig. 19.7 and answer the following:
1. What is the GDP per capita for most of the Mezzogiorno?
2. What levels of unemployment are typical for most of the Mezzogiorno?
3. From these maps, what are the major differences between the north of Italy and the Mezzogiorno?
4. Explain why unemployment is so high and income levels so low in the Mezzogiorno?

Almost 75 per cent of all new industrial jobs have been in large, capital-intensive sectors such as steel, chemicals and engineering. Most of these are state controlled and need a lot of investment. While each project provides many jobs, in general they have failed to create a lot of spin-off industries or jobs. This has led to the large-scale projects being called '**cathedrals in the sun**'.

While coastal zones have developed, inland areas remain depressed economically, so differences in levels of prosperity in the Mezzogiorno have increased. Some growth zones have been very successful in attracting industries. One of the best is the Bari-Brindisi-Taranto industrial triangle, where oil refining, chemicals and steel form the basis of a major industrial zone. Other successful zones are:

● around the major city of Naples
● the area immediately south of Rome in Latina
● the east coast of Sicily, centred on Siracusa.

Why are the giant new plants called 'cathedrals in the sun'?

Explain why there is a difference in prosperity levels between the coast and inland areas?

Find each of these zones on Fig. 19.6.

229

The Tertiary Sector

Transport

A key problem for the South is its peripheral location. To offset this, a major investment in transport infrastructure was needed to link the region to distant markets.

The *autostrada*, Italy's motorway system, was developed. The backbone of the system is the **Autostrada del Sole** (literally 'sunshine motorway'). It starts near the Swiss border and runs along the western side of the country, ending in Calabria in the 'toe' of Italy. This, and another *autostrada* (motorway) that runs along the east coast, provide fast, efficient links between northern and southern Italy.

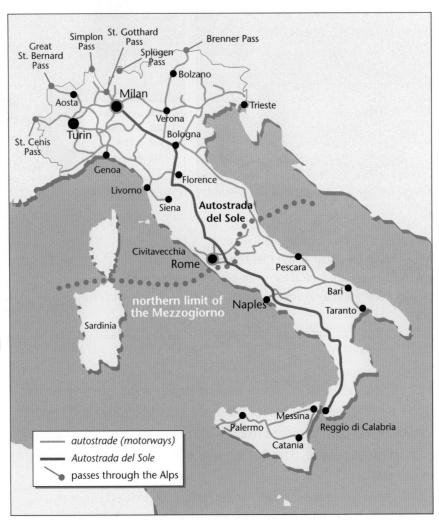

See how the major cities are linked by the Autostrada del Sole.

Fig. 19.8 Italy's *autostrada* (motorway) system

Activity

Look at Fig. 19.8 and answer the following:

1. Why are there more *autostrade* (motorways) in northern Italy than in the Mezzogiorno?
2. Why are there not many east-west *autostrada* routes across the Italian peninsula?
3. Suggest why modern motorways like the *Autostrada del Sole* are so important for the *Mezzogiorno*?

As well as upgrading the road system, large investments were made to modernise key ports. Several of the ports have become a focus around which successful growth centres have developed. These include the deepwater port at Taranto (essential for the country's largest iron and steel plant) and port developments along the east coast of Sicily, which has one of the largest oil and chemical complexes in Western Europe.

Tourism

Located within the Mediterranean Basin, the Mezzogiorno has much to offer tourists, including a hot, sunny climate, beautiful scenery, beaches and historic cities. It also tends to be cheaper and less crowded than the more commercialised tourist resorts of northern Italy and southern France.

As tourism is an international growth industry, planners for the Mezzogiorno have made great efforts to promote tourism as a basis for economic development. To achieve this, transport has been improved for easier access to the region and tourist facilities, such as hotels and recreation areas, have been upgraded.

This has been successful and the region has become more popular as a tourist destination. By 2000, over 12 million tourists visited the South, although 9 million of these were from the rest of Italy. More has to be done to raise the profile of the region with international tourists.

The *Autostrada del Sole* was constructed through very difficult landscape.
● *Why was this motorway vital for the development of the Mezzogiorno?*

Sorrento in the Bay of Naples is an important tourist centre in the Mezzogiorno. *What attractions does this area have for visitors?*

Remember almost 6 million foreign tourists visited Ireland in 2002.

HUMAN PROCESSES

The Mezzogiorno is similar to the rest of Italy in its language and religion. Italian is the language people speak and almost all of them are Roman Catholics. Rome, the centre of the Catholic religion, is located between the Mezzogiorno and the more developed northern regions.

Although the Mezzogiorno is a more rural society and economy compared to the powerful urban-industrial areas of Piedmont and Lombardy in North West Italy, the difference is closing. This is because there is strong urban growth in some Mezzogiorno areas, while the larger, long-established northern cities face problems of industrial decline.

The major differences in human processes between the North and South of Italy are now in **population trends.**

What caused the urban growth in the South? (Think about planning for industrial development.)

Population Processes

In the 1960s, the population in North West Italy greatly increased, while people continued to leave the Mezzogiorno. By the 1980s, these roles began to be reversed.

Five key factors explain these trends:

- Economic development
- Natural increase in population
- Internal migration
- Emigration
- Immigration.

Economic Development

> Think of how the *Cassa per il Mezzogiorno* and economic planning helped the South.

In the 25 years after the Second World War ended in 1945, the underdeveloped and rural-based economy of the South did not encourage population growth. This contrasted with the industrial regions of North West Italy (see Fig. 19.9). In the 1980s, traditional industries, including textiles, vehicle assembly and shipbuilding in cities such as Milan, Turin and Genoa, began to decline. This meant that the population growth in North West Italy was reduced. By this time, the South began to experience far more positive economic trends, linked to modernising agriculture and attracting new industries.

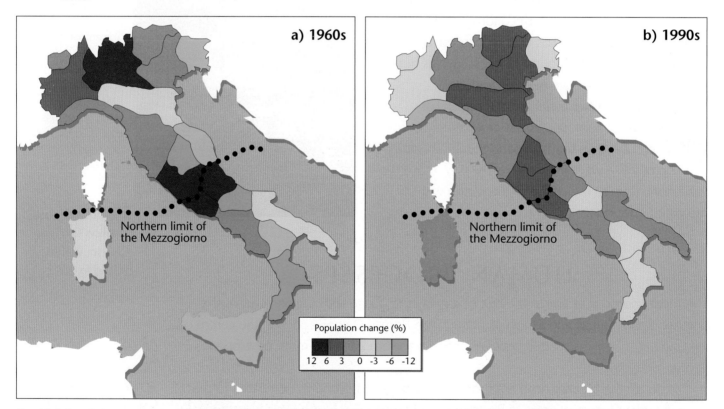

Fig. 19.9 Population changes in Italy in the 1960s and 1990s

Activity

Look at the two maps in Fig. 19.9 and answer the following:

1. What was the main trend for population change in the Mezzogiorno in the 1960s?
2. Suggest reasons for this trend, which is very different from the trend for northern Italy.
3. What are the major differences in population change in the Mezzogiorno in the 1990s compared to the 1960s?
4. Suggest reasons for these changes.

Natural Increase in Population

For a long time, a high rate of natural increase was associated with Italy because the birth rate was high. The situation has changed, and the Italian population is now not naturally replacing itself; there are not enough children being born. There are still big differences between the North and the South. This is highlighted if you compare selected provinces in both regions (see Table 19.4).

What does 'natural increase' mean?

Components of Population Change in Selected Regions of Italy in 2000 (per 000 population)		
	Birth Rate	Death Rate
North West		
Piedmont	7.4	11.5
Lombardy	8.4	9.0
Mezzogiorno		
Apulia	11.2	7.7
Campania	12.8	7.8
Mezzogiorno		
average	11.3	8.3
Italy		
average	9.7	9.8

Table 19.4

Activity

Look at Table 19.4 and answer the following:
1. Calculate the natural increase for each area.
2. What is the main difference between the North West and Mezzogiorno for each component of change?
3. Why is the birth rate higher in the Mezzogiorno?
4. What advantage do these figures for population change give the South? (Think about: age and labour force.)

Internal Migration

Internal migration is a major factor influencing population patterns in Italy (Fig. 19.10). It involves the flow of people from the countryside to cities in another part of the country, from the poor South to the richer cities of northern Italy. Between 1951 and 1971, over 4 million migrants left the South (**out-migration**) because of a number of **push factors**. Most of the people who left were attracted to cities (**in-migration**), such as Milan, Turin and Rome, by a variety of **pull factors**.

The out-migration to northern Italy continued up to the start of the 1990s; over a million people left the Mezzogiorno in the 1980s. The pull factors of northern cities have now been very much reduced, while modernisation of the South has reduced the push factors that encourage people to leave. Better job prospects in growth zones of the Mezzogiorno have reduced out-migration, but a 'trickle' of out-migration continues from this Objective 1 region because unemployment levels are still above Italy's national average.

The underdeveloped economy of the Mezzogiorno meant that large numbers of people migrated from overcrowded urban centres such as Palermo in Sicily.

Name some key cities in the Mezzogiorno growth zones.

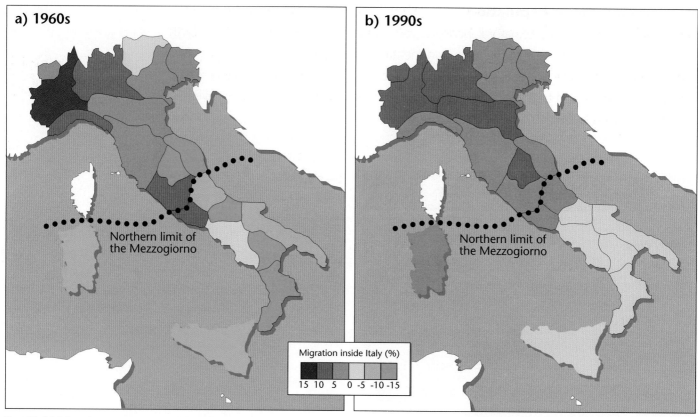

Fig. 19.10 Migration inside Italy in the 1960s and 1990s

What are **push and pull factors?** List three push and three pull factors that influenced migration from south to north in Italy.

Activity

Look at the maps in Fig. 19.10 and answer the following:

1. Was the net loss of population through migration from the Mezzogiorno larger in the 1960s than in the 1990s?
2. Suggest reasons for this.
3. Which part of the Mezzogiorno continues to have the most population loss through out-migration?
4. Compare Fig. 19.9 with Fig. 19.10. Do the migration trends help explain changes in the total population in the Mezzogiorno?

Emigration

For a long time it was a tradition in Italy for people to to go other countries, such as the USA and Germany. Since the 1970s, fewer people have left Italy (including the Mezzogiorno) because there are better job prospects in the country, and Italy's rate of natural increase has declined. For Italian people, this has **reduced the importance of push factors.**

Immigration

Since the 1980s, an increasing number of migrants from other countries have been attracted (pulled) to Italy. At first, the majority of them came from less developed countries in Africa and Asia.

234

In the 1990s, more and more people migrated to Italy from nearby countries such as Albania and the former Yugoslavia. Most of them were trying to escape from the poor economies and devastation caused by the fall of the Communist system and the outbreak of civil war in Bosnia and Kosovo. These refugees are not welcomed by the Italian (and EU) governments. It is difficult, however, to patrol all of the Italian coastline to keep out refugees who are determined to get into the country.

These migrants, or refugees, cross the narrow Adriatic Sea to get into Italy through ports along the east coast of the Mezzogiorno. Many of them see southern Italy as an easy way to enter the EU, believing that these coastal areas are less controlled than other parts of the EU. The east coast of the Mezzogiorno could be called the **'Achilles heel'** for migration into the EU.

Large numbers of refugees from Albania and other Balkan countries tried to gain entry into the EU through Italian ports such as Bari. Why?

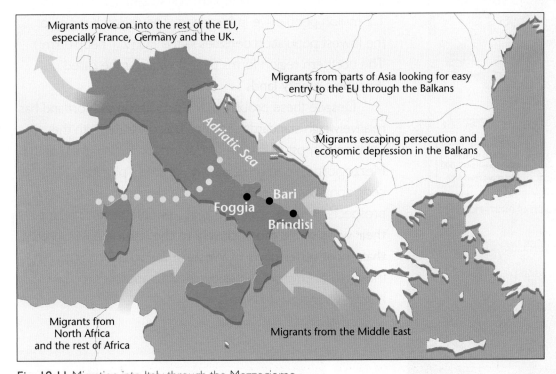

Fig. 19.11 Migration into Italy through the Mezzogiorno

Why could the east coast be called an Achilles heel? (Think about: a story in Greek mythology.)

As well as legal migration, up to 50,000 illegal migrants are estimated to enter Italy each year.

Activity

Look at Fig. 19.11 and answer the following:

1. From where do the majority of the 'new' migrants come?
2. Which part of the Mezzogiorno do they arrive in?
3. Why are these migrants interested in moving on to other EU countries?

TEST YOURSELF AT

my-etest.com

CHAPTER 20
NORRLAND

KEY IDEA!

The population of Norrland has adapted well to the extreme physical environment of this northern, peripheral region of Sweden.

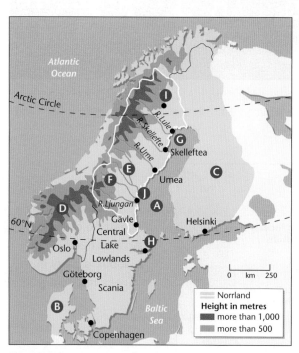

Fig. 20.1 Scandinavia and the region of Norrland

The many rivers and hydro-electric plants in Norrland provide the essential power sources for people to live and work in this region.

Norrland is the name for the region formed by Sweden's nine northern provinces. It covers almost two-thirds of Sweden and is to the north of latitude 61°N (see Fig. 20.1).

The region forms a major part of Europe's northern periphery. It is separated from both national and EU core regions by long distances. Although it covers an area as large as the United Kingdom (approximately 246,000 km²), only 1.2 million people live in Norrland. The region has one of the lowest population densities in the EU (2.1 people/km²). This northern region forms part of what can be called **'Europe's empty lands'**.

Despite these problems, the population of Norrland has relatively high standards of living. This contrasts with the situation in most of Europe's southern periphery, such as the Mezzogiorno. As in most peripheral areas, physical geography has a strong influence on development trends and prospects. In these northern lands, **people have to adapt their ways of life more closely to the natural environment than most other parts of Western Europe.** Understanding the physical environment is essential to appreciating the human geography of Norrland.

Activity

Look at Fig. 20.1 and use an atlas to identify:
1. sea area A.
2. countries B, C and D.
3. rivers E and F.
4. towns G, H, I and J.

Where is Sweden's core region?

PHYSICAL PROCESSES

Relief, Drainage and Soils

Norrland lies mainly on the Baltic Shield. This is the geological core of Europe and is composed of some of the oldest and most resistant metamorphic and igneous rock types, such as granites. Originally, the Shield was an area of high mountains, but long periods of erosion have reduced its surface to a gently undulating plateau. The plateau is tilted from west (600 m) to east, where it forms a coastal plain next to the Gulf of Bothnia.

The western edge of the plateau gives way to the high Scandinavian Mountains. These form part of Europe's north-east to south-west trending Caledonian Fold Mountains, and rise to 2,000 m above sea level (see Chapter 1, page 25).

The heavily forested but badly drained landscape of the Baltic Shield cannot support a dense population.

Most of the region's major rivers originate in these mountains. They flow to the Gulf of Bothnia, generally in a south-easterly direction, and cut steep-sided parallel valleys into the plateau. There are many waterfalls where the rivers cross rocks of differing hardness, as on the Angerman, Indals and Dal rivers. These locations are important for production of hydro-electricity (Fig. 20.6).

Much of the region's present surface was formed in previous ice ages. The region was covered by a great thickness of ice, and glacial erosion scraped and smoothed the whole land surface. A large number of glacial ribbon lakes were also formed, especially in the valleys of major rivers. As the ice sheets moved back, large volumes of glacial material such as sands and gravels were deposited over the landscape. This further disturbed drainage patterns, by blocking the rivers and added to the many lakes and poorly drained areas that are common in large parts of Norrland.

Climate

The climate of Norrland is shaped mainly by **two factors**:
● Northerly latitude
● Rain shadow and continental influence.

Northerly Latitude

The northerly latitude of Norrland, with a large area inside the Arctic Circle, makes for large differences between summer and winter, especially in temperature. In winter, the movement of the sun to the southern hemisphere means long hours of darkness and very little sunlight. In the most northerly locations, temperatures fall below freezing point for up to six months (Fig. 20.2).

During the summer months, temperatures are much higher. The return of the sun to the northern hemisphere gives 24 hours of daylight inside the Arctic Circle on 21 June, while the position of the overhead sun allows for more direct rays from the sun to reach the surface. Both these factors compensate for the northerly latitude and allow average summer temperatures to reach 17°C.

Remember your Junior Certificate. As you go north, the sun's rays shine more obliquely onto the earth's surface and give little heat.

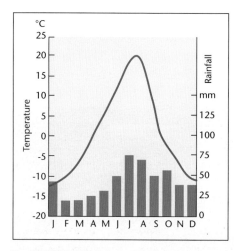

Fig 20,2 Climograph for Gällivare
(341 metres) 67° 20°E

Activity

Look at Fig. 20.2 and answer the following:

1. How many months record temperatures below freezing level?
2. Why is the winter season so long and severe?
3. In which season is the maximum precipitation? Why are total levels of rainfall quite low?
4. Contrast the climograph for Gällivare with Fig. 18.1 for Valentia (page 205) and Fig. 19.3 for Palermo (page 223). For each place estimate:
   a. the annual temperature range.
   b. seasonal patterns of rainfall.
   Describe and explain the main differences.

Rain Shadow and Continental Influence

Norrland is to the east of the Scandinavian Mountains. The rain-shadow effect of these mountains (see Fig. 20.3) means that rainfall totals are comparatively low in Norrland. While onshore south-westerly winds give rise to high precipitation totals of up to 2,000 mm along the western mountain slopes in Norway, annual levels of precipitation in Norrland are approximately 400 mm (see Fig. 20.2). This region, therefore, has a relatively dry climate.

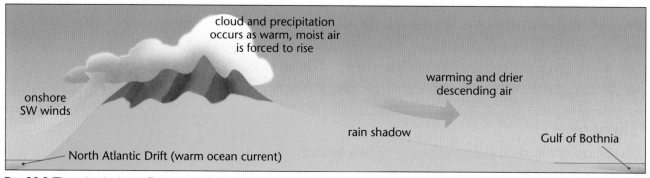

Fig. 20.3 The rain-shadow effect in Norrland

Activity

Look at Fig. 20.3 and answer the following:

1. What is a rain shadow?
2. Why is there a rain-shadow effect in Norrland?

Unlike the all-year precipitation along Norway's western seaboard, in Norrland most of the precipitation comes in summer. This, together with the higher temperatures, is vital for agriculture in these northern latitudes. Winter precipitation falls as snow.

The low winter temperatures and not having the moderating influence of the North Atlantic Drift (warm ocean current) mean that the Gulf of Bothnia is frozen in winter. This has important effects on trade.

ECONOMIC PROCESSES

The Primary Sector

Sweden has a well-developed economy. Much of the wealth is concentrated in the southern areas around Stockholm (the capital), the Central Lakes Lowlands and Scania. Norrland is less prosperous than the southern core but **is less underdeveloped than most peripheral regions in Europe**. This is due almost entirely to how successfully people have adjusted to the opportunities presented by their natural environment.

Norrland has a range of natural resources that form the basis for economic development. The most successful economic activities have been those based on natural resources: forestry and mining.

Being able to exploit these resources on a large scale and develop some successful industries depends on another natural resource: **water power.** Developing large-scale, cheap **hydro-electricity** allows the commercial extraction of natural resources, while also attracting major power-using industries to the region.

Norrland has three major natural resources:
- forests
- mineral ores, such as iron ore
- water power or HEP (hydro-electric power).

Farming

The freezing winter temperatures; thin, infertile acid soils; rugged landscapes and short growing season make profitable farming almost impossible. Farming is confined mainly to the narrow coastal plains and lower courses of major river valleys, such as the Angerman and Indals. Conditions are not suitable for cereal crops.

Although Norrland has over 50 per cent of Sweden's territory, only 10 per cent of its land is given over to crops. Pastoral farming is more common, especially dairying, although housing animals throughout the long winters adds a lot to costs.

Few people now work in farming. Those who remain in farming give over much of their land to forestry or look for part-time work outside the farm for extra income.

Forestry

North of 60°N in Europe, the dominant land use involves large areas of evergreen conifers. This includes Norrland, which is **the chief timber reserve** of the EU. Conifers, such as pine and spruce, are well adapted to withstand extreme winter temperatures and a relatively short growing season.

Conifers grow well in Norrland because:
- The Scandinavian mountains to the west shield the region from severe and strong winds.
- The land does not have a very steep and rugged relief.
- Needle leaves of conifers reduce transpiration (moisture loss).
- Conifers require fewer nutrients (than deciduous trees) from the soils.
- They are shallow rooting and grow well on thin, glacial or sandy soils.

Forestry dominates the land use of Norrland, and forests extend into the Arctic Circle. Trees grow less well to the north, as environmental conditions become more extreme. In Norrland, **the Angerman River** is usually the northern limit for intensive, commercial forestry.

Remember the boreal climate from your Junior Certificate.

What are the characteristics of a conifer tree?

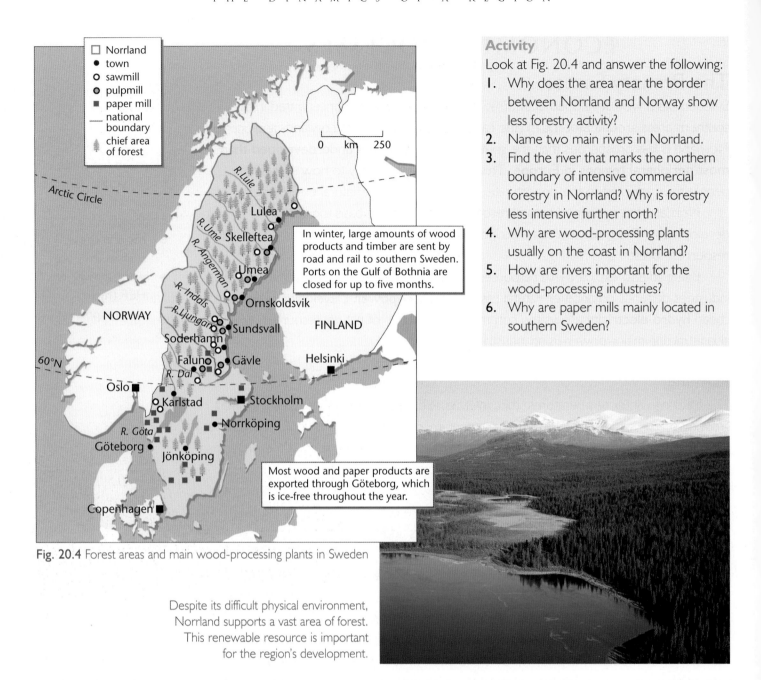

Fig. 20.4 Forest areas and main wood-processing plants in Sweden

In winter, large amounts of wood products and timber are sent by road and rail to southern Sweden. Ports on the Gulf of Bothnia are closed for up to five months.

Most wood and paper products are exported through Göteborg, which is ice-free throughout the year.

Despite its difficult physical environment, Norrland supports a vast area of forest. This renewable resource is important for the region's development.

Activity

Look at Fig. 20.4 and answer the following:

1. Why does the area near the border between Norrland and Norway show less forestry activity?
2. Name two main rivers in Norrland.
3. Find the river that marks the northern boundary of intensive commercial forestry in Norrland? Why is forestry less intensive further north?
4. Why are wood-processing plants usually on the coast in Norrland?
5. How are rivers important for the wood-processing industries?
6. Why are paper mills mainly located in southern Sweden?

In Sweden, forestry is seen as a valuable national resource, and an important element of their natural environment. It is a source of employment, especially in the more marginal farming areas, as well as generating important multiplier effects. Wood, for example, is the main raw material for wood-processing industries such as pulp and paper, while there is a growing interest in forest-related tourist activities.

The Swedish government has adopted a **growth strategy for forestry**. This is important for Norrland because expanding forestry and forestry-related activities are key elements in trying to stimulate the region's economy. The government has become increasingly involved in this sector, and large areas of forest are now state-owned. Incentives are also offered to private landowners to convert unproductive land to forestry. The forestry industry in Norrland, and the rest of Sweden, has moved away from being an industry that only exploits the natural environment to one that works on the **principle of sustained yield**.

Sustained Yield

Sustained yield forms part of a strategy of sustainable development. Its aim is to make sure that the earth's resources are not used up through exploitation now, so there will be not enough resources left for future generations. For a renewable resource like forestry, this means that trees that are felled are replaced by replanting. **Reforestation replaces deforestation.** In Sweden, 40 per cent more trees are now grown than are cut down every year to make sure that there is a long-term future for this important resource-based industry.

Prospects for forestry appear to be good. Demand for wood in the EU and the global economy is growing. The long-term success of forestry in Norrland will continue to depend heavily on the government commitment to sustainable yield. In addition, although output from forestry has grown, fewer people work in forestry as mechanisation has reduced labour in many operations. Government intervention is essential to diversify the region's economic base.

> Why is a policy of reforestation so important for Norrland?

> Why do you think demand for wood is growing? (Think about: paper, construction, population and deforestation in many parts of the world.)

Acid Rain

A recent threat to the forests of Scandinavia is acid rain. The main sources of this type of pollution are outside the region (especially from Britain and Germany). More effective international legislation is urgently needed to reduce levels of acid rain and to avoid large-scale damage to the forests of Scandinavia.

Mining

The most important mineral deposits in Sweden are in northern Norrland. Around the Skellefte River at 65°N, there are large deposits of a variety of ores such as copper, lead and zinc. These are mined at centres such as Boliden and moved by rail to major smelters at Skelleftea (see Fig. 20.5). Local HEP (hydro-electric power) is essential for the refining process.

Further north around Kiruna and Gällivare is one of Europe's most important deposits of iron ore (Fig. 20.5). This Lappland iron ore field has an estimated 3,000 million tonnes of high-grade magnetite ore. The bulk of the ore is mined underground, so mining is not disrupted by the severe Arctic winters.

> Magnetite iron ore contains over 70 per cent pure iron.

Acid rain causes serious damage to Norrland's extensive forests.

Despite their location in the Arctic Circle, the rich iron ore deposits at Kiruna are worked all year round and support large mining communities.

241

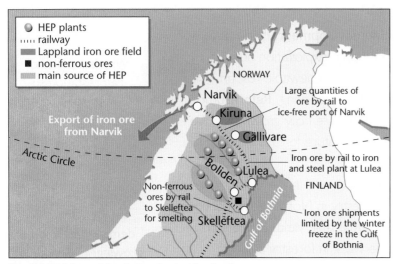

Fig. 20.5 Major mining industries in Norrland

Activity

Look at Fig. 20.5 and answer the following:

1. Why are large quantities of Swedish iron ore shipped through the Norwegian port of Narvik?
2. What are non-ferrous ores?
3. Why are these mining industries so important for Norrland?
4. What major industrial activity occurs in Lulea and Skelleftea?

The smelting plant at Skelleftea.
- *What locational advantages does this plant have for processing mineral ores?*

The steel plant at Lulea provides a regional market for some of the output of iron ore, although up to 80 per cent is exported. Most of the exported ore has to transported by rail to the ice-free Norwegian port of Narvik, as ports in the Gulf of Bothnia are frozen during the long winter months.

Recession in the global steel industry caused a decline in output, and employment is only about a third of the 1975 level, which was 9,000. This has had a major impact on local communities, which are strongly dependent on mining operations. Government finance has helped modernise the mines, and productivity levels have risen to help the mines compete internationally. In the 1990s, annual production stabilised at about 20 million tonnes.

Hydro-electric Power

> **Why is HEP an abundant and cheap source of power in Norrland?**

There is a long tradition of using HEP (hydro-electric power) in Sweden. This is partly because there are no fossil fuels but also because the conditions are suitable for generating HEP. Heavy and persistent rain and snow over the large catchment area of the Scandinavian Mountains feed the many major rivers that flow to the Gulf of Bothnia. Along these rivers a large number of HEP plants have been set up. These include the Indals, Angermann and Lule rivers.

About half of Sweden's electricity supply comes from water power. Over three-quarters of HEP-generating capacity is in Norrland, but most demand for power comes from southern and central Sweden. To transfer electricity from north to south, extensive transmission networks have been built.

There can be problems depending on HEP for energy because severe winter temperatures cause rivers to freeze. This disrupts the flow of energy at a time of the year when demand is highest. It also encouraged the government to develop alternative sources of energy, such as nuclear power, and to import energy from Norway in winter.

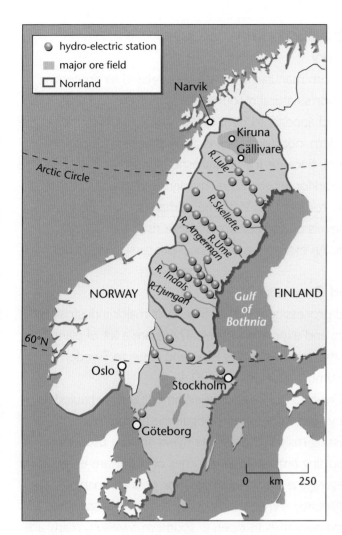

hydro-electric station
major ore field
Norrland

Narvik
Kiruna
Gällivare
R. Lule
R. Skellefte
R. Ume
R. Ångerman
R. Indals
R. Ljungan
Arctic Circle
NORWAY
FINLAND
Gulf of Bothnia
60°N
Oslo
Stockholm
Göteborg

0   km   250

Fig. 20.6 Hydro-electric installations in Sweden

Class Activity
Look at Fig. 20.6 and answer the following:
1. Why is the physical environment of Norrland so suitable for HEP?
2. Why is HEP so important for economic development in Norrland?
3. Name three industries in Norrland that depend on HEP as an energy source.

Despite these problems, HEP has been essential for developing Norrland.
Large and relatively cheap supplies of HEP have:

● Allowed a relatively large population scattered over a wide area to live in the region, despite severe winters.

● Facilitated the large-scale exploitation of Norrland's rich mineral resources. HEP stations along the Lule River provide essential power for the Lappland iron ore fields, while those on the Skelefte River are vital for mining operations in places like Boliden.

● Encouraged more diversified manufacturing to develop, although based mainly on the region's natural resources. These include wood processing (sawmills, pulp and paper) and metallurgical industries, such as the Lulea steelworks and smelting plants around Skelleftea.

Only 2 per cent of Ireland's energy comes from HEP. Can you suggest reasons for the difference beween Ireland and Norrland?

As Sweden is now committed to closing its nuclear plants, the country will have to import more energy from Norway.

In Norrland most sawmills are located at the mouths of major rivers and along the narrow coastal plain.
- *What advantages does this have for the industry?*

Wood provides the raw materials for many industries in Norrland, including construction.

Why is much of the Gulf of Bothnia icebound in winter, while the west of Norway is ice-free?

The Secondary Sector
Industry

Apart from manufacturing activities related to processing the region's natural resources and using cheap HEP, Norrland appears to have few advantages to attract a range of modern industries. This is a key problem for regional planners, because most established industries have reduced their workforce when they modernised operations to remain competitive. With the primary sector also losing jobs, levels of unemployment have risen throughout the region. An example is the wood-processing industries.

Wood Processing

Wood processing is one of Sweden's major industrial sectors and export industries. There are a lot of plants along the coastal zone of Norrland close to Sweden's major timber reserves (Fig. 20.4).

Over 85 per cent of felled timber is now hauled to mills by road rather than being floated down rivers to processing mills. Although the rivers are not used for transporting timber, large volumes of water are essential for processing the wood (especially for pulp and paper manufacture). While the flexibility of road transport has allowed new mills to open in southern Sweden, many are still located at traditional sites along the riverbanks or near the mouths of Norrland's major rivers.

This industry traditionally provided jobs and other spin-offs for communities in Norrland, which had few alternative opportunities for work. Rationalisation (modernising the industry to make it more efficient) of the sector has led to many of the smaller, less efficient mills being closed and production being concentrated on fewer, larger plants. Productivity has increased, but there are fewer jobs available.

In addition, while there are still many sawmills and pulp mills in Norrland, the higher-value paper mills now tend to be located in southern Sweden. This is the most urbanised part of the country and provides a major market for paper. It also has access to ice-free ports, such as Göteborg, to maintain year-round trade. Ports north of Gävle may be closed for up to five months each year.

Problems for locating modern manufacturing industries in Norrland
- Harsh, long winters
- Distance from southern Sweden and poor international connections from the region. Regional airports are small and are feeders to Stockholm. Ports are icebound in winter and roads are expensive to maintain.
- Few towns to provide a range of services and recreational facilities
- Low population numbers to provide a choice for employers in labour force (e.g. skills)
- Poor regional market, as there as are few people to buy products

> Suggest three ways that government planning can help offset these problems.

The Tertiary Sector

Despite Norrland's peripheral location, its social services are comparatively well developed. This is because Sweden has a commitment to providing high levels of social welfare for all its people. Decentralisation of government services and the importance of local government also add to the range of tertiary employment in Norrland. This is important in raising standards of living for the population spread across the region.

The range of higher quality services is, however, limited in comparison with the more prosperous and densely settled south of the country. This is a disadvantage when trying to attract new investment to the region.

> How would you define social welfare and tertiary employment? Do you see a link between these terms?

Transport

Norrland's isolated location is highlighted by its difficult and expensive transport links to the national core. Ferry services stop in winter because ports are icebound, while long-distance road links are disrupted by snow and freezing conditions. Despite these difficult environmental conditions, the rail network is well developed. The railways have an important role in developing the region's mineral base, providing services such as the rail link between the Lappland ore field and both Lulea and Norway's ice-free port at Narvik. Ore can be exported throughout the year.

> Why does density of population influence the range and quality of services available?

Tourism

Unlike the tourist industries in Europe's western and southern peripheries, such as Ireland and the Mezzogiorno, tourism in Norrland is underdeveloped. It also has a very different type of tourist potential.

The wilderness areas and forests of Norrland are important nature reserves, with a range of sensitive and interesting landscapes. To protect the environment, large areas have been designated as national parks and game reserves.

Ferry services provide a valuable link for the coastal communities in Norrland. In winter, freezing of the Baltic Sea disrupts these services and adds to the isolation of these communities.

Despite its difficult environment, Norrland has some important advantages for tourism.

● *Can you suggest any of these?*

These areas have great potential for tourism, although the scale and type of tourism will have to be carefully controlled to avoid disturbing these sensitive landscapes. The tourist season is also limited mainly to the summer months. Why?

HUMAN PROCESSES
Population

Norrland is part of 'Europe's empty lands', with 1.2 million people and a population density of only 2.1 people per km². About 80 per cent of people live in small towns that have been built up around the mills and mines that exploit the region's rich natural resources. These towns are located mainly along the coast and the valleys of major rivers. Most of the region is uninhabited and has extensive tracts of forest and wilderness.

For regions that depend on their natural resources, population trends are influenced strongly by world trade in these resources. During periods of growth and optimism in trade and development, Norrland generally shows some growth in population through in-migration and increased birth rates.

In contrast, a decline in demand and reorganisation of the industries to reduce output and employment levels tend to encourage out-migration and a fall in population and birth rates. These trends are shown in Table 20.1 for Norrbotten, which is the most northerly province in Norrland. The population peaked in 1994 at 268,000.

Selected Population Figures in Norrbotten		
	1991	2000
Population	265,000	256,000
Natural change	1,037	-348
New migration	80	-1,494

Table 20.1

Activity

Look at Table 20.1 and answer the following:
1. What was the main demographic factor accounting for population trends in 1991 and 2000?
2. In what ways did an increase in demand for the region's natural resources and optimism over plans by Sweden to join the EU affect Norrbotten's population in 1991?
3. How did tighter border controls for in-migration and poorer conditions for world trade affect Norrbotten's population in 2000?
4. Suggest other parts of Sweden to which young people in Norrbotten would migrate? Explain your answer.

Although some successes have been achieved by government incentives to support development, the region's peripheral location, extreme climate, low population densities and sensitive ecological landscapes make this region a continuing problem for Sweden.

The scale and type of these problems were recognised by the EU when Sweden joined the European Union in 1995. Norrland, along with similar areas in Finland, has an Objective 1 status. This makes Norrland eligible to receive structural funds to help promote a more effective infrastructure for the region and to protect its sensitive environment. This aid is essential for the long-term prospects of people living in this region.

Religion and Language

Sweden's main religion is Christian, with the Lutheran Church being the most important. In Norrland, there are some members of a small but distinctive cultural group called the Sami, who practise a more traditional religion (see Chapter 22). They have their own language called Sápmi, although Swedish is the dominant and official language of the state. Along the borders with Norway and Finland, people are also able to speak Norwegian and Finnish.

TEST YOURSELF AT
my-etest.com

CHAPTER 21
INDIA

KEY IDEA!

India is part of the world's most populated and poorly developed global regions. Its human and physical geographies have a strong effect on each other.

South of the great natural barrier formed by the Hindu Kush-Himalayan mountain ranges lies the natural region of the Indian subcontinent (this region is also referred to as South Asia). At the heart of this global region is the vast, triangular-shaped country of India. Stretching from approximately 36°N along its mountainous northern borders, this highly complex country reaches almost to the Equator, and divides the northern Indian Ocean into the Arabian Sea and the Bay of Bengal (see Fig. 21.1).

India is a region of different scale and type to the three case studies in Chapters 18, 19 and 20. With only 2.2 per cent of the earth's land area, India is home to 17 per cent of the world's population. Its population reached a billion in 1999. At present rates of natural increase, India will soon overtake China to become the most populous country in the world.

While the West of Ireland, Mezzogiorno and Norrland are problem regions for their national governments, they are all in countries that form part of the more prosperous and developed world. In contrast, India is a part of the less developed world, and the country faces huge problems of poverty and underdevelopment. Despite recent urban growth, India still has mainly a rural-based economy, and the average daily income per capita (per person) is only little over a US dollar (see Table 21.1).

Some Comparative Indicators of Development (2000)				
	Ireland	Italy	Sweden	India
Area (000 km²)	70	301	450	3,287
Population (million)	3.7	58	9	1,016
Density (per km²)	55	196	22	342
Percentage of urban population	60	67	83	28
GNP (Gross National Product) per capita (US$)	25,520	23,470	27,140	450

Table 21.1

Activity

Look at Table 21.1 and answer the following:
1. What percentage of the Indian population is rural?
2. In Europe, rural economies usually support only low densities of population. Is this true in India?
3. How much more prosperous is the average Swede compared to the average in India?

PHYSICAL PROCESSES

A country the size of India has a great variety of natural environments. This is a key factor in shaping the human geography of India, since almost three-quarters of the population live in rural communities and work mainly in agriculture.

Relief and Drainage

There are **three main landform regions** in India (see Fig. 21.1):

- Northern Mountains
- Indus-Ganges Plain
- Southern Plateaus.

Northern Mountains

These towering mountains form India's northern boundary zone. They extend from the Hindu Kush in the north west, through the Himalayas to the extreme north east of the country. The world's highest mountain ranges (including Mount Everest) came from the collision of two great tectonic plates, which compressed the earth's crust and resulted in the uplift of these fold mountains. They form one of the earth's most dramatic physical features and are the source of many rivers that flow south into India.

> See the collision of India and Eurasia in Chapter 1, page 15.

Indus-Ganges Plain

The Indus-Ganges Plain follows the Indus River Valley from Pakistan through the Ganges Valley to end with the double delta of the Ganges and Brahmaputra rivers in Bangladesh. About half of India's population lives in this lowland zone. This shows how important its role is in the human geography of the subcontinent.

The mountain ranges of the Himalayas form a northern boundary to the Indian subcontinent.

The earth movements that created the Himalayas also caused the Indus-Ganges Plain, a major depression to the south of the mountains. The main drainage of northern India and the nearby states is directed to this depression. It includes India's three most important rivers (Indus, Ganges and Brahmaputra) and their many tributaries.

These rivers are swollen by summer meltwaters from the surrounding mountains and with monsoon rains flood extensive areas of the lowlands. Large quantities of material eroded in the upper courses of the rivers are deposited along their lower courses as highly fertile alluvial soil. This has created one of the world's largest alluvial plains, which is able to support a very dense rural population.

> Locate the three major river valleys in Fig 21.1.

Southern Plateaus

Peninsular India (the southern part that projects into the ocean) is made up of a number of plateaus. The **Deccan Plateau** is the largest of these and is tilted from west to east. Drainage flows from the higher elevations in the west across and out into the Bay of Bengal. The coastal lowlands are relatively narrow, rising abruptly along both west and east coasts to form the Western and Eastern Ghats. Both of these coastal mountain ranges have an affect on onshore winds and rainfall distribution for peninsular India.

Activity

Look at Fig. 21.1 and at an atlas and name:

a. mountain area A.
b. sea area B.
c. rivers C, D and E.
d. cities F, G, H and I.
e. countries J and K.

Learn a simple sketch map that includes the major relief features and rivers of India.

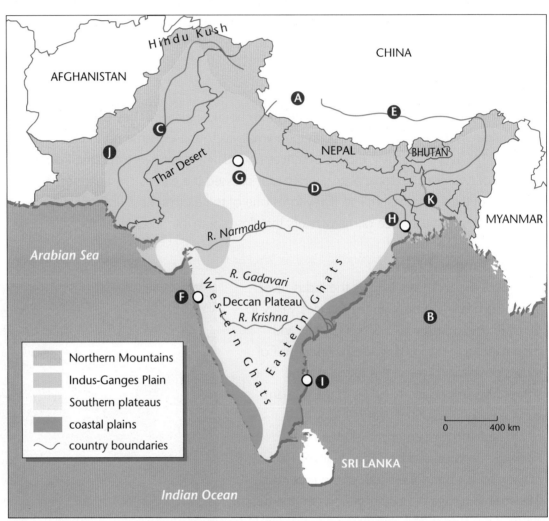

Fig. 21.1 The relief regions of the Indian subcontinent

Climate

Most of India is in tropical latitudes. Only the mountainous zones of the north and north west have frost. Temperatures year-round are relatively high, so the main climatic variable is precipitation and the **monsoon**. This shapes the patterns of development and livelihoods of the majority of people in India.

Monsoon comes from the Arabic word *mausin*, which means 'season'. The monsoon is a reversal of winds over the Indian subcontinent and elsewhere in South East Asia. The monsoon in India can be divided into **two** main seasons: **the dry and wet monsoon**.

Dry Monsoon

The dry monsoon occurs from October to June. It is caused by north-east winds that blow out from a high pressure area in the continental interior, north of the Himalayas (see Fig. 21.2). **From October to February,** these are very cold winds that bring freezing temperatures and snow to the mountains of northern India. Frosts can occur in the Ganges Valley. **From March to June,** these winds become warmer and, by June, temperatures in the Ganges Valley can reach 49°C. Coming from the continental interior, these winds are usually **dry**. Where these winds cross the Bay of Bengal and have to rise over the Eastern Ghats, this part of India receives a winter maximum of rainfall. The rest of India is dry.

> Why do these winds become warmer? (Think about the sun overhead.)

Wet Monsoon

From **mid-June to September**, warm ocean air is sucked into an intensive low pressure created in the continental interior (see Fig. 21.3). There are two branches to this monsoon.

One branch flows as a south-west monsoon across the Arabian Sea. Where these moist, warm winds are forced to rise over the Western Ghats, intense rain falls (more than 2,500 mm). A **second branch** crosses the Bay of Bengal and veers north to move along the Ganges. Torrential rain falls in the delta areas of the Ganges and Brahmaputra. In the hillier areas of north-east India, there can be more than 10,000 mm of rain in a period of six to eight weeks.

As these winds move westwards through the Ganges Valley, rainfall totals decline. In the extreme north west of India there are areas not affected by the monsoon. Here desert conditions occur, as in the Thar Desert.

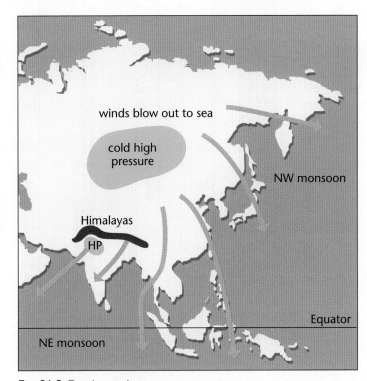

Fig. 21.2 October to June monsoon season

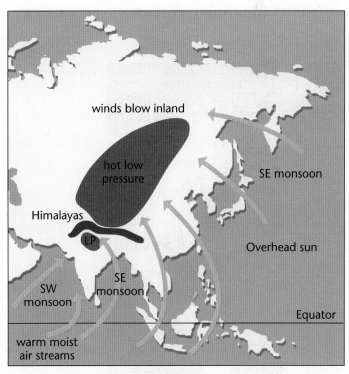

Fig. 21.3 June to September monsoon season

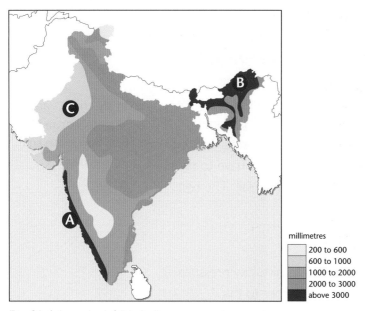

Fig. 21.4 Annual rainfall in India

Activity

Look at Figs 21.1 to 21.5 and answer the following about the Indian monsoon:

1. Does Fig 21.2 or 21.3 illustrate the dry monsoon? Explain your choice.
2. Look at where Mangalore (A) is located on Fig. 21.4. Explain why its region is so wet and why there is a high summer rainfall.
3. Look at where Cherrapunji (B) is located on Fig. 21.4. Explain why this is one of the wettest places on the earth.
4. Estimate the total rainfall in Cherrapunji in June. Compare this with rainfall totals in Dublin (Fig. 18.1 on page 205).
5. Give reasons for the desert region at C on Fig. 21.4.

While the monsoon rains are vital for agriculture in India, they also cause major problems and damage through flooding.

Almost 11,000 mm (or 425 inches) of rain fall each year at Cherrapunji.

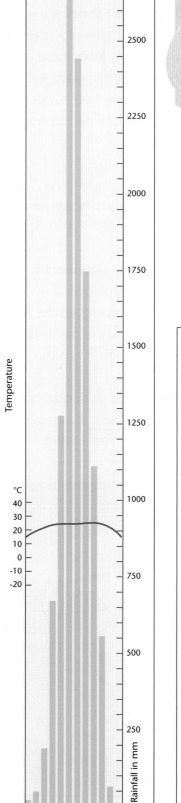

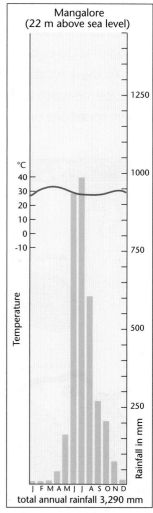

Fig. 21.5 Annual Rainfall in Cherrapunji and Mangalore

The regular monsoon rains provide for a rich vegetation cover on the Western Ghats, including tea plantations in the south.

Why are monsoon rains essential for India?

The people of the Indian subcontinent wait anxiously for the sudden burst of the summer monsoon. The timing and the intensity of the monsoon are very important for the livelihoods of hundred of millions of people:

- **Delay in the monsoon's arrival** affects planting of crops and the efficient use of irrigation systems. Harvesting can also be delayed.
- If the monsoon brings **poor rains,** it has an adverse effect on growing crops such as rice, which need waterlogged conditions. Low yields and poor harvests can lead to starvation for millions of farmers and their families who depend on the rice crop.
- When monsoon rains are **too heavy**, extreme flooding can occur and can wash away seeds, destroy villages and cause landslides.
- A **reliable, regular monsoon** is essential for India's agriculture and rural society. If the monsoon fails, it is disastrous for India. In 1987, a great famine followed the partial failure of the monsoon.

> There is no social welfare system in India. What does this mean if there is a poor harvest?

ECONOMIC PROCESSES

Despite the size of India, the country is underdeveloped. Income levels per capita (per person) are very low (US $450) and up to half the population lives in great poverty. There is some modern industrial development, but it is concentrated on relatively few city-based regions.

With only one in four people living in urban centres, the service sector also remains underdeveloped by international standards. India's economy is dominated by agriculture, and to understand the country's problems it is important to know about the nature and patterns of this sector.

The Primary Sector
Agriculture

The cultivated area of India (138 million hectares) almost equals the total area of land under cultivation in the European Union. A lot of the land has good agriculture potential, especially where water supplies are available. Only in the high mountains and the dry areas such as the Thar Desert along India's western border with Pakistan are conditions too extreme for productive farming. Arable farming, especially cereals, is the main type of farming.

Success in agriculture is very important for India's development:

- Two-thirds of India's huge working population depend directly on the land for earning a living.
- Agriculture provides the bulk of the country's food supplies.
- Food and other agricultural-based products, such as cotton, tea, leather, are important for export as cash crops.
- Taxes from agriculture provide government with money to invest in modernising the economy.

How does agriculture help India's balance of trade?

Trade in farm produce plays a vital role in the life of most rural communities, such as the port town of Malabar in Southern India.

Modernising Agriculture

When India became independent from Britain in 1947, the Indian government identified agriculture as a key sector for national development. Despite this, modernisation of the sector has been limited. An effective land reform programme has not been introduced to redistribute land from large estate owners to landless peasants.

In the 1990s, almost half of rural families had farms of less than 0.5 hectares, or no land at all, but a quarter of India's agricultural land was owned by less than 5 per cent of farm families. Most small farms are also broken up into tiny and scattered parcels of land. This reduces productivity even more and makes introducing modern farm practices, such as mechanisation, difficult.

The failure to modernise India's agricultural sector and raise levels of productivity for many key crops remains an important issue. The country's growing population places more demand on the food supply. If the farming sector fails to meet this demand, it can lead to large-scale famine.

The type of farming

Why are small and scattered parcels of land not suitable for productive farming?

The dominant type of farming throughout much of India is **intensive subsistence.** It is used especially in rural areas with high population density, where people depend on being able to feed themselves. Rice is the chief crop for this type of farming, especially in the flood plains of the Indus and Ganges rivers. Other cereals such as wheat and millet are grown in drier parts of peninsular India.

Almost all planting, weeding and harvesting is done by hand, with all family members being involved. Since plots of land are usually very small, no land is wasted. Roadways are narrow, and there are no field boundaries. Double cropping is also practised to make sure enough food is produced during the year to feed the farmer's family. While rice is grown in the wet monsoon season, alternative crops such as wheat and millet are grown in the drier months.

Although farming is intensive, it is not very productive and there is not much surplus food. Success with this type of farming depends very much on the natural environment and how reliable the wet monsoon is.

Why is the wet monsoon so essential for rural India?

Plantation farming is important in some areas. The crops grown include: tea, coconuts and cotton. Tea plantations of north-east India, especially in Assam, are major suppliers to the world tea trade. Coconuts are a speciality of the south-west coast, while cotton is important in parts of central India and north of Mumbai.

Wheat is the main crop in the drier north west of India. Crop yields are quite high, especially where land can be irrigated. The Green Revolution has helped increase productivity levels. Corn (maize) and chick peas are also grown in some parts of this zone.

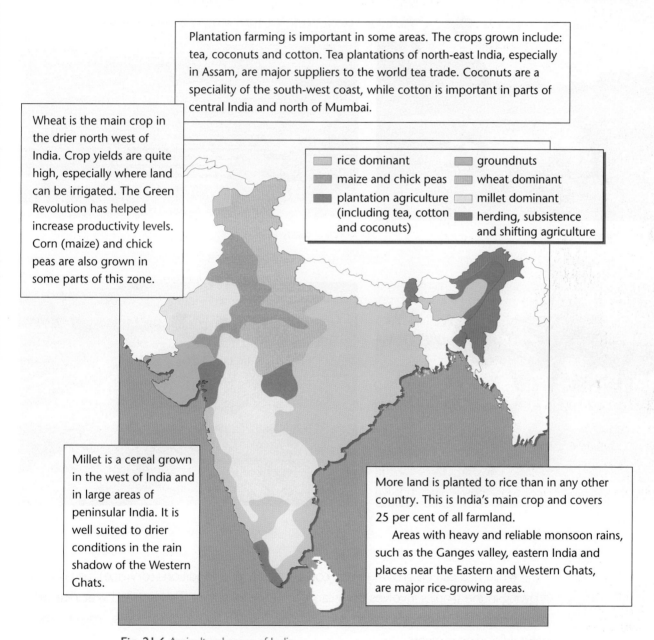

rice dominant
maize and chick peas
plantation agriculture (including tea, cotton and coconuts)
groundnuts
wheat dominant
millet dominant
herding, subsistence and shifting agriculture

Millet is a cereal grown in the west of India and in large areas of peninsular India. It is well suited to drier conditions in the rain shadow of the Western Ghats.

More land is planted to rice than in any other country. This is India's main crop and covers 25 per cent of all farmland.

Areas with heavy and reliable monsoon rains, such as the Ganges valley, eastern India and places near the Eastern and Western Ghats, are major rice-growing areas.

Fig. 21.6 Agricultural areas of India

Class Activity

Look at Fig. 21.4 and use it to help explain the patterns of farming shown in Fig. 21.6.

Rice Cultivation

Rice was domesticated in East Asia about 7,000 years ago. It is well adapted to tropical environments and produces more food per unit area of land than any other crop. As a result, it is a vital food crop for these densely settled parts of the world. Globally, over 2 billion people live by eating this crop.

Preparing the land for growing rice

Flooding paddy fields

Planting young rice plants

Harvesting rice

While rice can be grown under comparatively dry conditions (dry rice), usually rice growing in the tropics involves using large volumes of water. This is called **wet rice or paddy rice.** The rice fields, called paddies, are flooded by monsoon rains, irrigation or natural flooding of rivers.

Keeping a controlled depth of water is very important. Water not only provides the moisture but also nutrients (alluvial material) that promote growth, especially if chemical fertilisers are not used.

Preparing the land, planting, harvesting and controlling water levels is usually done by hand. The farmer and his family are all actively involved in this tedious and hard work. It is intensive subsistence farming.

Why are chemical fertilisers not used in most rural areas of India?

As the rice production techniques are primitive, the levels of productivity are low. There is great potential for raising production through more modern farming practices. Using fertilisers, better seeds and having larger fields, however, requires a lot of capital (money), and the people must accept the need for change.

The Green Revolution

India is a country that has benefited from the Green Revolution. The Green Revolution refers to the development and introduction of genetically-modified, high-yield varieties of staple crops, such as rice and wheat. These 'miracle crops' produce high yields and are resistant to many diseases and pests.

There have been important **benefits** in some areas of rice and wheat growing. This has helped India meet its needs for food production, and by the late 1990s the country became a net exporter of food.

Yet there are **many problems** linked to the 'green revolution':

- It depends on large inputs of chemical fertilisers and pesticides.
- Labour is often replaced with machinery, so rural unemployment goes up and more people leave the land and to go towns, increasing the rural-urban migration.
- Larger fields and farms are needed, so the number of farms is reduced.
- A well-educated farm population and capital (money) for investment are needed.
- It only benefits comparatively few, larger-scale farmers; large numbers of small-scale farmers are not able to participate in this process.
- There is environmental damage, for example, water and ground pollution from chemicals.

For a large number of Indian farmers a better solution to their problems would involve the use of more **intermediate technology** and a more effective programme of land reform. While the introduction of the Green Revolution has brought some important results, the vast majority of India's rice farmers use traditional farm practices, which depend heavily on the natural environment. The need to increase food production to match India's growing population remains a major concern for the government.

The Secondary Sector
Industry

When India became independent in 1947, it had only a limited range of industries, especially textiles and food processing. Only 2 per cent of the working population was employed in industry, which was concentrated mainly in the major cities: Bombay (now Mumbai), Calcutta (now Kolkata) and Madras (now Chennai).

On gaining independence, the new government was determined to encourage industrial development. The aim was to reduce India's dependence on imported industrial goods and to promote greater wealth and employment across the country.

Look at Fig. 21.6 and note the areas dominated by rice cultivation. Note the link between water supply and densely settled areas (see Figs. 21.4 and 21.10).

What are the benefits and problems of the Green Revolution? Are you in favour of this approach? Explain your answer.

What is intermediate technology? Give examples.

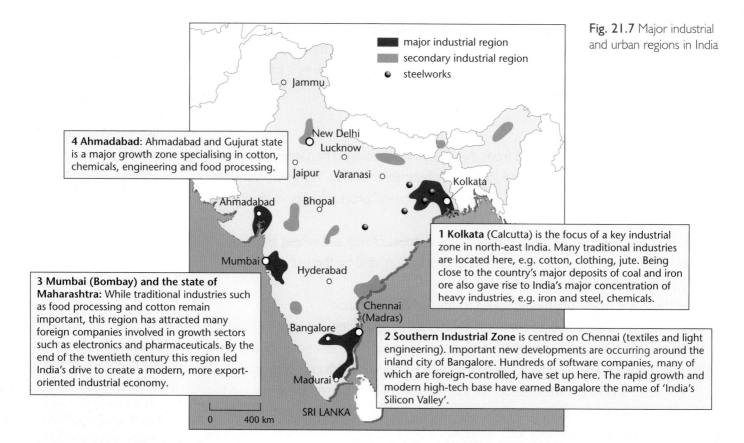

Fig. 21.7 Major industrial and urban regions in India

Legend:
- major industrial region
- secondary industrial region
- steelworks

4 Ahmadabad: Ahmadabad and Gujarat state is a major growth zone specialising in cotton, chemicals, engineering and food processing.

1 Kolkata (Calcutta) is the focus of a key industrial zone in north-east India. Many traditional industries are located here, e.g. cotton, clothing, jute. Being close to the country's major deposits of coal and iron ore also gave rise to India's major concentration of heavy industries, e.g. iron and steel, chemicals.

3 Mumbai (Bombay) and the state of Maharashtra: While traditional industries such as food processing and cotton remain important, this region has attracted many foreign companies involved in growth sectors such as electronics and pharmaceuticals. By the end of the twentieth century this region led India's drive to create a modern, more export-oriented industrial economy.

2 Southern Industrial Zone is centred on Chennai (textiles and light engineering). Important new developments are occurring around the inland city of Bangalore. Hundreds of software companies, many of which are foreign-controlled, have set up here. The rapid growth and modern high-tech base have earned Bangalore the name of 'India's Silicon Valley'.

0   400 km

Class Activity

Look at Fig. 21.7 and answer the following:

1. How many major industrial zones are there in India?
2. Which zone specialises in modern high-technology industries and which one in heavy industry?
   What are the growth prospects for these regions?
3. Suggest reasons for major industrial zones being located on or near the coast.

Major deposits of iron ore and coal near Kolkata gave rise to an important iron and steel industry. This was important for national development.

Jute is used to make mats and rope.

Two key factors helped India's programme of industrialisation:

- The size of India's population provided a large home market.
- The country has some important natural resources (coal and iron ore), a large and cheap labour force, and outputs from agriculture (cotton, jute). Mineral resources encouraged the government to develop heavy industries, such as iron and steel, shipbuilding and chemicals.

Despite these advantages, progress was relatively slow and helped only a small number of preferred growth centres. In addition, by the 1980s, many heavy industries were in decline. Industrial policy has changed to emphasise:

- **Agri-industries:** These include fertilisers, machinery and food processing, which can benefit rural communities.

258

- **Consumer goods industries and small-scale craft industries:** These are more labour intensive than large-scale, heavy industries, so more jobs are created. They also benefit from low labour costs and traditional skills, which make them competitive in export markets. Examples include: jewellery, clothing, leather goods.

- **Development in the countryside rather than the cities:** With more than 70 per cent of India's population living in rural areas, jobs need to be taken to these people, rather than encouraging migration to urban centres. This involves support for **community-based developments and self-help schemes** to improve facilities like basic health care and drinking water. Education schemes to improve skill levels are also important.

> Do you think that small-scale industries and rural-based development is better for rural communities than trying to set up large branch plants owned by multinational corporations?

A craftsman paints papier mâché toys. Often family members work together to produce their crafts.
- *Do you think the development of such industries is important for India?*

Although large-scale industries have developed in India and provide employment, many workers are paid low wages and continue to live in poverty.

- **High-technology industries:** These are attracted to India by the country's growing population of skilled workers, low costs and improved communication systems. These high value-added industries present a new and modern 'face' of India. They also suggest a brighter future for the country's industrial base.

> Give examples of high-technology industry.

India has emerged as a growing and significant manufacturer of computer software. Many major multinationals, such as IBM and Texas Instruments, have located in the country. Large numbers of locally-owned companies have also been set up to supply software components to Western markets.

India's Science Graduates

Although many people in the countryside are poorly educated, India has invested heavily in a well-developed education system, based largely in the cities. India now produces more university graduates than Canada and the USA combined, and 40 per cent of these are in science and engineering. A supply of skilled, English-speaking workers is attractive to international companies, especially as the cost of labour is low by Western standards. While a circuit board designer in California can earn between US $60-100,000, the salary in India averages about US $10,000.

Where Industry is Located

Note that the key city regions are the same as in 1947.

Although the government has tried to spread industry across the country, this growing sector remains concentrated in a small number of key city regions (see Fig. 21.7). The most important are Kolkata, Mumbai and its hinterland in the state of Maharashtra, and Chennai-Bangalore.

Modernisation of India's traditional industries, such as textiles, and the introduction of new high-tech industries, such as pharmaceuticals, provide a new basis for national development.

Services in many urban centres remain underdeveloped, reflecting the poverty of the population.

The Tertiary Sector
Services

India's service sector remains underdeveloped. About 70 per cent of the country's population lives in rural areas. As so many people are poor and depend on a subsistence economy they don't have the money for services such as schools, health care, banking, even if these were available. Many basic services are provided through self-help schemes and informal cooperation.

In India's cities, where most tertiary employment is located, there are **two** types of service activities. Large populations and more people with good incomes create demand for a full range of services. In the larger cities, there are job opportunities in services, such as government administration, finance and banking, retailing and education.

There is a second type of service activity in Indian and other cities of the less developed world. These services are in the **informal sector** (known before as the 'black economy'). Many people work as unlicensed sellers, offering a range of homemade goods and services. These services include street vendors, shoeshine boys and car repairs. Sometimes to survive the urban poor are forced to take part in more illegal activities such as drug dealing and prostitution.

In the absence of developed services, informal service providers are common throughout India. Here a herbal dentist practices his trade amid a crowd of onlookers.

Transport

Developing a country as large as India successfully needs an efficient transport system, but the government is not always able to find the money for improving transport. Transport systems in rural India are not well developed. One report suggested that by the late 1990s, half of the country's 600,000 villages did not have access to tarred roads suitable for motor vehicles. These communities use dirt-track roads and carts drawn by animals (usually oxen). It is unlikely that the transport networks in these areas will be modernised, especially in the short term.

Tourism

The size, history and variety of natural and cultural landscapes in India offer major attractions for the international tourist trade. International transport links to India have also improved in recent years, bringing more and more tourists to the country. For an underdeveloped economy, tourism offers many advantages, and the government actively promotes this industry.

What is your image of India as a tourist destination?

Among India's attractions for tourists are:

- The spectacular mountain ranges of the Himalayas.
- The vast number of palaces and fortifications that reflects the history of India.
- Many religious temples, highlighting the variety of religions – Hindu, Buddhist, Sikh and Muslim.
- Cultural landscapes that are not familiar to many people from the developed world.
- The great rivers and varied physical landscapes.

Activity

What advantages does tourism have for a country like India, especially for its less developed regions?

The Taj Mahal is one of India's most famous tourist attractions.

To succeed in promoting tourism as a basis for development, a lot of investment has to be made in upgrading internal transport links and tourist facilities, such as accommodation. Another aspect to consider is that some tourists may be put off by the sheer pressure of population and the obvious poverty of many people in India.

HUMAN PROCESSES

Population

The size and especially the rate of population growth in India is the key factor behind many problems facing the country. At the start of the twenty-first century, the national population was more than a thousand million. India has a comparatively high rate of natural increase (1.6 per cent a year) and its population could reach more than 2 billion by 2040.

The main reason for the rapid growth in India's population through natural increase is the high birth rate (see Table 21.2 and Fig. 21.8). The country has only recently entered the third stage of the demographic transition model, whereas more developed countries such as Ireland and Sweden are in the fourth or even fifth stage of this model (see Fig. 21.9). In India, while death rates have gone down a lot due to better health care, the birth rate remains high. The result is a high rate of population increase.

India has a large and rapidly growing population. In many rural areas children are often educated in open-air schools.

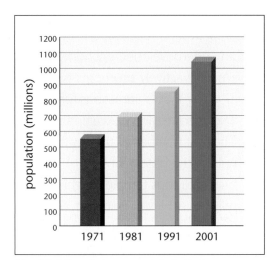

Fig. 21.8 Population growth in India from 1971 to 2001

Some Demographic Indicators for India, Ireland, Italy and Sweden				
	Birth rate (per 000)	Death rate (per 000)	Annual rate of natural increase (%)	Doubling time for population (years)
India	25	9	1.6	39
Ireland	14	8	0.6	139
Italy	9	10	-0.1	(population loss)
Sweden	10	11	-0.1	(population loss)

Table 21.2

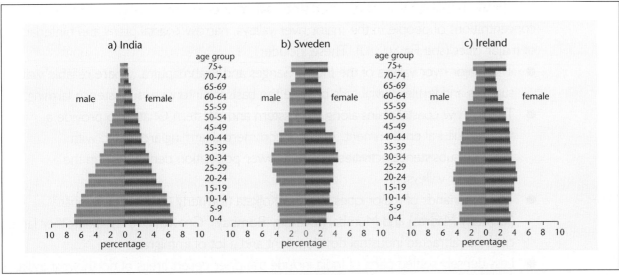

Fig. 21.9 Population pyramids for India, Sweden and Ireland in 2000

Activity

Look at Table 21.2 and Figs 21.8 and 21.9 and answer the following:

1. How many times higher is the birth rate in India compared to Ireland and Sweden?
2. Why will it only take 39 years to double India's population compared to almost 140 years in Ireland?
3. Calculate how many people have been added to India's population from 1971 to 2001.
4. Which of the three population pyramids best shows the fourth or final stage of the demographic cycle and which one shows stage 3? Explain your answer.
5. Do you think that a more effective programme of birth control is essential for India's future development?

> Remember the demographic transition model shows the stages a country with high birth and death rates goes through until it has low birth and death rates.

Population Growth in India from 1971 to 2001

The Indian government recognises the problems caused by the country's large and expanding population. These include:

● Pressure on farmland

● Making sure there is enough food

● Rural-urban migration

● Finding jobs for a growing labour force.

In the 1970s, the government started a campaign to reduce birth rates. They offered incentives to encourage people to use birth control (for example, a transistor radio for a vasectomy) and reduce average family size.

While the campaign had some success, it has been difficult to educate quickly large numbers of the population to the advantages of family planning. It is especially difficult in remoter rural communities, where large families are still seen in a positive way (for example, a sign of virility, help to work the land). Even with a slowdown in the rate of natural increase since the 1970s, the sheer size of the population and its young age profile have resulted in ever-greater numbers being added to India's total population. As urbanisation continues, it is thought that the birth rate will decline and help slow down the country's rate of natural increase.

> Why will urbanisation cause birth rates to go down?

263

India's population is not evenly distributed. There are many areas of very dense concentrations of people in the major river valleys, narrow coastal plains and hinterlands of major cities (see Fig. 21.10). These include:

- The major river valleys of the Indus, Ganges and Brahmaputra, where reliable water supplies and fertile alluvial soils provide the basis for intensive, subsistence farming.
- The narrow coastal plains along the Eastern and Western Ghats also provide a rich agricultural environment. Areas of commercial farming are mixed with intensive subsistence activities to give a lower population density than in the major river valleys.
- The hinterlands of major cities, such as Kolkata (formerly Calcutta), Chennai (formerly Madras) and Mumbai (formerly Bombay). Growth of these and other large cities has attracted industrial development and a lot of immigrants.
- Less densely settled parts of India include the drier desert areas of north-west India, such as the Thar Desert, and the mountainous zones on the northern border.

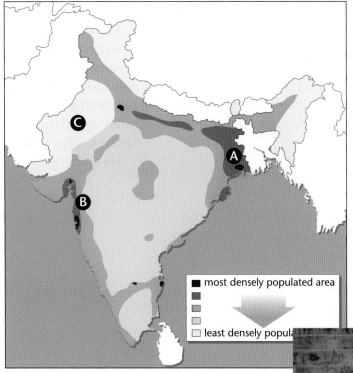

Fig. 21.10 Population density in India

most densely populated area

least densely popul[ated]

Activity
Look at Fig. 21.10 and answer the following:
1. Why are population densities so high in the region marked A?
2. Why do coastal areas such as B have a high population density?
3. Why is the population density in area C so low?

India has traditionally had a high birth rate. Recently the Indian government has tried to encourage birth control to restrict family size. Why?

SMALL FAMILIES, HAPPY FAMILIES

SOCIAL MARKETING

Culture

India's large population is made up of many different culture groups. The country's first civilisation originated in the Indus Valley several thousand years ago.

Three major outside influences have complicated India's cultural make-up, especially in language and religion. The main three external forces are:

● early Indo-European influences

● the spread of Islam

● British colonialism.

Languages

The population of India does not speak a common language. A wide variety of different languages is spoken:

● The Constitution of India recognises 18 languages.

● There are 1,600 minor languages and dialects.

● Schools teach in 58 languages.

● National newspapers are published in 87 languages.

● Radio programmes are broadcast in 71 languages.

This creates communication problems between different language groups and for effective government in India.

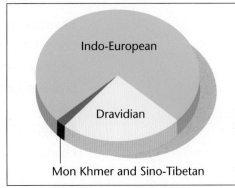

Fig. 21.11 The three main language families of India (English was also introduced through British colonialism.)

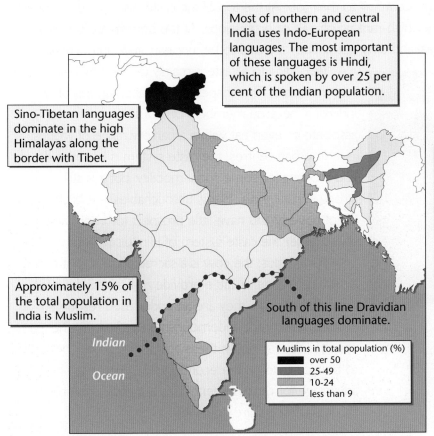

Most of northern and central India uses Indo-European languages. The most important of these languages is Hindi, which is spoken by over 25 per cent of the Indian population.

Sino-Tibetan languages dominate in the high Himalayas along the border with Tibet.

Approximately 15% of the total population in India is Muslim.

South of this line Dravidian languages dominate.

Indian Ocean

Muslims in total population (%)
over 50
25-49
10-24
less than 9

Fig. 21.12 Language regions and main areas where Muslims live in India

What problems can be created by having many different languages in one country?

Class Activity

Look at Figs. 21.11 and 21.12 and answer the following:

1. What are the two dominant language families in India?

2. What is the official language of India and to which language group does it belong?

3. What is the main religion in most of India?

4. Does the very high concentration of Muslims in the far north west of India give rise to problems? (See Chapter 28.)

5. Can you suggest a reason why there is a relatively high number of Muslims living in a zone going west to east across northern India? (Think about: trade routes.)

The various languages of India are based on three language families (see Fig. 21.11). The Indo-European language group dominates in India. This can be traced to migrants who entered the north west of India from Europe. Hindi is the largest and single most important language and is spoken by over 250 million people. It is the official language of India. Dravidian languages are spoken by about 200 million people, who live mainly in the south.

Although only 2 per cent of the population speak English, it is still an important language. Introduced under British colonial rule, it remains the language of business and the educated classes.

Although Hindi is the official state language, this is resented by many cultural groups. Bitter and often violent rivalries exist between language groups. Language is clearly a powerful expression of cultural differences, and, as well as religious divides, often emphasises the divisions within India rather than the unity of the state. This is a major problem for the development of India.

Religion

Hinduism

Indo-European influences also shaped the basis of **Hinduism**. This is the dominant religion in India and shapes much of the social and political life of the country and its people.

Hinduism introduced a multi-layered social system (or caste system). Individuals are grouped into a caste according to their job. At the top of the caste system are the priests (Brahmins) and other high-ranking officials or professions. At the bottom are the low castes that do menial and dirty tasks. They are said to be 'unclean' and 'untouchable'.

This street sweeper is one of the millions of 'untouchables' who live in extreme poverty in India.

● *Explain some of the reasons for this.*

Explain what is meant by a 'parasite on the economy'.

Belonging to a caste is mainly decided by being born into that caste. This shapes the social prospects of an individual because members of a caste can only marry, associate or even eat within a narrow range of groups.

In urban centres, the caste system is breaking down and allowing for some social mobility, but it is still very strong in rural India. Many 'untouchables' are limited to a life of poverty and have little prospect for improving their status under the caste system of Hinduism.

For Hindus, the cow is a sacred animal, so it cannot be killed. While the cattle provide milk, dried dung for fuel and pull carts, they are an under-used resource. Many poorly bred, undernourished cattle roam the countryside. For many, these animals could be considered to be a parasite on the economy, rather than an advantage for development. This is a good example of the impact of culture on development.

Minority religions in India

Although dominated by Hinduism, India also contains several important religious minorities.

- **Islam:** There are almost 200 million Muslims, mainly in northern India. Islam arrived in India in the tenth century from the north west and through trade links. Many people living in the great river systems of the Indus and Ganges converted to Islam, but not many converted from Hinduism to Islam in peninsular India. One of the major attractions of Islam for the low castes and 'untouchables' was that it rejects a rigid caste system and all converts are considered equal.

- **Buddhism:** The Buddhist religion started in India in the sixth century BC and later spread to other parts of the East. There are many Buddhists in the very south of India.

- **Sikhism:** This religion, founded in the fifteenth century, combines ideas from Hinduism and Islam. It does not have a caste system. The Sikhs are a powerful group centred in the Punjab (north-west India).

- **Christianity:** The Christians in India are linked to the time when India was a colony of Britain. There are small numbers of Christians scattered throughout India (and Pakistan and Bangladesh).

People who practise the Islamic religion are Muslims.

Political-Religious Divides in India

India was a colony of Britain for centuries. After independence in 1947, two states were created. These were based on religious divides. India became a Hindu state, while Pakistan was Islamic.

Drawing political boundaries on the basis of a majority religion was very difficult, and large numbers of minority religious groups were left in both countries. This led to rioting and large-scale migration. More than 15 million people moved, as Muslims went from India to Pakistan, and Hindus from Pakistan to India.

Pakistan was based on the majority Muslim population living in the Indus and Ganges river systems. As a result, this state was split into two parts, separated by a long distance with northern India in between. This was not practical and, in 1971, Pakistan broke up into two distinctive states: Pakistan (around the Indus Valley) and Bangladesh (associated with the lower Ganges Valley – Fig. 21.1). Tensions between India and Pakistan remain high, especially over the disputed territory of Kashmir (see Chapter 28).

Muslim men at prayer in Northern India, where this religion is concentrated

Hinduism is the dominant religion in India. Here Hindus bathe in the holy river of the Ganges.

Do you see any similarity over religious divides between India and Ireland?

Urban-Rural Development

The process of **urbanisation** is continuing strongly in India, especially because of large-scale rural to urban migration. Large numbers of people move (pushed) from poor rural communities by hope (pulled) of better prospects in growing cities. Approximately 270 million people lived in India's towns and cities at the start of the twenty-first century.

While urbanisation has a long tradition in India, the present patterns of urban development are linked to **two processes**:

- **British colonialism:** This emphasised the development of key ports and centres of administration such as Mumbai, Kolkata and Chennai.
- **National planning:** Following independence, national planning recognised the importance of modern urban centres for promoting industrial development. Large-scale investment was made to upgrade the infrastructure (e.g. transport) of key centres. When a new capital was set up at New Delhi (near Delhi), this also had important implications for the pattern of urban growth.

While there are towns and cities throughout India, regional concentrations are based on developments at **four** main cities (see Fig. 21.7):

- On the west coast around Mumbai (population 18.1 million).
- The southern tip of the peninsula linked to Chennai (6.6 million) and Bangalore (5.5 million).
- Kolkata (12.7 million) in the north east.
- Delhi – New Delhi (11.7 million).

Mumbai is India's largest city and has grown rapidly since independence through both in-migration and natural increase.

These four main urban regions have grown rapidly and have attracted many manufacturing and service industries. They also have huge problems of squalor and poverty linked to large-scale in-migration. The government faces major challenges in dealing with the urban poor, including housing, employment, health and education.

Although urbanisation is growing, about 760 million people still live in rural areas. Studying the villages of rural India is important in understanding India's problems of development. Villages in rural India:

- Have a very conservative and traditional society; they resist change.
- Have a rigid caste system, which limits people's social and economic progress.
- Are very dependent on the natural environment (especially the monsoon rains) and can be exposed to problems of famine.
- Have a subsistence economy, which means a hand-to-mouth existence for the people living there.
- Are self-sufficient. They make goods and supply services for themselves, with little surplus for trade and interaction with outside areas.
- Are often overpopulated, especially as there is a limit to the amount of land available.
- Lack the money (capital) to invest in basic facilities.

Rural poverty and other related issues, such as rapid population growth and a reluctance to adopt more modern farming practices, are major issues for the government of India. Dealing with these problems will not be easy and will not happen in a short time period. Do you agree with this conclusion? Explain.

SECTION 6 (CHAPTERS 22–24)
THE COMPLEXITY OF A REGION

This section builds on the section The Dynamics of a Region, which highlighted how a combination of complex interactions gives a region its individual identity. You will see examples at different levels in this section. For smaller regions, we shall look at Ireland and the Sápmi region in northern Norrland. On a large scale, we will review the relationships and structures that will shape the future of the European Union.

This section has three chapters:

- Chapter 22   Economic, Political and Cultural Activities in Regions
- Chapter 23   Cultural Groups and Political Regions
- Chapter 24   The Future of the European Union

Flags of EU members

Northern Ireland football supporters

Anti-ETA demonstration in Spain

CHAPTER 22
ECONOMIC, POLITICAL AND CULTURAL ACTIVITIES IN REGIONS

KEY IDEA!

The study of regions highlights how complex are the ways that economic, cultural and political processes act on each other.

Regional identities in geography are usually developed through studying **complex interactions** both within a region and between that region and its surrounding areas. While a large number of processes interact in forming a region's identity, **the most important are economic, cultural and political activities**.

In this chapter, **two examples** are used to show how economic, cultural and political activities affect each other to make a region's special identity:

● The Republic of Ireland and Northern Ireland
● The Sápmi region.

IRELAND'S CHANGING RELATIONSHIPS ON THE ISLAND OF IRELAND

At the start of the twentieth century, the two islands of Britain and Ireland were controlled by a powerful and centralised government in London. In 1922, Ireland gained political independence from Britain. Six north-eastern counties, however, remained as a part of Britain, and a new political boundary was created to separate what is now the Republic of Ireland from Northern Ireland (Fig. 22.1). This division of Ireland has strong historical roots and has had major implications on north-south relationships on the island of Ireland.

Ireland before independence and partition

The population of the north-eastern part of Ireland had historically built up a culture and economy that was very different from the rest of the island. For example, large numbers of English and Scottish settlers were brought to the region during the **Ulster plantation** of the seventeenth century. These settlers had a different culture and religion to the local Catholic population.

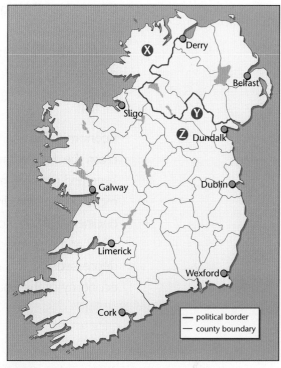

Fig. 22.1 The political divide in Ireland

The north-eastern region was also the only part of Ireland to experience large-scale industrialisation in the nineteenth century. So, at the time of partition in 1921:

● Two-thirds of Northern Ireland's population were Protestant, while the rest of Ireland was overwhelmingly Catholic.

● Northern Ireland was a prosperous industrial economy with strong trade links to Britain.

● The rest of Ireland was a depressed rural economy.

● The Protestant majority benefited from links with Britain, while the rest of Ireland associated British rule with poverty, migration and the suppression of Gaelic culture.

The majority of Ireland's population saw political independence from Britain as essential for their economic and cultural development.

In the 1921 Referendum the Protestant majority in six counties chose to keep their union with Britain, and became known as Unionists.

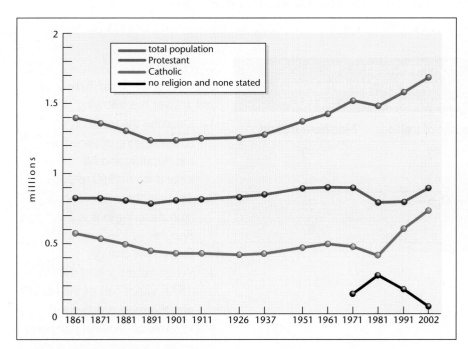

Fig. 22.2 Catholic and Protestant population trends in Northern Ireland

Changing Relationships between the Republic and Northern Ireland

The creation of the political boundary between the Republic and Northern Ireland emphasised long-standing political, economic and cultural differences. Since the 1960s, however, these differences have been reduced. Much of this has been due to the **modernisation** of the Republic's economic, cultural and political systems.

Economic Trends

From the 1960s, the Republic has attracted many foreign industries and has built up a large and modern manufacturing economy (Chapter 18, pages 212 to 216). In contrast, most of Northern Ireland's old, traditional industries, such as textiles and shipbuilding, declined. Furthermore, the period of civil disturbances (the 'Troubles') that began in 1968 and continued into the 1990s discouraged foreign investors. The result has been a depressed regional economy in the North as opposed to the prosperous Celtic Tiger economy of the South (Figs. 22.3 and Table 22.1).

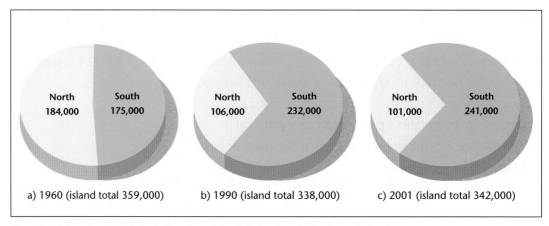

| North 184,000 | South 175,000 | North 106,000 | South 232,000 | North 101,000 | South 241,000 |

a) 1960 (island total 359,000)   b) 1990 (island total 338,000)   c) 2001 (island total 342,000)

Fig. 22.3 Manufacturing jobs in the Republic of Ireland and Northern Ireland

GDP Per Capita in the Republic of Ireland and Northern Ireland as a Percentage of GDP in the EU		
	Republic of Ireland	Northern Ireland
1973	59	79
1980	63	62
1990	68	74
2002	125	82

Table 22.1

Class Activity

Look at Fig. 22.3 and Table 22.1 and answer the following:

1. Describe the trends in manufacturing employment in the Republic and Northern Ireland from 1960 to 2001.
2. Estimate the proportion of manufacturing jobs in the Republic in 1960 and 2001. Explain the change.
3. When Ireland joined the EU in 1973, which part of the island was the most prosperous?
4. In terms of personal prosperity is the Republic still 'the poor relation of the North'?

Cultural Changes

While there are still cultural differences between the north and south, they are now less marked. Much of this has been linked to changes to more modern attitudes and ways of life in Ireland, especially in the Republic.

Political Interaction on the Island of Ireland

Political tensions between the Republic, Northern Ireland and Britain have been harder to resolve. This was especially the case during the 'Troubles', when a state of almost civil war existed between extreme Nationalist and Unionist groups (see Chapter 14, page 181).

During the 1990s, significant efforts were made to improve the political situation. In 1998, a major step forward occurred with the signing of the **Belfast Agreement** (also called the Good Friday Agreement). This created **three** new political bodies to act as the basis for what are called **strands** (see Fig. 22.4). These strands are designed to link together the political capitals of Belfast, Dublin and London. **In this way, inter-relationships are stressed rather than political division.**

> How would more prosperity and urbanisation, together with the Catholic Church having less influence in shaping people's lives in the Republic, help reduce the sense of difference between north and south?

> Do you think that an all-Ireland approach is the best way to address problems on the island of Ireland?

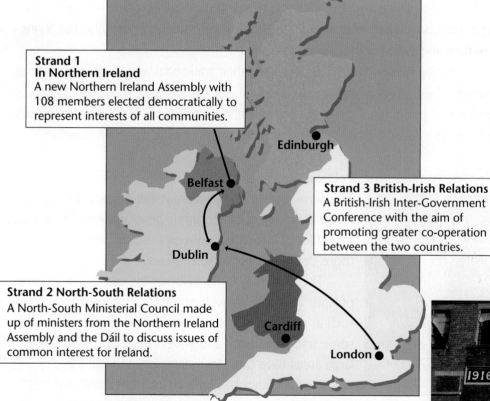

**Strand 1
In Northern Ireland**
A new Northern Ireland Assembly with 108 members elected democratically to represent interests of all communities.

Strand 3 British-Irish Relations
A British-Irish Inter-Government Conference with the aim of promoting greater co-operation between the two countries.

Strand 2 North-South Relations
A North-South Ministerial Council made up of ministers from the Northern Ireland Assembly and the Dáil to discuss issues of common interest for Ireland.

Fig. 22.4 The three strands of the Belfast Agreement

In spite of movements to integrate, signs of political and social division are still strongly evident in the landscapes of Northern Ireland.

Activity

Look at Fig. 22.4 and answer the following:
1. Why is the word 'strand' appropriate for this process?
2. What two strands operate within the island of Ireland.
3. Where in Belfast does the Northern Ireland Assembly meet?

THE SÁPMI REGION

In Chapter 20, we studied the regional geography of Norrland. In Norrland there is a small but distinctive cultural group called **the Sami (or Lapps)**. These people live not only in northern Sweden but occupy the northern parts of three other countries (Fig. 22.5). **This region is called Sápmi.**

Fig. 22.5 The area where the Sami live in northern Europe

Cultural Activities

About 50,000 to 65,000 Sami live in Sápmi. They have a strong tradition in art, music and handcrafts, as well as their own language. This distinct cultural group are, however, a minority people within their region because many 'outsiders' (Swedes, Norwegians and Finns) have migrated into these northern lands to access natural resources, such as forestry and iron ore (see Chapter 20).

> **What are the four countries in which the Sami live?**

> **What do you think 'living within nature and with the help of nature' means?**

Economic Activities

Living conditions in northern Scandinavia are severe, but the Sami have adapted well to their difficult Arctic environment. Hunting, fishing and especially herding reindeer have long been the basis of their economy. As a people they have been described as **'living within nature and with the help of nature'**.

It is becoming harder for the Sami to keep their traditional way of life and make a living from it. The traditional primary activities are not attractive for most young Sami. They prefer to work in the large, resource-based industries such as mining and forestry that have set up in their region, or migrate to the larger cities in southern Sweden.

About 3,000 Sami herd 260,000 reindeer over large areas of Norrland. It is a difficult lifestyle and today only one in five Sami is involved in reindeer herding.

Political Activities

The Sami receive comparatively little government support, especially in terms of economic development. This reflects a **conflict of interests** between the Sami way of life and more powerful economic interests.

The Sami way of life involves the use of a large area of land. This conflicts with other potential uses for the land, such as mining and forestry. While Sami rights of access to some traditional lands and waters have been guaranteed, large areas have been lost, especially to large forestry operations. Without a more co-ordinated and stronger approach by the four national governments to the needs of the Sami, the future of this distinctive cultural region may be in question.

TEST YOURSELF AT
my-etest.com

CHAPTER 23
CULTURAL GROUPS AND POLITICAL REGIONS

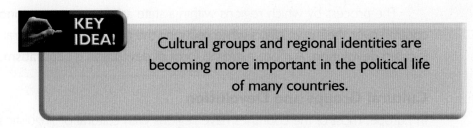

Cultural groups and regional identities are becoming more important in the political life of many countries.

Europe is a patchwork of different cultural groups and political units. The interaction between these is essential for understanding Europe as a distinctive region. There are **three** terms that are important:

● nation state
● state
● nation.

Nation State

The ideal nation state is defined as a country that has political boundaries containing a population with a high level of **cultural sameness**. It should also have a sovereign government with the authority to organise the population within the state.

State

A state is a politically organised territory that is administered by a sovereign government.

Nation

A group of tightly-knit people who have a common culture: language, ethnicity, religion and other cultural values. Many nations have gained political recognition and have become nation states. Other nations, however, have not yet established their own sovereignty and live within another internationally recognised state. An example of this is the Palestinians, who do not yet have a homeland.

Activity
Which of the following can be best described as a nation state, state or nation?
a. The Basques
b. France
c. Switzerland
d. Belgium
e. Scotland
f. Sweden
g. Ireland

Although most of Europe's countries are considered to be nation states, they all have **cultural minorities**. Generally, these groups identify with the state they live in and add to the strength and character of the state. For example, the German-speaking minority living in eastern Belgium think of themselves as Belgians. Second-generation Turks born in Germany probably regard themselves as German first, and Turkish second.

> A sovereign government is one with supreme power within its territory.

> 'Cultural sameness' generally means a population that has the feeling of being a nation because it has a common language, culture and history.

> 'Ethnicity' means belonging to a cultural group.

> Would second-generation Irish born in Britain regard themselves as British or Irish? What about in the United States?

275

Separatism sees devolution as a stepping stone to independence and the emergence of a new nation state.

There are some examples of minority culture groups, especially those with strong identities, who feel their interests are ignored or threatened by the dominant culture group. In such cases, the links that tie the state together become weakened. **Nationalist groups** can emerge to represent their interests and **begin to look for greater powers of self-government**. These groups include the Scots and Welsh within Britain, and the Basques and Catalans within Spain.

The process by which regions within a state ask for greater **autonomy** (political control) over their own affairs while reducing the powers of the central government is called **devolution**. A more extreme form of devolution is **separatism**.

Cultural Groups and Devolution

In Europe, most of the countries have regions with cultural or linguistic minority groups. Fig. 23.1 shows regions where people are asking for greater autonomy (self-government) from central government. These regions are usually located on the margins of the state. The people who live there feel that their cultural and economic interests can be better served by more self-government.

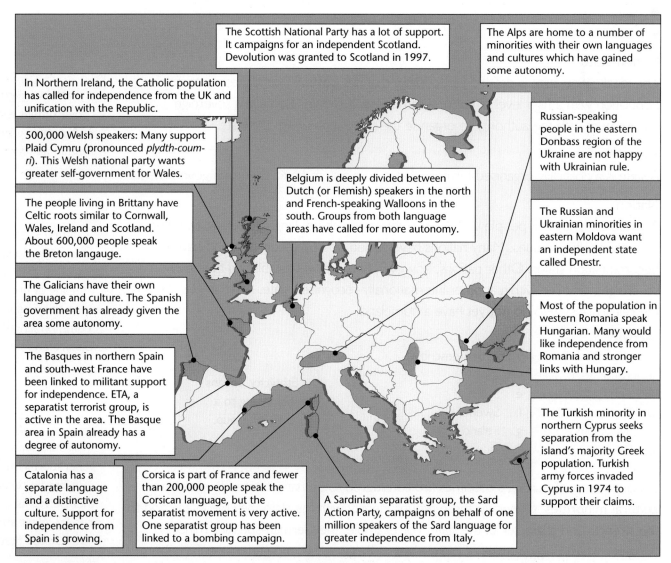

Fig. 23.1 Cultural groups in Europe which have demanded greater autonomy from central government

In some cases, national governments have accepted the demands for greater self-government and these regions have been given more autonomy. Examples include Scotland and Wales in Britain and the Basque Country and Catalonia in Spain.

In other cases, central governments cannot accept the levels of self government some nationalist groups demand. This is especially the case where these groups demand independence and the break-up of an existing country. Where this happens, cultural and political relationships between the region and the central government can become violent. The result may be extremist groups leading terror campaigns against the official government, as in the Basque Country in Spain.

Support for the Basque separatist group ETA displayed in San Sebastian, in the Basque region of northern Spain

Case Study: Cultural Groups and Devolution in Spain

In Spain, the government has been centred on the capital, Madrid, for centuries. Although the central government is still powerful, Spain has several well-defined cultural groups that have their own language. The best-known groups are probably in the Basque Country and Catalonia.

Each of these regions has been given powers by the central government to administer a range of key functions, such as cultural affairs, education, economic development and the environment. Both regions have their own parliaments. Their distinctive languages, Basque (called Euskera in the Basque language) and Catalan, are co-official languages with Spanish.

The Basque Country is perhaps the Spanish region that is best known for demanding independence from Spain. As a people, the Basques are a distinctive cultural group that occupy an area on each side of the Pyrenees in northern Spain and south-west France. The core of the Basque area is in northern Spain and has a population of 2 million. Bilbao is the largest city in the region (Fig. 23.2).

> The Basque region is located mainly in northern Spain, although a large number of Basques also live in south-western France.

Activity
Look at Fig. 23.2 and answer the following:
1. What are the main cities of the Basque Country and Catalonia?
2. Where are the two regions located in Spain?

The Basques in northern Spain:
● Have lived in the area for about 10,000 years, so they have developed their own special cultural identity.
● Are a distinctive ethnic group.
● Speak a language (Euskera) that is not like any other European language.

Above all, **it is because the Basque language has survived that this is a distinctive cultural region**. Under past Spanish governments, the

Fig. 23.2 The location of the Basque Country and Catalonia in Spain

In their attempts to gain independence from Spain, ETA has used violent tactics such as car bombs in Madrid.

Euskera language was illegal, and large numbers of Basque nationalists were put in prison for calling for independence and for their cultural roots to be recognised.

One reaction to government repression was the extremist nationalist group called ETA (*Euskadi ta Askatasuma*), which declared war on the Spanish state. ETA has been, and continues to be, involved in a large number of bombings and assassinations in its drive to gain independence from Spain.

In 1979, the Basque Country in Spain was granted a high level of autonomy. This weakened public support for ETA in the area because it seemed that democratic means were working in gaining self-government for the region. The cultural strength of this region has been the basis for gaining the Basques a more equal relationship with the national government in Madrid.

Catalonia is another Spanish region that has gained a lot of regional autonomy because it has a distinct cultural identity. Centred on the major industrial and trading city of Barcelona, the Catalans have a strong sense of nationalism. They have their own language, Catalan, and have a very prosperous economy.

Although it has only 6 per cent of the Spanish population, Catalonia accounts for nearly 40 per cent of Spain's industrial exports. It attracts high-technology industry, has strong trading traditions, and Catalonia has emerged as **one of the four motors of the EU** (see Fig. 15.3 in Chapter 15).

With Catalonia's economic success, its pride in its cultural distinctiveness and the strength of feeling to achieve independence from Spain, it is not surprising that the Spanish government has devolved power to Catalonia to keep this important region within Spain.

Do you see any similarities between Ireland and the Basques in their efforts to achieve autonomy or independence?

The Catalan demands for greater political autonomy are supported by a much stronger economic basis than in the Basque region.

The modern cathedral of Sagrada Familia in Barcelona stands as a symbol of a strong and growing Catalan identity and culture.

TEST YOURSELF AT
my-etest.com

CHAPTER 24
THE FUTURE OF THE
EUROPEAN UNION

KEY IDEA!

Future developments in the European Union will have a major influence on the economics, politics and sovereignty within Europe.

In 1957, the Treaty of Rome brought together six countries to form the European Economic Community (EEC). The aim was to develop the economies of the member states and unite Western Europe after the Second World War. This process was successful, and by the mid-1990s the original six countries had expanded into a **European Union** (EU) of 15 member states.

The fall of the 'Iron Curtain' separating East and Western Europe in 1989–1990 presented opportunities for further developments. It encouraged:

- Further enlargement.
- Further integration.

Look at Chapter 27 to learn more about how the EU was formed and when different countries joined (enlargements).

Further Integration in the EU

By the 1990s, the EU realised that if it was to grow as a leading world region it needed to strengthen its policies and institutions. **Three** treaties have been important in this process.

The Maastricht Treaty (1992)

This treaty established **three pillars** as the basis on which the EU would work in the future. To be effective, the EU could no longer be based only on economic objectives, such as free trade (Fig. 24.1).

- The **economic pillar** emphasised the continued importance of economic development, through the Single European Market (SEM) and Economic and Monetary Union (EMU) (see page 280).
- The **political pillar** recognised the need for the EU to strengthen its role in foreign affairs and defence (see pages 281–282).
- The **social pillar** was to give more social benefits to EU citizens and to deal with crime and immigration problems.

What is free trade?

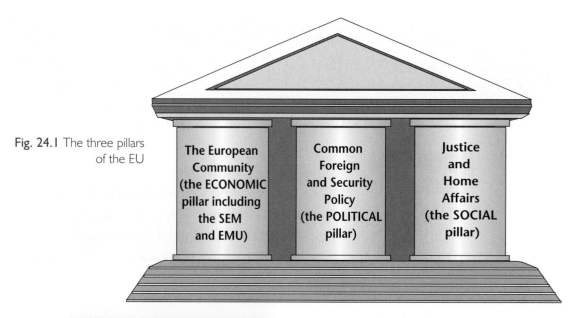

Fig. 24.1 The three pillars of the EU

| The European Community (the ECONOMIC pillar including the SEM and EMU) | Common Foreign and Security Policy (the POLITICAL pillar) | Justice and Home Affairs (the SOCIAL pillar) |

Before EMU and the introduction of the euro, each EU member state had its own currency and exchange rate.
● *Did this have any disadvantages for the EU?*

What advantages does a single currency have for the people and economies of the EU?

The Amsterdam Treaty (1997)

Social concerns were emphasised in this treaty. It placed employment and citizen rights at the 'heart' of the EU.

The Nice Treaty (2002)

This treaty focused on the need to change the institutions and voting systems to allow for further enlargement of the EU.

Together, these three treaties have important implications for the future of the EU, especially as they influence:

● Economic union
● Political union
● Sovereignty.

Economic Union

In 1993, the Single European Market (SEM) was established. This allowed for the free movement of goods, services, capital and people within the EU. It reduced costs of production and improved the competitiveness of the EU in world trade.

Most governments felt that for the SEM to be effective, it was also necessary to introduce a **single currency**. The idea of an **Economic and Monetary Union (EMU)** was agreed under the Maastricht Treaty. In 2002, the new EU currency called the **euro** was introduced.

The size of the Economic Union increased following enlargement in 2004. This will increase further in 2007 when Bulgaria and Romania are expected to join (see Table 24.1 and Fig. 27.1). Turkey's application for membership is still being discussed. Although economic opportunities will increase for many industries because the size of markets is larger, the underdeveloped economies of the new member states will pose many problems for the EU.

Some Development Indicators of New and Projected Member States of the EU and Turkey						
Country	Area in sq km	Population (millions)	GDP per head as % of EU average	Unemployment (%)	Agriculture as a % of GDP	Agriculture as a % of employment
Bulgaria	110,912	8.2	24	16.4	15.8	11.3
Cyprus	9,251	0.8	83	3.4	3.5	9.2
Czech Republic	78,884	10.3	60	8.8	3.4	7.4
Estonia	45,100	1.4	38	13.7	4.7	7.4
Hungary	93,032	10.0	52	6.4	3.9	4.8
Latvia	64,600	2.4	29	14.6	4.0	13.5
Lithuania	65,200	3.7	29	16.0	6.9	19.6
Malta	316	0.4	53	4.5	2.0	1.9
Poland	312,685	38.6	39	16.1	2.9	18.8
Romania	238,391	22.4	27	7.1	11.4	42.8
Slovak Republic	49,012	5.4	48	18.6	4.1	6.7
Slovenia	20,265	2.0	72	7.0	2.9	9.9
Turkey	774,815	65.3	29	6.6	11.2	34.9
Total/Average	1,003,000	171.0	33	12.5	6.9	27.8
EU (15)	1,317,000	375.0	100	8.2	2.0	4.3

Table 24.1

Class Activity

Study the data in Table 24.1 and suggest some of the advantages and problems that enlargement might bring to the EU.

Political Union

In the 1990s, debate increased within the EU over the need to strengthen its process of political integration. This took account of developments such as the collapse of Communism, wars in former Yugoslavia and the Middle East and the threat of international terrorism. It was important that the EU should take a stronger role in world affairs.

This led to the introduction of **a Common Foreign and Security Policy (CFSP)** under the Maastricht Treaty. Progress has been made, and the EU has shown signs of 'speaking with one voice' in a number of international areas. Examples include peace-keeping duties in Bosnia, discussions over world trade and concerns over the world's environment. Discussions for an EU constitution have also included creating a new position of Foreign Minister for the EU.

In the 1990s, soldiers from different EU countries took on peace-keeping duties in Bosnia on behalf of the United Nations.

281

Keeping control over their foreign policy remains a sensitive issue for most EU governments, as member states often have different political agendas and are very reluctant to allow the EU to make decisions for them. Suggestions for a common defence arrangement have also given rise to differing opinions between member states. Neutral countries, such as Ireland, have a major problem with any military role for the EU.

A lot of work still remains before the EU can achieve a political union that works as well as its economic union. And, the task will get harder with further enlargement.

> Differences over a common EU foreign policy were highlighted by Britain's support of the USA in the war with Iraq in 2003.

Sovereignty

A key feature of the Treaty of Rome (1957), which created what is today called the EU, was that member states had **to give up some degree of sovereignty, or decision-making powers**, to this new international organisation. This was necessary if the EU was to function efficiently.

Four main institutions are involved in making decisions in the EU (Fig. 24.2):
- European Commission
- European Parliament
- Council of the European Union, also called the Council of Ministers
- European Council.

At first, these institutions had few powers but as the EU has evolved they have gained more importance.

> The EU now has many more decision-making powers. As a result, the member states have less sovereignty than before.

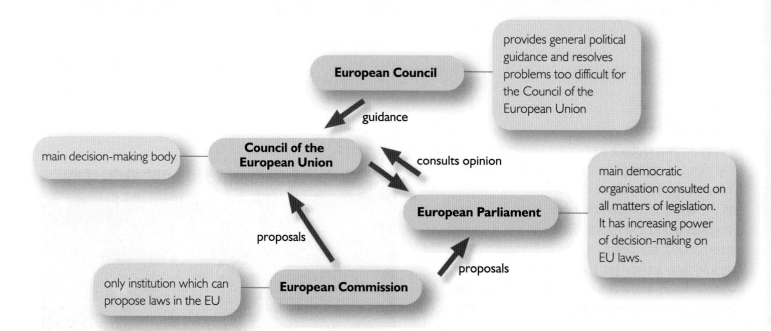

Fig. 24.2 How decisions are made in the EU

The European Commission

The main functions of the Commission are:

● It is the centre for EU administration.

● It represents the interests of the EU and is independent of national governments.

● It monitors EU policies to see that they work effectively.

● It is the only EU institution that can propose new legislation but it has
no decision-making powers.

The Commission is headquartered in Brussels, and is divided into sections called **directorates** (something like government departments). Each directorate is headed by a **commissioner**. At present, all member states can nominate at least one commissioner and the role of commissioner is regarded as being very important.

Proposals have been recently made to **reduce the number of commissioners**. This could mean that in an enlarged EU some countries, especially smaller member states, will not have a commissioner. Ireland and other smaller states are very keen to keep their commissioners.

> Why do smaller member states want to be able to carry on nominating a commissioner?

The European Parliament

This is the key forum for democratic debate in the EU. Since 1979, voters in all EU countries elect members of the European Parliament (MEPs) for five years. After enlargement in 2004, the number of MEPs will increase from 626 to 732.

At first, the European Parliament had limited powers. Since the Maastricht Treaty, it has gained increasing powers, including being able to approve or reject the EU budget. In particular, the European Parliament now has a joint decision-making role with the Council of the European Union in a growing number of policy areas.

> Ireland has 15 MEPs, but at the next election this will be reduced to 12 MEPs.

The Parliament has three separate locations: Strasbourg, Brussels and Luxembourg. Different sessions of the Parliament are held in Brussels and Strasbourg, and the Secretariat is located in Luxembourg. Each month, on average, MEPs spend two weeks in Brussels, a week in Strasbourg and a week in their constituencies. This is very inefficient, but none of the three cities, or their national governments, will give up the prestige and benefits of being linked to the European Parliament.

The European Parliament building in Strasbourg

A cartoon by Plantu for the French newspaper, *Le Monde*.

Activity

Look at the cartoon and an atlas and answer the following questions:

1. Find the three cities on a map of Europe.
2. Why is this arrangement expensive and inefficient?
3. What benefits do you think these cities gain from being linked to the European Parliament?

> The Council of the European Union is also called the Council of Ministers. It is the main decision-making body in the EU.

The Council of the European Union

This is the main decision-making institution for the EU. Each member state sends to the Council its minister responsible for the policy area to be discussed. For example, ministers for agriculture attend Council meetings that debate agricultural policy.

Each member state takes over the Presidency of the Council for six months. This is a very powerful role within the EU, especially for smaller member states, such as Ireland.

The European Council

Although this was not one of the original EU institutions, it has become more important. Since 1974, the heads of EU governments have met twice each year at a European Council, or summit. The political leaders debate the EU's overall political programme as well as helping to resolve complex or difficult issues on which the Council of the EU cannot agree. For example, it is the European Council that has to approve any enlargement of the EU.

TEST YOURSELF AT
my-etest.com

HOW REGIONS CHANGE OVER TIME

Regions change over time, especially when they are defined by human ideas, including religion and languages. This is because of how the processes that we looked at in the sections The Dynamics of a Region and The Complexity of a Region work together. As people migrate, the size of cultural regions changes. As transport systems improve, city regions spread out. On an international scale, the growing size of the European Union highlights the way political boundaries can change.

This section has four chapters:

- Chapter 25   Changing Boundaries in Language Regions
- Chapter 26   Urban Growth and City Regions
- Chapter 27   Development and Expansion of the EU
- Chapter 28   Changing Political Boundaries and
               Cultural Groups

Military patrol on the Line
of Control in Kashmir

Breaking down the
Berlin Wall in 1989

CHAPTER 25
CHANGING BOUNDARIES IN LANGUAGE REGIONS

KEY IDEA! The size and shape of language regions can change over time.

The regional boundaries of human activities change a lot over time. This is due mainly to **two** processes:
- Push-pull forces of migration
- The effect of strong external forces.

The **push-pull forces of migration** cause people to move from one region to another. When more people move into a region than leave, the region usually expands its boundaries. For example, rural-urban migration (when people move from the country into towns) often creates population pressure in the urban area, which then expands outwards into suburbs and rural areas around the town.

On another scale, the widespread migration of Islamic people to areas outside the Middle East has resulted in a large increase in the regions influenced by the religion of Islam (see Chapter 14, Fig. 14.3).

Strong external forces affect a region's identity. Stronger and more aggressive cultural forces can work to reduce the importance and regional patterns of minority cultures. For example, modern communication systems (radio, television and the Internet) have allowed the importance of major world languages, especially English, to increase. This often reduces the status of minority languages.

The decline of Irish and Welsh are examples of how both processes have changed the regional boundaries of these ancient Celtic languages.

Irish emigrants sailing for New York from Cobh early in the twentieth century
- *Why have so many people emigrated from Ireland?*

Boundary Changes of Gaeltacht Areas

In 1851, the census of Ireland recorded 1.5 million people as speaking Irish. Large areas along the southern and especially the western coastline kept Irish as their majority language (Fig. 25.1).

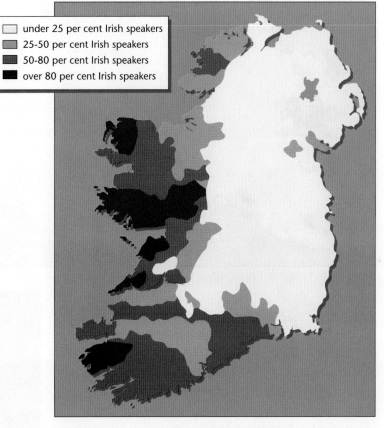

Fig. 25.1 The Irish-speaking population in 1851

Legend:
- under 25 per cent Irish speakers
- 25-50 per cent Irish speakers
- 50-80 per cent Irish speakers
- over 80 per cent Irish speakers

Activity
Look at Fig. 25.1 and and answer the following:
1. Which parts of Ireland in 1851 show more than 50 per cent of the population speaking Irish?
2. Why was so little Irish spoken in eastern and northern Ireland?

The Irish Language from 1861 to 1926
In the period from 1861 to 1926, the number of Irish speakers declined to 544,000. The changes were greatest in Munster and Connaught, provinces that traditionally had the most Irish speakers (Figs. 25.1 and 25.2). Declines in these core regions for the Irish language were so strong that many people felt that the Irish language would become extinct in the twentieth century.

The decline in the area and numbers of Irish speakers was due to:
- large-scale emigration
- the growing dominance of English.

The Irish Language from 1926 up to now
On gaining independence from Britain, the new government committed itself to supporting the Irish language as an essential part of national identity. This support took several forms:
- Irish became the official language of the state, and being able to speak Irish was essential for many jobs, especially in government administration and public services.
- Irish was included as a compulsory subject in the school syllabus.
- An official Gaeltacht area, set up in 1926, has been strongly supported by the government.

These measures were aimed at reducing the dominance of the English language. Irish would be the majority language in the Gaeltacht and would act as the core regions to preserve and promote the Irish language.

At one level, the measures to support the Irish language appear to have been very successful. The numbers of people claiming to speak Irish in Ireland have increased from 589,000 in 1946 to some 1.57 million today. Interestingly, the largest numbers are located in Leinster. This reflects, perhaps, the fact that some knowledge of Irish is needed to work in government and administration, which is concentrated in Dublin.

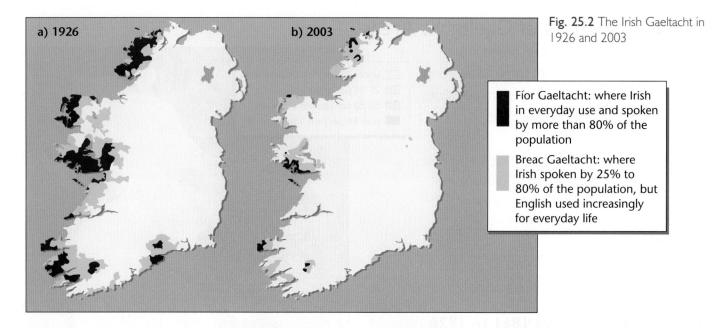

a) 1926

b) 2003

Fig. 25.2 The Irish Gaeltacht in 1926 and 2003

Fíor Gaeltacht: where Irish in everyday use and spoken by more than 80% of the population

Breac Gaeltacht: where Irish spoken by 25% to 80% of the population, but English used increasingly for everyday life

Activity

Look at Fig. 25.2 and answer the following:

1. In 1926, which counties were identified most with the Fíor Gaeltacht?
2. What major changes took place to the boundaries of the Irish-speaking region from 1851 to 1926?
3. Where would you locate the core areas of the current Irish-speaking population?
4. In what ways are these different to 1926?

The boundaries of the Gaeltacht have changed. Various initiatives, such as the launch of the club SULT for young Irish speakers in Dublin, are being made to increase the use of Irish in non-Gaeltacht areas.

● *How effective do you think these will be in reviving the Irish language?*

While a growing number of people in Ireland claim an ability to speak Irish, relatively few are fluent and use Irish on a daily basis. English is by far the dominant language of Ireland's population.

This is highlighted by the big change in **the boundaries of the Gaeltacht** where Irish is the majority language (Fig. 25.2). Compared to 1926, the present Gaeltacht has been reduced to relatively small and isolated areas that occupy the peninsulas of the west coast of Ireland. Even these areas face an uncertain future because the English-language culture is so strong.

TEST YOURSELF AT
my-etest.com

CHAPTER 26
URBAN GROWTH AND CITY REGIONS

 **KEY IDEA!** The growth of urban areas and the expansion of city regions are key features of development.

World Urbanisation

Up until 1950, levels of global urbanisation were low and showed only a slow rate of increase (Table 26.1). Since then, however, there has been a massive increase in urbanisation. By 2000, almost half of the world's population of 6 billion lived in urban areas.

How Urbanisation Has Developed	
Year	% of people living in cities
1800	5%
1950	6%
2000	48%
2025	65% (estimated)

Table 26.1

Levels of urbanisation are highest in the more developed countries of the world (Table 26.2). Urbanisation is growing fastest, however, in the less developed regions. **By 2025, some 80 per cent of the world's urban population will live in less developed regions of the world.**

> Urbanisation measures the proportion of a total population living in an urban area.

Trends in global urbanisation 1970-2025						
Region	Urban Population (millions)			Urban Share (%)		
	1970	1995	2025	1970	1995	2025
More developed regions:	677	868	1,040	68	75	84
Europe	423	532	598	64	73	83
North America	167	221	313	74	76	85
Japan	74	97	313	71	78	85
Less developed regions:	676	1,653	4,025	25	37	57
Africa	84	240	804	23	33	54
Asia	428	1,062	2,615	21	32	54
Latin America	163	349	601	57	74	85

Table 26.2

Half the world heads for life in the big city
Within six years more than half of humanity will live in cities for the first time in history. . . . Increasing urbanisation will see growing concentration in the largest cities, with more than a quarter of people in settlements of more than 1 million by 2025.

The world will be increasingly dominated by vast conurbations in Asia and Africa. . . . The populations of new giant cities such as Lagos (23.2 m) in Nigeria and Mumbai (26.1 m), plus 25 other cities will pass 20 million. Such cities will prove increasingly difficult for poor countries to maintain. The poor will increasingly be concentrated in their own neighbourhoods characterised by high rates of crime, violence and social disaster.

[Despite this] from 2015 the bulk of population growth will occur in urbanised areas, thus guaranteeing that the human future will be an urban one.

Sunday Times, 2 September 2002

Class Activity
Study Tables 26.1 and 26.2 and the newspaper extract and answer the following:
1. What percentage of world population currently lives in urban areas?
2. In 1970, Europe and Asia had almost the same total urban population. Contrast the trends for these regions for 1970 to 2025.
3. Which continents will be dominated by conurbations (very large cities) in the future?
4. What problems will these large cities be exposed to?

Urbanisation in the European Union

The EU has many large and important cities, and 80 per cent of its population live in urban areas (Fig. 26.1). Most of these cities continue to grow in population, and their built-up areas now extend well beyond their administrative boundaries. This is called **urban sprawl.**

In addition, modern transport and communication systems have allowed these cities to have an important influence over an extensive area or hinterland (for example, travel to work and shop). This is called the **daily urban system.** For large cities like London this can extend to about 150 km, while for Dublin it is some 80 km.

Two case studies are introduced to illustrate the growth and expansion of city regions in the EU:
● Randstad
● Dublin.

Car ownership has been a key factor in enabling large-scale urban sprawl to develop.

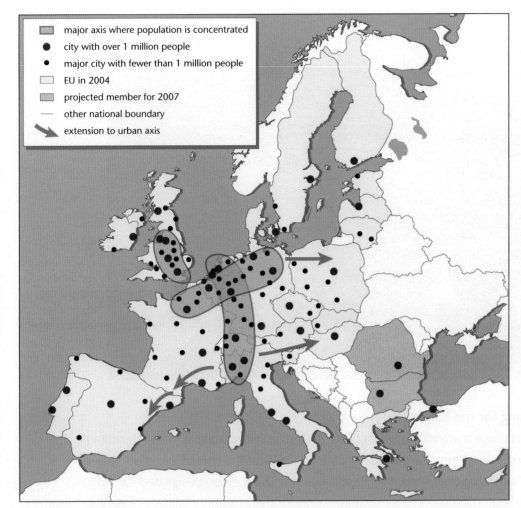

major axis where population is concentrated
● city with over 1 million people
• major city with fewer than 1 million people
▢ EU in 2004
▨ projected member for 2007
— other national boundary
➤ extension to urban axis

Fig. 26.1 Urbanisation in the EU and applicant countries

Look at Fig 26.1 and describe the patterns of urban development in the EU. Suggest reasons for the expansion of the urban axes in the directions shown.

Case Study: Randstad Holland

The western part of the Netherlands is one of the most urbanised regions in Europe. Most of the country's major cities are in this area, which has a radius of about 50 km. The growth and expansion of the towns and cities in this small area have resulted in a sprawling urban region called Randstad Holland.

The **Randstad** is shaped like a horseshoe, with an open end in the less populated east. It is a **polycentric city** region, which means it is made up of a number of major cities, with no single city being dominant. At its centre is an important agricultural and recreational area. This is the **Greenheart** of the Randstad (Fig. 26.2).

Since the end of World War II, the Randstad has grown rapidly. This has been due to the region's strategic location within the core of the EU, its excellent transport systems and Rotterdam, the EU's largest port.

As this urban region developed, competition for land increased and caused urban sprawl to occur around the Randstad cities. In particular, it put huge pressure on the Greenheart.

The **Randstad** contains 40 per cent (6 million) of the Dutch population living on only 17 per cent of the country's land area. Locate the **Randstad** on Fig. 26.1.

Increased demand for housing, industry, transport and recreation all contribute to the problems of congestion and urban sprawl.

The town of Zoetermeer in the Randstadt is separated from other urban centres by the green belt in the background.

Planning for the Randstad

Planners face many difficulties in trying to overcome problems in the Randstad. The focus has been placed mainly on trying to limit the spread of urban sprawl.

At the **national level**, five regional centres have been designated for major investment in infrastructures such as transport and housing. Planners hope that these regional centres will become a stronger attraction for people and economic development, and reduce pressure on the Randstad (see Fig. 26.2).

In the **Randstad**, some high-density development will be allowed close to the major cities, but urban sprawl will be strongly controlled by using **buffer zones**, also called **greenbelts**. Urban developments will also be encouraged along the eastern edge of the Randstad to close off its 'open' edge.

Buffer zones, or **greenbelts**, are important for planning. The idea is to try and limit urban sprawl by creating special areas where there can be no urban development. This is essential for the Randstad, if the Greenheart is to be protected.

EU Concerns About Randstad Growth

For the **EU**, controlling the expansion of the Randstad is also important. If uncontrolled urban growth is allowed eastwards along the Rhine river, the Randstad could eventually join up with the expanding cities of the Rhine-Ruhr (see Fig. 26.2). To the south, unplanned expansion could link up with the Brussels-Antwerp-Ghent growth zone of Belgium.

The result would be a **West European megalopolis**, with a huge concentration of population and economic activities in one vast and almost continuous urban sprawl. This would be an environmental disaster and will require strong planning controls to keep open spaces between these expanding urban regions.

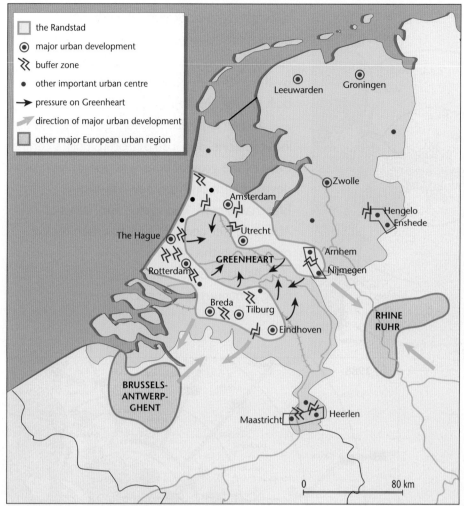

Fig. 26.2 Planning for Randstad Holland

Activity

Look at Fig. 26.2 and answer the following:

1. What planning tools are being used to reduce the amount of urban sprawl in the Randstad?
2. If there are no strict planning controls, which two major urban regions could spread and merge along the Rhine Valley?
3. Is urban sprawl putting pressure on the Greenheart?
4. Why is it important to ensure that the Greenheart remains as a significant area in the Randstad?

A west European megalopolis could result if the Randstad, the Rhine-Ruhr and the Brussels-Antwerp-Ghent growth zones are allowed to expand without careful planning.

Case Study: Dublin

Ireland's urban system is dominated by Dublin, which is a **primate city**. Since the 1960s, its built-up area has expanded rapidly. In addition, Dublin's zone of influence has increased strongly to create an urban region (or daily urban system) that extends some 80 km from the city centre.

Three factors, in particular, have contributed to the expansion of Dublin's urban region:

- Focus of the country's transport network
- Dominant employment centre
- High cost of land in the city.

Before World War II, Dublin was a compact city. The built-up area did not extend more than 5 km from its centre (Fig 26.3a). In the 1960s a period of significant growth began. Most of this expansion occurred within 8 km of the centre.

Expansion of the Dublin urban region has led to a great increase in journeys to work and therefore more traffic congestion at peak times.

- *Suggest how this problem can be resolved.*

293

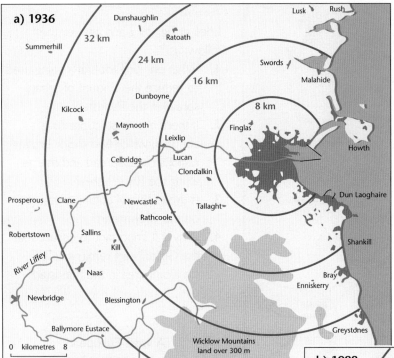

Fig. 26.3 Built-up areas in the Dublin region

It involved the relocation of inner-city populations to large new housing estates and apartment complexes, such as Ballymun. By the 1980s, this zone was almost entirely built up (Fig. 26.3b).

Urban expansion continued in the 1970s into the zone 8 to 16 km from Dublin's centre. Most of the growth here was due to the development of **three new towns**: Blanchardstown, Clondalkin and Tallaght. About 40 per cent of Dublin's urban region now lives in this zone.

As competition for land and the cost of living continues to rise in Dublin, more people

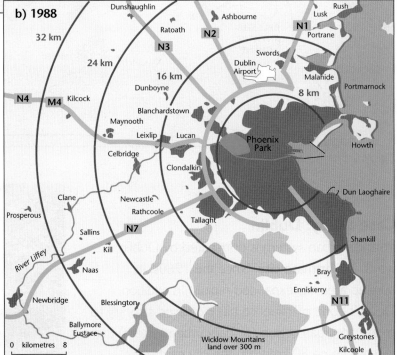

Class Activity

Look at the two maps in Fig 26.3 and answer the following:

1. Is Dublin's continuous built-up area larger in 1988 than in 1936?
2. In which direction has the urban area expanded the most? Why is further major expansion to the south of Dublin likely to be difficult?
3. Give examples of towns that have grown significantly because they are located on or near major roads that converge on Dublin.
4. Why are improved transport links important in extending Dublin's urban region?

Discuss how:
● the focus of the country's transport network
● Dublin's dominance as an employment centre
● the high cost of land in the city have influenced Dublin's urban region.

are encouraged to look for homes further from the city. Many small towns and villages more than 16 km from the centre of Dublin have, therefore, increased in size, especially if they are located on or near a transport route to the city. For many people living in such places, **long-distance travel to work to Dublin has become an accepted part of their daily routine** (Fig 26.4). This has been an important factor in the way the boundaries of Dublin's urban region have been extended.

Clondalkin is one of the three new towns built in the 1970s to accommodate Dublin's increasing population.
● *What evidence is there in the photo that this is a new town built around an old village?*

Long-distance travel to work involves a journey of more than 16 km.

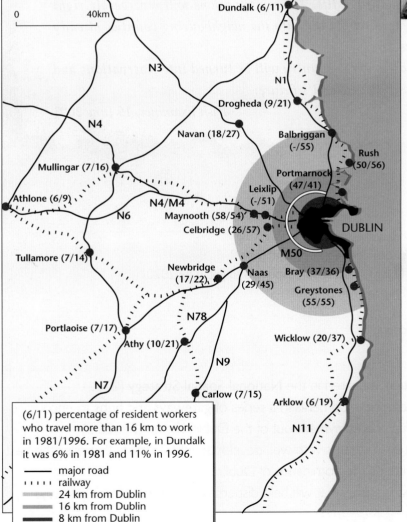

(6/11) percentage of resident workers who travel more than 16 km to work in 1981/1996. For example, in Dundalk it was 6% in 1981 and 11% in 1996.

——— major road
ııııı railway
▓▓▓ 24 km from Dublin
▓▓▓ 16 km from Dublin
▓▓▓ 8 km from Dublin

Fig. 26.4 Long-distance commuting from towns with a population of more than 5,000 in the Dublin urban region in 1981 and 1996

Class Activity

Look at Fig 26.4 and answer the following:

1. Which three towns in 1981 had 50 per cent or more of their resident workforce commuting long distance?
2. Compare the percentage figures for all towns for 1981 and 1996. What do they tell you about trends in long-distance commuting?
3. As you travel from Naas to Portlaoise along the N7, what do the percentages show about the relationship between levels of commuting and the distance from Dublin?
4. Do railways as well as roads have an influence on commuting and the growth of towns in Dublin's urban region? Explain your answer.

A Solution to Dublin's Continued Expansion?

The need for an urgent solution to the continued expansion of Dublin's urban region is highlighted in the press cutting from the *Irish Examiner*.

Don't let isolated rural areas become ghost towns

Dublin will continue to suck life out of major areas of the country unless there is a meaningful government intervention aimed at beefing up other regions...

It appears Ireland's lopsided development is destined to continue apace. Relentlessly, the population explosion of the capital and its sprawling hinterland along the east coast will accelerate unless urgent measures are introduced to redirect development from areas already mushrooming out of control.

The reality is that thousands of people in outlying regions have yet to hear the Celtic Tiger purring. While other cities and towns have benefited, the Tiger's economic impact is concentrated in and around Dublin.

Based on CSO figures, the population of the capital will tip 1,500,000 by 2020. That means traffic gridlock and a serious erosion of quality of life. The repercussions will reverberate right across the city, rippling outwards to greater Dublin and into the neighbouring counties already being turned into commuter dormitories.

Unless the trends are reversed, large areas of the country will be turned into reservations and stripped of people who are the lifeblood of the Ireland's future.

Irish Examiner, 19 June 2001

Activity

Read the newspaper extract and answer the following:
1. What does Ireland's 'lopsided development' mean?
2. By what amount is Dublin's population expected to grow by 2020?
3. What problems will this growth bring to:
   a. Dublin?
   b. the rest of the country?

The most recent solution appeared in the **National Spatial Strategy** (2002).
This proposed large-scale developments in a series of **gateways** and **hubs** to encourage dispersal of population and employment out of the Dublin region (Fig. 26.5).

- **Gateways:** Large urban centres with well-developed infrastructure that offer the best prospects for countering the dominance of Dublin.
- **Hubs:** Smaller urban centres that will help disperse development from gateways into their regions.
- **Strategic road corridors:** Important for providing efficient links between gateways, hubs and Dublin.

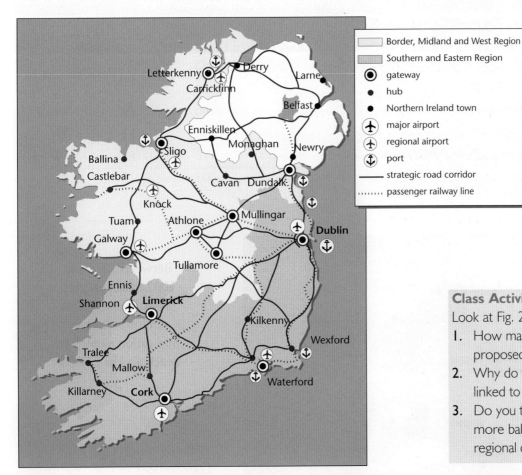

Fig. 26.5 Ireland's National Spatial Strategy, 2002

Class Activity

Look at Fig. 26.5 and answer the following:

1. How many gateways and hubs have been proposed?
2. Why do you think three towns have been linked to form a gateway in the Midlands?
3. Do you think this strategy can help a more balanced pattern of urban and regional development?

Administration Reform in Dublin

An important result of the increasing population and urbanisation within Dublin City and County has been the need to reform its local authority structure. Local authorities are responsible for supplying a range of essential services for the wellbeing of the population living in their area. Until 1994, the local authorities responsible for those services in Dublin were: Dublin County Borough, Dun Laoghaire Corporation and Dublin County Council.

In 1971, two-thirds of the total population of Dublin City and County lived in the city (see Table 26.3). The dominance of the city declined, as more of Dublin's population chose to live in the county's growing towns and rural communities. It proved increasingly difficult to serve the needs of such a large population growth, which was spread out across the county. As a result, it was decided to abolish Dublin County Council and Dun Laoghaire Corporation.

Three new counties were created: Fingal, South Dublin and Dun Laoghaire-Rathdown (see Fig. 26.6). These, together with the newly named Dublin Corporation, provide a more evenly distributed area and population for more effective administration of Dublin's changing population patterns. Dublin County Borough has been renamed Dublin Corporation.

Local government has to be local! Why do you think it becomes less effective if it tries to operate over too large an area and for too many people?

Population Trends in Dublin's Administrative Areas				
	1971 ('000s)	1981 ('000s)	1991 ('000s)	2002 ('000s)
Dublin County Borough/Corporation	568	545	478	495
Dublin County	284	–	–	–
South Dublin	–	165	208	240
Fingal	–	115	153	196
Dun Laoghaire/Rathdown	–	178	185	191
Total	852	1,003	1,025	1,122

Table 26.3

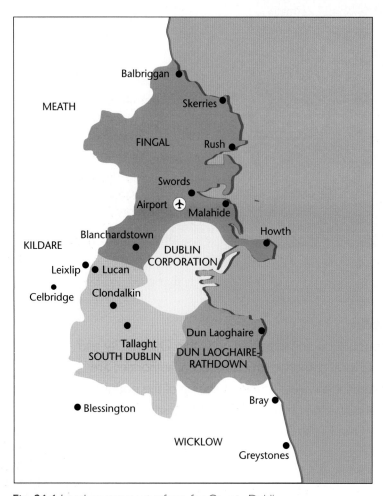

Fig. 26.6 Local government reform for County Dublin

Between 1996 and 2002 Lucan was the fastest growing area in Ireland. The population trebled to reach almost 22,000.

Class Activity

Look at Table 26.3 and Fig. 26.6 and answer the following:

1. What share of the total population lived in the Dublin Corporation area in 2002 compared to 1971?

2. Has population increased in all of the three new counties: Fingal, South Dublin and Dun Laoghaire-Rathdown?

3. Which of the new counties has the largest and fastest-growing population? Explain your answer. (Think about: new towns.)

4. Do you think it was necessary to reorganise the local administration in Dublin? Explain your answer.

TEST YOURSELF AT
my-etest.com

CHAPTER 27
DEVELOPMENT AND EXPANSION OF THE EU

KEY IDEA!

The European Union has expanded from six to 25 member states and is now the world's largest trade bloc.

Following the destruction that occurred during World War II, prospects for development within Europe seemed limited.

● The economies of most countries were devastated.

● A new political boundary, called the Iron Curtain, divided a democratic Western Europe from a Communist-dominated Eastern Europe.

From this uncertain time, a new, confident and prosperous Europe emerged. The basis for this began in Western Europe and involved **a process of economic integration**. At first, it included only six countries but by 2004 had expanded to 25 member states. As a result, **the European Union (EU),** as it is now called, **is an excellent case study of a region that has expanded its international boundaries.**

In 1957, the Treaty of Rome created the European Economic Community (EEC). This was a small, compact group of six countries located in the core region of north-west Europe (Fig 27.1a). The main aim of the EEC was to increase trade between its member states and their level of economic development. It has been successful and this encouraged other European countries to seek membership. As a result, the European Union is now the world's largest and most prosperous trading bloc.

There have been **five enlargements** of the EU that have expanded its international boundaries (Fig 27.1).

● **1973**: A **westwards enlargement** that expanded the core area of the EU in north-west Europe.

● **1981 and 1986:** The second and third enlargements expanded the boundaries of the EU into Mediterranean Europe. This **southern enlargement** was considered to be 'troublesome' due to the underdeveloped economies of the new member states.

● **1995:** This was mainly a **northern enlargement** as the EU expanded to include most of the Scandinavian peninsula. It also expanded the EU into Alpine Europe.

● **2004:** The largest single expansion of the EU involves ten new member states from Central and Eastern Europe. This **eastern enlargement** will be difficult due to the underdeveloped economies of all these countries.

In 1990, East Germany was reunited with West Germany (see Chapter 28). This did not, however, increase the number of countries in the EU. It was seen only as an existing member increasing its territory. The **reunification of Germany** increased the population of the EU by 17 million.

The EEC has now become the EU.

The EU is a very important world region.

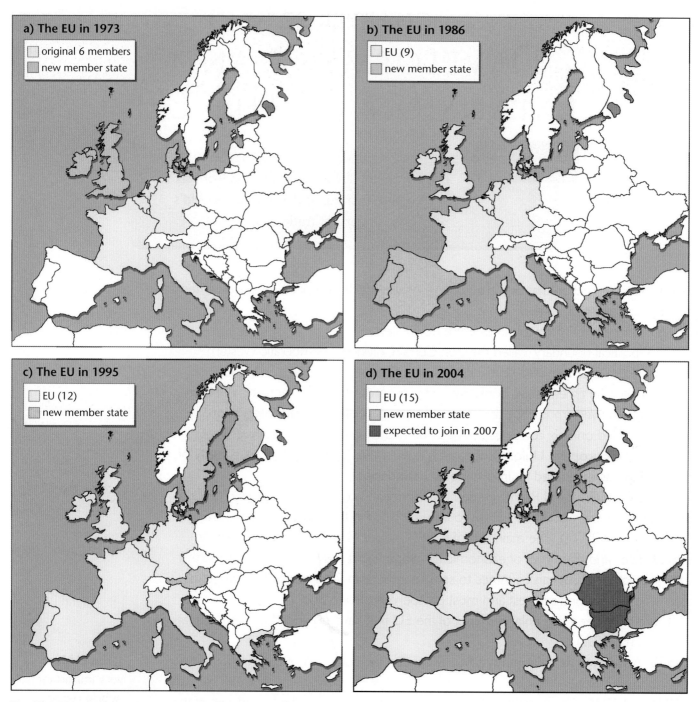

Fig. 27.1 Enlargements of the European Union

Can you suggest why Turkey may have to wait to become an EU member?

Bulgaria and **Romania** have been accepted for membership and are expected to join the EU in 2007. **Turkey's application for membership,** however, has met considerable opposition from many EU states. It is, therefore, unlikely to become a member in the near future.

The boundaries of the EU today are very different from those in 1957, which enclosed a relatively small core group of countries in north-west Europe. **Through a series of enlargements, the EU now covers almost all of western, southern, northern and eastern Europe. Its boundaries stretch from the Arctic to the Mediterranean, and from the Atlantic to the Russian border.**

Selected Data for the Enlarging EU				
European Union	Increase in area (%)	Increase in population (%)	Increase in GDP (Gross Domestic Product) (%)	Change in GDP per person (%)
EU (6) to EU (9) (First enlargement)	31	32	29	−3
EU (9) to EU (12) (Second and third enlargements)	48	22	15	−6
EU (12) to EU (15) (Fourth enlargement, including German reunification)	43	11	8	−3
EU (15) to EU (27) (expected in 2007)	34	29	9	−16

Table 27.1

Class Activity

Look at Fig. 27.1 and Table 27.1 and with the help of an atlas answer the following:

1. Locate and identify the six countries of the original EEC.
2. For each enlargement, locate and name the new member states.
3. Which two countries will join in 2007?
4. In the first enlargement, which new member state was responsible for the large increase in population and GDP?
5. Why should enlargements in the 1980s and in 1995 result in a decline in the average population density for the EU? (Think about: growth in area compared to population.)
6. Why do you think the enlargements in the 1980s and especially in 2004 are troublesome for the EU?
7. Name the two major countries in Western Europe that remain outside the EU?

There will be strong competition for funding between the 'old' (Atlantic and Mediterranean) and 'new' (eastern) peripheries of the enlarging EU.

TEST YOURSELF AT
my-etest.com

CHAPTER 28
CHANGING POLITICAL BOUNDARIES AND CULTURAL GROUPS

Changes in political boundaries can have an important affect on cultural groups.

How do you think the lives of people living in Northern Ireland have been affected by the creation of a border separating it from the Republic?

Changes in political boundaries often have major impacts for people who, as a result of boundary changes, find themselves living under a different political system. Their economic prospects, cultural experiences (language and religious beliefs) and human rights can all be affected by these changes.

This chapter will present **two** case studies to show how changing political boundaries affect cultural groups:

● Kashmir: An example of a violent clash of cultures after British India broke up and new political boundaries were drawn up.
● A reunified Germany: The peaceful reunification of East and West Germany.

Case Study: The Problem of Kashmir

In Chapter 21 about India, important religious and other cultural differences were highlighted. These led to the partition of the subcontinent into three independent states, based primarily on religion: India, Pakistan and Bangladesh.

The differences are still strong and continue to give rise to tensions between different cultural groups. Nowhere is this more marked than in the Kashmir region where India and Pakistan have fought three wars to settle their claims to this disputed border zone (Fig. 28.1).

On gaining independence from Britain in 1947, the states of the Indian subcontinent had to chose whether to form part of Pakistan, dominated by Islam, or India where Hindu was the majority religion.

In the Kashmir Valley, violent conflict broke out between the minority (25 per cent), Hindu population and the majority (75 per cent), Islamic population (see Fig 21.12, page 265). The Hindu minority looked to India for support, while the Islamic population were supported by Pakistan. This resulted in war between the two newly independent states. Many civilians were killed and large numbers of people fled from areas where they were of the minority religion.

India is a country dominated by Hinduism, while Pakistan is an Islamic state.

The United Nations negotiated a ceasefire line to end the conflict. This **Line of Control** was to be temporary, but it has remained as the dividing line between the two cultural groups.

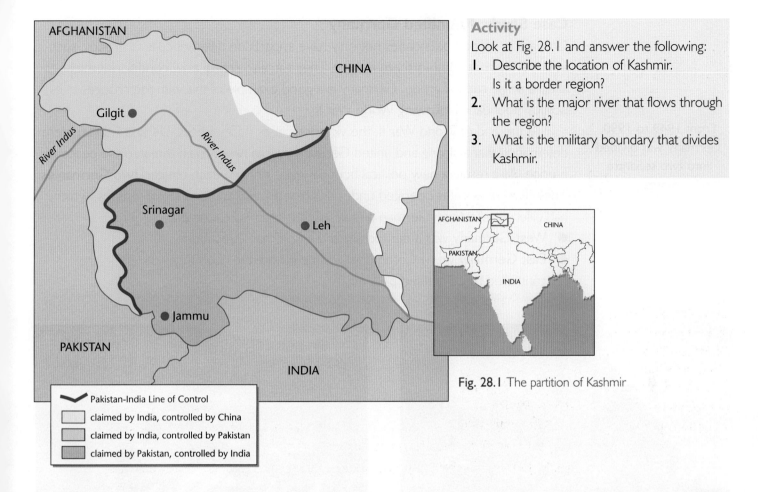

Fig. 28.1 The partition of Kashmir

The situation in the region remains sensitive because:

● India controls about 80 per cent of the Kashmir population, including large numbers of Islamic people.

● Pakistan and the majority Islamic population do not accept this. They want to integrate Kashmir into Pakistan.

● The Indus River and several of its large tributaries originate in Indian-controlled Kashmir. Pakistan wants to gain control over this essential water resource (for irrigation and industrial development).

● In the 1990s, an increase in Islamic fundamentalism has led to more fighting in the region.

● Both India and Pakistan have nuclear weapons. It is, therefore, a potentially dangerous situation when both countries come into conflict in this contested cultural and political border region.

Why is India more willing than Pakistan to make the Line of Control a permanent boundary?

Bill Clinton, a former US president, described the Kashmir as 'the most dangerous place on earth'. Why?

Case Study: Reunified Germany

Changes in political boundaries not only have impacts on different cultural groups, such as in the Kashmir and Northern Ireland. They can also create new conditions which affect a single cultural group. Germany is a good example of this with the changes in its political boundaries following World War II.

From 1949 to 1990, Germany was divided into two separate states.

At the end of World War II, the victorious allies (USA, USSR, UK and France) were determined that a strong and united Germany would never again threaten the peace of Europe. As a result, a new political boundary was drawn which created **two Germanies.** These two new states operated under different political and economic systems, which had different effects on German people living in the two countries.

● **West Germany** was a democracy and a free market economy.

● **East Germany** was a Communist regime where the economy was controlled by centralised planning.

Images of the two Germanies. Drab state-built worker apartments and underdeveloped services in the east (left) contrast with the prosperity of Munich in the west.
● *How did 'Ossies' react to such differences?*

Ask your teacher about:
● democracy
● a free market economy
● Communism
● centralised planning.

West Germany's economy developed strongly and became the largest and most powerful in the EU. Its industries were very competitive and the population enjoyed a high standard of living. Population totals also increased from 50 million to 62 million between 1950 and 1989. Much of this increase was due to large numbers of migrants, from countries such as Turkey, who were attracted to this prosperous country (Table 28.1).

In contrast, the East German economy was relatively inefficient, quality of life poor and personal freedom was limited. Although the state provided its people with basic services, such as housing and health care, most East Germans looked with envy at those living in West Germany. Their population also declined from almost 20 million to 17 million between 1950 and 1989.

Comparison of Some Economic and Social Indicators for East and West Germany in 1989		
	East Germany	West Germany
Gross Domestic Product (billion Deutschmarks)*	353	2,111
Per capita GDP (Deutschmarks)*	21,500	33,700
% unemployment	-	6.9
% children under 3 years cared for in crèches	56	2
Doctors per 10,000 people	24	29
Hospital beds per 10,000 people	24	110
*The Deutschmark was the currency in Germany before it changed to the euro in 2002.		

Table 28.1

Class Activity

Look at Table 28.1 and answer the following:

1. Which of the two Germanies was the largest and most prosperous economy?
2. Why did the East German population have relatively good access to a range of basic services?
3. Which of the two Germanies would migrant workers find more attractive?

A Reunited Germany

In 1989, the Communist government in East Germany collapsed, and in 1990 the political boundary that had separated the two Germanies was removed. Although now a single country, forty years of separate national identities had given rise to major differences between the **Ossies** (people from former East Germany and pronounced oss-sees) and **Wessies** (West Germans and pronounced vess-sees).

> In 1990 Germany was reunited, with its capital in Berlin.

At first, there was considerable optimism that a reunited Germany would succeed in reducing east-west divisions. This has not occurred. In particular, the expectations of the Ossies that their standard of living and job prospects would rise quickly to those of the Wessies have not been met.

Two main factors are responsible for this:

- **Free market forces** have meant that many of the older, less efficient industries located in East Germany were closed due to competition. Unemployment increased rapidly.
- **Freedom of movement** meant that large numbers of young East Germans migrated to western Germany leaving behind an ageing and economically depressed community.

Therefore, rather than becoming equals within a united Germany, **Ossies felt that they were being treated as second-class citizens in their own country** (Figs 28.2 and 28.3). Meanwhile, many Wessies felt that Ossies were ungrateful given the high costs the West German government and citizens paid for reunification.

Fig. 28.2 Unemployment percentage in German states (Länder) in 2001

German average: 9.4%

- 0–4.9
- 5.0–9.9
- 10.0–14.9
- 15.0–19.9
- former political boundary

Following reunification, an unprecedented consumer and construction boom, boosted by aid from the west, produced modern roads, sleek office buildings and shopping malls throughout East Germany. Easterners discovered the joys of fast cars and designer clothes. Their Communist-era apartment blocks were given more colourful facades. For a while they seemed happy.

The merger, however, meant that western employment policies were extended to the east, where industries soon lost their competitive edge to Poland and the Czech Republic. Unemployment in eastern Germany has grown to 18%, more than twice the western level and higher than in most of eastern Europe.

'Just look out there', said Manfred Geiger, behind the counter of his empty cafe in Reichenbach's central square. 'There are no young people here any more. They've gone. The east is dying.'...

The German government has done nothing even while a 'brain drain' was depriving some eastern towns of doctors and dentists. Migration westwards, at more than 200,000 people a year, is greater now than in the years after the fall of the Wall.

'A collective depression has set in,' says Karen Retzel, the mayor of Cottbus, whose population is shrinking by 7% a year. 'The promises of reunification have not been fulfilled.'

Sunday Times, 8 September 2002

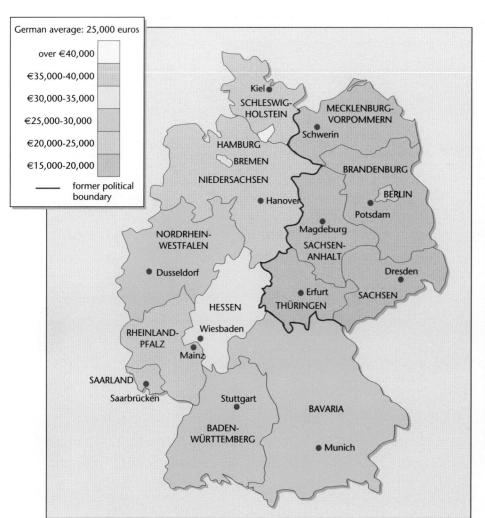

Fig. 28.3 GDP (Gross Domestic Product) per capita in German states (Länder) in euros

Legend:

German average: 25,000 euros

- over €40,000
- €35,000–40,000
- €30,000–35,000
- €25,000–30,000
- €20,000–25,000
- €15,000–20,000
- —— former political boundary

Class Activity

Study Figs. 28.2 and 28.3 and the newspaper extract and answer the following:

1. Is unemployment higher in eastern or western Germany? Suggest reasons why.
2. Do per capita income levels suggest that the former East Germany is still underdeveloped?
3. Is migration from eastern to western Germany a problem? Why?
4. If you were an Ossie, would you agree that the promises of reunification have not been met?

Ethnic Germans living in other countries

Over the centuries, Germans have migrated and settled in many countries of Eastern Europe and throughout the former USSR. When the Communist system changed and the political map of Europe was redrawn, this affected the people who came from Germany originally.

Under German law, anyone who can prove to be of German descent has a right to become a German citizen. With the Iron Curtain gone, large numbers of **ethnic Germans** chose to leave their home countries to take up their right to live in Germany. In the 1990s, the main source country of such migrants was Russia.

Although officially German, ethnic Germans have posed problems for the German government. They are often poor, have little or no knowledge of the German language and prefer to remain in their own tight social groups. They form a cultural group that are outsiders in their new homeland.

One estimate has suggested 10 million ethnic Germans lived outside Germany. About 2.5 million lived in the former USSR.

TEST YOURSELF AT
my-etest.com

307

FIELDWORK INVESTIGATION

Students should read carefully the guidelines set out by the syllabus for the geographical investigations.

THE GEOGRAPHICAL INVESTIGATION

The geographical investigation is a core area of study, and all students have to carry out a fieldwork exercise and write a report on it. Field studies and investigations using primary and secondary sources are a very important part of studying geography. These practical investigations allow you to apply the core geographical skills you have studied and practised through all units of the syllabus. The investigation also encourages you to **experience and question relationships and issues in your own surroundings**.

To carry out the geographical investigation you have to:

- Devise a strategy for it and **identify aims** and **objectives** to allow an effective investigation of the topic.
- **Select methods of collecting and gathering information** that are appropriate to the investigation topic.
- **Use suitable methods for gathering and collecting information**.
- Write a report.
- Analyse and interpret results and draw valid conclusions.

Structuring and Organising the Investigation

You choose your investigation topic from a list put together by the Department of Education and Science. You have to complete your investigation by 1 December of Leaving Certificate year two. Although you may work in class groups, for assessment purposes each student must present their own full and complete report. No group projects are accepted.

Higher Level students are expected to write a report of between 1,500 to 2,000 words, while Ordinary Level students should aim for a report of between 1,000 and 1,500 words. The investigation report must be presented in A4-size format.

For your investigation you must use primary and secondary sources of information. These should be approximately **60 per cent from primary sources** and **40 per cent from secondary sources**.

Primary sources give information that comes directly from the time or place that is being studied. These include original photographs, newspaper reports and maps of the time, and old buildings. Secondary sources are ones that may be written after the time period being studied but indirectly give us information about a time or place. These could include parish journals, historical accounts or interviews.

The geography teacher and school principal will verify that the investigation has been carried out by each Leaving Certificate candidate. The Geographical Investigation and Skills core unit allocates 20 per cent of marks at both Higher and Ordinary level.

The grid below shows the different steps of the geographical investigation and how many marks are allocated to each part. The different approaches to geographical skills for Ordinary and Higher level students are shown in the way marks are allocated for each part of the investigation.

Stage	Activities	Proposed Assessment Weighting	
		Ordinary Level	Higher Level
Introduction: Posing the problems and devising a strategy	● Selecting a topic for investigation ● Clear statement of the aim ● An outline of the objectives ● Identifying the types of information required	5%	5%
Planning and preparing the work to be carried out	● Selecting methods for collecting and gathering information ● Designing a questionnaire or recording sheets ● Deciding on locations for the investigation	5%	5%
Collecting data	● Using instruments to make measurements ● Records of observations made in the field ● Using questionnaires and surveys, as appropriate ● Using a variety of secondary sources, e.g. documentary sources ● Discussing the problems encountered	30%	30%
Preparing the report: presenting results	● Organising data ● Using illustrations, graphs, maps and tables ● Using ICT, where appropriate, to prepare and present results and conclusions	40%	20%
Conclusion and evaluation for the report	● Analysis and interpretation of results ● Drawing valid conclusions ● Comparison of findings with established theory ● Evaluation of the hypothesis ● Examining the validity of the investigation and suggestions for improvements	20%	40%

To help you see how to plan and carry out your geographical investigation, here are two examples of fieldwork activities: one is in an urban area and the other is a river study.

Tips for a Fieldwork Exercise in an Urban Area
Aims and Objectives
a. To discover how the land use in a village or defined area in a town has changed over time.

b. To discover and explain why these changes have occurred.

c. To learn to work with maps of different scales: updating, amending and orientating.

d. To observe and use sketches, cameras and research to record present and past building uses in the area.

e. Use computer software to create charts and images to improve the way you present your group's findings.

When doing a fieldwork exercise certain information must be gathered and recorded. There are four important points to remember.
- What information is needed and why.
- Where the information will be collected and why.
- How the information will be collected and why.
- When the information will be collected and why.

Make sure that you identify clearly the areas or activities of fieldwork that you take part in or contribute to.

Other fieldwork exercises might include:
- Traffic management
- Land environmental issues
- Changing settlement patterns in a local area
- Physical processes in a river, coastal, glacial or karst environment
- Changing demographic patterns in a local area.

Planning and Preparing for the Fieldwork
- The class should work in groups to prepare maps and organise fieldwork exercises and distribute work fairly and equally, using the skills of the group in the best way and making sure that all parts of the exercise can be completed well and on time.
- Create a system for double checking each group's findings.

Preparing for Mapwork
- Define the region to be studied by each group.
- Identify old land uses from maps, photographs and records and choose a colour code for displaying and letter code for surveying.
- Check that you understand the map symbols for individual buildings, yards, etc.
- Practise map orientation in the school grounds by using a simplified map of school buildings.
- Outline the recording methods you will use when surveying and in the classroom.
- Practise drawing bar and pie graphs manually and by using computer software.

Collecting Data

- Research old 1904, 1932, 1940, 1990s or other town maps to a scale of 1:2500 to discover past land uses, buildings and structures.
- Use library records from old books or local historical magazines to record past land uses, buildings and structures.
- Record present land uses in modern maps of the urban area chosen.
- Use any available census information and the age-sex structure of the residential population in the past and at present in this area.
- Research the type of accommodation available to residents over time and the reasons for this type of accommodation.
- Find out if any financial incentives to encourage change were used by the local authority in this area.
- Identify present land uses and changes to buildings or urban renewal and street changes.
- Draw or transfer maps and land uses to your own hand-drawn maps, marking the north sign (direction of north), streets, buildings, etc.
- Take photographs, draw or sketch relevant buildings of architectural value.

Results

- Record all the information using:
  - Pie or bar charts of land use for the past time periods being studied and at present.
  - Sketches of changes: new and old buildings.
  - Photographs of changes.
- If possible, note the age-sex structure of residents and how it may have changed over time.
- Describe these changes.
- Each group presents its findings so that results and conclusions can be drawn from the information gathered.

Conclusion and Evaluation

Each student should write a report that includes:

- Relevant and logical conclusions from the material gathered.
- Identify reasons for any changes in land use and the age-sex structure over time.
- Identify skills you have learned.
- Identify areas that could be improved when carrying out a similar survey and fieldwork.

Tips for a Fieldwork Exercise on River Study
Aims and Objectives
a. To understand the energy of running water and the factors that affect this energy.
b. To identify landforms that result from variations in the energy of a river.
c. To develop surveying skills, such as measuring, recording and sketching skills.
d. To develop map-reading orientation skills.
e. To gather and record information carefully.

As for the urban area study, when you do a fieldwork exercise certain information must be gathered and recorded. There are four important points to remember:
- What information is needed and why.
- Where the information will be collected and why.
- How the information will be collected and why.
- When the information will be collected and why.

Make sure that you identify clearly the areas or activities of fieldwork that you take part in or contribute to.

Planning and Preparing for the Fieldwork
1. In class, review information on rivers, river features and river processes.
2. Choose a short section (about 200 metres) of a shallow river suitable for the fieldwork. A shallow stretch of the river **with at least one bend** is usually the best choice for river study. This kind of river allows you to cross from one bank to the opposite side and makes precise measurement of depth, cross section and pebble size easier.
3. Make copies of a map of the river section 1:2500.
4. The class should work in groups:
- Group A focuses on river bend(s).
- Group B focuses on transportation by the river.
- Group C focuses on the speed of river flow.
- Group D focuses on the volume of river flow.

With your teacher make sure that the preparation is followed by co-ordinated activities to check that the fieldwork exercise goes according to plan.

Collecting Data
Group A

This group makes a cross section of the river. You can practise this by making a simple cross section of a slope in a grassy area or a slope in a field near the school buildings or schoolyard.

- Use measuring poles, line-levels, tape and cord to carry out this exercise.
- Indicate fast, medium and slow areas of the river by marking wide, medium and thin arrows on 'section line/tape'.
- Choose two points at A and B where there are significant bends in the river and follow through with skills learned in class or in a preliminary activity.

Group B

This group examines the material that the river carries. Bring to school samples of pebbles and stones taken from a riverbed near your home. Examine each sample and explain why they are rounded.

- Focus on cross-section skills and measuring poles, and find the depth of water at various points on the river at the location chosen. (This could be done in parallel to the cross-section line for Group A.)
- Measure and find the average diameter of stones, and their minimum and maximum sizes.
- Create a chart with the following headings:
  - Section
  - Depth
  - Pebble Diameter
- Create a graph, using pebble size and depth to see if there is a relationship between the water depth and pebble size.

Group C

This group aims to identify factors that influence the speed of the river. The exercise can be done in the river at various points in a particular location. This could be a few yards upstream or downstream from the cross section area of Group A or at a bend or another point.

- Research ways of measuring the speed of flow where the river is:
  a) fast
  b) slow
  c) still.
  This can be done using a drain in the school yard, a gallon or bucket of water, a cork, a stopwatch and a tape.
- Observe the size of pebbles at various speed locations and see if there is any relationship between speed and pebble size, or the width, speed and pebble size.
- Observe and debate factors, such as riverbed roughness, which might affect the speed of river flow.

Group D

This group aims to measure the cubic flow of water in a river. This can be done by:

- Finding the average depth and width across the river at the three crossing points chosen.
- Choosing the crossing points. Each crossing point should be about five metres across.

To calculate the cubic flow of water of the river along each section chosen, use the formula:

Volume = Speed (metres/second) x depth x width.

All Groups

All groups should make photocopies of a map of the river from a 1:2500 OS sheet.

- Mark each area being studied on the core map. (Your teacher may explain and practise map orientation with you.)
- Note the direction of flow.
- Take photographs of the sections of the river needed for each group.

Results

- Each group should record their findings carefully on charts. A group leader can give a brief description of each fieldwork activity on site, once each group has completed its work. This is to make sure that each group is aware of each other's work and how it is relevant for the fieldwork activity.
- Each group records and presents its findings so that results and conclusions can be drawn from the information gathered.

Conclusion and Evaluation

Each student should write a report that includes:

- Relevant and logical conclusions from the material gathered.
- Identify reasons for any changes in surveying methods.
- Identify skills you have learned.
- Identify areas that could be improved when carrying out a similar survey and fieldwork.

SAMPLE FIELDWORK EXERCISE REPORT

The following is a sample fieldwork exercise report using some of the tips mentioned previously. It is based on a small village that we will name 'Moher', but it could be applied to a section of a town or city. It is a simple exercise but nevertheless involves lots f map skills, observation and recording and measuring in the field. It would involve about two weeks' work during geography class time and lunch hour to survey the area and another week to finalise drawings and results in the classroom.

As the Department of Education will now supply a list of varied fieldwork exercises it will allow teachers scope to choose one that suits them and their students.

Individual input by students in new projects will be very important for future fieldwork reports and so where this occurs it should be emphasised by each student.

Title: Moher . . . A Change in Plan and Function Over Time

Aims

1. To see how the plan/layout of Moher village has changed over the past 150 years by examining past and present Ordnance Survey maps.
2. To find out how land uses of the ground floors of buildings in the village have changed since 1925.
3. To learn mapping skills, such as: orientation, accurate recording of information, measuring and observation of different building styles and land uses in the field. To use maps of different scales and from different centuries. To practise sketching some shop fronts of particular character.
4. To learn associated computer skills, such as the creation of charts, spreadsheets and graphs using Microsoft Works and to present findings in a professional manner.

Preparation

- Four maps of the village were located. One of these dated from the 1850s. A second map was dated 1904, a third map 1925 and a fourth map 1994. The 1994 map was the most up-to-date map that could be found. This meant that the 1994 map had to be updated to present times to achieve our aims. The old maps were small and so fitted on an A3 sheet. However, the 1994 map had to be photocopied and the sheets joined accurately to include the whole village. I attached these maps by cutting overlapping sections and used Sellotape to join them at the back. I then attached them to our drawing board. Each map was placed directly underneath the other with the oldest at the bottom and the most recent at the top.
- Our class was divided into groups of three and one group of two students. Each group was assigned a particular section of the village to record the present land uses first and later the past land uses. Some groups were given the same section of the village because buildings were difficult to identify in that area. But we had to survey the section from opposite ends so we could compare our findings and ensure accurate recording.

- We made a list of all the services/functions of the present village. We did this in a brainstorming session. We then grouped them under eight headings: Religious, Business/Sole Traders, Health, Financial, Education, Industry, Community/Public Facility, and Residential. We gave each category a letter, for recording our findings in the field, such as 'R' for residential, etc. and a corresponding colour for marking in on the maps. Then we learned how to identify the various categories of land uses/functions.

- Finally we learned how to measure accurately with a trundle wheel and measuring tape and record accurately our measurements in a notebook. I measured the basketball court in our school using the trundle wheel. Then, by using a scale rule we learned how to adapt these measurements to the 1994 map. A sharp pencil could only be used because this ensured neat work and accurate transfer of measurements.

Careful Gathering and Recording of Material

- Each group went to their designated starting points. We stopped at MacCarthy's corner shop in the centre of the village. We were expected to survey the buildings on the opposite side of the street to MacCarthy's shop. In this way we had a clear view of each building as the village street was narrow. Each of us had a photocopied map of our section of the village and it was attached to hard cardboard with gum. This allowed us to write our findings on the map. We orientated our maps so we could record easily and accurately. Each map was enlarged on the photocopying machine in school so we could record the appropriate letters for the present land uses on our map. We would repeat this for past land uses at a later time.

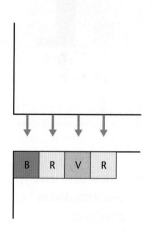

Fig. 1

- After orientating our maps we checked each building carefully to see if it matched the present buildings on the street. Where it did not match we had to find out why this was so. For example, where a building was demolished we noted that with a letter 'D'. If an extra building was added, we measured the frontage and spaces between it and adjoining buildings and recorded the measurements in our notebook. This process created an updated map and made us familiar with each building on the street. Then we returned to our starting point to observe land uses.

- There were a number of arches through the line of houses for access to the rear of some buildings and some narrow alleys broke the street front into sections. The arches were marked by an x symbol on the maps. Both the arches and alleys were used to check for accuracy. When we reached one or other of these we checked back to the previous arch or alley to see if our building numbers were correct. We were also able to check our findings with the other group who had surveyed from the opposite end of the street. We continued in this way until we completed our section.

- Our third surveying task included observation and judgement skills as above. However, a more advanced skill in observing was needed to identify the past use of each building. Using the 1925 map, we had to identify old shops by checking plaster details and repair marks on the walls of the buildings. We also had to check that the buildings marked on the 1925 map matched the present-day buildings. If they did not, we had to indicate what the difference was and why this change had occurred. Was it a shop before and not any more? Was the old building demolished and replaced by a newer one or ones? This proved very difficult in some instances. In any case the appropriate letter for what we decided on was marked into the old map. Any information we gathered of the individual buildings from old people in the village was noted in our notebooks.

● I used the digital camera in school to photograph our section of the street buildings. I printed them off in our computer room. Each group did this for each of their sections. This helped us to double-check our work in the classroom if a dispute over land or a particular building use arose. It was also helpful on wet days when we were unable to go outside. I also sourced old photographs that indicated some past land uses.

Preparation of our Results

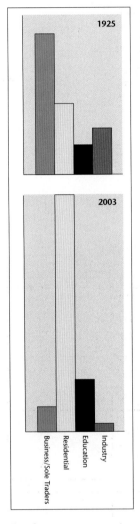

Fig. 2

● Other land uses also included in class graphs.
● Sample bar charts not drawn to scale due to limited time available but shows how residential land use within the village has increased while businesses have closed down.

Fig. 3

● Four maps of our village were placed on the drawing board in our classroom. The centre of the village of each map was placed directly underneath the other so comparisons could be made of the changes to the village over time. The bottom map was the oldest map of the 1850s. Directly above this was the 1904 map, then the 1925 map and, finally on top, our updated map from 1994.

● After surveying the present land uses, each group – after consultation with each other – marked on the updated map each building land use according to our findings in the field. We repeated this for the 1925 map again according to our own observations and information recorded from older people.

● We counted each colour and noted their total numbers. This gave us the number of buildings associated with each land use/function. By keying in these numbers on a spreadsheet in the computer room we created varied charts and graphs to show the difference between the 1925 map and the updated 1994 map. We also created

Land use changes in Moher, 1925–2003

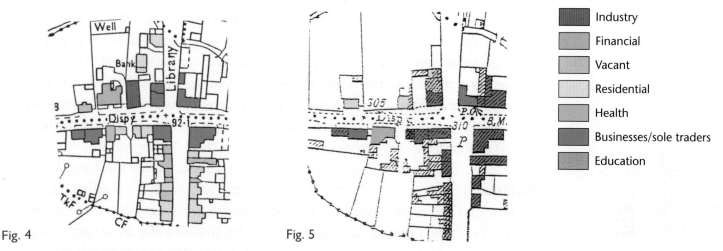

Fig. 4   Fig. 5

Industry
Financial
Vacant
Residential
Health
Businesses/sole traders
Education

(Students could also draw a simpler version of these maps.)

bar graphs in the classroom to show how these land uses had changed. We created a table to show the numbers of land uses in 1925 and 2003.

- Some old buildings had features of great character. These included some shop fronts with plaster barges and owners' names. Other buildings included a small grain mill where grain was crushed for local farmers. We made drawings of three of these buildings to show how building styles had changed over the years.

Results and Conclusions
Shape and Size

The village of the 1850s was very small. It showed just twenty-five buildings. Most of one side of the modern-day village did not yet exist at all. The 1925 plan showed a much larger village. Long, rear gardens were added to many houses. The basic village plan of this time was quite similar to that of the present day. The updated 1994 map showed the greatest change. The houses had now spread out along the roads that lead into the village. The housing estates had added to the size and changed the shape and area of the village.

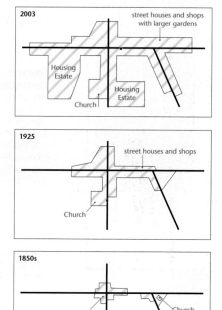

Fig. 6 Change over time

Housing

The type and number of houses was the most notable change in the village. Three housing estates had been added to the village since 1925. One of these was built in the 1960s. It was an estate of fifteen semi-detached houses. The second was a much larger estate of forty houses that included some semi-detached and terraced houses. This housing estate was built by the County Council in 1989. The third estate was built only six years ago for elderly people of the area who wished to live in the village. These were community houses. In addition, many houses were built by individuals at both ends of the village, some of which were old, while others were relatively new.

319

Land uses

The land use of many buildings had changed over time. Many buildings that are now dwellings were once shops. Most people today shop in the city, which is only 9 km away. They are mobile shoppers and so are not tied to their local village as much as the older generation were. So there is less need for small shops as there was in past times. So many of them have closed. Large shop windows were replaced with smaller ones more suited to a home. The remaining space differences were blocked in and plastered. This gave some buildings an uneven plaster effect on the outside. Because of this change, upstairs windows did not necessarily match up with ground-floor windows.

Facilities

Since 1990, a community hall and GAA sports field were added on the south side of the village. The library, CBS and secondary school, a playschool, a doctor's surgery, two garages, a chemist shop and a bank were not present in 1925. However, five bakeries, ten shops, a blacksmith's workshop and a row of six tiny houses with no backyards had either closed or were demolished.

Picture Credits

For permission to reproduce photographs and other material, the authors and publisher gratefully acknowledge the following:

PHOTOS: ALAMY IMAGES: 182, 203BR, 216, 222, 228, 253 © Alamy Images ARDEA.COM: 48B © Valerie Taylor PETER BARROW PHOTOGRAPHY: 195, 197, 198L, 218, 293, 295 © Peter Barrow Photography CAMERA PRESS IRELAND: 93L, 180R, 285T © Camera Press Ireland CORBIS: 1T, 1BR, 23T, 24C, 32T © Roger Ressmeyer; 1BL © Ralph White; 3 © Michael T. Sedam; 16B, 94T © Lloyd Cuff; 24T © Amos Nachoum; 24B/97T, 36, 42, 43, 120, 155B; © Corbis; 29 © Sergio Pitamitz/Corbis; 39BR © DiMaggio/Kalish; 39BL © Lanz Von Horsten/Gallo Images; 41 © Lester V. Bergman; 45 © James A. Sugar; 52 © Annie Griffiths Belt; 54, 226, 255TR © Hans Georg Roth; 57T © Michael Nicholson; 57BL © Ric Ergenbright; 60 © Bettmann; 62 © Rougemont Maurice/Corbis Sygma; 67L © Sylvain Saustier; 67R © Paul Almasy; 71 © Stephen Frink; 75 © Bryan Pickering/Eye Ubiquitous; 84 © Macduff Everton; 85 © David Muench; 86 © Wolfgang Kaehler; 89 © Tom Nebbia; 92T © Andrew Brown/Ecoscene; 93R, 94C, 176C © Galen Rowell; 100, 144B, 201T and C, 278B © Yann Arthus-Bertrand; 104R © Paul A. Souders/Corbis; 127T © Darrell Gulin/Corbis; 148 © Keren Su; 150T © Lance Nelson; 150B © Kraft Brooks/Corbis Sygma; 153 © Patrick Ward; 159R © Dallas and John Heaton; 159L, 196 © Jason Hawkes; 164 © Alan MacWeeney; 176L © Tom Bean; 176R © Roman Soumar; 178 © Tim Thompson; 179 © Olivier Hoslet/Van Parys; 180L © Enzo & Paolo Ragazzini; 186T © Setboun; 186B © Adam Woolfitt; 190, 202 © Peter Turnley; 200B © Mark L. Stephenson; 203BC, 264 © David H. Wells; 225 © Fulvio Roiter; 227 © Vittoriano Rastelli; 231T © David Lees; 231B © Paul Thompson; 233, 304R © Jonathan Blair; 235 © Patrick Durand/Corbis Sygma; 241T © Erik Schaffer/Ecoscene; 244B © Michael Boys; 254 © Charles & Josette Lenars; 255BR © Bennett Dean/Eye Ubiquitous; 259L © Lindsay Hebberd; 258 © Colin Garratt; 261T © Earl & Nazima Kowall; 261B © Jeremy Horner; 262 © Vince Streano; 267T © Zen Icknow; 269BL © Despotovic Dusko; 273 © Alain Le Garsmeur; 274 © Tiziana and Gianni Baldizzone; 277 © Jacques Pavlovsky/Corbis Sygma; 278T © Duch Dany/Corbis Sygma; 281 © Chris Rainier; 285B © Owen Franken; 304L © Shepard Sherbell ESLER CRAWFORD PHOTOGRAPHY: 26, 59 © Esler Crawford Photography KEVIN DWYER: 80R, 81, 213 © Kevin Dwyer ECOSCENE: 191 © Rosemary Greenwood FLPA: 70R, 147 © Roger Wilmshurst HUTCHISON PICTURE LIBRARY: 268 © Christine Pemberton IMAGEFILE IRELAND: 180C, 200T, 249, 252, 260 all, 267B, 269T, 283 © Imagefile Ireland INPHO.COM: 269BR © Inpho IRISH IMAGE COLLECTION: 44R, 64BR, 70L, 73, 91, 128, 133, 141, 160, 162L, 166, 169TR, 170, 171, 198R, 203T, 204, 208L, 208L, 210, 211, 217T, 220 © Irish Image Collection IRISH PICTURE LIBRARY: 286 © Fr. Browne S.J. Collection NATURFOTOGRAFERNAS BILDBYRÅ: 203BL, 240 © Tor Lundberg; 237 © P. Roland Johanson; 241B © Jonas Forsberg; 242 © Peter Lilja; 244T © Goran Hansson; 246 © Tore Hagman NORDIC PHOTOS: 245 © Linda Thompson FINBARR O'CONNELL AERIAL PHOTOGRAPHY: 193 © Finbarr O'Connell ORDNANCE SURVEY IRELAND: 65, 80L, 82 © Ordnance Survey Ireland PANOS: 255TL © Caroline Penn; 255BL, 266 © Mark Henley PA PHOTOS: 169TL © Chris Bacon PHOTOCALL IRELAND: 162R, 288 © Photocall Ireland PHOTOLIBRARY WALES: 177 © Jeff Morgan REUTERS: 94B © Andreas Meier; 96B © Mario Laporta REX FEATURES: 97B © Mauro Carraro; 175 © Rick Colls; 183 © Hatami Collection; 201B © Leon Schadeberg; 280 © Nils Jorgensen SCIENCE PHOTO LIBRARY: 22T © Krafft/Explorer; 22B © B.Murton/Southampton Oceanography Centre; 23C © Prof. Stewart Lowther; 23B © GECO UK; 32B © David Leah; 39T © Michael Barnett; 47T, 56 © Bernhard Edmaier; 47B © Alfred Pasieka; 48T © Dr Jeremy Burgess; 57BR © Martin Bond; 61 © George Bernard; 63 © Tony Craddock; 64T, 111C © Simon Fraser; 127C © Sinclair Stammers; 132 © Michael Marten; 144T © Kaj R. Svensson; 155T © John Howard; 236 © Alex Bartel SIMMONS AEROFILMS: 92B, 109 © Simmons Aerofilms SKYSCAN PHOTOLIBRARY: 292 © Aerophoto Schiphol STILL PICTURES: 259R © Chris Caloicott WALKING WORLD IRELAND MAGAZINE: 83, 88, 90, 98, 102, 104L, 106B, 110, 111T and B, 113, 114, 116, 119, 127B, 135, 156B, 157 © Eoin Clarke; 131 © Gareth McCormack

OTHER PHOTOS: 16T © Marie Tharp; Oceanographic Cartographer; 44B, 64BL, 106T, 118, 129, 130 all, 143 courtesy of Pat O'Dwyer; 50 © Chrysalis Books Archive; 95 courtesy of the Geological Survey of Northern Ireland; 96T © Peter Foss/IPCC (Irish Peatland Conservation Council); 103 © University of Cambridge; Committee for Aerial Photography; 156T © ECOPRO Code of Practice/Department of Communications, Marine and Natural Resources; 181 © Jason South/*The Irish Times*; 188, 189 both © DG REGIO, European Commission

Map extracts are reproduced by permission of Ordnance Survey, Ireland.

T = top, B = bottom, L = left, R = right, C = centre

The authors and publisher have made every effort to trace all copyright holders, but if any has been inadvertently overlooked we would be pleased to make the necessary arrangements at the first opportunity.